The Education of Things

A VOLUME IN THE SERIES
Childhoods: Interdisciplinary Perspectives on Childhood and Youth

EDITED BY
Rachel Conrad, Alice Hearst, Laura Lovett,
and Karen Sánchez-Eppler

The Education of Things

Mechanical Literacy in British Children's Literature, 1762–1860

ELIZABETH MASSA HOIEM

University of Massachusetts Press
Amherst and Boston

Printed in the United States of America

ISBN 978-1-62534-755-8 (paper); 756-5 (hardcover)

Designed by Sally Nichols
Set in Fairfield LT Standard
Printed and bound by Books International, Inc.

Cover design by adam b. bohannon
Cover art: *Ladder of Learning* ([London]: ca. 1850).
Cotsen Children's Library, Courtesy of Princeton University Library.

Library of Congress Cataloging-in-Publication Data

Names: Hoiem, Elizabeth Massa, author.
Title: The education of things : mechanical literacy in British children's literature, 1762–1860 / Elizabeth Massa Hoiem.
Description: Amherst : University of Massachusetts Press, [2023] | Series: Childhoods : interdisciplinary perspectives on children and youth | Includes bibliographical references and index.
Identifiers: LCCN 2023027641 (print) | LCCN 2023027642 (ebook) | ISBN 9781625347558 (paperback) | ISBN 9781625347565 (hardcover) | ISBN 9781685750374 (ebook)
Subjects: LCSH: Children's literature, English—History and criticism. | Machinery in literature. | Work in literature. | Material culture in literature. | Reading (Primary) —Great Britain—History. | Technical education—Great Britain—History.
Classification: LCC PR990 .H65 2023 (print) | LCC PR990 (ebook) | DDC 820.9/9282—dc23/eng/20230906
LC record available at https://lccn.loc.gov/2023027641
LC ebook record available at https://lccn.loc.gov/2023027642

British Library Cataloguing-in-Publication Data
A catalog record for this book is available from the British Library.

For my daughters, Isla and Rowan, with love

Contents

CONTENTS

Supplementary materials are available online at https://umpressopen.library.umass.edu/projects/the-education-of-things.

Illustrations

Preface

This book brings labor to the forefront of our investigations into children's literature and material culture. Since one undercurrent is the relationship between learning from books and learning from experience, I want to explain how this project reflects my work experience. From the first semester as a graduate student at the University of Illinois, I taught two writing classes as the instructor of record, performing work as a "teaching assistant" but given the same responsibilities as a professor or adjunct instructor. Before I arrived, the doctoral students secured official recognition from the State of Illinois for their union, the Graduate Employee Organization (GEO), after a protracted legal process, during which the Illinois Educational Labor Relations Board initially refused to consider doctoral students as employees. GEO gained recognition in 2000 only after the Illinois Court of Appeals returned the case to the labor board with instructions to allow doctoral student employees to unionize in cases where their work did not significantly overlap with disciplinary training. I arrived in 2004, the same year the university finally followed the court's directive to bargain with the GEO after students occupied the administration building.

As this case illustrates, one challenge of unionizing for graduate students is that teaching, research, and education are not easily separated, leaving unclear whether to categorize what they do in the classroom as learning or labor. Our tuition waivers depend on teaching these courses, which also prepares us with essential job skills. Humanists have the added challenge of teaching about books, media, and art—things we love to share, which makes our work seem like good fun. All of this makes graduate student labor difficult to distinguish from leisure or professional development, at least for those not doing the work. Which of these labels was foremost in the minds of upper administration seemed to change depending on context. When we presented at conferences or won awards, we were researchers who supported the university mission. When we negotiated a living wage and better health insurance, we were students learning to teach.

In November 2009, while reading Andrew Ure, Peter Gaskell, and catalogues from the Great Exhibition of 1851, and taking a Victorian industrial fiction class with Eleanor Courtemanche, I attended contract negotiations. Several years later participated in a strike that successfully protected tuition waivers for doctoral students with teaching appointments. I want to thank my amazing cohort, who learned labor law and negotiating tactics while writing their dissertations, especially lead negotiator, Christopher Simeone, and the bargaining team, who listened to everyone's perspectives at each stage in the process, right up until midnight, crowded together to share our priorities before walking out. You gave all of us an object lesson in democracy. Although we could unionize because Illinois recognized my work at a public university as labor, the National Labor Relations Board under the Bush administration in the 2004 Brown University case reversed previous precedent by reclassifying doctoral student labor at private universities as training. The ambiguity between education and labor had consequences for New York University (NYU) graduate students, who finally succeeded after years of work actions, petitions, legal pressure, and protests in gaining recognition for their union from NYU in 2013.

After the GEO strike, I was curious what working children thought about playful pedagogies that offer engaging ways to learn, since blurring distinctions between tasks and toys seems like a terrible position for labor negotiation. Although childhood is associated with play and learning, our conceptions of child agency and leisure emerged from labor debates. Early nineteenth century English law initially recognized apprenticeship, then child labor in general, as "unfree" labor because children negotiate their contracts under coercion from various adults. Whereas regulating "free" labor was regarded as an inexcusable interference, those who perform unfree labor merited legal protection. This logic supported later efforts to limit children's work hours and require school attendance. Instead of insisting on boundaries and definitions between labor, learning, and leisure, this book tries to point out the power given to those who decide when we are doing work, and how these distinctions reflect hierarchies between adult and child, teacher and student, which complicate whether children engage in activities autonomously or automatically, as we might say in the language of machines.

This book is also a steampunk love letter of sorts, from a reader confused by the disdain for anything "mechanical" that I found in otherwise fascinating scholarship, notably Michel Foucault's *Discipline and Punish*. (If you are wondering at its absence, here is your confirmation of my anxiety of influence with that work.) I read my first story about automata, "The Artist of the Beautiful," in an undergraduate course on Nathaniel Hawthorne with Robert Daly at SUNY Buffalo. The story about lifelike art crushed by a child's hand must have stuck with me through my master's program at Carnegie Mellon University (CMU), where my husband was a doctoral student in the Robotics Institute studying computer vision, and where our literature classes met in a converted factory building. I read Chaucer and postcolonial theory surrounded by students enthusiastically designing bridges, creating digital performance art, and programming robot dogs to play soccer. I am grateful to my CMU teachers, especially Christine Aguilar, Peggy Knapp, Kristina Straub, and Michael Whitmore, and, at the University of Illinois, to Robert Markley, in whose class I read Maria Edgeworth's *Belinda*, found more robots, and went off on a tangent reading the "Rosamond" stories. Thank you to the many people who supported me at Illinois, especially Eleanor Courtemanche, Jed Esty, Lauren M. E. Goodlad, Jim Hansen, Robert Markley, Justine S. Murison, Hina Nazar, Michael Rothberg, Julia Saville, and Gillen D'Arcy Wood. Special thanks reserved for my advisor, Ted Underwood, who generously critiqued my drafts and provided encouragement when I doubted my project.

One reason I connected with *Belinda* is that my dad, like the Percivals and Clarence Hervey, performed little experiments around the house on pretty much everything. Growing up with "familiar science," I recognized my dad's calculation of the depth of an Ithaca gorge, or his explanations for why pectin makes strawberry jam firm as his eccentric expression of love. We did not have any automata, but we had a large family. My dad had three daughters, then three more stepchildren, then half a dozen high school exchange students, and he tutored all of us in physics, chemistry, and math. I remember these lessons with the emotions that other people recall reading picture books on their parent's lap, and that comparison has made me alert to the shared spaces of literacy and science instruction. Thank you to my dad and all of my siblings, Christine, Rebecca, Jonathan, Kris, and Mackenzie, and my moms, Donna, Pat, and Dietlind, for everything you taught me.

I owe much to my new family who sustains me, my husband, Derek, and my daughters, Isla and Rowan, who were born while I wrote this book. Getting to know my own children gave me a different appreciation for the individuality of children's responses to books and objects, and the difficult, long process of learning letter sounds and patching them together into words. I appreciate the people who have cared for my children while I wrote this book and taught them many things, but especially love, patience, and kindness: Destiny Gardner, Margot Rossignon, Chris Wilson, Valinda Peat, Brekke Day, Taylor Lancaster, and their grandmother Dietlind Hoiem. I am thankful that several academics helped me after maternity leave to reconfigure my work schedule, including Michelle Martinez, who saved my sanity by driving me to a Victorian Studies conference while I nursed Isla, and Cynthia Oliver and Shelly Weinberg for talking me through ideas I had put on hold.

The archival dimension for this project was made possible by librarians who supported my research, beginning with Andrea Immel at the Cotsen Children's Library at Princeton. I first read Jane Marcet's *Willy's Travels on the Railroad* at Cotsen, and I gathered images of people working from production stories, although I did not know what to call them yet. Suzan Alteri welcomed me to the Baldwin Library of Historical Children's Literature at the University of Florida, gathering hundreds of inventor biographies, travel books, production stories, and physics textbooks, while pointing out unique marginalia. Her bibliography of nineteenth-century women science writers for children enabled the interdisciplinary turn of this project, alongside encouragement from Alan Rauch. Thank you to Erin Chiparo, Jody Mitchell, and Sarah Mitchell at Lilly Library at Indiana University, Bloomington for sharing their collection of boardgames and literacy aids, and to librarians at the Rare Book & Manuscript Library at the University of Illinois at Urbana-Champaign, where I found new editions of materials I first read elsewhere. I initially read cooperative periodicals at the Cambridge University Library, where I called up various education treatises. Sophie McCulloch at The

National Co-operative Archive in Manchester assisted with historical periodicals and George Jacob Holyoake's writings, while staff welcomed me to the New Lanark World Heritage Site. Thank you Marlène Rüfenacht Archiviste-Documentaliste at Musée d'horlogerie du Locle—Château des Monts for assistance with the history of Swiss automata.

Several organizations provided financial support for this project at various stages: the Illinois Program for Research in the Humanities (IPRH), now the Humanities Research Institute (HRI), whose fellowship and community supported my writing for a year; the Friends of the Princeton University Library, whose Library Research Grant allowed me to use the Cotsen Children's Library collection and covered the cost of including images in this book; a National Endowment for the Humanities in the Arts (NEH) fellowship and an Illinois Humanities Released Time (HRT) Campus Research Board fellowship together provided teaching release to focus on writing. Several people helped me draft my materials and encouraged me to apply, including Maria Gillombardo, Craig Koslofsky, and Carol Symes. Craig read early summaries of the project and advised me to focus on social class to create a straightforward argument out of the interdisciplinary knots.

Over the years, I collaborated with and learned from a host of enthusiastic friends and colleagues who revived my spirits or offered ideas when I had so little time to express my appreciation, especially Teri Chettiar, Ryan Cordell, Irvin Hunt, Emily Knox, Mariah Kupfner, Jennifer Lieberman, Bonnie Mak, Michelle Martinez, Judith Pintar, Lisa Ann Robertson, Sarah Sahn, Jodi Schneider, David Sepkoski, Sara Weisweaver, and Jessica Young. I owe a special debt to childhood friend Christina Szakaly, to Stephanie Clark for her kind mentorship and friendship during lonely times, and to Guy Tal for modeling loyalty and intellectual curiosity to everyone he meets. Several children's literature scholars introduced me to this field; others generously provided mentorship, letters or support, feedback, friendship, and kind words: Minjie Chen, Alisa Clapp-Itnyre, Karen Coats, Sarah Park Dahlen, Patrick Fleming, Fiona Hartley-Kroeger, Mary Hilton, Jackie Horne, Katharine Kittredge, Kyungwon Koh, Alaine Martaus, Elissa Myers, Kate McDowell, Hina Nazar, Kenneth Parille, Julie Park, Donelle Ruwe, Lara Saguisag, Joe Sutliff Sanders, Celestina Savonius-Wroth, Sara Schwebel, Deborah Stevenson, Laureen Tedesco, Ralf Thiede, Alan Rauch, and

Laura Wasowicz. I cannot imagine where I would be on this project without careful feedback and questions from Jamie Jones, who helped me figure out the confusing thoughts colliding in my head. Joe Sutliff Sanders and Katharine Kittredge offered recommendation letters and encouragement back when I first attended the Children's Literature Association. Other senior scholars showed up at my panels consistently, offering feedback and kindness, which I so deeply appreciate even if I cannot list you all.

Finally, my editor, Matt Becker, and series editor, Karen Sánchez-Eppler, believed in this book and made it happen, while my astute peer reviewers waded through the early manuscript and offered incredibly kind and practical advice. Rachael DeShano, Julie Shilling, Sally Nichols, and Sandy Sadow helped make this book. The digital humanities supplement to the book would not be possible without the training I received from the scholarly communications and publishing division at the University of Illinois at Urbana-Champaign Library on fair use and copyright from Sara Benson, and digital publishing from Daniel Tracy, with additional advice from Mary Ton, Spencer Keralis, and John W. Randolph, and images assistance from Owen Monroe and Helen Salkeld.

The Education of Things

INTRODUCTION

Elizabeth Hamilton's Philosophical Piano Stool

The novelist Elizabeth Hamilton in her *Letters on the Elementary Principles of Education* (1802) provides mothers with practical nursery advice founded on Dugald Stewart's philosophy of mind. In one anecdote, her sample conversation between a wise mother, Mrs. Z, and her son, shows how nursery play teaches through everyday objects:

> "Here is a pretty box, mama; but it won't open for all that I can do."
>
> "That box, my dear, won't open by force; the lid is screwed on, and it must be turned in such a manner as to take out the screw. Observe. There—it is opened—now see how the part that fixes, is cut in the manner of a screw."
>
> "Oh, yes, now I understand it, for I remember what papa told me one day about the cork-screw, when I was looking at it: but I thought there was no use of screws, but to draw corks."
>
> "All screws are made upon the same plan, or principle, as it is called; will you remember that word?" . . . "A piece of furniture that is just by you, is made upon the principle of the screw; and if you will find it out, I will give you a kiss."
>
> "I see! I see! It is the stool on which my sister sits at the piano-forte. It turns and rises just like the lid of this box."

As an exemplary mother-teacher, Mrs. Z allows her son's curiosity about an object he explores (the box) to guide their inquiries (he asks how to open it); then she provides a general principle (the screw) exemplified by this particular box lid. They apply this principle to his memory of a similar object (the cork screw), and she tests his mastery of the principle by asking him to find more screws (the piano stool). Beginning with a single instance of a screw, the child assembles knowledge about screws in general. Mrs. Z "taught her son the properties of one of the principles of mechanics, in unscrewing his toy," merely one example of how she guides his "accurate examination of every object that came within the sphere of their observation."[1]

Mechanical philosophy books for children typically begin with "simple machines" (screw, pulley, inclined plane, and wedge), but, despite teaching about screws, Hamilton is more concerned with reading. As a result of Mrs. Z's conversations, "Reading was taught with ease, a privilege, rather than a task." But why would "the principles of mechanics" help with reading? According to Hamilton, children develop the faculty of "perception" first (used to gather observations) and "reflection" last (used for abstract thought, or general principles). Therefore, God designed the world itself as "a school of virtue," where "the objects that inspire delight are liberally scattered on every side." By appealing to "the objects of sight and sound, before the mental faculties have begun to open," mothers prepare their children's minds for reading. Since mechanics bridges manual manipulation and observation with abstract mathematical principles, the subject gently guides children from the infant world of sensation to the literary world of symbols and imagination. Hamilton warns that "little books . . . given to children at an early age" are "so many destroyers of their faculties." Children should exercise their minds on "material objects" first, then "fiction."[2] In this respect, Mrs. Z's son is like his toy; she cannot "open" him "by force," meaning she cannot teach her child something before he is developmentally ready.

Hamilton's conversation illustrates one of the key insights of this book. By the close of the eighteenth century, learning to read and write texts became closely associated with learning directly from the material world. Mrs. Z prepares her son for reading by teaching him what I call "mechanical literacy," or an understanding of the principles governing the physical world: *the regular laws that explain how objects are sensed, manipulated, created, manufactured, distributed, and exchanged.* Mechanical philosophy (or the natural laws governing matter in motion) was a valued component of British nineteenth-century education curricula; so was mechanical literacy. Mechanical literacy encompasses a constellation of skills and knowledge areas thought to empower industrial-era youth to navigate the complex systems in which they participate. The study of biological and heavenly bodies, manufacturing and political economy—even child education—all concerned material bodies in motion. By reconvening these knowledge areas using the term "mechanical literacy," I consider the mutual influences between the physical sciences, economics, and human development. These intersections allowed ideas about labor and play to translate between disparate contexts. Materials for teaching human anatomy or steam engines, for instance, speak to debates over child labor or education.

This book investigates where alphabetical literacies intersected with mechanical literacy in the toys and books that taught children reading, physical sciences, manufacturing, political economy, and grammar. I begin with the commercialization of children's publishing in the late eighteenth century and conclude with the approach of universal primary school in Britain in 1870 and the expansion of male suffrage with the Second Reform Act of 1867. During this period, many British author-educators urged parents to combine book learning with active lessons that used the child's body to explore their environment, resulting in a convergence between traditional alphabetical literacies and new literacies for an industrial economy. What started as a movement in bourgeois nurseries and Dissenting academies to make knowledge tangible, sensible, and playful, as suggested by John Locke, Claude-Adrien Helvétius, Jean-Jacques Rousseau, Maria and Richard Edgeworth, and Johann Heinrich Pestalozzi, and many others, then spread after 1820 to infant schools and mechanics institutes, becoming pervasive in the education systems of Great Britain and the United States by late century. This pedagogical movement inspired new materials for children—games, alphabet tiles, puzzles, cards, lottery sheets, movable books, wall prints, microscopes, model machines, panoramas, wooden blocks, maps, and specimen boxes—all sold alongside "toy books" for children.

Teaching children through observation, experimentation, and practical experience is an effective, child-centered approach, one that empowers students as partners in discovery with adult teachers. Yet social hierarchy and economic inequality were originally built into these pedagogies by design and occluded through egalitarian rhetoric. Initially, exploring the material world firsthand offered an attractive alternative to learning from books, a corrective that many English bourgeois radicals and Scottish

Enlightenment authors believed could circumvent received wisdom from the past, with its errors and prejudices, and create a new society of critical thinkers, their ideas sharpened by observation. Following the Reign of Terror in France and the decline of English constitutional reform, this revolutionary dream of learning directly from the material world was tempered by the realization that objects are far from ideologically neutral alternatives to texts. Children use objects to learn about social class and property ownership, which informs their embodied reading practices. By recovering the forgotten politics of experiential and haptic learning, I show how these pedagogies were used for varied political aims, by free-market liberals to defend child labor as instructive, by wealthy landed families to teach children lessons in the sciences, by bourgeois radicals to train future industry innovators, and by leaders of the cooperative movement to cultivate politically active youth.

Children's Material Culture and the Politics of Play

Scholars have shown the remarkable extent to which observation, manipulation, and experimentation contributed to children's instruction and entertainment. Jill Shefrin's survey of over four thousand educational aids produced by a single English publishing family, the Dartons, indicates the vast array of materials sold alongside children's books. Barbara Maria Stafford's *Artful Science* and Jessica Riskin's *Science in the Age of Sensation* describe Enlightenment-era public lectures with captivating experiments or visually stunning exhibitions of natural and mechanical wonders, which inspired children's lessons for activating the *sensorium commune*.[3] Over the next century, children's publishers commercially produced domestic-friendly kits or toys based on these public entertainments, designed for use in nurseries and classrooms. Megan Norcia examines how travel and adventure themed boardgames made geography tangible to young people, along with conflicting messages about British and US imperialism. Sarah Anne Carter's impressive *Object Lessons* recovers how late nineteenth-century US primary school instructors used specimens from natural resources and industrial processes to teach children critical thinking about their everyday surroundings. These studies collectively demonstrate the importance of objects for teaching children about race, class, gender, and Indigeneity. Carter shows, for instance, that Native Americans both learned with object lessons and served as object lessons for non-Native students.[4] This wealth of scholarship reinforces Robin Bernstein's appraisal "that the union of literature and material culture has defined children's literature since 1744" when John Newbery packaged *A Little Pretty Pocket-Book* (1744) with a ball or pincushion, and has only "broadened and intensified over the past two and a half centuries."[5]

The invention of rational playthings for use with children's books is instantiated by John Newbery's 1765 paragon of schoolteachers, Goody Two-Shoes, whose students learn to read by running about the schoolroom to find alphabet letters posted on the walls, and who devises a barometer to help farmers harvest their hay before it rains, proving her, in Seth Lerer's words, "a mistress of empiricism: an observer of the world, a maker of the tools of measurement." (The villagers call her a witch.)[6] If we have taken so long to notice Goody's multiliteracies, which enable her shoe-strapping social mobility, some blame falls, according to Lissa Paul, to the anti-commercialist sentiments of modern scholars, for whom "advertising and education are mutually exclusive categories," since "innocent children" are "too pure to be the objects of grubby marketing practices." She points out that publisher Benjamin Tabart inserted brazen puff pieces into children's stories to connect reading with the maps, microscopes, and educational playthings he sold.[7] More than mere accessories, these items, like Goody's barometer, are legible objects and powerful portents. Their close companionship with books remind us that Goody's alphabet, too, is "an artifact" whose "physicality" recalls the printing processes that produced it. "It is an object, held in little hands."[8] Scholars in childhood studies have embraced material culture for its ability to reframe debates over the adult-driven educative project of making media for children. Meredith Bak regards commercial toys of the past, like visual media today, as neither "exclusively disciplinary or liberating," asserting that "children had the capacity to be consumers, experimenters, and makers, exercising multiple forms of agency."[9] The same could be said of the multisensory playthings that accompanied the first century of children's book publishing.

Paying attention to material culture cuts a straight path between texts and actions in the world, helping us imagine how children's literature "actually functions in the everyday lives of children."[10] The torn, colored, and broken pages described in Hannah Field's *Playing with the Book* bear witness to the actual children who used and abused their novelty books in novel ways unanticipated by adults. Their joyful physicality in eating or breaking their treasures prizes gimmicks over narrative in defiance of adult expectations that children mature beyond mechanical features toward enjoying the intellectual contents of books. Children's material culture, says Field, tacitly shares a common premise advanced by Michel de Certeau in *The Practice of Everyday Life*, that cultural consumption is never entirely passive. Drawing a similar idea from media studies, Jacqueline Reid-Walsh refers to child readers as "interactors" and categorizes moveable books with today's multimodal texts and computer games as "a type of interactive narrative media-text on paper platforms" or "supports."[11] Although concerned with more conventional books, M. O. Grenby prefers "user" over "reader" in *The Child Reader* to acknowledge the variety of unapproved things children do with books besides read them, for his expansive overview of who purchased these books, how children used and stored them, and what they wrote in their margins.[12]

In the company of objects, books and their readers are more lively than we thought. Through everyday actions, children claim books and toys for their own by signing bookplates, doodling in margins, tearing pages, breaking delicate features, coloring illustrations, singing songs, creating parodies, and rewriting narratives. If inscription claims books, performance claims stories. Marah Gubar suggests investigating how children interact performativity with texts to claim ownership of them, expanding the boundaries of children's literature to include works (and objects) that children found meaningful for their purposes. Andrew O'Malley explores the playful responses to *Robinson Crusoe*, an adult novel claimed by children through abridged chapbooks and paraphernalia, but also by playacting the story. Even children's hymns, too easily dismissed as staid didactic materials, call out for raucous performances, according to Alisa Clapp-Itnyre, creating space for children's consolation, political agency, and creative expression. Performance theory also underwrites Robin Bernstein's method for reading artifacts as "scriptive things" that invite play from child users, who may choose to act out racist performances or resist these affordances.[13] Together, these many playful artifacts provide a better understanding of the ways children creatively altered what adults provided for them, but also the complex politics of play.

One undercurrent of these studies is that play requires privilege. The recreational epistemology popularized by Locke worked best for families who carved out an early childhood dedicated to spontaneous exploration, free from compulsory labor. Learning from at-hand objects appealed to the precariously situated, mobile middle classes, those largely responsible for the period's pedagogical and didactic literature. Andrew O'Malley argues that embracing Locke's concept of children born as blank slates, deficient in reason but capable of improvement, helped the middle classes differentiate themselves from social stations above and below them and replace inherited privilege with economic competition as a more "justified and morally acceptable inequality."[14] Extending this argument to Locke's "playthings," we might say that baubles and alphabet tiles taught the same middle-class values of self-reliance, thrift, charity, and piety that O'Malley and Isaac Kramnick identify in early children's literature. If the work of children is play, it must be self-improving, virtuous, productive play. This kind of play teaches mechanical literacy as the groundwork for learning to read, but it also teaches about the child's place among material goods.

Through play, children practice their social station by interacting with play objects or identifying with fictional characters. As Michelle Beissel Heath explains, "Play and literature are consistently deployed in tandem in attempts to create ideal citizens—though what those ideals were varied greatly and were dependent on factors such as gender, ethnicity, colonial status, and class."[15] Play creates social identity, allowing for children to perform who they might become, and, as Christopher Parkes points out, children's literature has much to say about what kinds of play prepare children to become good capitalists. Challenging British Romanticism's concept of "childhood as separate and apart from capitalist society," Parkes argues that a middle-class vision of children as ideal innovators and self-improvers "displaced" competing working-class depictions of children as victims in the late nineteenth century, so that childhood became "synonymous with capitalism."[16] Similarly, Karen Sánchez-Eppler considers how play and leisure in the United States provided children with opportunities to perform class identities while learning what leisure activities and behaviors others considered appropriate, given their social position. Middle-class children learned they were supposed to engage in "culturally valuable play" through "depictions of working-class children" that contrasted with their own improving leisure activities—among these, reading imaginative literature to learn how to empathize with working street children.[17] Her pithy observation that "poverty, like childhood, is merely a stage to be outgrown," and "class conversely" is "an identity to be grown into," could as easily describe early nineteenth-century Britain, when reformers expressed moral objections to mistreatment, dangerous conditions, and long hours for children, but accepted child labor as necessary. As Pamela Horn explains, "They merely wished it to be regulated in order to eliminate the worst abuses." Even late Victorians believed the half-time system (days split between school and work) was beneficial to children and therefore they resisted implementing child labor regulations.[18] Under these circumstances, labor's exclusion from the boundaries of playful learning constituted a strategic move in a contest over what actions in the world produce knowledge.

The intersection of labor, commercialism, and objects is the territory of thing theorists. Bill Brown and Lorraine Daston have used literature to explore the lives of nonhuman objects, drawing on Marxist traditions of historical materialism and Heideggerian philosophy to decenter humans and explore nonhuman material things that speak, act upon, and shape human subjects.[19] Igor Kopytoff and Arjun Appadurai suggest recovering the varied life cycle of "specific things, as they move through different hands, contexts, and uses," resisting commodity fetishism through "methodological fetishism," or by ironically treating objects as if they are living people who relate their autobiographies.[20] While loosely inspired by these theoretical approaches, *The Education of Things* recovers epistemological and ontological insights from the nursery, using children's books about mechanical philosophy to discover what children, parents, and practitioners actually learned about matter in motion. This thing theory from below investigates marginalized voices (mothers, children, working-class teachers) and genres (radical periodicals, science textbooks) to generate new theoretical insights about labor and play, which prove useful for interrogating established pedagogical authorities (Pestalozzi, Rousseau) and reexamining canonical authors. Joining together children's literature and childhood studies with the histories of popular science and working-class print culture, I investigate children's authors like Maria Edgeworth, Anna Letitia Barbauld, Priscilla Wakefield, Rev. Isaac Taylor, John Ayrton Paris, Henry Cole, and George Jacob Holyoake, who taught children about the material world and integrated this knowledge with reading and writing. Despite their differences, these author-educators all studied science and economics, connected with philosophers of mind and manufacturers, and embraced embodied learning while challenging the classical curriculum of landed gentlemen. While the breadth of my archive prevents delving into histories of knowledge by Lorraine Daston, George Levine, Mary Poovey, and Barbara Herrnstein Smith, I investigate how children learned to produce and claim ownership of knowledge through labor and play.[21]

Reading Class Politics in Texts and Objects

In keeping with my argument about integrated literacies, my method of analysis interprets children's books as one of many interactive, legible material objects. Hamilton's anecdote becomes more meaningful, for instance, considering a literacy toy familiar to her readers—an alphabet, printed on round cards, with a letter on one side and an object printed on the reverse, the cards stacked in a cylindrical box with a screw-top lid. Using this toy, Mrs. Z's son must, quite literally, learn mechanics to access his alphabet. When finished, he puts his letters, along with their object pictures, in a box that symbolizes his mind. This concretization of learning as collecting teaches children that knowledge is analogous to physical property, a point reinforced by the common practice of using wooden storage boxes for alphabet tiles or card cabinets to play forfeits. In this memory game, a child tries to name the letter indicated by another player, and, depending on the response, either collects or forfeits a letter from the box.

FIGURE 1. The Picture Alphabet (Birmingham: Kendall & Son, after 1840). Children's alphabet counters stored in a turned wooden box with screw-top lid. Cotsen Children's Library. Courtesy of Princeton University Library. The image on the lid is an example of an interlocutor gesture (see chapter 1), in which a mother or teacher presents an instructional toy in the same image composition used for presenting a book.

One description of forfeits that uses letters appears in *The Art of Teaching in Sport* (1785) by Lady Ellenor Fenn, written to accompany her set of grammar, spelling, and arithmetic toys. The self-styled "rational dame" advises that mothers give their child a box and "let him call it his own; as he acquires a knowledge of the letters let him deposit them in his box . . . If he should forget a letter, then he forfeits that one till he recognizes it . . . Children love property; the box will be often produced, its contents displayed;—'these letters,' (the happy child will say) *'are my own!'"* [Fenn's emphasis][22] The child's earnest pronouncement of his status as a literate property owner is quite distinct, in Fenn's account, from the carnivalesque attitude toward property in other forfeit games of folk origin in which children forfeit small treasures but earn them back via silly dares or mock punishments meted out by a child judge chosen among her peers.[23] Fenn's game is about the child's slow and proud progress toward adult literacy as measured by steady accumulation. The double status of Fenn's letters, as texts and as manipulable toys, reinforces the child's association of reading with property, since acquiring literacy is so clearly commensurate with acquiring objects. For Fenn, Hamilton, and their contemporaries, toys and books not only teach children messages about property, they *are* personal property. For those who could not purchase letter tiles of their own, schoolchildren received rewards for good behavior, through a practice called "dab." The lucky child sticks a pin into a book, pinning through the pages to capture one of the lotto object images hidden in the book, which they receive as a prize in exchange for the pin.[24] The added tangibility of literacy toys reinforces connections between reading, manipulation, and property, while teaching mechanical and alphabetical literacies together.

By using their books and toys to acquire ideas, children also learned to regard physical things as exterior markers of interior moral qualities and mental processes. Just as stories in books favor metatextual commentary on the making and consumption of texts, objects designed for children favor metacognitive learning, which elevates mere "sensation" of external objects (to use Locke's terms), into "reflection," or "the *Perception of the operations of our own Minds* within us."[25] Literacy toys are first grasped by children, then they become a child's first metaphors for the workings of his mind. As Mrs. Z's son demonstrates, toys held, manipulated, and owned are knowledge held inside the mind, but also stand-ins for the mind itself as a storage container for representations of objects. The ability to "read" and control bodies—one's own body among other material bodies—is associated with elite property owners. Among other things, Mrs. Z's son learns that people with philosophical piano stools possess a theoretical understanding of matter, which they use to move objects strategically, rather than merely "by force." Like alphabetical literacy, mechanical literacy was conceptualized in ways that maintained class distinctions, despite the rise of mass literacy, by reserving a particular kind of mastery over objects for people of property.

The politics of learning directly from objects is clear from the case of Elizabeth Hamilton, who not only supported mass literacy but promoted instructing poor children about the material world. A volunteer in Monitorial schools, she became the first British writer to suggest using German educator Johann Heinrich Pestalozzi's "object lessons" to correct the debilitating effects of raising children in homes without alphabet cards and philosophical piano stools.[26] Her *Hints Addressed to the Patrons and Directors of Schools* (1815) insisted that poor children, especially girls, who "have their sense of sight perpetually occupied in a narrow sphere," only seem incapable of learning to read because of their barren home environments, but with proper education "the intellectual faculties appear often strong and vigorous." Through exercises that teach "an attentive observation of these objects" children are "led to the acquirement of new ideas, till, step by step, they arrive at those in the want of which their apparent stupidity originated."[27] In sum, she argues that the availability of diverse objects accounts for class and gender differences in intelligence and suggests ways for schools to provide a stimulating environment that prepares poor children for reading. With its deficit undertones, Hamilton's *Hints* advocates for training children with objects to save minds degraded by object poverty while reinforcing the assumption that large homes filled with diverse and curious furnishings are the ideal educational environment that classrooms should aspire to imitate.

For Hamilton's contemporaries, exploring the world prepares children for reading because mechanical literacy, like reading and writing, signals the rational self-governance and extensive property ownership of the ruling elite. The full significance of Mrs. Z's dialog unfolds in a well-stocked nursery, where children organize their little treasures in specimen boxes and spell with alphabet card "cabinets," perhaps themed as natural history collections, and where children play memory games passed down in oral history using objects and cumulative rhymes. These kinds of nurseries—the ones where parents could afford those little wooden alphabet boxes with screw-top lids—were part of larger homes or country estates, where owning, collecting, and knowing seemed necessarily connected with moving, manipulating, and commanding the world by harnessing the general principles of matter. The identification of these mechanical competencies as essential for self-fashioning maintains social distinctions between the mechanically literate and the mechanic. At a time when artisan work contributed more significantly to national wealth, these distinctions between different ways of using the body to learn determined whose manual skills have social capital. As portrayed in children's literature and educational materials, the ability to control matter, to own things—one's self included—is a sign of self-governance. Women, youth, or working-class characters thus challenged their presumed child-like, hand-to-mouth existence, and proved their capacity for governance, by demonstrating their command over matter. Those who acquire mechanical literacy transform themselves by comprehending bodies in motion, human and nonhuman. Once they can "read" complex systems with moving parts, they can navigate them; no longer mechanized, they leverage the physical world.

Histories of Literacy and Inequality

By calling the ability to "read" the physical world a "literacy," I want to suggest that mechanical literacy prefigures today's emergent digital and cultural literacies, functioning as an essential skillset taught alongside reading and writing, one that transformed established paper technologies. Additionally, the critical examination of "literacy myths" in the field of new literacy studies is useful for interrogating the cultural beliefs surrounding mechanical knowledge in the sciences, engineering, and political economy. A bureaucratic term first used in the late nineteenth century, "literacy" captures the cultural meanings and metrics of reading and writing. Once associated with Christian spiritual merit, literacy increasingly became associated with secular achievements, such as the potential for social mobility, and the self-reflexivity of those capable of writing their lives through autobiography. According to Harvey Graff and Brian Street, literacy is culturally situated, associated with powerful mythologies about the origins of Western civilization in the all-powerful written word. People commonly believe that acquiring literacy brings spiritual freedom and economic opportunities, even though these rewards are dependent on cultural contexts and may never materialize for people marginalized by their gender, race, ethnicity, or class.[28] Always accompanied by its shadow (illiteracy), literacy is used and misused to winnow the so-called educated from the ignorant, the literacy haves from the have nots—a distinction maintained over time by shifting the goalposts of what constitutes literacy, maintaining a "literacy crisis," where skills lag behind ever-increasing demands for technological competencies.[29] The distinction between the literate and the illiterate has been leveraged, in the United States, as a proxy for enforcing racist immigration policies through literacy tests, or to suppress African American voters through poll tests.[30] Withholding literacy from Black Americans helped enforce slavery and racial oppression, while at the same time, teaching English literacy in Indian Boarding Schools was a tool for erasing Native American cultures.[31] In early nineteenth-century Britain, the abbreviated curriculum offered to poor children was cited as a reason for limiting their political participation and suppressing the working-class press. As narrowly defined and quantified by state institutions, literacy can legitimize and rationalize structural inequalities by tracking students into professional or trade employment, based on a meritocratic veneer that hides structural inequalities through suspect metrics. Nevertheless, a belief in the power of the written word can be a self-fulling prophesy, aiding freedom seekers to escape from slavery and circulate their stories. For any individuals who gain literacy, there is always the possibility of adapting skills for their own purposes, or to resist oppressive narratives.[32] Like alphabetical literacy, mechanical literacy developed its own mythologies derived from a similar set of beliefs about the progress of European civilization through machines and the superior mechanical genius of British inventors, which justified its imperialist project. Mastery over machines explained the rising wealth of an industrial middle class, while applying machinery principles to organizing schools promised to make reading and writing cheaply accessible to all. Implying both social stratification and the march of progress, mechanical literacy was mythologized as indispensable for social advancement, rational thought, self-reflection, and moral autonomy.

Since mechanical and alphabetical literacies are interconnected, beliefs about the power of objects and the power of the written word mutually reinforce the association of literacy with owning property.

In *Reading Children*, Patricia Crain describes the prevalent cultural belief in nineteenth-century America that reading grants children "self-possession," what John Locke describes as a person's ownership of the self, because reading "was associated with property."[33] In Great Britain, reading was associated with a governing class whose membership primarily included male landed property owners, then, after the 1832 Reform Act, men with the required minimum of capital. While the Scottish kirk provided reading instruction to all children studying their catechism, English working-class families relied on a hodgepodge of dame schools and day schools, which children attended for an average of two to four years, often noncontiguous, before entering the workforce around age ten. Literacy rates in England fluctuated around 30 to 45 percent until the introduction of universal primary school in 1870.[34] Instruction in the "higher subjects" of classical languages, geometry, and English grammar was reserved for the few elite boarding schools for boys, while newer Dissenting academies served the wealthier mercantile and professional families with a revised curriculum of applied sciences and vernacular languages. The ability to express one's ideas in writing was, therefore, synonymous with having a political voice. When debating whether to fund national schools, some members of parliament tried to regulate social mobility by limiting mass literacy, arguing that if the poor could read, they would no longer plow, and if they could write, then they would commit forgery. This preoccupation with counterfeits betrays anxieties over the possibility that one class might resemble another if everyone possessed a written voice, challenging the existing economic system and mode of governance.[35] Similar debates considered whether new scientific discoveries would threaten agrarian traditions in the name of railroad tracks and steam engines, or whether science writing provided safe, apolitical reading for intelligent workers who might otherwise burn ricks and break machines. For others still, understanding the material world provided insight into how to address poverty or reform the machinery of government. Amidst these political disagreements over who can access knowledge and for what purpose, children's books performed a gatekeeping function across multiple subject areas by indicating what kind of literacy is appropriate for readers of various social stations.

Work and Play as Everyday Learning

In the term "mechanical literacy," the word "literacy" calls attention to the ideological beliefs surrounding children's technical and scientific competencies, while "mechanical" brings labor into dialog with play. The mechanical manipulation of objects was a form of liberatory educational play, but also a form of physical labor performed by "mechanics." Both of these meanings operate in the context of experiential education, where learning-while-doing can be strangely difficult to distinguish from child labor. Experiential learning reframes work usually performed for subsistence as educational play. The establishment of an educational category of labor—performed voluntarily or spontaneously, in a space designated for learning—implicitly creates an opposite category of labor, conceived as intellectually degrading, mechanical, automatic, and subordinate. This division between the mechanically literate and the mechanic appears over and again in children's books and materials. In Lucy Wilson's *A Visit to Grove Cottage* (1823), for instance, Caroline and Emily Summerset travel with their father from London to Cumberland. They stop in Birmingham to witness "the grand toy-shop of Europe," where the girls can "see children of your own age employed in making watch-chains, bracelets, necklaces, buttons, snuff-boxes and buckles, and using their little fingers with as much dexterity as you do in dressing your doll, or playing a game of drafts."[36] This comparison between two class-specific interactions with material culture—child play and child labor—sets apart Caroline and Emily, who visit factories for an educational tour, maybe try their hand at making something, from the children working six days a week assembling watch chains and buckles. Through a curious alchemy, this distinction transmutes the ignorance of these privileged children about the lives of Birmingham factory children into a kind of aesthetic distance through which they can appreciate the work of others as an empowering practical lesson. Meanwhile, the development of children who actually make things receives little narrative attention. And how can it, when they are the object in another child's lesson?

What does it mean that recreational, experiential, and haptic learning flourished during a time of such divisions in how British children used their "little fingers"? While research in children's print culture has yielded fascinating explorations of book-making processes and publishing houses, we have struggled with how to join children's literature and material culture with the history of labor, even though when child characters learn through play, they compare themselves with people who work. Consider how labor and play are woven together in *The New Picture Book: Being Pictorial Lessons on Form, Comparison, and Number, for Children under Seven Years of Age* (1858), published in Edinburgh and translated from German educator Nicholas Bohny's *Neues Bilderbuch* (1850), which reached at least nine British editions in a dozen years, its popularity amplified by enthusiasm for Pestalozzi's object lessons and the kindergarten movement.[37] The cover depicts an ideal classroom environment reminiscent of Mrs. Z's nursery, where children of various ages engage with age-specific toys (blocks, architecture models, drawing), while a female instructor shows *The New Picture Book* to children ages three to eight gathered casually about her. The preface advises educators to harness children's enthusiasm for tinkering with everyday things. Experienced teachers who "have taken interest in the early acquisitions of children" know that "they easily comprehend objects, pictures of them, and find delight in examining them and speaking about them." (Here, "early acquisitions" refers ambiguously to ideas or collected objects.) Children should experience this book as a social and sensual activity, learning "the habit of observing accurately, yet with readiness—a habit acquired by the exercise of attention, through the eye, on visible objects." As the author explains, "All objects have form, are presented in different positions, and are one or more in number. In these properties of objects lie the germs of thought and knowledge; and in the perception of these, combined with the use of speech in describing them, we have a sure foundation upon which to rear a solid superstructure of education. Nor can we over-calculate the detriment arising from the neglect of this habit of readily and with accuracy observing the qualities and relations of objects."[38] If thinking begins with the "properties of objects," the preface suggests, then, without objects, and without guided practice describing them, children cannot properly think.[39]

Whereas counting books typically feature similar repeated objects, *The New Picture Book* invites interpretive creativity from readers through variety, with images of everyday objects and people at play or work. The opening page progresses from "one" as conceptually singular (a single horse), to "two" as intimate and confiding (two horses greeting each other), to "three" as social (three horses engaged in social grooming). A full page dedicated to "five" compares five male deer, their antlers splayed out from their heads, while the row underneath shows five fallen trees resembling the deer, their bare branches stretched toward the sky while loggers cut them apart. Suggested questions for instructors, in small script under each image, include, "How many trees do you see in this row? Are they standing? Why have they been uprooted?" Below the trees, three butterflies, one caterpillar, and one chrysalis make five.[40] As children move down the page from deer, to trees, to butterflies, they face increasingly complex problems of categorization, form, and identity. Are some of these butterflies the same animal, despite their radically different forms? And if an animal who changes form retains its identity, what are we to say of the dead trees, branches splayed like deer antlers, which the loggers cut apart to make into wooden furniture? And what of the chrysalis, a discarded dead thing, while the butterfly lives? And what of the child reading this book? These clever illustrations feature living and nonliving items on the brink of transformation. While devising descriptions about the "properties of objects," children use this book to facilitate their own transformation, but also to observe themselves as living objects transformed. Just as Mrs. Z's son resembles his literacy toy, the readers of *The New Picture Book* narrate their own development by creating object descriptions, rehearsing a process for consciously shaping themselves using the material world.

This common analogy between sculpting and teaching, or labor and learning, raises the question of whether artisan labor, or physical labor more generally, is a catalyst for self-development—whether children need to play-act work in order to make themselves. In addition to playing or attending school, children in *The New Picture Book* sew and spin in scenes juxtaposed against adult workers cutting apart fallen trees or carpenters shaping wood in their workshops. By linking together physical labor with education, such illustrations suggest comparisons between children who spin their own chrysalis then leave it behind and adult artisans who create objects by shaping once-living wood. This juxtaposition of early childhood play with labor depends on

FIGURES 2–3: Nicholas Bohny, *The New Picture Book: Being Pictorial Lessons on Form, Comparison, and Number, for Children under Seven Years of Age* (Edinburgh: Edmonston and Douglas, 1858), cover, 9. Cotsen Children's Library. Courtesy of Princeton University Library. This copy is signed, "to Isabella Napier Wilkin from her loving Auntie, Jane Rigby, 1st January, 1860."

the cultural construction of both children and working-class adults as embodied learners—as "primitive" in their relationship to the material world, which they experience in terms of immediate needs (hunger, warmth). Thus Pestalozzi credited one of his assistants, a local illiterate man named Kresi, with discovering the "elementary principles of intellectual action" (a phrase that implies the mind's movements, like matter, are subject to regular laws), presumably because Kresi has the advantage of existing in a closer mental state to the orphan students they teach. As paraphrased by Pestalozzi, Kresi explains his discovery of how to use objects to expand vocabulary: "I did with my children, as nature does with savages, first bringing an image before their eyes, and then seeking a word to express the perception to which it gives rise."[41] Nor is Pestalozzi the only author-educator to make problematic comparisons between children, laborers, and non-Europeans. There is a general tendency for such books to contain ideological messages about work, inflected by class, race, and gender, because physical labor shapes the material world just as much as educational play.

The tangled relationship between work and play has lain at the center of experiential education and haptic learning since Jean-Jacques Rousseau's *Emile* (1862), the novel of education that provides the title for this book and a cautionary tale. Emile's tutor, Jean-Jacques, uses object lessons to free his pupil from subordination to his adult instructor by making Emile obedient to the material world instead. Unlike his predecessor, John Locke, who advocates shame and praise in place of physical punishment, Rousseau considers psychological or corporeal discipline equally dangerous, as they teach children to rely on the judgment of others. Rousseau's solution, what he calls "the education of things," limits young Emile to learning from "objects of sense." Rather than command Emile to do things, Jean-Jacques secretly influences his actions through the orchestration of his environment, arranged "so that on all sides he perceives around him only the physical world."[42] The object lessons that Jean-Jacques designs for his pupil separate "the education of things" from "the education of men," meaning that Emile learns from the natural consequences of his actions, without any awareness of Jean-Jacques's behind-the-scenes manipulation. "Never present to his undiscriminating will anything but physical obstacles or punishments which stem from the actions themselves and which he will recall on the proper occasion." By learning from "the force of things alone," or "only from experience," Emile obeys the constraints of the physical world rather than the capricious will of a human instructor.[43] Raised this way, Emile will not try to control other people and force them to provide for his needs. Emile avoids the tyrannical codependency between master and servant, teacher and pupil, child and parent because he submits himself directly to material circumstances rather than to another person. Incidentally, this teaching method supports a political theory in which submitting to authority is consistent with Emile's freedom if government is aligned with the laws of nature.[44]

As many of Rousseau's British readers objected, the division between "things" and "men" is, practically speaking, impossible. Moreover, literary scholarship on it-narratives and commodification by Jonathan Lamb, Mark Blackwell, Elaine Freedgood, Lynn Festa, and John Plotz explore the liminal divide between humans and objects during a period when enslaved persons were legally defined as property and when wives were the property of their husbands and children the property of their fathers.[45] As long as social hierarchies depend upon the objectification and commodification of human beings, experimenting with the material world cannot offer a more liberatory alternative to other forms of education. What children learn about their relationships to material objects helps them conceptualize social hierarchies, especially given the scientific method underpinning Rousseau's epistemology, where knowing means observing, grasping, and speaking for inanimate objects. Emile learns from building furniture and planting crops, yet Rousseau distinguishes these object lessons from the labor they resemble. He compares Emile to a so-called "savage," questionably romanticized as a person "without prescribed task, obeying no one," honing his intelligence, because he is "forced to reason in each action of his life"; he also contrasts Emile with a peasant, "doing always what he is ordered or what he saw his father do or what he has himself done since his youth." Whereas Emile commands himself, the peasant "works only by routine; and in his life, almost an automaton's, constantly busy with the same labors, habit and obedience take the place of reason for him."[46] Rousseau thus distinguishes between the work performed by an internally motivated pupil, who understands and guides his own actions, from the same work performed by a peasant, whom he compares to an "automaton," an obedient machine created by another person. Although Rousseau eliminates books from Emile's environment to prevent subordination through received knowledge, the command Emile establishes over material things reintroduces the social hierarchies he erases. Similarly, when Caroline and Emily watch children making toys and buckles in Manchester, they establish their own mechanical literacy, in contradistinction to the children who make toys and buckles, whose labor, by comparison, seems thoughtless and mechanistic; and the woodsmen sawing at fallen trees in Bohny's picture book serve a similar function.

Class divisions in everyday life actually deepened during this period, as wealthier families invested more in the formal education of their children, creating private bedrooms, nurseries, hobby workshops, and gardens devoted to teaching their children. Despite the fashion for Rousseauvian simplicity, teaching through everyday experience meant purchasing miniature wheelbarrows, home chemistry sets, children's microscope manuals, wall prints, model steam engines, and alphabet blocks. The exemplary mother from Stéphanie-Félicité de Genlis's popular epistolary novel of education, *Adèle et Théodore, ou, Lettres sur l'éducation* (1782), exemplifies how domestic consumption could be framed as a praiseworthy alternative to fashionable society. Retreating to her country estate to educate her children, Baroness d'Almane designs every part of her home to optimize its educational value, which she describes in letters to her Parisian friends. She landscapes hills for physical exercise, embroiders curtains and furniture with historical dates and names, paints mythological wall murals, and writes, like the celebrated author herself, her own children's plays, history books, and didactic fiction. Her children watch artisans in their workshops by visiting a utopian village founded by a local aristocrat couple, who study manufacturing methods and teach them to whomever comes searching for work.[47] In the final stage of her daughter's education, the baroness presents her daughter with a girl from a poor family whose education she supervises, an episode Jane Austen satirizes through Emma Woodhouse's friendship with Harriet Smith. In didactic fiction from this period, rational parents teach their children through factory tours and home science lessons, family gardening or botany excursions, curiosity cabinets and alphabet samplers. Jacqueline Reid-Walsh provocatively compares this new commercial market for didactic playthings with what Henry Jenkins describes as the slow replacement of folk culture with commercial culture.[48] Locating child agency in creative interactions with open-ended moveable texts, Reid-Walsh imagines children manipulating toys much like Ellenor Fenn, whose infant claims letters "as my own," while playing her commercialized variant on the folk game forfeits. If play and labor are both ways of interacting with the world, however, I wonder how we might examine material culture from a perspective that values physical labor as a source of knowledge.

Radical Mechanical Literacy

There is another way of conceptualizing mechanical literacy, which acknowledges that life events have greater influence on children than do adult-planned lessons dependent on personal property. An article by James Mill in *The Encyclopedia Britannica* (1816–24) provides an already widely accepted definition of education as "every thing" that "operates" on the child's mind "from the first germ of existence, to the final extinction of life," which implies that formal schooling accounts for very little of what children learn.[49] James Mill connects early impressions with morality (and sanity), since the child repeats in his thoughts the succession of events he senses from the natural world, internalizing an awareness of causality that creates awareness of what is right: "Children ought to be made to see, and hear, and feel, and taste, in the order of the most invariable and comprehensive sequences, in order that the ideas which correspond to their impressions, and follow the same order of succession, may be an exact transcript of nature, and always lead to just anticipations of events."[50] Mill credits David Hartley, Étienne Bonnot de Condillac, and Claude-Adrien Helvétius for these insights and recommends Maria Edgeworth's literature for laying the groundwork of benevolence in children, explicitly because her works are founded on these scientifically based theories of mind.

This way of conceptualizing education—as a causal series of events recorded in the body—was prevalent among bourgeois radicals and Dissenting Protestants, among them Joseph Priestley, the cofounder of the Unitarian Church, who edited and republished classic works by Anthony Collins on determinism and the physician David Hartley on the association of ideas. A sort of scientific Calvinism, philosophical determinism proposes that ideas in the mind are subject to the same natural laws of "cause and effect" that govern inanimate matter, meaning our actions at any one moment, although experienced as freely chosen, are determined by the sum total of our experiences—by education—and are predictable to an omniscient being. As the industrial philanthropist Robert Owen argued, one practical implication of determinism is that a person's character or habits are the product of their circumstances, and therefore universal schooling should supersede the criminal justice system. Hartley's association of ideas provides a physiological explanation for how life experiences create an individual's personality by proposing that the body stores causal chains of associated thoughts and feelings generated during past events, which a person recalls automatically under similar circumstances. Hartley optimistically proposed that social interaction helps individuals temper their prejudices by exchanging associations between persons, producing "a tendency to reduce the state of those who have eaten of the tree of the knowledge of good and evil, back again to a paradisiacal one."[51] Exploring the political implications of associationism, David Hume considered the "association of ideas" the "source of all the relations of interest and duty, by which men influence each other in society, and are plac'd in the ties of government and subordination."[52] Kings, masters, or husbands command obedience by perpetuating social habits that have the *appearance* of natural law, but these cultural beliefs could be changed by introducing children to new experiences that are calculated to form different mental habits or social behaviors. Together, associationism and determinism account for James Mill's "just anticipation of events," or the predictability of human behavior. And since experience is stored physically in the body machine, children's earliest impressions from physical objects have great significance, providing the key to human perfectibility and political reform.[53]

By this way of thinking, philosophical piano stools and literacy toys are immensely important, but they make less of an impression on children's minds than the entirety of life experiences. Addressing upwardly mobile parents in her Dissenting community, Anna Letitia Barbauld in her "Essay on Education" cautions against staged domestic simplicity of the sort made fashionable by "Rousseau or Mme. De Genlis," wherein "you take a country-house in a good air, and make [your child] run, well clothed and carefully attended, for, it may be, an hour in a clear frosty winter's day upon your graveled terrace . . . and you think you have done great matters." In affluent households, this false performance of peasant life has limited influence next to a family's pervasive signs of wealth: "Above all, your rank and situation in life, your house, your table, your pleasure-grounds, your hounds and your stables will educate him . . . the education of circumstances—insensible education . . . This education goes on at every instant of time; it goes on like time . . . Poverty educated you; wealth will educate him."[54] By Locke's accepted wisdom, her phrase "insensible education" is an oxymoron, since all knowledge enters through the senses, and Locke pronounced unconscious sensation impossible. By the "education of circumstances," therefore, Barbauld suggests that children internalize class through the quiet accumulation of infinite details in their surroundings. These influences are beyond "sensation" because their significance is not easily recognized by those most affected by them. Barbauld finds hope by reflecting that an omniscient God designs the world itself as a learning environment—what she calls "the education of events"—as an alternative to Rousseau's education of things. Private families have limited control over their children, because "the education of your house, important as it is, is only a part of a more comprehensive system."[55]

Where Rousseau's education of things resembles a science experiment, Barbauld's "education of circumstances" or "events" is more like a picaresque novel, or a walk in the woods.[56] It speaks to a growing awareness of another kind of "comprehensive system"—the material conditions responsible for constructing political subjects. William Godwin prefers to describe this insensible stuff as "political education," defined as the "modification our ideas receive from the form of government under which we live." Everything that enters our senses takes on a political hue that we cannot escape: "politics and modes of government will educate and infect us all."[57] In working-class print culture, the phrase "education of men and things" suggests a similar concept, that knowledge of things is necessarily social and political. If a child's material environment is not just a stockpile of purchased objects, but a relationship between things, a "system" for interacting with the world, then children ultimately gain agency over who they become by changing that "more comprehensive system," or reforming the "government under which we live." This way of thinking about education appears in radical print culture because it potentially recognizes poverty and physical labor as legitimate sources of theoretical knowledge about "men and things," without romanticizing hardship or labor as an adequate replacement for learning.

Here is an object lesson about labor that suggests changing the system: A series of "fables" from the September 1832 issue of Robert Owen's newly founded cooperative newspaper, *The Crisis*, uses the classroom practice of object lessons to illustrate the social meanings of things. The fables suggests that working-class readers have a more accurate understanding of the material world, which they can use to question the value assigned to commodities. Each short article follows a common practice in primary school classrooms where students hold an object in their hand, accurately describe its parts and properties, explain the origins of its materials and associated uses, and conclude with inferences or moral reflections drawn from their observations.[58] In this case, the author observes a lady's gold watch, a silver tongs and poker, and a mariner's compass, and for each one concludes that "iron," which represents the working classes, is more valuable than other metals for powering these machines. The ship at sea, for example, depends upon "something in the box that speaks to the man who holds the helm. This something, diminutive in size, and simple in appearance, in not made of gold or silver, or brass, but of IRON. It is the NEEDLE in the compass." This "friendly hand" (another name for a worker) represents "labour, the only source of wealth" who "unites continents together." The fable's concluding moral suggests that iron hands are valuable precisely because they follow the magnetic pull of the material world, whereas society's gold and brass are divorced from reality: "Matter is right and mind is wrong." Yet despite its affinity with matter, "LABOUR, the only source of wealth, is lightly esteemed; while MONEY, the mere representation of wealth, is sincerely worshipped." The ship of state "must be wheeled round," and *The Crisis* will help it change course.[59]

On a pedagogical level, this object lesson is familiar. Watch, compass, and shovel and tongs are common objects regularly featured in reading lessons and lotto sheets with similar phrasing concerning their parts and materials. Yet it is hard to imagine a more unconventional lesson than heeding the iron hand's voice on matters of political economy. Written object lessons typically model how teachers and students should perform real-life exercises, but here, the three fables "on the true value of things" invite a different audience interaction with the text. The fables were published alongside articles announcing an experiment conceived by Robert Owen to create an alternative to gold-backed paper currency called "Equitable Labour Exchange Notes." Representing hours of labor, this print currency allowed workers to exchange their goods at a cooperative bazaar. One nearby article explains through a dialogue between a manufacturer and a farmer that gold is "based on men's opinions," and may lose its value if the productive classes refuse to trade goods for it, forcing the wealthy to make something of value themselves, while other articles transcribe meetings held to establish the bazaar. In this company, the fable's satirical adaptation of a classroom genre reclaims control over the school curriculum for the "productive classes," reappropriating material objects to observe a fundamental reality that many working people cannot meet their basic needs however hard they work. Insisting on this fact requires joining mechanical and alphabetical literacies—reclaiming the ability to create knowledge from the world and express observations in print. In the reader's hands, object lessons teach that the value of gold currency is vulnerably dependent upon coerced participation in capitalist economies. If mechanical literacy means understanding *the regular laws that explain how objects are sensed, manipulated, created, manufactured, distributed, and exchanged*, then a radical mechanical literacy means deriving this understanding from everyday play and labor, preparing working-class youth to critique social systems and design new ones through collective action. In this case, "friendly hands" fashioned an alternative system for more equitable exchange.

Chapter Overviews

Departing from a strict historical chronology, chapters explore a distinct subject area and the genres that teach it:

1. Reading and writing (interactive books and literacy aids)
2. Mechanical philosophy (science textbooks, amateur crafts, inventor biographies)
3. Manufacturing and political economy (production stories)
4. Autonomy/governance (domestic fiction, automata)
5. Grammar/politics (radical grammars)

Children acquire mechanical literacy by learning these interconnected knowledge areas, each of which imparts self-awareness by helping children identify as agents within complex systems. Nevertheless, I organize these chapters to roughly make sense chronologically by confining chapter 1 to earlier examples from my archive before exploring a full century in chapters 2 and 3 and concluding with author-focused studies in chapters 4 and 5. While social class remains a consistent lens, I use an intersectional approach with closer attention to gender in chapters 2 through 5, and race and colonization in chapters 3 and 4. Book chapters iteratively present mechanical literacy from different ideological perspectives, exposing the tacit politics behind mainstream material lessons through contrast with radical sources that resist established genre patterns. The many books and materials I examined in archives offer compelling visual evidence, only some of which could be included in this book. I encourage readers to browse the extensive online supplementary resource featuring additional analysis of educational materials, available at https://umpressopen.library.umass.edu/projects/the-education-of-things.

Chapter 1 argues that commercial materials designed to accommodate children's small, moving bodies made the resemblance between playful learning and physical labor more obvious and contentious just when industrial economies created greater demand for mechanical knowledge. Amidst these changes, author-educators like Maria Edgeworth, Ellenor Fenn, Priscilla Wakefield, and Anna Letitia Barbauld promoted multisensory learning practices that combined reading with haptic learning and scientific observation. They did this through books that call users out into the physical world, and toys or learning aids that call users back to books. This back-and-forth between learning mediums acclimates children to creating their own knowledge by literally collecting and gathering objects, which materializes the mental process of synthesizing information they later perform through writing. Interacting with texts and objects thus provides children with tangible meta-representations of their inner mental processes, adding a dimension of self-reflexivity associated with play. Influenced by Locke, these authors theorized learning as a kind of object-tinkering akin to labor, where mixing the body with the material world creates ideas in the mind as intellectual property. I conclude with someone who questioned equating knowing with owning: Catherine Whitwell, a cooperator and teacher whose classroom specimen tables teach children to critically examine the economic principles behind learning with things. The reciprocal relationship between written texts and the physical world is important for understanding why ideas about ownership and sensation easily migrated between the discourses of work and play and those of reading and writing.

Chapter 2 examines the class politics of Newtonian physics books for children. Analyzing over a century of children's books and materials that teach mechanical philosophy, I identify concepts about matter in motion that influenced the new world of playful books explored in chapter 1. From Enlightenment-era textbooks to Victorian engineer biographies and armature craft books—the similarity between play and physical labor is on full display. To learn mechanical philosophy, child characters from wealthier families go out into the world and watch moving bodies, human and nonhuman, and compare chopping wood or breaking rocks to their own childish games. Identifying with these characters, readers learn to transform their subjective observations of matter in motion into theoretical "mechanical philosophy," which these books distinguish as a higher form of learning from what wage laborers comprehend when they move things. Mechanical philosophy books thus helped create a cultural mythology around middle-class white boys, who tinker with machines and understand how things work, and whose mechanical know-how signifies their ability to govern themselves and others. By the Victorian era, working people and girls are marginalized in these fictional stories, their bodies often reduced to sources of knowledge for boys who imagine themselves becoming heroic engineers. These books reinforced distinctions between theoretical and practical mechanics, with real consequences. Opponents of child labor regulation used these playful pedagogies to misrepresent long hours of physical labor as playful "education," while radicals sought to limit working hours to protect the leisure to learn.

Chapter 3, "The Empire of Man over Material Things" investigates the books and games that taught middle-class children about manufacturing and political economy. I argue that "production stories," or stories about how everyday things are made, teach mechanical literacy by providing children with material models of complex, global economic networks. Detailed descriptions and copious illustrations of people working in print shops and pottery manufactories, mining salt and coal, harvesting sugarcane and tea, then shipping these products abroad for further processing, provided early Victorians with a sense of mastery over industries that spanned multiple continents and employed workers of different races and nationalities. This mode of visual empowerment positions privileged white child readers as knowledge-makers, trained to observe working people and gather natural resources. The material aspects of these media reinforce the child user's sense of control, as the interactive affordances of books and games create an embodied sensation of agency over intangible economic systems. During a period of heightened class conflict, production stories connected people of different classes and nations, occasionally exposing labor exploitation and slavery. Influenced by abolitionist and conscious consumerism movements, production stories depict girls as morally responsible for regulating the market through informed, ethical consumption, while boys improve their nation's technological edge. With close readings of information books by Isaac Taylor and fiction by economist Jane Marcet, this chapter investigates the relationship between physical labor and playful learning through the genre most concerned with the pleasure and power of watching people at work.

Chapter 4, "Self-Governing Machines," explores mechanical literacy through automaton exhibitions, arguing that memetic machines model how children are supposed to fashion themselves as self-aware agents in a material world. Offering a single-author case study for the arguments laid out in previous chapters, I focus on fiction by leading "practical education" expert and children's author Maria Edgeworth, whose father was inspired to learn mechanics by viewing William Bridges's automaton clock. Like her father, the protagonists in Maria Edgeworth's books redirect their lives after formative encounters with automata: Rosamond, a girl from a wealthy family, gains moral autonomy by building her own compass and visiting factories; likewise, Jervas, a child who works in the Cornish mines, raises his social standing by building an automaton that he exhibits in India while teaching in Andrew Bell's Madras school, where the "educational machinery" of Monitorial schools originated. Rosamond and Jervas thus capture how mechanization marks racial and class inferiority, whereas owning, controlling, and modeling machines indicates social mobility and self-governance. Addressing class, race, and gender in colonial settings, this chapter explains how Edgeworth uses machines to depict some women and girls as capable of rational thought, yet she avoids acknowledging the mechanical expertise of people from other marginalized groups.

Chapter 5 on radical grammars identifies oppositional radical voices of the 1840s Chartist and cooperative movements, who demanded wider access to a practical curriculum of hands-on learning, but who resisted associating literacy with property ownership. I explore how grammars for working-class youth by George Mudie and George Jacob Holyoake challenged the political meaning of interactive techniques first designed by Ellenor Fenn and Jane Marcet for middle-class mothers teaching grammar to young children. Instead of connecting the manipulation of matter with children's play, Mudie and Holyoake connected it with work. In doing so, they pushed back against the tendency to consider mechanical labor as intellectually degrading, insisting that such work prepares youth to analyze political systems and suggest new governing laws. Radical instructors reminded their students that by working with their hands, they learn more about the world around them, making them astute observers with privileged access to practical "knowledge of men and things." Physical labor provides empirical evidence needed to create more equitable economic principles for how resources are assembled, circulated, and exchanged. This chapter thus explores a countercultural perspective on mechanical literacy, with natural laws of matter derived from everyday working-class life.

Although this book takes a historical approach, my hope is that readers will consider implications for work and play today. In the United States, where I grew up and live with my children, middle-class parents spend quality time with their children picking apples on a fall afternoon, while migrant children may work up to ten hours a day harvesting produce; while one high school student takes an enriching "alternative spring break" to build homes in a poor community, another student must work an after-school job in landscaping. The flexibility in how we interpret these activities as education or work has its origins in the historical period when hands-on learning first became a widespread pedagogical approach. The fraught relationship between work and play in this earlier period helps to explain why humanities scholars portray education today alternately as an ideological state apparatus used for control or our best hope for empowering the oppressed. Returning to when these polarized conceptions of education begin, this book investigates the consequences of predicating child agency on an object theory derived from Enlightenment science, which creates active child subjects by pacifying the world of things. When applied to human beings, this way of thinking construes all learning subjects as either omnipotent or powerless, with wider implications for how workers of different genders, races, nations, and ethnicities are treated, especially whether their expertise is recognized and compensated, and whether their children experience learning as pleasurable.

Learning through experience continues to form an important part of our education at every level, as institutions, including universities, strive to incorporate the strengths of community-based, informal learning practices into classrooms, yet we often devalue the same skills that youth pursue independently. Blending active learning with book learning should ideally encourage young people to develop intrinsic motivation inspired by the practical and political relevance of what they learn in their lives. The ambiguities between work and play can be used, however, to arbitrarily discredit knowledge gained informally or to withdraw protections from people who find their work abruptly redefined as training or apprenticeship. Over the course of the nineteenth century, one kind of mechanical knowledge was appropriated and elevated as cultural capital, its dissemination relocated into educational institutions and used to defend the genius and political advent of a powerful class of industrialists and science professionals—while another kind of mechanical knowledge remained associated with physical labor, its cognitive benefits regarded with skepticism and its practitioners excluded from political representation. We might ask whether the same divisions appear today in how educators, employers, and families assign value to cultural literacy, digital literacy, or information literacy, or fail to recognize where these skills and others of equal importance flourish outside of channels sanctioned by white middle-class culture.

CHAPTER 1

What Children Grasp

The Tangible Properties of Objects

The Interlocutor Glossary to *Practical Education* (1780)

Eighteen years before Maria Edgeworth coauthored with her father, Richard Lovell Edgeworth, their influential education treatise *Practical Education* (1798), Honoria Sneyd Edgeworth, her father's second wife, wrote a children's story by the same title. Only a half-dozen copies of the second volume of the two-book set *Practical Education; or, The History of Harry and Lucy* (1780) survive today. Privately published with a glossary composed by Richard Lovell, it tells the story of two children as they explore their environment from sunrise to sunset. Lucy investigates how cream is made in her mother's dairy, while Harry observes how bricks are made.[1] The book begins with instructions for its use: "The asterisk in the text refer to the Glossary; and when the Child is directed to ask to see any thing, it is hoped, that his teacher will shew him what he asks for, and let him handle and examine it." The appended glossary defines words from the stories, with a penchant for sensory terms: "observation," "perceived," "sweet," and "shape," whose entry reads, "You must look at things and touch them, and you will then know their shape." Whenever the glossary lists a common object, it withholds a definition and asks readers to find one for themselves. The entry for "Hammer" reads, "Ask to see Hammers of different sorts, and to be told their uses," while the entry for "oven" simply reports, "Ask to see an oven," with similar entries for "Hartshorn," "Housewife," "Heap," "Digging," "Clay," and "Pit."[2] The story and glossary hypertextually reference the sensual, material world of

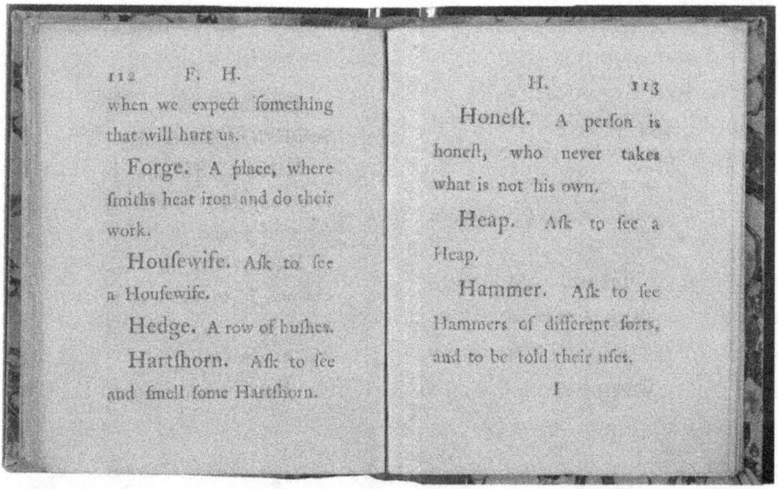

112 F. H.

when we expect ſomething that will hurt us.

Forge. A place, where ſmiths heat iron and do their work.

Houſewife. Aſk to ſee a Houſewife.

Hedge. A row of buſhes.

Hartſhorn. Aſk to ſee and ſmell ſome Hartſhorn.

H. 113

Honeſt. A perſon is honeſt, who never takes what is not his own.

Heap. Aſk to ſee a Heap.

Hammer. Aſk to ſee Hammers of different ſorts, and to be told their uſes.

I

FIGURE 4. Glossary pages from Honoria Sneyd Edgeworth and Richard Lovell Edgeworth, *Practical Education: or, The History of Harry and Lucy*, vol. 2 (Lichfield: J. Jackson; J. Johnson, 1780). Cotsen Children's Library. Courtesy of Princeton University Library.

child readers, inviting them to imitate Harry and Lucy by asking adults about the things they see, hear, touch, taste, and smell.

The book's dedication declares its pedagogical inspiration: "This little book, written upon the Principles of ASSOCIATION, Is inscribed to Dr. Priestley." Consistent with physician David Hartley's theory of association, which Richard Lovell's friend Joseph Priestley republished in 1775, the story combines things and words, responding to his concerns that children might learn words as mere symbols or sounds without meaning.[3] The story begins at sunrise in the familiar domestic space of Harry and Lucy's bedroom, where the children wake from sleep before they explore outward to unfamiliar places. After visiting the forge, dairy, meadow, and brickmakers, the children reconvene at their house, where they play at making bricks and construct a small house. At the conclusion of the book, Harry and Lucy enter the symbolic world of texts as they read a story with their mother about a man who helps a chimney-sweep boy, who later saves the gentleman from drowning. The children discuss this story of cross-class reciprocity, a metatextual moment that points to the physical world outside the story, where child readers might discuss these sibling characters. In a single day, Harry and Lucy recapitulate human history while presenting a microcosm of a child's development from a creature of sensation to one of reflection.[4] Implicitly, the child audience for *Practical Education* learns that reading books is related to the hands-on learning enjoyed by Harry and Lucy, and the glossary also suggests that they turn from their books to examine the world around them.

This chapter explores the mutual influences between children's books and educational objects, along with philosophies and practices behind using them together. I theorize common rhetorical maneuvers used to refer children from immersive reading to object observation, and from toys and experiments back to reading. Children's literature of this period supports learning from other media by redirecting readers' attention outside the book, using what I will call "interlocutor gestures." I borrow this term from art history, where it refers to a figure in Early Modern art who breaks the fourth wall by locking eyes with the audience outside the world of the painting and gesturing toward something of interest inside the artwork. For our purposes, interlocutor gestures are the "object" equivalent of metafiction; they call attention to the book's kinship with other manipulable objects in the child reader's environment. The covers and frontispieces of books provide interlocutor gestures when they portray children learning from multiple mediums, or when their titles—"mother's gift," "child's cabinet," "little plaything," and so on—assign books toy names. A story may provide similar self-referential moments by directing children, in the second person, to perform the same experiments as fictional families or to turn a page or to examine an illustration, or by referring to objects that are likely in the child reader's vicinity. Books with interlocutor gestures point children toward "reading" the world, what Thomas Bewick called "the unerring and unalterable book of the Deity," or they incorporate conversational and experiential teaching methods into the book.[5] As a result, reading is an interactive activity that extends beyond the text, into the world.[6]

These interlocutor gestures imply corresponding "developmental gestures," or references to the child reader's interior growth. Whereas interlocutor gestures help users to integrate alphabetical and mechanical literacies, developmental gestures add the element of self-reflexivity to object reading that David Vincent ascribes to "literacy" as a "tool for enabling individuals and social groups to extend their understanding of themselves and their world," while "amongst the objects of comprehension" is "literacy itself."[7] As an understanding of the laws governing the natural world, mechanical literacy is equally self-reflexive. When the glossary to *Practical Education* (1780) redirects readers to examine objects using their eyes and hands, it calls children's attention to their embodied reading and their reliance for ideas on sensing their surroundings. Together, interlocutor and developmental gestures encourage children to connect discoveries in the world with internal growth; they observe nonhuman material things to achieve self-knowledge.[8] Moreover, learning from objects is itself an object of contemplation. The self-reflexivity of object reading encourages children, as they learn from objects and spaces owned by themselves or their families, to consider the close relationship between grasping, knowing, and owning—which suggests that people own knowledge, including literacy, as a kind of private property stored inside of themselves.

To make this case, I explore how children took apart, reassembled, manipulated, observed, and collected their books, and where such activities draw from the affordances of toys. Beginning with frontispieces and toy packaging, I argue that illustrations from these transitional spaces affirmed children's media-switching behaviors and normalized interrupted reading. Next, I analyze children's books and toys that make language tangible by recalling boxes, specimen containers, and exhibition spaces while also providing models for the child's developing mind. The book wrapped in dutch papers or the toy packaged in a box are collected together by booksellers or family consumers into little cabinets or children's libraries, forming object assemblages that organize the world in much the same way that children are supposed to organize mental images inside their minds as they learn to read. The cabinet or box connects books and toys with collection practices used outside the home in public exhibits that children visited with their families. Home, book, and box are so many exhibition halls that proudly display knowledge as property, acquired and lodged within children's bodies, a comparison that makes domestic learning seem commensurate with British trade and imperialism.

These books and toys idealized ways of learning from material culture practiced by children of leisure, who, like Harry and Lucy, appropriated the learning practices of artisans and cottagers into their domestic spaces. Granted, combining mechanical and alphabetical preliteracy skills makes sense given that infants can explore things before they can read. Nevertheless, the growing market for children's educational materials reinforced the perception that purchasing toys and other domestic goods nurtures the ability to make rational moral judgments. Just as reading was associated with virtuous behavior, mechanical literacy became associated with owning and controlling moving bodies—with governance over oneself and others. While some educators used these pedagogical philosophies to justify social inequality within a divinely ordered material world, others experimented with learning from objects to support radical ideas about property.

Observation: A Profitable Interruption to Reading

Learning with objects as a complement to reading has its own visual rhetoric. Containers for toys feature illustrations of children absorbed in reading objects with books discarded by their side, or several children engaged in both reading and play: On the lid for Spelling in Play (ca. 1830), an alphabet card game, a mother hugs a young girl, a book left open and neglected at their feet, while two nearby siblings spell words with alphabet cards, and, within a decorative frame around this central image, a boy whips a top and a girl regards her doll; on the screw-top lid for The Picture Alphabet (ca. 1840), children eagerly gather around a schoolteacher who holds out alphabet counters for them to explore, while behind them, older children work at their seats; on the game sleeve for The Elegant and Instructive Game of Useful Knowledge (ca. 1819), a boy regards a hot air balloon through a telescope while a girl draws with a compass; on the lid for the card collection The Infant's Cabinet of Trades (1802), a man gestures with an open hand for a boy to examine people at work in the city shipyards.[9] These images resemble the iconic illustration featured on the frontispiece to John Newbery's books, of a mother seated with a book on her lap while she teaches a child to read, but in these cases, a parent directs the child to examine an object or scene.[10]

The prevalence of both kinds of images on children's materials—children reading, and children observing—suggests that these are closely related activities. A series of five infant primers by Jacob Abbott, reprinted as "Harper's Picture Books for the Nursery" (1855–1857), indicates a conscious attempt to create parallel imagery. The prolific American author of the Rollo books, Abbott wrote over 180 books in which observation and experimentation figure prominently, many republished in London.[11] His pedagogical approach reflects his early career as a professor of natural philosophy at Amherst College prior to founding and serving as the principal of three children's education institutions. He coauthored a treatise on school management with Charles and Elizabeth Mayo, English advocates of Pestalozzian object teaching.[12] In the frontispiece for *Learning to Talk*, a mother holds her toddler as they peer into each other's faces; in *Learning about Common Things*, a mother directs her three- or four-year-old infant to examine a tree by holding her shoulders while she points; in *Learning to Think*, a young girl sits sewing by herself; and in *Learning to Read*, a girl follows the text with her finger in a book held by her mother. The succession of images depicts the evolving relationship between the mother/teacher and her child as their face-to-face intimate communication becomes mediated, first by relationships to the material world, and finally by work, contemplation, and reading. The repetition of the mother's gestures, first pointing to the tree, and later pointing to the text, create what I have come to think of as the classic interlocutor gesture, where a parent guides the child's observational activity by carefully focusing their attention on a single object in the same way that they guide the child's first introduction to books by pointing to a single letter or word. Although there are no images in the glossary to *Practical Education* (1780), the command to "ask" to see or handle particular items and discuss their use suggests adult guidance.

More often, children's materials refer to a picture of an object to suggest a method for observing and chatting about whatever is in the child's environment. Small pictures of isolated objects, or "sensible signs," are a common feature of children's toys and education aids, and children themselves pasted these paper objects on toys and scrapbooks. Patricia Crain describes the "objects" in alphabets as "atomized, adrift on the page. . . . in an aesthetics of accumulation and accretion," but a similar aesthetic dominates lotto prints, conversation cards, game boards, and spelling cards, all of which feature little objects floating in white space, as if children's minds are cabinets that organize and store what they pick up from the natural world, gathering quotidian detritus on the way to adulthood.[13] One children's boardgame, The Elegant and Instructive Game of Useful Knowledge (ca. 1819), implies as much by creating a game path out of such images. The complete randomness of the object selections (umbrella, snail, letter, carrot), each with no obvious connection from one to the next, replicates the eclectic visual impression of lotto sheets or object alphabets and provides insight into how these sensible signs supported children's cognitive development. Like table games of the period, Useful Knowledge is a variant of the Game of the Goose, where players advance along a coiled path by rolling a many-sided top, or teetotum, then following the instructions for each space where they land.[14] Here, child players gather practical things, advancing along the object-chain path toward a central image of schoolboys presenting their slates to a schoolmaster. The architecture of the school, along with careful details (children grouped at the walls), indicates the school depicted uses the methods of Quaker educator Joseph Lancaster, whose classroom materials were printed by this game's publisher, the Dartons. One method of rewarding students in Lancastrian schools was giving out tickets or lotto prints, which could be accumulated and exchanged for prizes, including books.[15]

The game path uses a chain motif to connect and contain each object, which recalls David Hartley's associationism, also mentioned in the dedication to *Practical Education* (1780). A medical doctor, Hartley suggested that sensations of objects become organized in the mind along "chains of associations," enabling future encounters with objects or people to recall engrained responses. As Catharine Macaulay explains, teachers "fashion the mind of his pupil" toward excellence by deliberately forming these associations whereby "a single impression calls up a host of ideas, which, arising in imperceptible succession, form a close and almost inseparable combination."[16] The game's visual design suggests that children must build these associations before they learn to read, just as they collect lotto prints for prizes. The game makes an interlocutor gesture to the player's accumulated property (books, prizes), and a developmental gesture to accumulated mental associations between common objects formed in preparation for reading.

FIGURE 5. The Elegant and Instructive Game of Useful Knowledge; Designed to Impart Information to the Minds of Youth of Both Sexes (London: William Darton, ca. 1819). Cotsen Children's Library. Courtesy of Princeton University Library. Typical of engraved games, this one is printed on paper, hand-colored, and cut into nine pieces that are glued onto linen to create a foldable, durable board. The board and likely a booklet (not surviving) are stored in a paper slipcase (not shown here) with a front image showing two boys learning with scientific instruments before a natural backdrop. One boy with a compass and sextant references celestial and terrestrial globes, while another boy uses a telescope to see a balloon.

The placement of these images—at the culmination of a game path, at the beginning or end of books, or on toy lids and envelopes—anticipates child users who transition between reading books and manipulating toys by presenting them with illustrations of children doing the same. The frontispiece for *Mamma's Present* (1801), a small book the size of a child's palm, shows an infant daughter grasping a book gifted by her mother, who blesses her. The girl's horse and doll

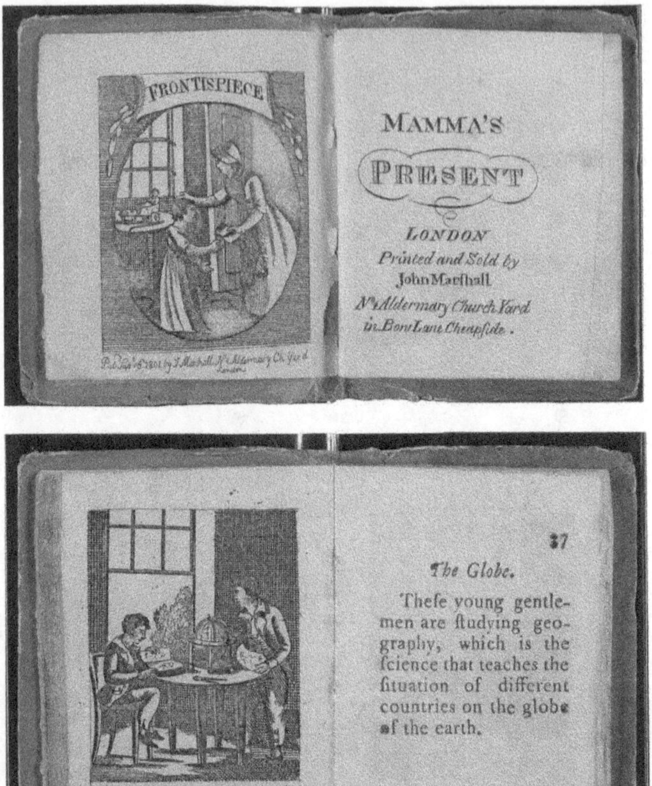

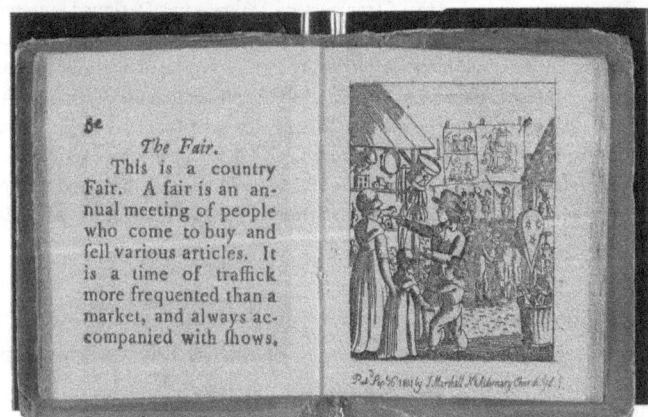

FIGURE 6. *Mamma's Present* (London: John Marshall, 1801). Cotsen Children's Library. Courtesy of Princeton University Library. This frontispiece provides a classic interlocutor gesture, with a book presented to a child as a replacement for toys. The mother's substitution is foiled on later page spreads in which other playful mediums replace the book.

carriage lie abandoned on the table behind them as she turns her attention to reading. The primary placement of this image may seem to prioritize book learning, but successive page spreads show learning with other media or experiences, including "The Globe," "The Walk in the Park," "The Pleasing Tale" (reading), "The Magic-lantern," and "The Fair," each of which could be interpreted as an adult's "present." As children put down their toys and pick up their books, they were greeted by interlocutor images like these, which endorse moving between mediums. Other illustrations depict children who read and play at the same time without distinguishing between these activities. The sliding lid to the wooden box for Marshall's The Alphabetical Cabinet (ca. 1815), a set of illustrated alphabet cards (each with a letter and object) accompanied by a small reading book, shows a girl standing outdoors in a country estate, cards spread at her feet as she holds a book aloft while pointing to the text and boasts her literacy to the family cat. A path leading behind her into a gardened landscape suggests a connection between literacy and her family's estate. Standing confidently, in the landscaped garden, the girl claims possession of her affluent space and uses her illiterate subordinate, the cat, to foil her ability to read as the source of her authority. In this case, the alphabet cards are her toy, which she uses along with her book, gesturing to them both, suggesting that children using The Alphabetical Cabinet imitate her behavior, which is itself a playful imitation of an interlocutor gesture. Children who use Marshall's Alphabetical Cabinet would need to slide open the box lid with this image of multimodal reading to discover both toy and book nestled together inside. The cards allow caregivers or children to make the same gesture themselves, isolating a child's attention by handling or viewing one letter at a time with its corresponding image of an object. Such illustrations function as complex interlocutor gestures that suggest approved ways of combining toys and texts.

While encouraging children to lay aside their toys for reading may come as no surprise, book frontispieces quite commonly show the reverse, with an adult gesturing to an educational aid or pointing outside.[17] The cover of *The Parlour Book* (ca. 1835) shows two children chatting with their father while gesturing to a large globe, discussing places mentioned in the story; the frontispiece for *The Young Travellers* (1816) illustrates a scene of the four Longland children organizing their grandmother's loose natural

FIGURE 7. The Alphabetical Cablnet (London: Marshall & Co., ca. 1815). Cotsen Children's Library. Courtesy of Princeton University Library. The building in the background could be a symbolic temple of wisdom or a gazebo, which suggests learning letters leads to spiritual and worldly advances.

history specimens into labeled cabinet drawer sections that display "order, neatness and taste."[18] With book reading profitably interrupted by observation, manipulation, collection, and play, children center their education around reading the world of things. Switching the emerging child reader between reading and observation can, according to Richard Lovell, "give him a habit of commanding his attention," which improves longform reading.[19] The children work independently at a pleasurable activity

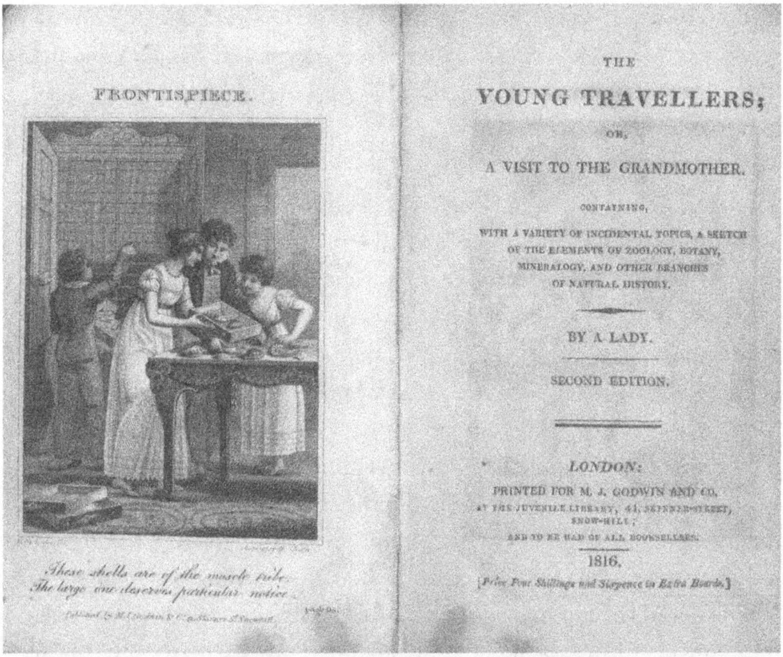

FIGURE 8. Frances T. Jamieson, *The Young Travellers; Or, a Visit to the Grandmother: Containing, with a Variety of Incidental Topics, a Sketch of the Elements of Zoology, Botany, Mineralogy, and Other Branches of Natural History*, 2nd ed. (London: M. J. Godwin and Co., 1816). Frontispiece engraving. Courtesy of Baldwin Library of Historical Children's Literature, George A. Smathers Libraries, University of Florida.

suggested by adults that facilitates their mental organization of what they learned during their visit.

Interlocutor gestures referring to objects in the reader's environment also appear in books for older children, especially textbooks, encyclopedias, science experiment books, and instructional fiction, suggesting that early literacy toys scaffold more advanced information-seeking behaviors that combined reading with observing God's book of nature. As natural theologian Rev. John George Wood explains in his best-selling *Common Objects of the Country* (1858), there are two kinds of illiteracy, both equally debilitating: "To one who has not learned to read, the Bible itself is but a series of senseless black marks; and similarly, the unwritten Word that lies around, below, and above us, is unmeaning to those who cannot read it." Children require "proper teaching" in how to interweave these activities, interrupting their reading with sensory modes of learning.[20] The revised edition of Priscilla Wakefield's *Mental Improvement, Or, the Beauties and Wonders of Nature and Art* (1784, 1840) opens with a striking engraving showing a child interrupted while reading. Seated at a writing table, holding a quill in one hand and an open book in the other, her intense gaze is arrested by some object outside the frame. What is remarkable about this image is the child's deep attention. She wears the rapturous expression we might expect to see on the face of a child lost in a book, but, instead, she is lost in observation. The frontispiece asks child readers to imitate Wakefield's characters, the Harcourt children, who learn about everyday objects from their father's "agreeable evening conversations." Beginning with the production of whale oil, which, significantly, provides evening light to see, Mr. Harcourt entertains Sophia, Cecelia, Henry, Charles, and their neglected cousin, Augusta (whose mother has died and whose father manages their West Indies estate), ages nine through sixteen, with accounts of mining, agriculture, and artisanal processes—provided they finish, during daylight, their lessons with their "writing master." The children choose a topic inspired by their curiosity about an everyday object (such as tea and coffee at breakfast), then search for answers in the family library and conduct experiments, convening to share their findings around the fireside.

This method of multimodal learning transforms the Harcourt children from passive vessels into active researchers who decide what to investigate and how to synthesize knowledge gathered from different sources, a process similar to the way Wakefield described writing her books, by adapting material spliced from multiple adult texts. As her preface explains, children should learn to think about the material world using varied mediums and sources:

> The art of exercising the faculty of thinking and reflecting upon every object that is seen, ought to constitute a material branch of a good education; but it requires the skill of a master's hand, to lead the minds of youth to the habit of observation. Dr. Watts says there are four methods of obtaining knowledge: observation, reading, conversation, and meditation. The first lies within the compass even of children, and from the early dawn of reason, they should be accustomed to observe every thing with attention, that falls under their notice. A judicious instructor will find matter for a lesson among those objects that are termed common or insignificant.[21]

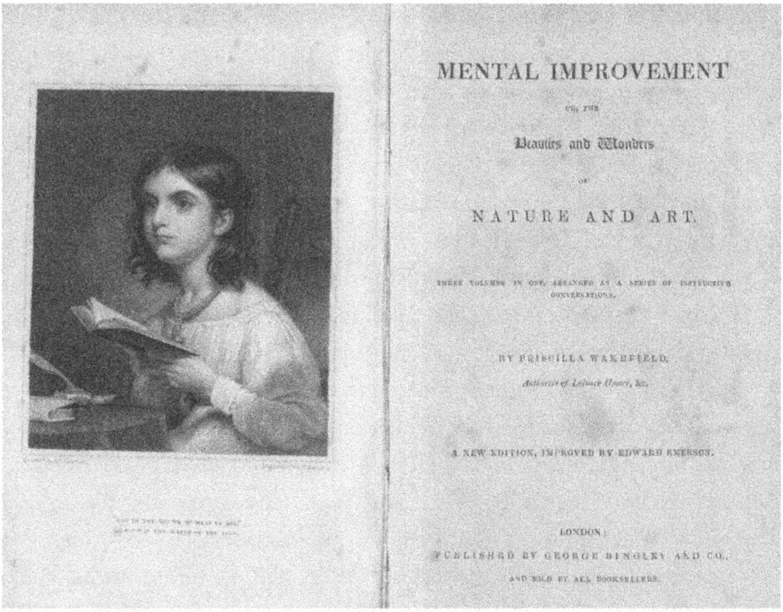

FIGURE 9. Priscilla Wakefield, *Mental Improvement: or, the Beauties and Wonders of Nature and Art*, 1794, new edition, revised by Edward Emerson (London: George Bingley, 1840). Courtesy of Baldwin Library of Historical Children's Literature, George A. Smathers Libraries, University of Florida. The frontispiece is "painted by A. Robertson" and "engraved by J. Thomson." The child's indeterminate age and gender leaves open whether this is one of the Harcourt children or the book's reader.

Wakefield paraphrases Isaac Watts's *The Improvement of the Mind* (1741), a collection of essays on education that inspired the title of her own work. As Samuel Johnson recognized, Watts's *Improvement* is a practical implementation of John Locke's description of learning through the senses. "It is Observation that must give us our first Ideas of Things," Watts explains, "as it includes in it *Sense* and *Consciousness*" or all that "Mr. Locke means by Sensation and Reflection." Observation is the first way that we learn; it "lays the Ground-work and Foundation of all Knowledge." Without first learning a "Variety of sensible and intellectual Ideas by the *Sensation* of outward Objects," we cannot learn from people or books. Unfortunately, few children, Wakefield laments, receive adequate training in how to observe their surroundings, and consequently, youth with "a considerable degree of classical learning, are unacquainted either with the materials of those things they daily use, or the methods of manufacturing them."[22]

Her *Mental Improvement* models how parents might teach habits of observation to children who can already read, correcting the mental limitations left by memorizing classical literature. The owner of one copy at the Baldwin Library shows a teacher who took her suggestion to heart, signed: "Presented by Mr. Clery / to / Master John Lawson, / Second Place in the / First Greek and Fourth / Latin Classes. / Byethorn Academy / 24 July 1840." Like the Harcourt children, John Lawson could enjoy Wakefield's conversations after finishing his Latin.

Readers who switch between reading, conversation, and observation remix and remake knowledge—a mode of active reading that Watts distinguishes from memorization as "deep reflection," without which, "I do not see what title your head has to true learning above your shelves."[23] A child who memorizes is like a bookshelf, but a child occupied in "deep reflection" refashions ideas born of sensation into new, more complex ideas. This point Watts borrows from Locke, who describes creative thought as acting, mixing, recombining ideas, depending upon a varied "stock" gathered through sensation.[24] Tinkering with objects furnishes the mind with material for thought, while thinking is itself a form of mental tinkering that produces intellectual property. Counterintuitively, deep reflection is a habit formed by interrupted reading.

Taking Apart and Assembling books: Mechanical Literacy in Early Childhood

For younger children, dismantling objects and assembling new ones is a fun activity with printed material—and a useful one that scaffolds the organization of information from multiple sources. The mind's creative fashioning of ideas takes physical form in toys and books that require cutting apart and reassembly for proper use. Families purchased maps, picture sheets, and lotto sheets with thumbnail images printed on a grid to be used for crafting, coloring, decorating walls, making puzzles, or scrapbooking. Some behaviors that fall under what Leah Price calls "rejection history," such as tearing and destroying books, are the same creative "modding" behaviors described by Jacqueline Reid-Walsh—copying, adapting, and "repurposing" existing books to make homemade books.[25] Cutting things apart also allows children to try new combinations and collections of objects. I have seen object alphabets and lotto prints, for example, pasted onto linen scrolls, or decorating a Jacob's ladder, or pasted into scrap books.[26] As Hannah Field argues in *Playing with the Book*, children learned from adults to carefully handle their books to avoid destroying them, especially moveable books with delicate mechanisms. While harshly using books was frowned upon as destructive, books and toys also invited sanctioned behaviors for taking apart and assembling pieces as a matter of course. Children are expected to scatter, shuffle, then put away their cards, tiles, dolls, games, and pictures back into decorative storage cabinet boxes or paper envelopes.[27] Similarly, inexpensive unbound chapbooks, sold by peddlers as single flat sheets, required purchasers to fold, sew, and cut the pages at home. Infants (or their parents) cut apart sheets printed with the alphabet to make letter tiles and cut out paper dolls from book pages.[28] And if scrapbooks are any indication, children sometimes cut apart their books to repurpose the illustrations.

Tinkering with books has been part of infant reading since the beginning of the children's publishing industry. M. O. Grenby argues in *The Child Reader* that during the second half of the eighteenth century, children were increasingly likely to learn to read through alphabet toys instead of books, but he cautions that such methods did not replace books in most families.[29] Another possibility suggested by Heather Klemann is that books for infants absorbed some of the affordances of toys, blurring distinctions between them, beginning with John Newbery's *A Little Pretty Pocket-Book* (1744), a children's miscellany with alphabet and short stories, sold with a ball or pincushion, that deploys haptic learning for didactic ends. Newbery instructs children to use the ball or pincushion like a Protestant autobiography by sticking pins into the toy to record their good and bad deeds, an appropriate activity in part because children also used pins to point to letters when learning to read.[30] There is also a second game included in Newbery's book, a set of alphabet tiles printed as part of the book itself. Sometime before 1743, Benjamin Collins printed an alphabet game "upon the plan of Mr. Locke" that invites children to rearrange letters to spell words, as described in his treatise *Some Thoughts Concerning Education* (1693). The accompanying directions suggest "cozening children into a knowledge of the letters" through "play or recreation." Collins's game became part of Newbery's *A Little*

Pretty Pocket-Book under the heading, "The Great Q Play." Children could cut out the letters from the miscellany to play the game or buy a separate set of manipulable letters, meaning they could take apart their book and remake it into a toy.[31]

Over the next century, children's publishers produced thematic alphabet cards based on Locke's plan, usually featuring an image of an object that begins with each letter and a short rhyme for advanced reading. These cards, sold as boxed sets, resemble the alphabets printed in children's miscellanies, and the pages of these miscellanies could be cut apart (as Newbery suggested) to make alphabet tiles and cards. In library collections today, these miscellanies are catalogued inconsistently as realia, ephemera, or books, because their current form depends on what families did with their purchase.[32] Anticipating these choices, *The Child's New Play-Thing* (1742), a miscellany "designed for the USE of SCHOOLS, or for Children before they go to School," suggests in the preface that parents cut out the object alphabet and put it "into a Hat or Box, and let the Child draw the Letters out one by one," providing two copies of the same alphabet to accommodate cutting them, with the object images printed on the back of the corresponding letter. With these varying options, one 1763 copy at Princeton's Cotsen Children's Library binds all the pages together into a book, while another copy survives entirely as a set of cards, including the alphabet, the emblems, and the short reading lessons from the end of the book.[33] Interestingly, creating these cards is *not* suggested by the book's preface, but a reader familiar with commonly available instructional card sets decided to make one. As its title suggests, the miscellany allows readers to determine its form: either book or "plaything." In addition to multiple formats, literacy materials offer conflicting affordances so that an item's status as book or toy depends on what a child does with it at any moment. If a child eats his gingerbread hornbook, for example, without thinking about the letters printed on it, is it still a hornbook? Other toys provoke similar questions. A wooden jumping jack (1810), also held at Cotsen, allows toddlers to chew the figure or pull the string to make it dance or discover the alphabet carved into the horn piece on its torso.[34]

Handmade literacies exhibit these same ambiguities, especially those books modeled on popular toys.[35] One innovative family cut out illustrations from children's books and pasted them onto cloth pages they sewed together into a book. Each page has ribbon pull-tabs for moving dozens of little paper figures across the page along tracks cut in the cloth. One ribbon sends a sailboat skipping across the waves while another guides a farmer with his cow across a meadow. The complexity of this creation, with hundreds of figures and ribbons spilling from its pages, suggests willing participation from older children or adults who approved of cutting apart books to make this new book-toy hybrid. The moveable manuscript's pull-tab ribbon draws the figures along cut paper tracks in the same manner as a moving panorama, a street entertainment featuring small wooden figures that move across a painted scene, powered by a crank or clockwork instead of a ribbon.[36] Similarly, another home-made book, *Little Miss Kitten Come and Read* (ca. 1850), is designed like a literacy toy. The book is constructed of paper "pages" pasted onto a long piece of linen and rolled together into a scroll. Readers slowly unroll each page until the full book unwinds as a panoramic sheet, similar to a scroll alphabet, a literacy toy resembling alphabet cards printed successively on a linen or paper strip that children uncoil from its cylinder case and then crank back inside for storage. Appropriately enough, the story follows a mother cat's patient attempts to teach reading to a playful kitten who keeps pawing distractedly at passing scarves and shoelaces. Matching form to content, *Little Miss Kitten* compares infants to restless kittens, acknowledging the difficulty of sitting still for lessons while presenting a solution: a book built like a toy that requires unique exploratory movement to access its contents.

By combining physical and mental exercise through literacy toys, children reinforced the connection between training their bodies and learning about the world around them. Another kind of literacy toy, called the "posturepedic alphabet," commonly produced as prints, puzzles, and cards, forms each letter out of children's bending bodies. Children can rearrange pieces from the Posture Master's Alphabet Jigsaw Puzzle (ca. 1800) like alphabet cards, or assemble the puzzle pieces in order, or imitate the illustrations with their bodies.[37] Recommending these activities, one miscellany from 1790 recounts: "I have two little boys, who have learned the Alphabet in capitals in a week, by turning themselves into various postures, agreeable to the different shapes of the letters. It is not two days since I met one of them in the garden, with my boots on his head."[38] These literacy toys and games offer children

FIGURE 10. Catalogued in Cotsen Children's Library as Scrapbook of Moveable Collages, this item was likely created in England before 1845. Courtesy of Princeton University Library.

images of themselves as movable bodies, which they imitate or control as they learn letters in their minds. They also normalize interrupted reading by suggesting activities for children to perform during their lessons, much like Miss Kitten batting at string.

Encouraging young children to move while they learn reflects a new appreciation for distinct developmental stages of childhood and a willingness to accommodate behaviors considered natural to infants.

FIGURE 11. *Little Miss Kitten Come and Read* and *The Story of the Small Brown Mouse that Kitten Saw*, likely created in England, ca. 1850s. Cotsen Children's Library. Courtesy of Princeton University Library.

Paraphrasing Locke, Rousseau, and François Fénelon, Catharine Macaulay insists that "the laborious task of learning" should not replace "bodily exercises which are so necessary to corporal health and strength." Boys need to move, and even "little Miss" should not be censored for "her locomotive tricks."[39] Inviting movement into reading lessons may seem, nevertheless, an unlikely method for teaching the deep reflection valued by Watts or Wakefield. Yet Macaulay explains that moving around lays the foundation for deep reflection as adults. Although the "child's brain" is not ready for the extended attention necessary for study, fortunately, "the curiosity of children is eager and insatiable," and, therefore, they easily give extended attention to their physical surroundings. Through curiosity, children learn the "habit" of "attention to all the objects which surround us."[40] When permitted uninterrupted deep attention to things, children grow into lifelong observers, "stimulated" not only to reading, but to "the study of nature, and the productions of art."[41] Counterintuitively, objects profitably interrupt children's reading to teach them sustained attention, not exclusive to reading but toward any purposeful project. As a result, reading lessons tend to focus an infant's attention on just a few letters or words while enabling prolonged attention on the environment more generally. They meet children where they are at: in the physical world, immersed in their sensations. Anna Letitia Barbauld—who suggested that parents direct infants' attention using paper with a small hole to reveal single letters or words on a page—created age-graded reading books with fictional family characters to suggest an ideal balance between short reading lessons and longer periods of experiential learning. Her *Lessons for*

Children from Two to Three Years (1778–79) begins by describing a reading environment with "mamma's lap," "your book," "the pin to point with," and the family cat, but young Charles spends only a short time immersed in these tools and sensations before mother commands him to play. For the rest of the book, Charles focuses his attention on a series of objects, each singled out from the clutter so he can easily concentrate. He holds a comb, examines father's watch, sets cutlery on the table, goes for a walk in the field, and finally examines different coins used at the fair, covering a full developmental trajectory from home to abroad and from family exchange to neighborhood trade. Even though Charles reads his lesson from a book, the rudiments of language remain integrated with other experiences that prioritize embodied learning.[42] His method of reading—first letters, or single words, as directed by his parent who points to each with a pin—is quite similar to the progress he makes on objects, beginning with a simple comb (a single object, directly related to his body), and concluding with a fair, where many objects gather from far and wide, tangled together with all the complexity of a novel. His mode of learning is an implicit model for parents using Barbauld's age-graded books to teach their own infants to read texts and objects.

Interrupted reading works especially well for information books. The stigmatization of avid novel reading, especially for young women, may explain why science-minded educators revalued playfulness in young child readers as a positive early indicator of future literacy expertise. Adults who study nature or make art are more likely to engage in what Louise Rosenblatt calls "efferent reading," or reading with another goal in mind besides the pleasure of reading itself. Instead of losing themselves in an engrossing story, efferent readers pause to write notes or marginalia, test ideas through experiments, pace the room, or switch between sources.[43] This kind of reading is underexamined in the history of children's literature because today educators assume immersive, imaginative fiction inspires a love of reading, while we fear that skimming on screens may herald the death of deep reading. For scholars of Romantic literature, these concerns sympathetically align with antipathy for didactic informational texts expressed by canonical male poets. When Maria Edgeworth compares Rosamond's education to "annealing," or hammering hot metalwork while alternating between the fire and cold water, we cringe at the migraine-inducing metaphor for what

Samuel Taylor Coleridge insists should be an organic process. These materials are made by the author-educators whom William Wordsworth derisively called "those who manage books and things / and make them act on infant minds."[44] Admittedly, that is exactly what they did.

Collecting Things in Books and Acquiring Knowledge

If Barbuald's student Charles is any indication, objects have a way of gathering together into machines and markets, like images pasted in a scrapbook—or letters collected into words. Collecting together manuscripts was a conceit commonly used by children's authors to explain the origins of their story compilations. John Aiken and Barbauld's *Evenings at Home; or the Juvenile Budget Opened* (1792–96) begins as a game among the Fairbourne family, who collect manuscripts written by visitors in a "budget," or treasury box, drawing a story each night to read. Charles and Mary Lamb's *Mrs. Leicester's School* (1807) compiles stories told by students and recorded by their teacher, who binds them together as gifts for her students. Like authors, children take apart and put together information from books, an approach to written knowledge that takes after the tinkering affordances of toys and printed material. Assembling literary collections is a logical extension of dismantling print media to make new books and toys.[45] The similarity between child reading practices and dismantling books is itself examined within such story collections. In Lamb's case, one girl recalls in her autobiographical story, "The Little Mohometan," combing unchaperoned through a large library, where she reads information from a torn history volume and struggles to determine the authenticity of what she learns; likewise, readers must decide to what degree the student autobiographies in the collection are altered by their tellers or censored by the teacher who compiles them.

This kind of information gathering is scaffolded by the early literacy toys and children's libraries created for infants that introduce children to book and object collections. Beginning in 1800, John Marshall began publishing libraries of miniature books, housed in a wooden cabinet with a sliding lid resembling a bookcase. Competitors John Harris, Darton and Harvey, John Wallis, Mary Jane Godwin, Benjamin Talbert, and many others quickly created similar offerings, diversifying languages and book sizes and including alphabets, storybooks, and sets of instructional textbooks (on birds, beasts, flowers, British monarchs, and so on). Although larger palm-sized volumes offer coherent fiction, smaller one-inch volumes place isolated objects, floating in space, opposite a short descriptive sentence or alphabet letter. The "infant prattle" used in these smaller books, such as those from John Marshall's *The Infant's Library* (1800–1801), suggests that adults shared them with children while chatting informally about the pictures or whatever objects are at hand around the room: "Here is a coffee-pot, my dear, there are also coffee-urns which I believe are not more used," or "This is a carriage . . . If it were a real one I suppose you would like to have a ride in it."[46] As evidenced by Jane Johnson's literacy materials created for her son, mothers created these materials well before their commercial production. Brian Alderson surmises that children used doll-sized libraries to perform teacher with dolls, as illustrated on the sliding lid for *Doll Casket* (ca. 1819), thus imitating instructional practices modeled by mothers, using their toys and pets as captive audiences.[47]

Miniature libraries deploy a complicated array of interlocutor gestures that accustom child users to finding information about their

FIGURE 12. *The Book Case of Instruction* [London: John Marshall, 1801–1813]. Courtesy Lilly Library, Indiana University, Bloomington, Indiana.

immediate environment inside of books. The library box announces this pedagogical purpose through its design, which nests things inside books, inside cabinets. Children access the miniature books by sliding open the wooden cabinet's lid, illustrated to look like a bookcase, usually with drawers for objects on the bottom and bookcase shelves on top. The split cabinet prepares children to approach each book inside, with their tiny lotto cuts and brief text, as their own little collection of legible things, while books themselves are legible objects stored inside library cabinets. The sliding lid for a copy of Marshall's *The Infant's Library* features an illustration of a young mother-teacher holding a book while she looks up into the face of the central figure, a boy, who points with both hands to a globe held in a younger child's lap. The globe is a legible model of the physical world, a miniature book of nature. The three figures, mother pointing to child pointing to infant, gesture back in time developmentally to the origins of book learning in an infant's manipulation of the material world. The family are seated on a path leading to an estate, indicating that reading objects and books prepares this boy for his inheritance and for his mastery over the physical world.[48] Like other alphabet toys, miniature libraries combine a developmentally appropriate lesson with an ideological one. They teach children to learn from books and experience and connect these literacies with property ownership by pointing out that books can be stored in the same manner as coffee pots and carriages.

Such lessons extend across the nursery through a wide range of toys and books that connect mechanical and alphabetical literacies with property by asking children to gather objects and texts into "collections." In addition to miniature libraries and alphabet cards, Marshall produced infant cabinets—The Infant's Cabinet of Fishes; Flowers; Birds; Insects; Animals; Trades and The Infant's Cabinet of Various Objects (1800–1801)—each of which contains a thematic picture card deck accompanied by two miniature books (volumes one and two), all housed in a wooden box. Referencing conventions for specimen display, the illustrated sliding lid depicts the view through an oval sash window. The Infant's Cabinet of Birds, for instance, shows one bird perched on a nest with eggs and another flying above, turned to display its identifiable beak and plumage; The Infant's Cabinet of Fishes shows a bowl with fish placed on a small table and displayed in a classically landscaped garden. A child user would slide open the cabinet's lid to see their own collection of specimens, neatly arranged on individual engraved cards, each labeled with its name and a page reference for the descriptive text in the accompanying two miniature books. Like the miniature library, the infant cabinet carefully connects books with objects through a series of interlocutor gestures. While these cards could have included the short blurb on the card itself just below the image, the separation of the illustrations from the text requires users to move between the cards and the two books just as a child might consult a book to explain something she found.[49] This movement between image and text, card and book, would be doubly reinforced for children who own specimen boxes or curiosity cabinets for storing the little treasures they find on walks—or who presents these objects and books to

FIGURE 13. The Infant's Cabinet of Various Objects (London: J. Marshall, 1801). Courtesy Lilly Library, Indiana University, Bloomington, Indiana. The lid's illustration displays the interlocutor gesture of a mother handing two children this object cabinet while outside. The composition imitates the conventional frontispiece image of a parent giving a child a book while indoors, as shown on *Mama's Present.*

a doll, who mirrors both the child (as instructional audience) and the book (as mimetic object).

Marshall's miniature libraries and cabinets prepare infants for a way of learning that extends throughout their childhood. After their libraries, children can read fiction that revolves around collection, with titles like "rural rambles," or "country excursions," or a "visit" to a relative's house. The typical plot, first established by such authors as Sarah Trimmer, Anna Letitia Barbauld, Charlotte Smith, Mary Wollstonecraft, Frances T. Jamieson, and Jane Webb Loudon, features an exemplary rational instructor who converses with young siblings about plants, animals, and the natural world, providing a mix of natural history and moral lessons adapted to the children's various capacities. Inevitably, one child is a neglected cousin of dissipated tastes whose senseless consumption is put to rights, demonstrating the moral benefits of learning about everyday things. By the nineteenth century, such books teach popular science by portraying the family gathering specimens during country walks or purchasing goods in towns. The children document items and experiences, thus reproducing the author's own writing practices and inviting reader emulation. For instance, Jeanette writes about what she discovers while traveling in Jane Gardiner's *An Excursion from London to Dover* (1806), or, much later, in American author Mary Ellen Bamford's *The Look-About Club, and the Curious Live Things They Found* (1887), the Perry family moves to the country, where the children begin a family club for journaling about all the interesting plants and animals they find, modeling for children how to make their own notebooks and cabinets.[50]

The plots of these stories configure the book itself as a collection. In a geology book by E. W. Payne, *Earth's Riches: or, Underground Stores* (1860), Mr. Goodman, who oversees the education of his large family, writes to friends for "minerals peculiar to different localities, and of widely different composition and use," which the children assemble into a "friendship grotto," complete with rustic furniture. The family then gathers regularly in the grotto, where the specimens inspire questions for Mr. Goodman—himself a living grotto of knowledge, whose "mental stores, and still lively taste, rendered him a fountain of wisdom."[51] The book itself is thus represented within the story, remediated as a grotto, just as children reading the book might translate the story into "labour of the hands," as Payne calls it, by collecting specimens and having similar conversations in a space all their own. This interchangeability between textual and material worlds is reinforced by the way such information literature was written, by collecting bits and pieces from adult nonfiction, retaining some paragraphs almost verbatim, and binding these loosely together inside a children's fictional story frame. In other words, the process used to create children's information literature is a textual collection practice much like Mr. Goodman's friendship grotto, with Mr. Goodman standing in for the author.

Emulating their teachers, children in such stories create their own nursery cabinets. They acquire objects and learn their properties in order to stock their minds. In *The India Cabinet Opened* (1823), the first novel by travel writer and naturalist Lucy Sarah Atkins Wilson, Ellen and her family gather natural history specimens during their country walks while vacationing in Cumberland. Back home in Devonshire, her mother unlocks her curiosity cabinet, revealing "three shelves, containing a choice collection of nature's ever varying productions, nicely arranged," and they unwrap the contents over several weeks, each item inspiring her mother's stories. Ellen's mother also gives her a numbered book in which she has recorded each specimen and where it was gathered, allowing Ellen to find the locations on a wall map. Like Marshall's card cabinets, Ellen's cabinet refers to her own experiences collecting specimens, as well as other print media in her home; she has to search around in literature, just as she searched the Cumberland hills, justifying her father's comparison between books and nature: "Nature is the first and best volume of instruction: it is always open to you, and will undoubtedly repay your attention by inspiring an early spirit of piety and devotion." After the cabinet's contents are exhausted, Mother assures Ellen that she will always carry the cabinet with her through "the knowledge" she has "acquired."[52]

In *The Mind Is a Collection*, Sean Silver investigates such physical metaphors of the mind, including Locke's mind-as-cabinet, arguing that Cartesian dualism dissociated the mind from matter so thoroughly that dualist thinkers used ready-to-hand objects and spaces to re-materialize the mind.[53] According to Anke te Heesen, pictorial encyclopedias like the picture academy for the young, an eighteenth-century German education aid that forms the center of her study, organize information about the world in storage boxes that represent the student's mind.[54]

These ways of materializing mental processes inform how British children's books and material culture use curios and workshops to materialize learning as mental acquisition. For naturalists, books themselves actually functioned as containers for collecting botanical specimens, held neatly pressed between pages, demonstrating the book owner's organized mind and their knowledge of classification systems, with specific class connotations. Using books and collection boxes, argues Anne Secord, distinguished between collection for work or leisure, "between artisanal and genteel ways of seeing. For formally educated collectors, whose observation was shaped by classificatory systems, collections became the *basis* of their knowledge of nature; for artisans, whose knowledge of plants usually preceded their understanding of classification, collections were viewed as the *product and result* of the knowledge of nature."[55] This distinction is especially noticeable in the learning process represented in books for children, since wealthy child characters like Ellen simultaneously gather specimens while learning classification and organizing their specimens. From the disorganized splendor of Cumberland's hills, Ellen's mind arranges its contents as neatly as her mother's cabinet. As a reward, Ellen will make "some additions to it" when they visit the seashore.[56] She assumes control over her mind's future accumulations. So do genteel readers, who, having learned classification, may carry out Ellen's activities outside the book, adding chapters from their lives to Ellen's story collection, and specimens to their nursery cabinets.

By the Victorian period, children's materials connect these collections with British imperialism, which enabled the collection of cultural and scientific specimens, many stollen through conquest, for display in educational spaces. One of the clearest examples of this are the toys created by industrial designer Henry Cole, who drafted the organizational exhibit schema of the Great Exhibition of 1851 and advocated for its crystal palace design. During the previous decade, Cole wrote more than a dozen children's books under the pseudonym Felix Summerly.[57] In *An Alphabet of Quadrupeds* (1844), Summerly creatively combines alphabetical and mechanical literacies while connecting the home with global trade. Summerly pairs each alphabet letter with an animal illustration, faithfully copied from paintings displayed at the British museum, accompanied by a short natural history lesson detailing the animal's habits and its uses in manufacturing (E is for Elephant, whose "tusks are of ivory and are very useful for handles of knives"). The subject (animals or quadrupeds) is a common one for alphabet card cabinets, suggesting that Summerly's book is itself a little cabinet collection between two covers. To round out the metaphor, the opening dedication to the author's daughters emphasizes ownership and collection: "This book puts you in possession of a little Picture Gallery of your own." Readers can add to the book by drawing their own "good copies" of the animals. By making "your own 'Gallery,'" readers participate in a collection tradition modeled by the British Museum, which displays objects collected through imperial conquest, and by Summerly, who collects the best animal images for his book.[58] By adding their own art, the children's home becomes a domestic museum and an extension of a global empire. Home, museum, and book all become metaphorical cabinets that organize the alphabet in the mind while connecting that alphabet to real animals, objects, and their visual representations. The mind is a microcosm of the world—a little *Orbis Pictus* that calls forth mental representations neatly connected with the right alphabetical signs.

The aesthetics of collection concerned Felix Summerly, who believed in its moral import. When his children were young, Cole (as Summerly) published fables and fairy tales, but also travel literature, such as visitor guides to Westminster Abbey and Hampton Court. Drawing on this expertise, Summerly's children's books ask readers to make something at home, then find the real thing exhibited in public. He patented and produced two sets of children's toys for "creating a taste for beauty in little children" that work just like his alphabet book: the *Tessellated Pastime* (1843), which teaches design principles by inviting children to arrange colored triangles into mosaic patterns after designs by Owen Jones, and the *Architectural Pastime* (1845), which provides simple blocks for erecting buildings. Both are part of his Home Treasury series, along with nonsense and fairy tales, a redeployment of traditional nursery fare heralded by Harvey Darton for rescuing children from unimaginative matter-of-fact tales. Geoffrey Summerfield argues that Summerly "marked the emergence of emphatically nondidactic books for children," anticipating the Golden Age of cultivating child imagination through artistic folklore—an assessment selectively focused on one aspect of Summerly's work. Although Cole objected to

Peter Parley–style information books, his approach to art remains didactic, and by organizing mental images in relation to real-world collection spaces, he borrows the pedagogical practices of those he opposed. Reconsidering Cole's toys in design history, Ezra Shales notices continuities with didacticism through the influence of Richard Lovell and Maria Edgeworth's *Practical Education*, Pestalozzian object teaching, and John Locke's philosophy of mind.[59] An accompanying booklet for each toy contains suggested patterns for mosaics and buildings, plus descriptions of public buildings from which the designs are copied and short children's stories that illustrate the moral benefits of aesthetic toys. Children can use Cole's toys to approximate real architectural art specimens, just as *An Alphabet of Quadrupeds* encourages them to draw animals while looking at art from the British Museum. By claiming to support children's moral development, Cole defends aesthetic exercises as a mode of organizing the mind through the arrangement of miniature blocks.

These collection metaphors entered into common purveyance with the Victorian children's "treasury" or "cabinet"—books filled with playful activities and experiments. *The Illustrated Girl's Own Treasury* (1861), a book of games, knowledge, and activities for girls, begins with the arrival of "a most exquisite piece of furniture in English oak, inlaid and carved," sent by the children's aunt along with a key. The mother unlocks and opens the doors,

> and revealed a Book-case and Cabinet; the former furnished with richly-bound and illustrated volumes, and the latter with a great variety of objects suitable for feminine employment and recreation, all arranged in the daintiest order imaginable, on shelves or in drawers, glass cases, and little odd nests and nooks. Over the whole ran an ornamental scroll, in old English letters, // The Girl's Own Treasury.[60]

An image of this imposing piece of furniture forms a frontispiece spread for *The Illustrated Girl's Own Treasury*, so that readers open its doors when they open the book. The device is remarkably similar to the infant cabinets created by Marshall sixty years earlier. Now a shorthand for children's literature with an experiential component, the "treasury" connects books with activities by remediating a familiar nursery toy while representing leisure as the privilege of cabinet owners. The mother opening the children's neatly arranged cabinet suggests a display of domestic leisure activities reminiscent of Cole's exhibition schema for collecting specimens of raw materials, tools, machinery, and finished products from around the world in a "crystal palace" like an enormous curio cabinet. Book or toy—cabinet or museum—exactly where one ends and the other begins is hard to say.

Manipulating Books like Playthings; or, the Mechanics of Learning

As educators emphasized the productivity of children's play, the class connotations behind the labor of learning informed theories of reading. In the first chapter, "On Toys," from *Essays on Practical Education* (1798), Maria Edgeworth praises the child with the "sense and courage to destroy" his "frail and useless" toys: "He breaks them, not from the love of mischief, but from the hatred of idleness," desiring to discover "how they are made, or whether he can put them together again." He takes apart his little mechanical birds to see how they warble. And the same for his books: his parents "throw him an old almanac to tear to pieces."[61] These broken toys are the opening anecdote for a curriculum of natural philosophy founded on observation. Toys lay the foundation for her second chapter, "On Tasks," which covers languages and concludes with rational argumentation. It is helpful to consider these two chapters as another version of Hamilton's anecdote about Mrs. Z, who teaches the principles of the screw prepare her son for reading. Edgeworth integrates the languages and sciences through an infant play curriculum. Indeed, Edgeworth's third chapter is on "attention"—precisely the faculty that, according to Hamilton, Macaulay, Wakefield, and Watts, children develop by observing and handling objects. The attention necessary for reading and reasoning begins with toys: "When children are busily trying experiments upon objects within their reach," Edgeworth advises, "we should not, by way of saving them trouble, break the course of their ideas, and totally prevent them from acquiring knowledge by their own experience."[62] Allowing children to indulge in deep concentration creates habits of reflection they extend to other forms of study.

FIGURE 14. *The Illustrated Girl's Own Treasury, Specially Designed for the Entertainment of Girls, and the Development of the Best Faculties of the Female Mind* (London: Ward and Lock, 1861). When assembling, dismantling, and collecting appear endemically across children's information books like these, references to locked cabinets and orderly compartments differentiate the labor of learning from physical labor performed for wages.

The toys that Maria Edgeworth recommends develop mental faculties while also giving that developmental process a physical form. To cite Locke's favorite metaphor, her toys look suspiciously like manifestations of the mind as an "empty Cabinet," "furnished" with "Ideas" through "sensation" and "reflection."[63] The child commences with simple building blocks, "pieces of wood of various shapes and sizes, that they may build up and pull down, and put in a variety of different forms and positions; balls, pulleys, wheels, string, and strong little carts." Parents should give their children empty specimen cabinets to organize their "little treasures," and empty doll houses along with materials to make their own furnishings. They love chatting about common "objects which are familiar" in prints, making baskets, and modeling with clay. They eventually build "models of architecture," then "models of simple machines," and, finally, "models of more complicated machinery" used by "manufacturers and artists," including miniature "spinning wheels, looms, paper-mills, wind-mills, water-mills." Model machines prepare children to learn mechanics, chemistry, and natural philosophy as they begin to "class particular observations gradually under general principles" before they visit factories first-hand.[64] As metaphors for the mind, machines work somewhat differently than the natural history specimen boxes, suggesting the mind "tinkers" with sensations to create an organized relation between knowledge, toward some useful function.

This progressive exploration of toys assembles objects and organizes them into purposeful machines. Although these "wheels" and "looms" are designed to model industrial machinery, they just as easily model child mental development. As described by Locke, the mind of "a *Child* from its Birth" gradually "comes more and more to be furnished with *Ideas*, it comes to be more and more awake; thinks more, the more it has matter to think on." The mind begins using other "Faculties of *Enlarging, Compounding*, and *Abstracting* its Ideas, and of reasoning about them, and reflecting upon these."[65] The children's nursery, with its little alphabet toys, its collecting cabinets, its miniature libraries, and its model machines partitions and arranges the natural world outside its walls in the same way that a child's mind aspires to organize its ideas. As one advertisement for an infant's catechism on "common things" explains, "Between a mind taught at random and a mind educated there is a vast difference. As much as there is between a lumber room and a store room—a book manufactory and a library."[66] An ordered mind is one capable of imposing order on its environment as an outward sign of self-governance. In Edgeworth's progression of nursery toys, the most orderly child's mind works like an industrial engineer, building then overseeing its mental machinery.

According to Edgeworth, these toys prepare children for reading because language itself is a kind of model machinery, put together by humans to create representations of real things. Her toys thus scaffold lessons in the physical sciences, but also lessons in language. Infants begin learning language with "the names of things" that "can be easily produced for examination," and they learn to read not with whole-word recognition, but with letter sounds and phonetical groupings (sion, th, sh). These are the building blocks of language. Children master communication by adding complex associations to a word just as they use bits of wood to make larger structures. Edgeworth gives "gold" as an example: children can point to gold, but they do not grasp the reason for its value until they learn "all the properties of gold," and "in what it differs from other metals, to what uses it is applied in arts, manufactures, and commerce." Eventually, children grasp concepts that cannot be described in words and have no physical manifestations, such as "surprize, joy, grief, pity." Like pieces of machinery, words and ideas join together in meaningful relationships that reflect material reality. A child raised by this method will speak the truth and reason with accuracy. "Let us then take care that their simple ideas be accurate, and when these are compounded, their complex notions, their principles, opinions, and tastes, will necessarily be just." The result of carefully scaffolding a child's alphabetical and mechanical literacies is a correct comprehension of an ordered world where clear communication resembles an honest financial transaction, and where the cost of an item accurately reflects its value. Words without ideas are "counterfeit coin," but "words which really represent ideas" are "of sterling value; they not only shew our present store, but they increase our wealth by keeping it in continual circulation; both the principal and the interest increase together."[67]

Edgeworth's financial metaphors for learning language and acquiring knowledge through tinkering subtly rely upon Locke's concept of owning property. According to Locke, a person claims personal property for their own use by adding the "labour of the body, and the work of the hands," removing it from what belongs "to all in common."[68] Something similar happens with ideas. The "stock" or "furniture" of the mind belongs to the child because his hands and his senses grapple with these objects to make something external into an idea stored inside the mind. Tinkering claims physical objects as property and creates new ideas—creates knowledge-as-property, held inside the child's mind, born by mixing the child's senses with external objects. Seizing property is a creative act akin to accumulating ideas through haptic learning and refashioning them through reflection. We gather, remix, and make. Educators describe learning with the language of property, with the mind as a storehouse, collection, or box, and ideas as accumulating stores, furniture, or treasure. Paraphrasing Locke, Isaac Watts describes "observation" (or sensation and reflection) as a constant on-going accumulation of property, "every Moment of our Existence we may be adding something to our intellectual Treasures."[69] Since we own what we make, Locke posits that parents own the bodies of the children they make, while God owns each person's life, for humans are "all the workmanship of one omnipotent, and infinitely wise maker," and therefore are God's "property, whose workmanship they are."[70] In the image of their maker, humans make knowledge into property, whereby children claim ownership of themselves as creatures of their own making. Learning through observation and manipulation of objects practically manifests these artisanal metaphors of self-fashioning as self-ownership.

Owning knowledge as a kind of intellectual property begins with the child's exploration of an ecology of objects. This connection between tinkering and property surfaces whenever authorities on education describe observation. Give children "objects that belong to them, and instruments which they may dispose of as their own property," advises the Abbé Pluche in *Le Spectacle de la Nature* (1732–43), a children's encyclopedia that Denis Diderot used as a model, strongly recommended in *Practical Education* (1798). "Give them an old-fashioned clock, a small timber-framed house put together with removable pegs, a jack, a small crane, rammers, and all the engines for driving piles into the ground to be taken apart, with each piece numbered in order to put the whole thing together again."[71] To understand how these machines are made, a child must take them apart and become their maker, as

God the Creator knows all His creation.[72] Likewise, a children's biography of James Watt describes how the inventor of the steam engine "used, when quite a boy, to take his toys to pieces; examine how they were made, and then put them together again" to learn "the principle on which they were constructed."[73] Curious manipulation confirms children's ownership of their machines and the concepts they embody, just as Ellenor Fenn recommends learning the alphabet with manipulable letters that children regard as their property.

Understanding the general principles of movement not only prepares children for reading, but confirms their identities as property owners. Nursery practices based on this philosophy of mind socialize children into accepting what C. B. Macpherson calls "possessive individualism," the liberal idea that humans own their capacities, knowledge, and labor, and they relate to one another as equals in a rational marketplace where they freely exchange this property, unfettered by power relations.[74] In a society that mistakes possessive individualism for virtue, poverty reflects the moral failings of individual members, who are easily dehumanized.[75] Through the logic of possessive individualism, a child's developmental progress using haptic exercises might be regarded as a process of becoming human (a rational adult). Not born "in the state of equality" but born "to it," as Locke says, children obtain freedom from the "bonds of subjection" to their parents as "age and reason" loosen them—as they, too, become makers. These bonds are "like the swaddling-clothes they are wrapt up in, and supported by," a metaphor that Jean-Jacques Rousseau literalizes (and note how frequently metaphors about the mind are used literally in nurseries), when he recommends preserving Emile's freedom by removing his swaddling and letting Emile explore the world unimpeded. In other words, a child's haptic learning begins his transition toward "rational" adulthood, when he will have "liberty to dispose and order as he lists his person, actions, possessions, and his whole property" and to contract his own labor.[76] In an unacknowledged circular argument, the home, garden, and the nursery itself are so many microcosms of God's divinely ordered world, providing scientific evidence that confirms possessive individualism as the law of nature. The general "law" of nature, as well as moral law, asserts one natural philosophy textbook, "is in the constitution of things."[77] In other words, moral principles are legible in the arrangement of physical objects and their movement in the world. Children explore their environment to develop sound judgment through an organized, disciplined mind.

These ideas could be taught through Pestalozzian object lessons, widely used in British schools after 1820 to unite experiential learning with reading and writing. In the Pestalozzian methods recommended by English teaching manuals, children draw lines, circles, curves, and various other shapes, and they practice finding these "pure forms" in buildings, trees, food, and so on, before they consider the same forms within the alphabet. Similar to how Maria Edgeworth introduced reading and engineering with tactile play, Pestalozzi divided alphabetical knowledge into tangible composite pieces, while students performed math using manipulatives (identical small objects for counting) before reading numbers.[78] Even the children's aerobic exercises were broken down into "the alphabet of abilities," which included "*striking, carrying, throwing, pushing, pulling, turning, twisting, swinging*, &c." Described as an "apprenticeship of virtue," these basic motions formed an ordered series for students, organized "according to the structure of the human body."[79] Pestalozzian lessons are designed to transition children from sensation to reflection by learning the ABCs of adult rational thought.

Pestalozzi developed his object teaching methods while working with war orphan children. Suffering from "privation and want," these students had "a knowledge of the essential relations of things" but they could not connect their lives with rote lessons from books, which they repeated without understanding.[80] Pestalozzi began teaching using "those objects only which immediately encircled my pupils," or what they already know and can describe with accuracy, before gradually expanding their knowledge in concert with their experience. Working with a three-year-old, Pestalozzi recalls, "Very soon I was obliged to lay aside the alphabet, that first torment of youth; he felt no interest in those dead signs; he would have nothing but things, or pictures of things."[81] The purpose of this method, according to historian Sarah Anne Carter, is to scaffold right moral action: "Children were first to develop sensation, then perception, notion, and finally volition, learning how to act morally based on an individual view of the world."[82] Explaining Pestalozzi to British readers, George Eduard Biber describes how in learning language "the child is to be raised above the mere perception of the senses" and "led to the consciousness of an immortal soul within himself." Object lessons teach a child "consciousness of his powers, and a tendency to mental self-activity," enabling his "moral ascendance." Biber exclaims passionately against rote learning, the empty "repetition of hollow sounds!" Instead, instructors should follow the "unalterable nature of things."[83] Learning from things is not a rejection of language, but an alignment of words with God's creation to reduce falsehoods born of miscomprehension. For English teachers applying Pestalozzian techniques, tying words to things agrees with John Locke's argument for "the imperfection of words": Even the Bible, though "infallibly true," relies on a comprehending reader, "fallible in the understanding of it," so that the "will of God, when clothed in words" is like Christ taking human form, "subject to all the frailties and inconveniences of human nature," whereas an illiterate person may read in the world, without error, "such legible characters of his works and providence."[84]

The moral importance ascribed to combining alphabetical and mechanical literacies may be judged from the interlocutor gestures widely deployed in children's books. A humble collection, such as *The Keepsake, or, Poems and Pictures for Childhood and Youth* (1818), contains two symmetrical poems that call readers into the book and send them away. In "Mary's Lesson," Mary must complete her reading lesson before she goes outside to play, while in "Alfred" a boy considers the relationship between reading and observation. The child speaker asks his mother, who sews by the fire:

> How can I the south from the north ever know,
> When there is no S in the sky;
> Oh! How can I tell the east from the west
> When not the least mark I can spy?

The question suggests Alfred learned directions by reading a compass, but he does not yet grasp the relationship between an instrument and the world it measures. Rather than teach her son to use a compass, the mother suggests a new way of reading the world, by finding an alphabet in the sky:

Whenever the sun rises, there is the east,
Now that is both easy and clear;
Wherever at ev'ning he sets from your view,
The west, my beloved, is there.

Now you know where to find both the west and the east,
We soon shall discover the rest:
To the left is the south, to the right is the north,
When your face is turn'd full to the west.[85]

In the illustration, the mother faces the fire, seated "at her work" (rather than reading), while Alfred gestures outside of the window, creating a visual interlocutor gesture. Through identification with these characters who move outside the home, the poem pushes parent and child readers outside the text in front of them. The mother's explanation of the cardinal directions, in turn, points back to reading.

Orienting emerging readers spatially by compass directions appears in several books designed for young children, including Barbauld's infant lesson books and Jane Marcet's *The Seasons* (1832–34). In classrooms, some teachers spatially oriented students before they began to read by asking about their position in the room. An exercise from Samuel Wilderspin's infant school manual, published in the following decade, describes using children's directional awareness to orient them within their physical space during a reading lesson. With an eerie resemblance to Bill Martin Jr. and Eric Carle's 1967 picture book, *Brown Bear, Brown Bear, What do you See?*, a teacher equipped with twenty-six alphabet cards, each with a letter and object, questions students:

> *Q*. Where am I? *A*. Opposite to us. *Q*. What is on the right side of me? *A*. A lady. *Q*. What is on the left side of me? *A*. A chair. *Q*. What is behind me? *A*. A desk. *Q*. Who are before me? *A*. We children. *Q*. What do I hold up in my hand? *A*. Letter A for apple . . .

The questions continue by exploring the apple itself, as an object available to the senses.[86]

Wilderspin's reasoning behind this exercise may sound familiar.

Teachers should tie alphabet letters, or any reading lesson, to information about objects to ensure that children's knowledge of words does not outpace objects presented to their senses. "It is the object of our system to give the children a knowledge of things—and then a knowledge of the *words* which represent those things," so that words call forth an "ideal representation" of the thing, making it "present in the mind of the child." In other words, alphabet exercises that move children between letters and objects, or between reading and the physical space of readers, approximate what should happen inside children's minds as they hear a word and form a mental representation of an object previously examined. Children who become complacently satisfied with vague knowledge lose their inclination to ask questions about "visible things." Furthermore, using words unsupported by experience endangers moral development by allowing children to speak vacuously about "abstract" concepts, such as "love, kindness, religion." Experiencing love or kindness first ensures that "virtue" may not be "an empty sound amongst men" but "an active principle."[87]

Various Pestalozzian schoolbooks published in Britain in the following decades also provide instructors with questions to help children investigate objects in the room, proceeding outward away from their bodies. Horace Grant's *Exercises for the Improvement of the Senses* (1848) for example, begins with "Hands," an exercise that instructs children, "Open your hands—shut them—touch something—hold something—lift something—clap your hands—close your hands together," before addressing other body parts, then proceeding to colors and properties of objects. With the third series of exercises, children are told to "saw the air in this manner, back and forwards with your hand" and "strike the table with your hand" to learn "different substances," or states of matter. Students study the physical sciences to gain awareness of their bodies in relation to other material bodies using immediate examples to deduce general principles.[88] Object lesson pedagogy established its credibility by drawing from mechanical philosophy. Speaking with another teacher, Pestalozzi reportedly described the scientific basis for his system as "the existence of certain physical and mechanical laws, to which our mind is subject in the receiving and fixing of external perceptions," to which his friend Mr. Glayre responds, "Vous voulez mécaniser l'éducation" (You want to mechanize education). Pestalozzi agrees, but qualifies what he means by "mechanism": "My intention was to bring the different means of education and instruction into regular courses adapted to the nature and progressive development of the human faculties."[89] Children are themselves little bodies in motion, following natural laws.

Returning to young Alfred, it becomes clear he has learned his cardinal directions as "empty sounds," by reading "S" on the compass without first grasping directions relative to his body. The mother's response also hints at the moral benefits of extending reading practices from books to the reader's environment. Instead of giving him a compass, she tells him how to read the landscape, because a child who makes his own compass demonstrates moral autonomy. Many child characters, including Rousseau's Emile and Edgeworth's Rosamond, build a compass, which represents following the dictates of one's conscience. The poem's interlocutor gestures thus help to orient child readers of *The Keepsake* within their legible world, binding together alphabetical and mechanical literacy in a common purpose of moral education.

The Matter of Virtue: Learning Religion through Work and Consumption

One of the peculiarities of the history of European pedagogy, as Jill Shefrin points out, is the resurgent call as far back as classical Greek education texts for practical teaching methods that value physical engagement over memorization.[90] These teaching practices take a particular form, however, under the influence of British Dissenting Protestants, who created many eighteenth-century texts for children.[91] A century before either the Edgeworths or Pestalozzi, John Bunyan considered the benefits of observation for teaching children to contemplate abstract theological concepts. He connected reading the Bible with observing the world itself as a legible book, created by God. The poems in his emblem book, *A Book for Boys and Girls: or, Country Rhimes for Children* (1686, republished as *Divine Emblems*), help children to find God's purpose in common objects, such as vines, birds, and trees. The book promises to teach "all Sorts and Degrees, / From those of Age, to Children on the Knees . . . to mount their Thoughts from what are childish Toys. / To Heaven." Just as God took the form of a child, insignificant objects and childish poems are mediums for divine wisdom, for "Great things, by little ones, are made to shine."[92] If moral judgment is dependent on the right education with things, then religion itself should be available to the senses.

In teaching religion and morality through objects, Protestant skepticism of religious imagery gave way before recommendations to provide children with models or images as substitutes for things themselves. Following *Orbis Sensualium Pictus* (1658), the illustrated encyclopedia by John Amos Comenius, educators defended representations or "sensible signs" as long as these worldly things support abstract, spiritual thinking.[93] Isaac Watts recommends using "sensible things and corporeal images for the illustration of those notions which are more abstracted and intellectual," especially "emblems of virtues and vices," which teach children more effectively than "abstracted discourses." But Watts cautions against immersing "the mind in corporeal images" so far that a person never learns to think abstractly, or forms "wrong conceptions of immaterial things" by mistaking symbolic representations for literal things.[94] A father explains the same principles to his daughter, Cecelia, in John Aiken and Barbauld's dialogue "On Emblems" from *Evenings at Home*: Some "notions that we form in our mind" without "any of our senses," such as "Virtue, Vice, Honour, Disgrace, Time, Death, and the like, are not sensible objects, but ideas of the understanding." We give to them "visible form" with "something to the sight that shall raise a familiar notion in the minds of the beholders."[95] As they practice decoding emblems, Cecelia and her father carefully distinguish literal and figurative representations. The "sugar-loaves over the grocer's shop" are "the objects of sight," but an "anchor" is the "emblem" of a "sailor."[96] Such distinctions prevent the cognitive equivalent of idiolatry, or confusion between symbol and thing, which would prevent Cecelia from learning to think abstractly. By observing emblems and images, children sublimate their curiosity for material things into spiritual ideas.

The same principle informs their children's reading lessons. As a Unitarian schoolteacher well versed in philosophy of mind and a friend of Joseph Priestley, Barbauld designed her graduated reading books to provide a progression of curated sensations needed to comprehend complex theological ideas. Her *Hymns in Prose for Children* (1781) uses the love parents show by holding their child at night, the heat of the sun, the grains of sand at the seashore, and the grass that cushions a lamb's feet to accrue an experiential bases for abstract concepts like love, power, eternity, and forgiveness. Publisher John Wallis produced a rebus card edition of Barbauld's *Hymns* in which small images of everyday objects replace words or sounds, which embeds the material evidence of God's presence into her language. In addition to providing clever puzzles—such as the hieroglyphic letters William Darton wrote to his children—hieroglyphs were idealized as a primitive language, closer to nature, that directly represents objects, unlike the Roman alphabet's representation of sounds. At one time, Francis Bacon, whom rational educators frequently quoted, wanted to prevent "linguistic libertinism" by creating a language of pictograms or "written signs that attach to real things rather than the phonology of a particular word."[97] His dream may have inspired later educators who wanted to connect linguistic signs with some material presence to ensure children learn things themselves.

Barbauld's rebus hymns likely take after the rebus Bible, first created by Thomas Hodgson in 1783 and promoted for reading instruction. *A Curious Hieroglyphick Bible* makes history from "Creation" to the "Redemption of Mankind" accessible to "even the youngest children," so that "the History of the Holy Scriptures is imprinted into them in their younger Days." Promising "an easy Way of leading them on in Reading," the book offers select Biblical verses with words replaced by

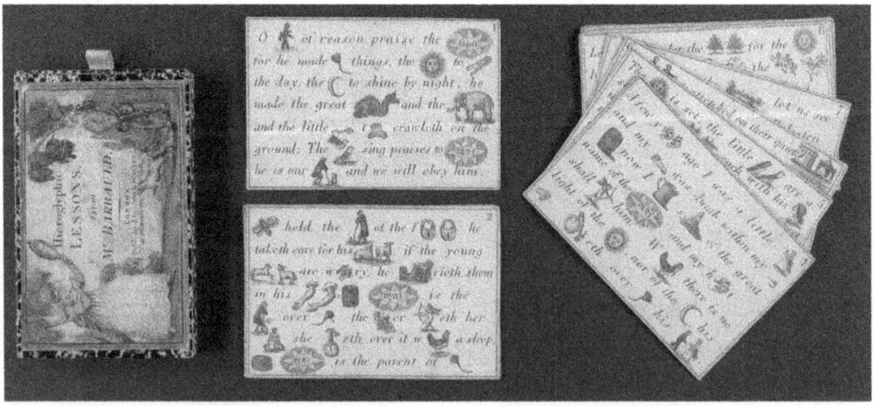

FIGURE 15. Anna Letitia Barbauld, Hieroglyphic Lessons from Mrs. Barbauld (London: John Wallis, 1812). Cotsen Children's Library. Courtesy of Princeton University Library.

"lively and striking Images" of "the most remarkable things that exist in the World."[98] The full text is provided at the bottom of each page, with the words replaced by images indicated in italics. Biblical truth is physically placed in children's minds, accommodating their limited capacity to grasp abstract religious concepts. Its method of representation shows sensitivity to the theological difficulties of representing Biblical subjects through illustration. Some images are simple object substitutes for nouns, while others depict full action scenes, such as Moses's mother placing him in the river.[99] The result is a graduated reading book that also teaches children to regard the physical world, created by God, as a legible book with hidden spiritual significance. Simple material objects, easily represented by a single image of the real thing, prepare children for finding allegorical meanings carefully deduced after long reflection. Unlike Bunyan's emblems, however, this late eighteenth-century book betrays a comfortable convergence between religious instruction and child consumer culture. Its concluding full-page illustration is a classic interlocutor image: A father holds a book, arm outstretched to bless a child during their Bible reading lesson, while around them his other children play with various toys. The scene depicts a family where Bible reading is interrupted by other forms of educational play, suggesting these activities are surprisingly complementary.

This new mode of combining play with spiritual contemplation reflects a privileged experience of leisure and work, made possible in families where children are not essential wage earners. In Bunyan's *Pilgrim's Progress*, Christian and Christiana's labor provides divine wisdom, while worldly Vanity Fair offers a dangerous distraction. By comparison, Georgian didactic fiction such as Mary Wollstonecraft's *Original Stories from Real Life* (1788, 1791) or Barbauld's *Lessons for Children* conventionally concludes with children attending a fair or exhibition, where they apply moral lessons in practical social settings. Rational educators embraced consumer culture for providing an invigorating variety of playful things for children to observe at home, where domestic collection practices mirrored those of public spaces such as zoos, museums, and national landmarks. This revaluation of child consumption reflects changes in wealthier families, whose children were more likely than previous generations to join parents in fashionable entertainments to make them less shy and awkward under public scrutiny, while they also enjoyed greater

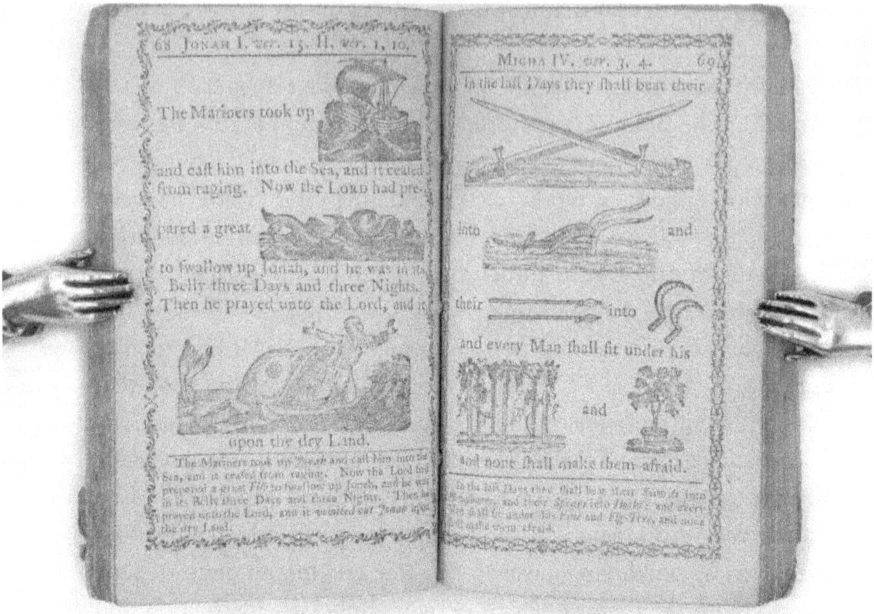

FIGURE 16. Thomas Hodgson, *A Curious Hieroglyphick Bible, or, Select passages in the Old and New Testament. Represented with Emblematical Figures, for the Amusement of Youth*, 20th ed. (London: J. Barker, 1812). Courtesy Lilly Library, Indiana University, Bloomington, Indiana. *Top*: A typical spread of words with hieroglyphs and full text along the bottom. *Bottom*: A father blesses his son, who holds a book, while two siblings play with toys, indicating an ideal setting for catechism instruction.

access to inexpensive, globally sourced commodities and manufactured goods.[100] For families whose children need not work, the ideal environment involved greater exposure to social gatherings, with private spaces of curated objects, such as nurseries, playgrounds, and schools, removed from adult workspaces. This idealization of a leisured childhood coincides with the stigmatization of labor for restricting children's observation to a narrow sphere, while workshops became architecturally separated from the hospitable sales rooms that displayed consumer goods.

No wonder that games and books for children portray young people's participation in commercial markets, where they use purchases to reflect interior development. *The Toy-shop, or, Sentimental Preceptor* (1787), adapted for children by Richard Johnson and published by Elizabeth Newbery, is an extended commentary on purchasing objects to acquire virtuous qualities. A mother, Lady Meanwell, brings her children, Horace and Belinda, to a special toyshop where the shopkeeper uses toys for didactic lessons; for example, a mirror mocks vanity, while a telescope allows people see their own faults reduced and those of others enlarged. Lady Meanwell praises the shopkeeper as "a new kind of satirical person; your shop is your scripture, and every piece of goods is a different text, from which you expose the vices and follies of the world, in a very fine allegorical sermon." The shopkeeper agrees, "I may, indeed, be called a parson," delighting to have "a full congregation in my shop." The toyman warns that "people sometimes condescend to take home the text, perhaps, but mind the sermon no more than if they had not heard one."[101] This extended analogy between toys and the Bible transforms the toyshop into a microcosmic book of nature, a commercial world in miniature. The toys are texts that, like God's creations, contain lessons for careful observers, and the children are natural philosophers.

Toy purchases mark the intellectual and moral development of the child protagonists, which culminates in trading their toys for books. Once they are old enough, Horace and Belinda imitate the toyman's satirical conceit by officiously thrusting their mirror and telescope upon their vain and gossipy playmates, and by creating their own morals for new objects they daily encounter. Some years later, Horace composes an it-narrative from the perspective of Belinda's old doll, allowing "the doll to appear to speak for itself," which they give to the toyman, suggesting Horace and Belinda may have written another of Richard Johnson's more popular works, *The History of a Doll* (1800). When they return to the toyshop as young adults and request something "above the common baubles," the toyman again presents them with what he calls "a Looking-glass," but instead of the same mirror he first introduced to the children, he hands them a book. "It is the Looking-glass for the mind, or Intellectual Mirror," he explains, referring to the English translation of Arnaud Berquin's *L'Ami des Enfans* (1782–83), a book described (in its English preface) as an "instructive Pocket Looking-Glass," or "a mirror that will not flatter them, nor lead them into error"—in other words, the textual equivalent of the actual mirror the toyman first sold them. Recommended by Catharine Macaulay's *Letters on Education* (1790), *L'Amie des Enfans* was popular for its depictions of everyday children's experiences, and indeed, the toyman praises the book for its material substance, by recommending it "to all those, who prefer useful knowledge to empty conversation, and substantial advantages to mere phantoms." The toyman advertises several other titles for sale "by Mrs. Newbery, the corner of St. Paul's Church-yard," revealing that the toyman represents Mrs. Newbery herself, making these child characters fellow customers with the readers who have purchased *The Toy-shop*.[102] The story asks readers to connect the toys from the story with real toys, and the toyman with Newbery's actual bookshop, just as Belinda and Horrace took what they learned in the toyshop and applied it within their home.

Patricia Crown deprecates such puff pieces, which blatantly flatter customers for their superior discernment in purchasing Newbery's wares, yet there is something admirably clever in this metatextual contemplation on how books and toys fix didactic lessons within collectable material objects.[103] *The Toy-shop* presents books, readers, children, and objects as strangely interchangeable, each speaking, acting, reading, and moralizing in turn. Books are mirrors, mirrors are books, and children's minds are mirrors; children are like dolls, while dolls can be made to speak like shopkeepers, who are actually booksellers, who sell toy books.[104] The toyshop is the new curiosity shop, replete with legible things, a child's cabinet of the mind. *The Toy-shop* is full of interlocutor gestures from book to things, because these gestures help child readers understand their own interior mental development as modeled in the object before them. The 1830 preface conveniently explains Dugald Stewart's philosophy of mind—that fiction develops control over mental images: "The attention may be thus insensibly seduced from the present objects of the senses, and the thoughts accustomed to dwell on the past, the distant, and the future."[105] Similar to Bunyan's emblems, *The Toy-shop* shapes readers minds into an "intellectual mirror" stocked with legible physical objects, which can summon or dismiss mental images without the object's presence.

Belinda and Horace (and readers) use their toys to transition from playing to reading, and from low objects to spiritual wealth. But instead of expressing skepticism of the marketplace, their educational purchases prove their moral superiority. Similar messages on moral consumption appear in quite different books.[106] For instance, the first flipbooks published for children, William and Stacey Grimaldi's *A Suit of Armour for Youth* (1821) and its companion book for girls, *The Toilet* (1823), are traditional emblems that ask youth to contemplate either various pieces of armor or beauty supplies, as so many representations of masculine and feminine virtue, which children place on their bodies.[107] A more literal representation of the market, *A Visit to the Bazaar* (1818) is about children who discuss the moral lessons of their purchases at a London Bazaar. The front cover features John Harris's bookshop, which contains a collection of textual mirrors of the legible world for children to purchase. Opening the cover of *A Visit to the Bazaar* is like entering Harris's shop; and by reading the book, children "browse" an imaginary bazaar, which, like the pages of the book, offers various objects for interpretive "reading." Purchases from the Bazaar are analogous to storing acquired knowledge inside the body, which expands the reader's moral lessons. Through such books, children learn that property kept close to their bodies reflects interior virtues. One whimsical edition of the Cries of London, titled *Figures of Fun; or, Comical Pictures and Drole Verses for Little Boys and Girls* (1833), communicates the same lesson with imaginative flare by depicting the vendors who hawk their wares as composed of the things they sell, an art form called "composite" or "emblematic" portraits. The Orangeman is an animated collection of oranges, while the knife seller is a rather intimidating jointed collection of kitchen implements. James A. Secord ascribes the popularity of Charles Tilt's emblematic portraits in 1820s and '30s Britain to crazes for scrapbooking and scientific collection, intellectual leisure activities that require physical labor. Typically featuring specimen collectors composed of shells or bugs, or working people composed of their wares, composite images satirically level all classes to their composite bodies.[108] In their own unique ways, each of these very different books uses interlocutor gestures to redirect readers' attention to the marketplace as a microcosm of the world, then back to the textual mirror.[109]

Tracking inner growth through purchases ties mechanical and alphabetical literacies with property ownership, since, implicitly, children with few toys and books remain childishly immersed in low objects. In their survey of teaching methods from 1770 to 1850, Steven Shapin and Barry Barnes find that regardless of vast pedagogical differences, nineteenth-century writings on education consistently reinscribe a "gnostic" / "banaustic" culturally constructed binary in human mentalities that corresponds to social hierarchies of race, class, gender, and age. The gnostic mentality, assigned to adults, men, Europeans, and wealthy classes, is verbal or symbolic and capable of abstract, complex thought, purposeful action, and self-control; whereas the banaustic mentality, assigned to children, women, and working classes, is primarily sensual or concrete, tending to superficial, non-symbolic thought and mechanical, automated action. According to this divide, the mental development of all persons in the banaustic category, adults included, seems equally child-like and "primitive." Because they are (supposedly) illiterate or disinclined to abstract thought, such people experience the world differently, engaging directly with objects and using fewer linguistic mediations. Whereas education for wealthier children focuses on raising children from a banaustic to a gnostic mentality, note Shapin and Barnes, education for women and workers rarely encouraged this transition up the hierarchy from concrete to abstract thinking.[110]

A story like *The Toy-shop* suggests, furthermore, that different ways of interacting with the material world were valued as intellectually stimulating depending on their association with gnostic or banaustic mentalities. Playing with a variety of purchased toys, for instance, transitions children from a banaustic to a gnostic mentality, while wage labor or childcare do not. The reason for these prejudicial contradictions supposedly had some basis in philosophy of mind. Locke posits that the failure to encounter diverse objects would be intellectually and morally damaging because "Men then come to be furnished with fewer or more simple ideas from without, according as the objects they converse with afford greater or less variety."[111] Since manual labor confines attention to the same objects (repeating a process to master a technique), working children supposedly fail to develop intellectually and morally, yet dabbling at carpentry or gardening is beneficial for wealthier children. If mixing labor with objects is necessary to annex them as property, but labor is potentially degrading, then play is an acceptable alternative way for children to mix their bodies with the world and the written word, grasping both as personal property. In other words, experiential education tended to devalue the working-class practices on which it relied in order to differentiate educational settings, where observation and manipulation are playful and instructive, from manual wage labor. From this deficit perspective, students from poor families live a material existence, yet, nonsensically, they lack access to educational objects or the right training in reflection.

This devaluation of working-class experience is evident from descriptions of plebian nurses and teachers who supplied the youngest children with their earliest and deepest impressions of things. Rousseau praises women who nurse their children, but wants a male tutor to step in as soon as possible, before she corrupts the child's mind; likewise, Maria Edgeworth, who warns that children should not learn from servants, takes pains to distinguish her recommended learning activities from the occupations they resemble. Chemistry can be taught with pastry cooking and logic through carpentry, but don't let your children learn either subject solely from cooks and carpenters. Children's books express these same reservations in how they represent working-class characters, dame schools, and workshops, as both sources of innovative teaching methods and corrupting plebian habits. One of Harvey and Darton's miscellanies, *The Rational Exhibition* (1800), for example, claims its eclectic readings were inspired by the author's visit to "a poor aged woman" who covered a wall inside her house "with printed papers and pictures," an anecdote in keeping with Margaret Spufford's research showing that many such women taught poor children to read using homemade literacies:

> She told me they were the collection of her children and grandchildren; who, instead of tearing them, had suffered them to be pasted against the wall; that they not only answered the purpose of covering the ragged places in the paper hangings, but afforded an opportunity for the children to read, and employed her frequently in giving them an account of many of the subjects depicted.[112]

The rest of the book proceeds as if browsing the dame's wall, presenting each selection as another posted text. A grandmother's homemade literacy, tacked on her cottage walls to hide bare places (a gesture toward respectable domesticity), becomes a "rational exhibition" when extracted from its context and published as a compilation. The book's frontispiece depicts not the dame's ragged wall, but a geometrically precise teaching aid resembling an enormous lotto print, with children gathered around while a teacher points to each pictorial lesson. Where the grandmother repurposed children's books for her wallpaper, *The Rational Exhibition* remediates a torn cottage wall as a lotto print and a children's miscellany. Its legitimacy rests, at once, on its authentic origin in the dame's kitchen and its separation from that space.[113]

I want to return to the first publication of *Practical Education* (1780), with its interlocutor glossary, because the story of Harry and Lucy performs a similar move. The siblings watch cheese making, bricklaying, smithy work, and so forth, which they replicate when they return homes, as educational play. Indeed, playing at building a brick house joins together the symbol of their family's property with artisanal knowledge learned from workers during the day, claiming both as their own. The impulse to consider brickmaking "fun," as Harry clearly does, is only possible because Harry and Lucy do not have to churn clay with their feet for wages nor do they have to run carrying heavy clay items—like the children who worked in pottery manufacturers—between a cold workroom and a hot drying room, where pots were fired. On the contrary, Harry is intrigued by the blacksmith's bellows, which he has never operated before, in the same way that children reading the story should, as the glossery suggests, "ask to see an oven." Like Harry and Lucy, the implied readers observe the material world while remaining far enough removed not to experience too much.

Shared Properties and Common Objects: The Cooperative Specimen Tables of Catherine Whitwell

Exactly how children's books gesture to other educational objects is important for understanding the socialization process by which children come to regard alphabetical literacy as their property. By alternately moving around books and things in corresponding ways, children extended their sense of ownership over personal objects to include texts, labor, ideas, and their own bodies, while misdirecting attention from this process by framing knowledge of the material world as somehow free of the social prejudices of class because it is more objective than knowledge received from books.

One educator whose work proves especially useful for exposing the class ideologies of mechanical literacy is Catherine Whitwell. Although one of the most influential teachers of her century, Whitwell is now almost forgotten, eclipsed by her employer, Robert Owen, the initial leader of the cooperative movement and originator of British socialism. According to Karl Marx, Owen's schools, which included the first universal infant and primary schools in Great Britain, reunite "productive labour with instruction and gymnastics" for "producing fully developed human beings."[114] Ian Donnachie suggests that credit for this whole-body curriculum should be shared with Whitwell, who, prior to her arrival in New Lanark, taught Robert Owen's daughters in London and likely collaborated with her cousin in the design of his model utopian villages. Sometime before the autumn of 1821, Owen hired Whitwell to teach at the infant school and lecture at the Institute for the Formation of Character in New Lanark and to create his classroom teaching aids, including paintings and scrolled canvases for the school's open plan hall, a space used for dance lessons, reading, singing, and lectures.[115] Owen regarded his school as an "important experiment for the happiness of the human race" to "ascertain whether the character of man could be better formed, and society better constructed and governed" if the institutions of society were "based on an accurate knowledge of human nature."[116] While none of Whitwell's visual aids survive, Robert Dale Owen describes them at length in *An Outline of the System of Education at New Lanark* (1824), a landmark work in the history of education that may have been collaboratively written with Whitwell:

> The walls are hung round with representations of the most striking zoological and mineralogical specimens; including quadrupeds, birds, fishes, reptiles, insects, shells, minerals, &c," along with "very large representations of the two hemispheres; each separate country, as well as the various seas, islands, &c. being differently coloured, but without any names attached to them.[117]

Whitwell received five hundred pounds for her most celebrated visual aid for teaching history: "Seven large maps or tables" painted on rolled canvas that "laid out on the principles of the Stream of Time," providing a grand visualization of history as branching rivers. Her artwork appears in iconic engravings depicting the school, where they form the background to students dancing in Highland-inspired robes. These descriptions have since been used to re-create Whitwell's learning aids for today's visitors at the New Lanark World Heritage Site. During the advent of the infant school movement, thousands of visitors, including Samuel Wilderspin, toured the classrooms featuring her materials.

In her education treatise, intriguingly titled *The Material and Intellectual Universe, from which the Object and End of Education May be Deduced* (1849), Whitwell claimed that observation-based instruction can accommodate children to competition and accumulation, which she deemed detrimental to their moral development. The present "object of education," she explains, is to teach children to value wealth above all else. "Acquisitiveness is the centre of our system," the "dark Planet around which all our actions and all our pursuits revolve. . . . . it hoards, it accumulates, it grasps, and it never rests." She connects the ascendency of capitalist values with a grasping "intellect," "enamored" of its own "powers of perception," that pursues knowledge without advancing the "moral powers." Creating an analogy between astronomy and education, Whitwell calls for a Copernican revolution that will replace the selfish "dark Planet" at the center of our moral universe with divine love: "And as every Material System in the Universe, is moving around a magnificent central body, so each Mental System should circle around our Lord Jesus Christ."[118] Her Owenite millennialism, expressed near the end of her career, is nascent in her earlier classroom lessons, which critically adapted object teaching to teach radical lessons on private property.

Whitwell's first treatise, *Her Education, An Address to Mothers in the British Empire* (1819), which she dedicated to Pestalozzi, describes the specimen tables she created as headmistress of a London female seminary, where she experimented with methods she used two year later with New Lanark factory children. Like her contemporaries, Whitwell expresses concern that memorizing words without training in observation creates a superficial appearance of knowledge devoid of understanding. She instructs teachers to set up three tables, at least two yards square, designated for the Animal, Vegetable, and Mineral kingdoms, and provide "at least one hundred objects" for each table, labeled on one side. She designed these exercises "to affix correct ideas to words, the signs of our ideas," by quite literally attaching words to objects. Since "the object and the sign will be in contact," she explains, children never learn words without acquiring knowledge of the thing itself. After learning the specimen names, the children "arrange the objects according to their respective classes" by placing them on the tables. In addition to teaching "a large portion of natural history," this method provides students resources for learning numbers by counting the specimens, or students can learn geography by consulting a globe to locate where specimens were gathered. To explore individual specimens more deeply, as "subjects of attention," they might use "a solar microscope" and observe their qualities.[119] Whitwell's table exercises thus integrate reading and math with geography and natural history, encouraging students to make connections between these diverse subjects. In doing so, she undermines hierarchies of knowledge that correspond to divisions of labor, which traditionally excluded certain subjects from female or working-class education.

At the time she created her specimen tables, Whitwell wrote one of the first astronomy textbooks for girls, *An Astronomical Catechism* (1818), which shows the close connection between human and heavenly bodies that informs Whitwell's teaching. The textbook begins with the "principles and laws of motion, by which bodies on or near the earth are governed," and concludes with these laws applied "in the organization of the human frame, in the philosophy of the human mind." Isaac Newton's insight that mechanical laws govern celestial and human bodies alike suggested to educators the possibility of regular laws for child development, making education an observation-based science. Whitwell also refers to astronomy as the basis for her educational philosophy in *Her Education*, which praises Newton for discovering the "fixed and invariable laws" that "bind the universe together," then commands teachers to learn the "principles" behind the formation of human "faculties." Effective teachers "must make *human nature their study*" to discover how "*our opinions and our conduct are the result of impressions made on our minds during the periods of infancy and youth.*"[120] The natural gravitational laws of the universe suggested to Whitwell that human nature has its own laws, which the current organization of society forces children to violate.[121] By "human nature," Whitwell refers to Owen's case for criminal justice reform and a national system of education, which he based on the "discovery" that children are "universally plastic"; they have their character formed for them by their environment, in a manner not of their choosing. We "train children to crime from infancy," and once they are grown, we "hunt them like beasts of the forests" until we catch them in "the toils and nets of the law."[122] By understanding of how character is formed, teachers can promote benevolence from infancy, enabling a new society where punishment is replaced by education and people live together in harmony.

This connection between Newtonian physics and human development may seem in accordance with the Edgeworths' approach in *Practical Education* (1798), but astronomy provided Whitwell with observation-based evidence that economies could be reorganized by educating children in kindness and cooperation. Whitwell thus designed her specimen tables in accordance with her cooperative beliefs, placing a premium on metacognitive skills to help children critically investigate how their minds observe objects. According to Whitwell, children learn language by progressing from "particular" nouns (fish) to "general terms" (animal). The specimen tables show children the "wonderful power of language, which renders the human mind capable of grasping at a vast multitude of objects" with a single categorical word.[123] By organizing the specimens, children can observe and manipulate physical representations of the cognitive work taking place inside of their minds. She suggests that students place objects where they choose on the tables, determine new categories for sorting items, then explain their choices to the class.[124] Since in many cases, children collaboratively determine the categories used to organize objects, the exercises teach awareness of the social construction of categories. In short, her students question the order of things.

The same principles of cooperation and reorganization guide other language exercises described in her book. In addition to the specimen tables, Whitwell describes methods for using "a black board and chalk" (a new classroom technology) for collaborative exercises in categorization, something like mind mapping, where the teacher writes the name of an object in a circle on the board. Students offer facts or observations connected with the object, which they write in bubbles that radiate out from the central concept. Showing the versatility of this exercise, Whitwell suggests writing dates at the center surrounded by historical persons or events, or an animal kingdom surrounded by animals belonging to it. She also suggests using "the objects of their daily attention," for instance collecting items that students observe on the way to school and categorizing them as "Food, Clothing, or Shelter."[125]

In some respects, Whitwell's mind maps and table specimens serve the same purpose as the bits of wood and model machines in Edgeworth's chapter on toys. For both educators, children gain self-awareness by manipulating objects that model invisible developmental processes. But where Edgeworth expects to find evidence for classical economic principles in the natural world, Whitwell helps children question how wealth is defined by society. In Edgeworth's account, a child first learns what "gold" is by holding a specimen before she slowly acquires "all the properties of gold," which allows the child to finally grasp why gold *must* be valued above other metals given its intrinsic properties. But what if a teacher wants pupils to question whether gold *should* be highly valued? The contingencies of Whitwell's specimen table or the dynamic process of mind mapping—which generate different possible connections constructed collaboratively by groups of pupils—disrupt deeply established cultural associations by making children aware of the social process of category formation.

This interpretation of Whitwell's methods is supported by the accompanying illustration in *Her Education*, which shows how mind maps can teach fine distinctions between similar abstract words, in this case "custom" and "habit." These two words carry considerable polemical baggage. In the 1790s political debates over the French Revolution and English Constitutional Reform, Edmund Burke passionately defended "custom" and "prejudice" as the basis for familial and national affections, while William Godwin theorized "habit" as automated action unaccompanied by thought. Mary Wollstonecraft and Mary Hays used these words to question what parts of education are "natural," or merely conventions worth discarding. By making "habit" and "custom" the focus of these analytical exercises, Whitwell suggests that students investigate how ingrained habits and unquestioned prejudices are formed.

These same exercises could be adapted for more advanced grammar and spelling lessons. Whitwell gives several examples of how to arrange facts onto simple visual diagrams as a memory aid—for example, words with similar spelling are placed around the line drawing of a house. "Any arrangement," she explains, is "better than allowing knowledge to float irregularly in the mind," because "the memory" is "strengthened by the association of ideas" and by "attention." Whitwell's exercises thus teach that language is a human technology, one students might critically investigate to determine why certain associations become mentally fixed. One use of her specimen tables, she explains, is to illustrate the "difference between the object, and the sign." Signs are arbitrarily constructed by people, whereas natural objects are God's creations that speak his "wondrous power" and "goodness."[126]

The approach to language and observation that Whitwell developed for middle-class girls ultimately informed her teaching at New Lanark. As described in *An Outline of the System of Education at New Lanark* (1824), Owen's school used Whitwell's learning aids to make language available to the senses by teaching "the *nature and properties* of the different objects around him, before we proceed to teach him the *artificial signs* which have been adopted to represent these objects." These object teaching practices reflect not only Robert Dale Owen's training with Pestalozzi in Germany, but Whitwell's influence. Instead of textbooks, teachers give "familiar lectures, delivered extempore," with "the use of sensible signs," a point Robert Dale Owen repeats each time he describes geography lessons with large globes, or history lessons with the Streams of Time (both aids created by Whitwell). Teaching children with books is "impolitic and irrational" while the words remain "unintelligible"; instead, children may learn from "conversation, and illustrated by sensible signs," priming them with enough curiosity about the world to sustain them through the frustrating task of learning to read. Even for older pupils, Robert Dale Owen reiterates that "children should never be directed to read what they cannot understand," and that they should practice paraphrasing passages as they read aloud to demonstrate the words are not "unmeaning sounds."[127] This approach at once generalizes object learning throughout the curriculum and integrates reading with other subject areas like geography, chronology, and natural history, which might otherwise be eliminated as unnecessary for working-class youth.

Whitwell's learning aides provide a better understanding of how classroom practices used to teach language, observation, collection, and categorization could reflect radical ideas about human nature and property ownership. Like other rational educators, Whitwell quotes Dugald Stewart, praises Bacon and Newton, consulted with Pestalozzians, studied materialist philosophies of mind, and references mechanical philosophy in her teaching materials. Despite these similarities, Whitwell draws her own conclusions about the moral arrangement of objects in God's universe, using the material world to suggest that established social hierarchies and the inequitable distribution of material goods have been mistaken for natural laws. In his description of Whitwell's teaching, Robert Dale Owen draws on Newtonian physics to explain her determinist theory of child development: "The law of cause and effect applies equally in the formation of the human character, as in that of a blade of grass or any other natural production."[128] Since children are formed by their material environment, Whitwill deploys words and things to teach methods of critically observing economic and political systems.

Conclusion

Educational materials designed for children invited a shared interactive repertoire for using books and other objects: collecting, assembling, grasping, handling, browsing, categorizing, storing, making, and naming. By teaching mechanical and alphabetical literacies together, children's books facilitated the easy transfer of beliefs about labor and ownership from the material world to reading and writing. When children go out into the world to find hammers and ovens, they bring back class-specific notions of property, work, and play to handling their books. The different ways that educators like Edgeworth and Whitwell taught mechanical literacy depended on their political beliefs, suggesting some awareness of what I am arguing—that lessons with objects should be handled carefully because they teach children about social stratification. Contrary to Francis Bacon's dream of circumventing past errors by learning through direct observation, reading God's book of nature merely produces another layer of culturally situated beliefs and prejudices that shape (and are shaped by) language.

One way that children's materials teach about social class is by defining specific, approved practices for acquiring mechanical literacy. By approaching mechanical literacy as a set of skills best taught through recreational and experiential learning, author-educators could distinguish the way children of leisure learn with their bodies from the work it closely resembled. Play was distinct from the mechanical compulsions of work as a self-aware, self-improving, and voluntary activity. Nevertheless, the similarities between work and play determined the value placed on these new pedagogies. Learning through play appeared practical and rational because it resembled work in its usefulness and productivity, and while dependent on inherited privilege, recreational learning offered a veneer of authenticity. Playful learning was, therefore, a way to train children of leisure to govern their own bodies while protecting them from the hardships of physical labor. In moving their bodies and manipulating objects in their environment, children engineer their own development and gain mastery over other bodies, human and nonhuman. This way of thinking brings human development into alignment with the physical sciences, which explains why someone like Catherine Whitwell first articulates her alternative approach to teaching with specimens while writing an astronomy textbook. I conclude, then, with my own interlocutor gesture—from toys and cabinets to the physical universe. In the next chapter, I reconvene reading and the natural sciences by investigating the class politics of Newtonian physics—the tops and balls, children's bodies, and working bodies represented in mechanical philosophy books for children.

CHAPTER 2

Moving Bodies

Manual Labor and Children's Play in Mechanical Philosophy Books

Class is built into the very definition of mechanics. In the preface to *Philosophiae Naturalis Principia Mathematica* (1687), or *Mathematical Principles of Natural Philosophy*, which introduces the law of universal gravitation, Isaac Newton distinguishes between "practical mechanics," used by artisans to maintain exact geometric proportions, and "rational mechanics," used to mathematically explain the general principles of matter in motion.[1] He ascribes this distinction to "the ancients," who "considered mechanics in a twofold respect; as rational, which proceeds accurately by demonstration; and practical. To practical mechanics all the manual arts belong, from which mechanics took its name." Children's books that teach mechanical philosophy use Newton's tenuous distinction between "practical" and "rational" mechanics to police boundaries between social stations, reserving the social prestige of rational mechanics (or mechanical philosophy), with all its cognitive benefits, for people of leisure, while disavowing the mental demands of artisan work.

These class divisions of knowledge are explained to readers in clear terms. Outlining the scope of his 1754 textbook, William Emerson, a mathematician and teacher who published a defense of Newton's *Principia*, defines mechanics as "a science that teaches the principles of motion, and construction of engines, to move great weights," while machines are "a mechanical instrument for moving bodies." Although all persons, "from the king down to the cobbler" use mechanics, and "the meanest artificier must work mechanically or not work at all," Emerson dismisses repetitive labor as "the lowest part of Mechanics, which concerns, manual arts or working by hand." He sees no need to cover the subject, "for there is no theory required here, but only a habit of working, to be acquired by constant practice."[2] In other words, physical labor performed using the body is thoughtless work for "low" mechanics, who have no business reading his book. Conversely, learning the "laws" or "principles" of mechanical philosophy enables children to direct moving bodies, both human and nonhuman, whether workers, machines, or commodities. The "art of mechanics" enables "all engines of war, ships, bridges, mills," and "grand works in building," and "clocks, watches, jacks, chariots, carts and carriages," also "the motions of the parts of an animal body," and "the motions of all the celestial bodies." Everything from "planets and comets" to the smallest "particles" moves by "mechanical principles."[3] Mechanical philosophy is an appropriate subject for Emerson's readers because it is a sign of rational self-governance and social command over laboring bodies and material goods. Such children's books display the social construction of two different kinds of mechanical knowledge: one for making with the hands, the other for thinking with the mind. Although beholden to the practical arts, only rational mechanics, by this logic, counted as mechanical literacy.

This chapter examines the class and gender politics of textbooks that teach mechanical philosophy either as a single subject or as a component of the physical or natural sciences. Since children's books about mechanics explicitly theorize concepts like matter, motion, bodies, and power, they helped shape the class ideologies of children's reading—especially the association between literacy, acquiring knowledge, and property ownership. By representing the study of the material world as a philosophical pursuit, these textbooks follow the same assumptions as those educators who suggested learning through observation, play, and experimentation as an unprejudiced alternative to books. Yet the prominence of social class in the way mechanics is defined, organized, and taught suggests that mechanical philosophy quietly provided an ideological framework for learning with objects, one that made existing social hierarchies seem as natural and inevitable as the unchanging laws that govern matter in motion. Together, objects and books reinforced a shared assumption that men of property own, generate, and circulate knowledge. The rising popularity of experiential education in eighteenth-century Britain thus provided a way to fold crucial new scientific and artisanal literacies into older traditional ones, securing both mechanical and alphabetical literacies as the property of dominant groups. During the following century, mechanics textbooks contended with the potentially destabilizing effects of science on national economies and theological beliefs by assigning a select portion of mechanical knowledge to people of different stations. While at the beginning of the nineteenth century, mechanical philosophy is closely associated with landed wealth in familiar science books featuring boy and girl siblings who playfully learn on family estates, Victorian books increasingly marginalize mothers and girls as middle-class men claimed professional careers that required mechanical expertise. Despite these changes, mechanical philosophy books consistently perform gatekeeping work, using playful learning to distinguish which characters can learn which forms of mechanical knowledge.

Although "mechanics" earn wages by manipulating matter, the exclusivity of mechanical literacy, as constructed by science writers, ensures that somehow their expertise is interpreted as the product of body repetition, skill, or practice, unaccompanied by any conscious understanding of their body's movements. *Evenings at Home* by John Aiken and Anna Letitia Barbauld (1792–96) includes a dialog in which a father defines "a manufacture" for his son, Henry, as "something made by the hand of man. It is derived from two Latin words, *manus*, the hand, and *facere*, to make." Skeptical, Henry asks whether making a watch requires as much thought as dexterity: "Does not the head work?" His father responds, "Once invented, the art of watch-making is capable of being reduced to a mere mechanical labour, which may be exercised by any man of common capacity, according to certain precise rules, when made familiar to him by practice."[4] The dialog differentiates workers who follow "precise rules" and learn through repeated operations from those who direct work performed by others and understand the general "principles" that govern all matter in motion. As an illustrative choice, the watch creates a comparison between divine and human making wherein God understands the laws He created to govern all creation, while humans who comprehend those laws can organize and remake His world. They have mechanical literacy; they own property, invent machines that make things, circulate goods, and govern the state.

In the first part of this chapter, I provide a brief overview of the various kinds of books that teach children practical and rational mechanics, and the contemporary debates about what scientific subjects are appropriate for students from different stations. Analyzing textbooks and learning aids that teach mechanical philosophy as an introductory component of the physical or natural sciences, I show how these books associate theoretical mechanics with the qualities of a ruling elite, such as self-awareness and self-governance. After surveying broadly applicable definitions and enduring genre patterns, the chapter follows a rough chronology, beginning with John Newbery's Tom Telescope books (1761) and concluding with Victorian inventor biographies and amateur craft books. Because of its association with industry and governing power, mechanics is coded as a masculine subject. Teacher-mentors are often fathers and gentlemen of science, with younger girls taking their lead from older male siblings. Gendering mechanical knowledge became more prominent as Victorian publishers distinguished between books for girls and boys, again limiting whose mechanical knowledge receives recognition.

The First Books on Natural Philosophy for Young Readers

Mechanics—the study of matter in motion—is one of first sciences that children learn, but also the most profound and complex, because it connects together all of the physical sciences. Samuel Goodrich's *A Glance at the Physical Sciences* (1844) boasts that "natural or physical science," the study of the natural world and causal relations (as distinct from metaphysics), is as "boundless in its scope as the extent of the universe, . . . it seeks out the hidden laws of the universe, the principles by which the Architect of the earth and heavens constructs and governs his boundless dominions."[5] Within natural philosophy, mechanics examines these "universal" Newtonian "principles" or "laws" ("Principia Mathematica") that tie together terrestrial and celestial bodies. Mechanical philosophy explains astronomy (the movement of planets) and animal anatomy (the movement of body parts). The astronomer James Ferguson describes these unifying principles as "those laws by which the material universe is governed, regulated, and continued"—"Laws" created by "the ALMIGHTY" and harnessed by engineers to navigate ships around the globe and plumb the depths of the earth, yet understood by a child who watches water boiling in a teakettle.[6] Mechanical philosophy is both accessible and powerful, ordinary and sublime. Explaining the theology behind Newton's mechanical laws of the universe, James C. Ungureanu concludes, "The new mechanical philosophy that emerged in the eighteenth century was not atheistic. For Newton, a mechanistic world was imbued with the presence of God."[7] Through the early nineteenth century, textbooks represent mechanical philosophy as the study of God's presence in the universe, through which observation of everyday objects may lead to sublime religious truths. As the author of Newton's laws, God "governs" all matter, meaning that governance on earth requires a similar power over the material world through a person's ability to create and manipulate matter.

The mechanics or physics textbooks for adults published during the eighteenth century are by popular men of science who delivered experimental science lectures for the general public or taught at a university: Thomas Rutherford, James Ferguson, William Nicholson, Rev. T. A. Parkinson, John Anderson, Benjamin Martin, and Adam Walker. While their books could be used in school or studied with parents or private tutors, they wrote for lay readers of all ages, serving a rising interest in public science. As the sciences joined other subjects taught at the private academies created for the middle classes, textbook authors wrote explicitly for youth audiences, including girls educated at home. William Enfield, a Unitarian minister and teacher at Warrington Academy, produced books on natural philosophy for schools, while Margaret Bryan, teacher and principal of a girls' school, created a natural philosophy book for young women. With the exception of Benjamin Martin, an itinerant lecturer, few eighteenth-century authors attempted to simplify mechanical philosophy for the youngest children before the publication of John Newbery's *The Newtonian System of Philosophy, Adapted to the Capacities of Young Gentlemen and Ladies* (1761), which sold 25,000–30,000 copies before 1800, with editions in Sweden, the United States, Italy, and Ireland. One of Newbery's bestselling titles, it remained in print for over eighty years.[8] This important physics book introduced a fictional child character, Tom Telescope, who performs salon-style lectures that demonstrate the principles of natural philosophy using his toys. In his longitudinal comparison of editions, James Secord argues that *Newtonian System* targeted a clientele of the "middling sort," yet depicts science as a gentleman's leisure occupation motivated by religious feeling and unconnected to the practical application of technology. Earlier illustrated editions depict Tom as an infant performing with tops and balls while he demonstrates proper deference for his host, a gentleman of science named Lord Galaxy, who provides expensive orreries and telescopes from his country estate. Beginning with the 1806 edition, however, publishers removed the original ending in which Tom imagines a future republic of reason, a nod to Bacon's vision of Solomon's house that struck readers as revolutionary in England's anti-Jacobin climate. In later editions, Tom ages into an older youth, while Lord Galaxy disappears as Tom's gentleman patron, until eventually, an informed adult character delivers lectures on Tom's behalf. These changes reflect the importance of natural philosophy for industry and its newfound association with the manufacturing class.[9] My broader survey of titles indicates a general transition in mechanical philosophy books for children, in which Enlightenment salon science is replaced in the Victorian Era, by practical applications and middle-class characters, in those nineteenth-century children's science books priced for middle-class purchasers.[10]

By the early nineteenth century, children's authors like Priscilla Wakefield, Richard Lovell and Maria Edgeworth, Jacob Abbott, William Martin, and Jane Marcet created natural philosophy lessons reframed as domestic dialogues between fictional characters who converse about natural philosophy while conducting home science experiments, traveling on vacation, or going on excursions.[11] As a popular form among children and lay readers alike, these "familiar science" books, according to Melanie Keene, create rapport between authors and readers by avoiding jargon, teaching through everyday objects, and portraying experiments conducted in a domestic setting.[12] The familiar science conversational format combined two eighteenth-century textual forms that used dialog: the children's conversational format, which represented fictional children learning in dialog with adults, and scientific articles, which reported the consensus reached by men of science who attended a particular experiment, enabling readers to mentally replicate the experiment through reading.[13] Familiar science books became so widespread after 1820 that families would be perplexed to choose from the wide variety of entertaining books for sale that contain a substantial measure of mechanical philosophy, which they might supplement with lighter fare: children's inventor biographies, craft hobby books, and illustrated science experiment books. To these were added cheap periodicals and compilations of "improving" information articles produced by the Society for the Diffusion of Useful Knowledge (SDUK), the Society for Promoting Christian Knowledge (SPCK), and the Religious Tract Society (RTS), which targeted a mixed audience of youth and working-class readers.[14]

This first golden age of information literature for children coincided with the emergent cultural belief that young children are scientifically minded and particularly drawn to mechanical philosophy. James Secord shows that John Locke, a correspondent of Newton, believed as much when he created an outline for teaching Newtonian philosophy for his private use. However, his posthumously published recommendations, which Newbery seems to have consulted for the subject outline of *Newtonian System,* only became popular nearly a century later, when educators expounded upon the object-mindedness of infants. As Adam Walker reminds parents in *A System of Familiar Philosophy* (1799), "At a time when a nurse supposes a child is only amusing itself by striving to catch hold of every thing within and without its reach, it is laying in a stock of important information!"[15] Children are tireless investigators who constantly perform experiments on surrounding objects, which adults readily dismiss as "play." Good scientists have this same childish quality, or, as one children's mechanics book suggests in a title page epigram from Francis Bacon: "To enter the kingdom of knowledge we must put on the spirit of little children."[16] Jacob Abbott, the American author of the Rollo books, goes one step further and defines natural philosophy in his textbook on the subject, *The Little Philosopher for Schools and Families: Designed to Teach Children to Think and to Reason about Common Things* (1829), by its accessibility to infants:

> WILLIAM. What is Philosophy, mother?
> MOTHER. It is the first thing which children learn.
> WILLIAM. Why, mother, the *first thing?* Then it must be the a, b, c. . . .
> MOTHER. No, William, you learned a great many things, long before you learned the a, b, c.[17]

The Little Philosopher also links the acquisition of mechanical philosophy with learning to read, as both mechanical and alphabetical literacies were taught to infants through manipulable objects. Abbott begins with a mother praising her baby for "tearing the newspaper all to pieces." She directs her two older children to follow the baby's example when they study the physical world, assuring them "it is not for mischief. A piece of paper is something new and curious to him; and he likes to shake it about to see how it will move; and to pull it to see how strong it is, and how easily it will tear. In that way, he is learning the nature of it."[18] Next, the destructive baby edges toward the footstool, which he throws down and drags about the room. Reduced to their material components, stool and text—those accoutrements of fireside child reading—find themselves repurposed for "questions," "explanations," and "little

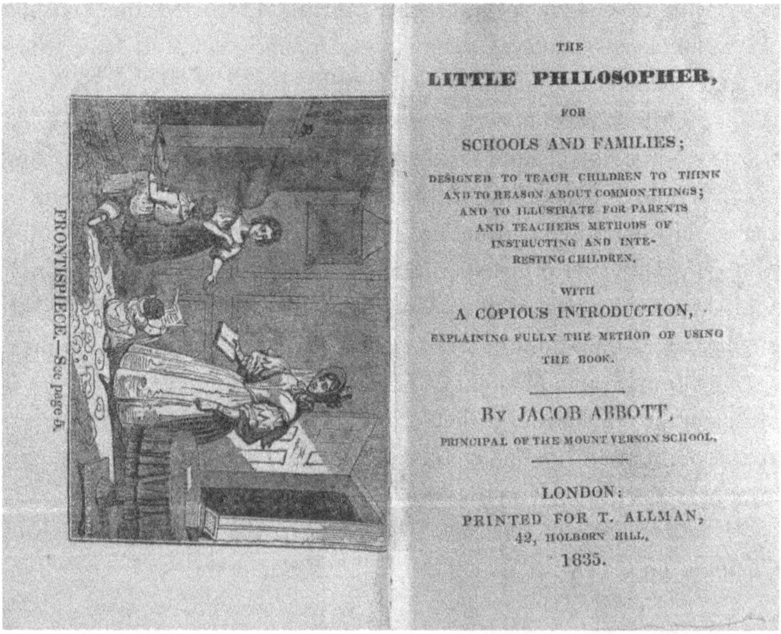

FIGURE 17. Jacob Abbott, *The Little Philosopher, for Schools and Families; Designed to Teach Children to Think and to Reason about Common Things* (London: T. Allman, 1835). Courtesy of Baldwin Library of Historical Children's Literature, George A. Smathers Libraries, University of Florida. The mother giving a book to a child is a common frontispiece. But here, the baby tears apart the newspaper while another child lights a fire with a bellows (a common experiment for teaching about air and fire). The interlocutor gestures reinforce Abbott's invitation to use his book to perform little experiments.

experiments." Abbott warns that under no circumstances should parents give his introductory natural philosophy textbook to their children to read alone; neither should parents read its questions "mechanically and rapidly," expecting rote answers. Rather, teachers and students should together explore their surroundings, aiming "*to think and to reason about common things*."[19]

Children are good experimental philosophers because they have no trouble collecting evidence before forming a hypothesis. Children are "peculiarly suited" to "experimental knowledge" because they "have no prejudices," write Richard Lovell and Maria Edgeworth in *Practical Education* (1798), "therefore they have the complete use of all their senses."[20] Early childhood is therefore the perfect time to learn mechanics. "Parents are anxious that children should be conversant with Mechanicks," advise the Edgeworths, and "certainly no species of knowledge is better suited to the taste and capacity of youth," nor as easily accessible to everyone, "by implements which are in every body's hands" and by "the daily occupations of mankind."[21] Children should also observe household repairs, investigate machine drawings, and eventually design their own machines that demonstrate mechanical principles. Jeremiah Joyce cites the Edgeworths to justify teaching natural philosophy through children's dialogues. Adapting Newtonian philosophy for the very young coincided with the creation of early literacy toys for infants, which prepared children for reading through conversations on common things. By the 1820s, learning with "common things" became proverbially associated with infant schools, while philosophy of mind urged connecting early language development with observing the material world. As a result, introductory physical sciences became closely associated with early literacy.

Who Should Learn Mechanical Philosophy?

The notion that young children should learn mechanical philosophy first, while they are still unlettered, influenced how different types of mechanical knowledge became coded by age, gender, and class. Although few textbooks are polemical, *Philosophy in Sport Made Science in Earnest* (1827) by John Ayrton Paris, plainly dramatizes political debates over who should learn mechanical philosophy and by what means, providing a key for interpreting subtler texts. The novel situates itself within a pedagogical tradition of teaching science to children through play, observation, and experiment. The eldest children, Tom and Louisa Seymore, frequently consult Jane Marcet's *Conversations on Natural Philosophy* (1819), a gift from their mother, and contest what adults tell them, after Montaigne's method, by referring to personal experience or devising their own experiments. In his preface, Paris dedicates *Philosophy in Sport* to Maria Edgeworth, whose "Harry and Lucy has shown how profitably, and agreeably, the machinery of fiction may be worked for the dissemination of truth."[22] Paris himself had a reputation for devising instructional machinery as the inventor of the thaumatrope, an optical device featuring two images, such as a bird and a cage, printed on opposing sides of a square paper or medallion. When the user rapidly twists strings attached to either side, both images become visible simultaneously, a phenomenon that demonstrates through play the scientific principle of persistence of vision. From the beginning, thaumatropes featured word play and political satire, a combination that Meredith Bak aligns with other mid-century visual and verbal literacy toys, such as alphabet blocks, rebus cards, and jigsaw puzzles, which combine learning with deciphering—toys that accord with Paris's satirical class commentary in *Philosophy in Sport*.[23]

Part novel of education, part textbook, with illustrations by George Cruikshank, *Philosophy in Sport* satirizes efforts by women and the working classes to learn science through self-education and criticizes the recently established mechanics institutes for upsetting social stations. The protagonist, Tom (of course), and his four sisters learn from their father, a gentleman landowner, "the first principles of natural philosophy, beautifully illustrated, by the common toys which have been invented for the amusement of youth."[24] Tom learns science through a combination of toys, conversation, and reading, but these pedagogical practices are determined by his class. As the son of a gentleman, his father teaches science using the trappings of landed wealth. This choice may seem surprising, given what Isaac Kramnick describes as the prominence of middle-class Dissenting propertied people, who "nearly destroyed aristocratic England and its traditional values," among children's literature authors, entrepreneurs, and industrialists, whose new academies trained children in the sciences.[25] But Paris seems to feature Tom's family for precisely this reason—the threat posed to the social order. Thus Tom learns from the Seymore garden, which contains a grotto with geological specimens "dedicated to the genius of geology," and a Linnaean "Horologe of Flora" (or "*botanical clock*") designed by Louisa under her mother's "direction" with flowers that bloom on each hour. Readers can make the clock by following appendix instructions, provided that they, too, have enough land for grottos and botanical clocks. Tom and Louisa's wealth is equally displayed by their attitudes toward learning through leisure. Mr. Seymore glosses Maria Edgeworth's opening chapter on "Toys" in *Practical Education* (1798) to support his method of playful learning: "*Play* and *work*—*amusement* and *instruction*—*toys* and *tasks*—are invariably but most unjustifiably employed as words of contrast and oppositions."[26] As a gentleman's son and heir, Tom cannot learn mechanics at his elite grammar school, which teaches classical literature, or from networks of artisan mentorship, since his only "work" is attending school. Play is therefore the perfect way for the leisured class to learn mechanics.

Mr. Seymore and his friend the Rev. Twaddleton defend playful science as their exclusive class privilege. In fact, their whole scheme to teach the children natural science is motivated by their disapproval of local women and artisans pursuing a similar education. The carpenter, Tom Plank, recently returned from the Mechanics Institute in London, has founded a "philosophical society" with the help of Miss Kitty Ryland, a gossiping old maid whose pretentions to learning occasion misogynist comedy. "Preposterous idea!" declares Rev. Twaddleton, "As if a block of wood could not be split without a knowledge of the doctrine of percussion, nor a pail of water drawn from the well, without an acquaintance with hydrostatics." Meanwhile, Roger Naylor, the blacksmith, "has been foolish enough to desert his forge, and open a school for elementary instruction."[27] Like Mr. Seymore, these town schools combine "play and work" by using practical experiences to teach philosophical principles to artisans, yet that is precisely the problem: learning philosophy merely distracts artisans from their real work of splitting logs and beating iron. The novel suggests that only people of property should learn mechanical philosophy, while carpenters and blacksmiths should confine themselves to practical mechanics.

So concerned is Rev. Twaddleton about the spread of philosophy that he initially warns Mr. Seymore that by teaching his children science, "you scatter the seeds of insubordination" and "manure the weeds of infidelity." But Mr. Seymore responds to his antiquarian friend, "Classical learning is, undoubtedly, essential to the polished gentleman; but science is the staff upon which he must rely for support." Faced with the threat of educated artisans, the Seymore children learn science to maintain their wealth and privilege. "Natural Philosophy" must spread among the "higher classes," Mr. Seymore frankly explains, because "it has now become essential to their very existence, and to the maintenance of their rank in the scale of society." At the end of the story, the family reinstates their power by hosting a local fair for the townspeople, a traditional safe amusement for working people that cements vertical loyalty. The children attend the various street entertainments and "point out successively the philosophical principles upon which each of the tricks might be supposed to depend." This conclusion to the book shows the children using their rational science to carry on old traditions, while proving their superiority to gullible village rubes.[28] Everything is put to rights. The people have their harmless amusements to distract them from foolish studies, while the next generation of wealthy landed gentry learns natural philosophy.

Mr. Seymore voices a widely held position on mass education and social unrest: the gentry cannot neglect mechanical philosophy without ceding power to Dissenters, artisans, and manufacturers. To have any influence at all, they had better lead education efforts than suppress them. From the Twaddleton point of view, the spread of mechanical philosophy, like all modes of education, threatens social cohesion because it supports upward mobility. But more subtly, mechanical philosophy was closely associated with the development of rational thought, self-governance, and moral judgement—the intellectual qualities attributed to the ruling classes. Mr. Seymore reclaims these qualities by distinguishing his playful lessons from the village's Philosophical Society. By the time Paris published on the eve of the 1832 Reform Act, reserving play for higher ranks no longer seemed likely or desirable, as a growing audience of middle-class readers embraced playful learning. An increasingly popular Whig position viewed the dissemination of cheap informational literature, including natural philosophy, as the solution to social unrest. After 1830, publishers served multiple lay audiences with cheap, apolitical information literature, repurposing text and illustrations from periodicals or encyclopedias to create new compilations for women, middle-class families, youth, or a newly literate workforce. This is especially true of the SDUK,[29] founded by Whig MP Henry Brougham in 1826, which tried to supplant the radical press but found a ready audience of middle-class youth. Under Charles Knight's leadership, the SDUK cultivated youth and working-class cross-readership using children's publishers Craddock and Joy. The same cross-readership developed for publications by the Society for Promoting Christian Knowledge (SPCK), a competing organization affiliated with the Religious Tract Society that published domestic science and manufacturing books for children.[30] Paris himself witnessed his creations reproduced as inexpensive mass printings, though he initially charged the high price of 7 shillings for his thaumatrope set before publishers rapidly produced inexpensive versions of these and other playful learning toys. Regardless of Mr. Seymore's reservations, rational play became more accessible over the following decades, with cheap wood-pulp paper and mass print, which, as Meredith Bak argues, "expanded the conception of literacy" for people of all classes.[31]

Targeting cross-class audiences, children's books about mechanics expressed multivalent class ideologies. While they embrace Newton's hierarchical division between applied mechanics and mathematical theory, they also stress a potentially democratizing idea stemming from Bacon's induction method—that anyone, even little children, or someone with no formal education—can derive mechanical principles through observation of everyday objects. Even before they can read, children begin to learn natural philosophy, since "observation," Priscilla Wakefield remarks (citing Isaac Watts), "lies within the compass even of children, and from the early dawn of reason, they should be accustomed to observe every thing with attention."[32] By this same logic, artisans and mechanics engaged in "the daily occupations" of manual labor are well positioned to learn mechanical philosophy. While some radical educators make this point, other proponents of popular education more often suggested that a little mechanical philosophy (and similarly, just a little reading) might save the working classes from the dilatory effects of repetitive labor, providing just enough rationality to prevent revolts without creating discontent with their station. In *The Wealth of Nations* (1776), Adam Smith argues that a national education system is necessary to maintain civil peace because the division of labor, accelerated by new machinery, creates a dangerous, widening gap in mental capacity between workers and wealthy elites, which foments unrest. Those with "leisure," he argued, have "an almost infinite variety of objects" to form their minds, and "contemplation of so great a variety of objects necessarily exercises their minds in endless comparisons and combinations, and renders their understandings, in an extraordinary degree, both acute and comprehensive."[33] By focusing on "objects," Smith implies that owning a variety of possessions and having the leisure to explore them makes wealthy people fit to govern, a claim he paraphrases faithfully from John Locke: "Men are differently furnished with [ideas], according to the different objects they converse with. Men then come to be furnished with fewer or more simple ideas from without, according as the objects they converse with afford greater or less variety."[34] However, Smith questions whether the division of labor creates ungovernable subjects, their minds vitiated by repeated exposure to the same objects. The "man whose whole life is spent in performing a few simple operations" is unfit for government because he "generally becomes as stupid and ignorant as it is possible for a human creature to become," "incapable" of "rational conversation" or "conceiving any generous, noble, or tender sentiment, and consequently of forming any just judgment concerning many even of the ordinary duties of private life. Of the great and extensive interests of his country he is altogether incapable of judging."[35] In short, performing repetitive labor is incompatible with governing one's self or family, let alone the nation.

As a solution to this object gap, Smith advocates teaching workers "the elementary parts of geometry and mechanics," because these subjects are useful in nearly any trade, where they would "gradually exercise and improve the common people in those principles, the necessary introduction to the most sublime as well as to the most useful sciences." Again, mechanics is both sublime and accessible, theoretical and practical. Because mechanics potentially bridges the labor of the hand and of the mind, the subject promises to raise working-class people, as it does young children, from material concerns into an abstract realm of higher moral thought. Surprisingly, mechanics, like poetry or fiction, opens the mind; it stretches the mind's ability to use everyday sensation to stimulate imaginative ideas.[36]

Smith's argument gained traction among progressive educators, who viewed the diffusion of "useful knowledge," including mechanical philosophy, as the key to improving the mental faculties of workers, while ensuring social cohesion between classes. James Mill revives Smith's argument in his article "Education" in the *Encyclopedia Britannica* (1816–24), praising "Dr. Smith" for defending public education to counteract the cognitive effects of the "division and subdivision of labour. . . . This confines the attention of the labourer to so small a number of objects, and so narrow a circle of ideas, that the mind receives not that varied exercise, and that portion of aliment, on which almost every degree of mental excellence depends. . . . The minds, therefore, of the great body of the people are in danger of really degenerating, while the other elements of civilization are advancing," unless we "counteract" these effects through "other instruments of education."[37]

This argument for mass education was adapted by working-class radicals for their own purposes. Speaking at the Manchester Mechanics' Institute in 1831, Rowland Detrosier, a self-taught manufacturer who helped found the institute, made the case for extending "moral" and "political" education to the working classes and blamed long hours of repetitive labor for deforming workers' minds. "They are human machines for the creation of wealth, whose physical education in the adaptation of their hands, &c. to mechanical purposes is all that is thought of." He notes that if humans are the "creatures of education and circumstance" and their entire lives are "labour," then they are kept in "political ignorance and moral degradation." Radicals like Detrosier differ, however, by advocating for shorter work hours, which provides time to pursue the sciences as a means of political empowerment: "Why not make public education a part of our scheme for obtaining political reform. . . . Let our Sunday-schools become the UNIVERSITIES OF THE POOR, in which the infant mind shall be taught to look through nature up to nature's source" through "natural philosophy."[38] Detrosier anticipates that learning natural philosophy will aid the moral and political ascendency of the working classes. Natural philosophy can transform the worker's mechanical skills, which he considers potential assets, into political power by helping workers understand the laws governing the economy.

Although these authors take different positions on teaching mechanical philosophy, they agree about its transformative power over the minds of people engaged in physical labor. These widely held beliefs influenced textbook authors. The same year as Detrosier's speech, Mary Somerville published at the request of Whig MP Henry Brougham and the SDUK an expanded translation of the first two volumes of the French mathematician Pierre Simon Laplace's five volume *Traité de mécanique celeste*. Her comprehensive theory of everything, titled *Mechanism of the Heavens* (1831), became a standard textbook on celestial mechanics at Cambridge. She followed this achievement with a book geared toward non-specialists, *On the Connexion of the Physical Sciences* (1834), which, like Smith and Detrosier, promises her readers social and intellectual elevation through learning mechanical philosophy.[39] According to her preface, mechanical principles *connect* profound cosmic wonders: "We perceive the operation of a force which is mixed up with everything that exists in the heavens or on earth; which pervades every atom, rules the motions of animate and inanimate beings." And through "delightful contemplation" of these truths, "the mind of man is raised from low and perishable objects, and prepared for those high destinies which are appointed for all those who are capable of them." By progressing from material objects to principles, the student of science is spiritually transformed in ways that imply a worldly elevation suggestive of the economic or political advances pledged to those who pursue self-education. Moreover, she insists these benefits are open to all readers, even to those who lack the "higher branches of mathematical and mechanical knowledge," because "general laws" can be extrapolated from everyday things: "Our knowledge of external objects is founded upon experience, which furnishes facts; the comparison of these facts establishes relations, from which the belief that like causes will produce like effects leads to general laws."[40] To make an elite subject open to all, Somerville, who had secretly taught herself as a child by smuggling books through her brother, advocates for everyday "experience" as a legitimate source of theoretical knowledge—a position that subtly erodes Newton's class distinctions between practical and theoretical mechanics. Although she did not write for children, Somerville personally taught her several children and tutored Ada Lovelace in mathematics, helping to cement her partnership with

Charles Babbage on the Difference Engine. She was close friends with the women children's authors responsible for developing information literature on mechanics, whom Bernard Lightman calls the "maternal tradition," including Henrietta Beaufort, Maria Edgeworth, and Jane Marcet.[41] James Secord explores the Whig politics behind these textbooks, including Somerville's investment in Unitarian philosophy and the theology behind her search for universal mechanical laws.[42] Her project underscores the extent to which mechanics textbooks reflected evolving political debates over mass education.[43] At 15,000 copies, *Connexion* became one of John Murray's bestselling books in any subject and defined "what constituted the physical sciences" for "almost three generations."[44] Tellingly, the eighth posthumous edition was edited by Arabella Buckley, a specialist in Darwinian evolution who authored popular children's fairy science textbooks.

Although aimed at an adult mass audience, Somerville's work articulates the moral purpose behind observing the physical world in terms familiar to children's authors of her century. The notion that mechanical philosophy stimulates a coming-of-age or mental maturation for the working classes was so widely credited because writers on education had already established the importance of exploring objects for child development. It was common knowledge that sensations gathered during infancy by observing a variety of things stimulate a child's moral and spiritual growth. To use Somerville's terms, children pass from "low and perishable objects" to "high destinies." This belief was supported by trends in education, but also by religious contemplation of God's truth in His creations. Adam Walker's physics textbook promises to place "the book of Nature before his readers," so that all may see the "foundation of morality is in the constitution of things."[45] Moral principles are legible in the arrangement of physical objects and their movement in the world because the world itself is a divinely ordered school.[46] Children explore their environment to develop sound judgment through an organized, disciplined mind.[47] Because manual workers were infantilized, their mental capacity associated with a state of childhood, it is impossible to separate this belief in children's moral development through object manipulation from Smith's concern for the intellectual degradation of workers through the division of labor—or the solution he proposes in learning mechanics. The narrative of personal growth so often associated with mechanical philosophy suggested that learning a little mechanics (but not too much) could counteract the feared degenerative effects of deskilled labor, producing subjects rationally submissive to governance; and, conversely, reserving advanced principles for children from wealthier families would reinforce existing social hierarchies.

Class Politics in Physics Textbooks

Steeped in this political climate, even textbooks that avoid polemical politics tacitly reinforce messages about class simply through how they organize and teach this material. There are several ways that mechanics textbooks link knowledge of mechanical philosophy with qualities associated with elites. First, they use comparisons between human and nonhuman bodies to establish that learning mechanical principles implies command over one's body, and, by analogy, over other working bodies and material objects. Second, they use metacognitive exercises to enhance children's self-awareness, which teaches children how to turn their subjective feelings into universal facts through reflective practices, while reserving this power for a select few. And third, the organization of natural philosophy books from simple to complex creates an implied narrative trajectory, where the reader builds/constructs/organizes himself at the same time as the world. When such texts embrace the exclusivity of mechanical philosophy, they imply that while all children have mechanical bodies and move in a physical world, only some children use their bodies to gain command over matter, to awaken consciousness, or to grow into rational beings. These books thus carefully distinguish the intellectual benefits of mechanical philosophy from the threat associated with repetitive mechanical labor. They often imply that "mechanics," or people who perform physical labor for wages, are largely incapable of understanding the principles behind their work by reducing them to moving bodies that demonstrate mechanical principles for the edification of children of leisure.

Human anatomy was once considered part of mechanical philosophy, and, therefore, human bodies are often used to illustrate laws of motion and simple machines. For instance, *Lectures on Natural Philosophy* (1806) by Margaret Bryan covers human anatomy under the chapter

PROPERTIES OF MATTER.

Matter is the general name which has been given to every species of substance, or thing, which is capable of occupying space, or which has the qualities of length, breadth, and thickness; consequently, every thing which can be seen or felt, is said to be matter. In describing the properties of matter, it must be understood that they do not apply to the masses, or substances, commonly met with, but to the uncompounded or primitive materials of which such substances are formed. These original component parts, of which all substances

FIGURE 18. Samuel Goodrich, *A Glance at the Physical Sciences, Or, the Wonders of Nature, in Earth, Air, and Sky* (New York: John Allen, 1844). The Rare Book & Manuscript Library, University of Illinois at Urbana-Champaign. The first chapter opens with definitions of matter as "everything which can be seen or felt," illustrated by stone breakers, an especially grueling form of labor.

titled "Man as a Machine," as a subtopic of mechanics. She also uses the reader's body as a convenient at-hand reference for demonstrations of mechanical principles. After teaching the mechanical powers, Bryan directs her students' attention to their own bodies: "Behold that various and complicated machinery, which forms the graceful column of man! Composed of bones, joints, and arteries; and clothed with muscles, veins, and teguments!"[48] Since human and nonhuman bodies move according to the same principles, objects and observers are theoretically interchangeable, each modeling the other's movements. Although comparatively simple, William Pinnock's *A Catechism of Anatomy* (1825), a widely circulating, cheap schoolbook, also defines two kinds of bodies: "natural and artificial." Natural bodies are "framed by the hand of nature" and "contain the unknown principle of life," while artificial bodies, such as a watch, "are made by men, and are set in motion by the material powers of gravity or elasticity." The last lesson asks readers to consider their own body as a "wonderful machine," made by "some superior Intelligence" whose "laws we are bound to obey."[49] Such comparisons between human and nonhuman bodies encourage child readers to consider object manipulation as an externalization of their self-development. They can see themselves in moving objects.

Because of this overlap with anatomy, authors can make mechanics more entertaining by inventing creative analogies between humans and machines. In *Art in Nature and Science Anticipated* (1833), a father takes his children to an automaton show, and then compares their body parts (created by God) with objects around their bedroom (created by people). The "pivot, or axle" of Emma's neck is like her piano chair, and her vertebrae are like a telescope's hinge.[50] Likewise, a mother in *Village Science* (1851) illustrates the "laws of motion" using God's "own works": the human arm is "a most powerful lever," while teeth "are a complete set of chisels, wedges, and saws."[51] Anatomy books make similar comparisons. In *Every-Day Wonders of Bodily Life* (1862), Anne Bullar compares human veins to leaves, the skull to a box, nerves to telegraph wires, joints to hinges, veins to pipes, and glands to little bags.[52] Such comparisons can include mimetic machines that model the complexity of human development. Characters in mechanics textbooks often build elaborate clocks, automata, and factory machines, which they compare to their own intellect. William Paley's *Natural Theology* (1802), required reading at Oxford, attests to the orthodoxy of these comparisons between God-designed human body and human-designed inventions. These metaphors help children understand invisible parts of their bodies through visible objects and suggest that children build/explore objects in order to fashion/know themselves.

As living bodies, humans are a peculiar kind of machine because they have sensation. Since all knowledge of the physical world is mediated by the senses, bodies are the only source of information we have about other objects. All knowledge thus begins with subjective experience.[53] As one father explains in a lecture on mechanical philosophy, "matter" is "that which either itself or by its effects is an object of perception to the senses of the body. This leaden ball, this bar of cedar wood, I can see them, I can feel them, I strike them together and my ears become witnesses to their existence, so also might my palate and nasal organs."[54] Accordingly, haptic exercises can help children understand and explain mechanical principles, transforming subjective feelings into objective facts; for example, children *feel* centripetal force while throwing a sling or sledding downhill, comparisons that American author Mary Swift illustrates in *First Lessons on Natural Philosophy for Children* (1836).[55] In the works of education philosophers, these sensations, especially touch, were credited with initiating human consciousness. According to Julia V. Douthwaite, "thought experiments of sensationist philosophers such as Buffon, Condillac, and Bonnet," such as statues coming to life, "were undertaken as a means of exploring the origins and processes by which human beings translate physical impressions into thought." French educational philosophers Condillac and Rousseau were fascinated by Ovid's Pygmalion myth because it seemed to illustrate the mystery of how mechanical sensations in the body generate complex reflections in the mind. Other works describe the birth of human consciousness in similar ways, from Frankenstein's monster experiencing the world for the first time, to Georges-Louis Buffon's Adam coming to life.[56] Physics textbooks allude to the power of sensation to generate conscious awareness when they ask readers to feel material forces and narrate those experiences. By touching things, children become less like dead objects and more like sensitive, thinking beings.[57]

Teachers devised remarkable ways for children to feel mechanical principles at work in their bodies, conferring a sense of adult self-mastery through self-awareness. One of my favorites is an educational machine called the "Panorganon," invented by Richard Lovell Edgeworth, for "giving a general notion of the mechanical organs" by allowing children to "*feel*" the "effect of his own bodily exertions with different engines." He describes experiments performed with the Panorganon that allow children to measure their comparative strength using pulleys, different sized levers, screws, and other simple machines, activities designed to "bring the sense of feeling to our assistance in teaching the uses of the mechanic powers." His instructions for building a Panorganon also appear in William Nicholson's *Journal of Natural Philosophy, Chemistry, and the Arts* (1801), as well as the *Encyclopedia Britannica*.[58] The Panorganon transforms knowledge about the physical world into a form of self-knowledge, as children explore how their bodies move in conjunction with the machine. The name "Panorganon," like its design, synthesizes all organs into a single sensory experience, from parts of the body, to the brain's mental organs, to the parts of the machine. When lessons are done, the Panorganon converts into a swing set.

Cumulatively, these comparisons between machines and bodies and between God-as-creator and human-as-inventor enhance the prestige of rational mechanics and associates it with mastery over the body's work. Those who possess mechanical literacy know how to enhance the body's energy and strategically direct its efforts, thereby manipulating the physical world to serve human ends. Controlling the world of objects is akin to controlling one's own body since both are subject to a reformative process, whether by clever gears and pulleys or by educational mechanisms. Moreover, mechanics aids self-awareness and creative expression, supporting self-fashioning and the development of moral consciousness. Mechanical knowledge signifies, therefore, not only the practical know-how of artisans and factory workers, but a wider comprehension of the principles behind manipulating the world of things, which signifies the sort of lively intellectual life of self-reflection and moral feeling that grants individual identity and permits participation in public life. In other words, mechanical philosophy develops mental qualities believed to distinguish the ruling elite. Granted, this social category expanded over the century to include middle-class professionals and small-property owners, which explains why ownership of mechanical knowledge is politically contested. As greater numbers of

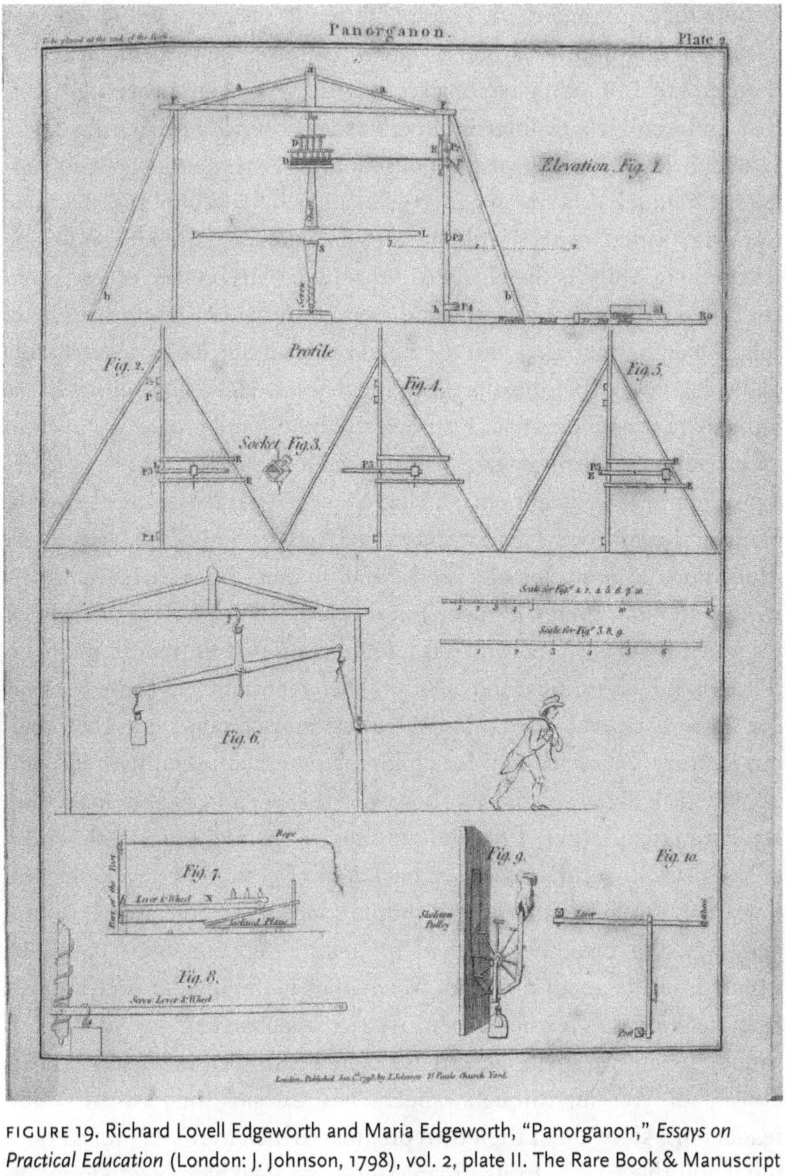

FIGURE 19. Richard Lovell Edgeworth and Maria Edgeworth, "Panorganon," *Essays on Practical Education* (London: J. Johnson, 1798), vol. 2, plate II. The Rare Book & Manuscript Library, University of Illinois at Urbana-Champaign.

middle-class and working-class people began to learn mechanical philosophy after 1820, they could use this knowledge to claim these same qualities while mobilizing for greater political power.

Natural philosophy textbooks also tell this story of self-empowerment in how they are organized. Young children are materially minded, and so natural philosophy textbooks start with objects they can easily sense, then progress to intangible objects or unseen forces (gravity, light, air) that children have to infer indirectly from observations. For instance, Jeremiah Joyce, a tutor in the household of Earl Stanhope (who supported Samuel Whitbread's 1807 education bill), begins his *Scientific Dialogues* (1800) with a volume on "mechanics," a field comprising "every thing which is the object of our senses." His preface offers extensive thanks to the Edgeworths and a nod to Anna Letitia Barbauld and John Aiken for inspiring him to imbed his scientific lessons into family dialogues. Joyce then breaks down mechanics. He begins with what is immediately tangible (matter, simple machines) and progresses to complex machines (steam engines) and invisible forces (electricity, magnetism).[59] Jane Marcet, a friend of Mary Somerville and Maria Edgeworth, likewise begins her *Conversations on Natural Philosophy* (1819) by explaining the definition of a "body" and "matter." Next she covers gravity and motion, then the mechanical powers—progressing from what we touch to how we move it—as a foundation for her final chapters on astronomy, hydrostatics, and optics.[60] The organization of these books is the same as several general audience textbooks produced in the previous century. Once adapted for children and embellished with illustrations and fictional characters, however, this seemingly unremarkable, standard organization of natural philosophy textbooks places the order of the natural world against the backdrop of children's developmental trajectory. While beginning with simple concepts is motivated by sound pedagogy, the meaning assigned to "matter" encompasses culturally situated beliefs about children. Mechanics is the first subject in most of these children's textbooks because it is "mechanical," in the sense of simple, repetitive, material, and associated with the body and working-class labor. Working through a mechanics textbook thus involves child readers in a story about their own progress, which they can project onto the world they study. In its progression from tangible objects to intangible forces, the mechanics textbook recalls the child's transformation from a mechanical creature of sensation into a thinking, rational, self-aware adult. This transformation implies the infantilization of people who remain "mechanics" as adults.

Where present, fictional plots communicate this progress story more

FIGURE 20. Science in Sport, or, the Pleasures of Natural Philosophy: A New & Instructive Pastime (London: John Wallis, 1818). Courtesy Lilly Library, Indiana University, Bloomington, Indiana. This engraved game is printed on paper, hand colored, and cut into nine pieces that are glued onto linen to create a foldable board, stored in a slipcase with a rule booklet. Lilly also has another 1806 copy, same board, but different slipcase. The center of the board outlines the same curriculum and organization as a textbook for young children. The central image shows "The Falls of Niagara," surrounded by portraits of Descartes, Boyle, Franklin, and Bacon. The rules or "Laws of the Game" are printed on the right, creating an analogy between following the rules of the game and learning the divine laws that govern nature.

plainly. Child protagonists begin their studies by expressing curiosity about everyday objects they see around them, often things that they eat or wear. Their instruction thus begins close to the body, or in the home, and it progresses outward into the world, leading to increasingly difficult lessons on abstract concepts or intangible forces. William Martin's *The Parlour Book* (1835), for instance, begins at the "breakfast table," where the children ask about the china, tea, sugar, and coffee, before they tour a brickyard, farm, brewery, and mill. In later chapters, the children perform experiments with a barometer and an air pump, learn optics, and build steam engines. Home is a place for metacognitive activities, where child characters write journals, perform experiments, build models, and organize curiosity cabinets. This plot formula—search outward, reflect at home—may repeat each chapter, creating continuity between what children discover in "the visible world without" and "the invisible world within," reinforced through interlocutor and developmental gestures. Concluding chapters introduce children to socio-economic contexts by visiting crowded environments away from home, such as science museums, automata exhibits, factories, or centers of trade (like the Seymore family's neighborhood fair in *Philosophy in Sport*). Martin devotes the last fifty pages of *The Parlour Book* to the family's visit to "The Gallery of Practical Science" in London, an exhibit devoted to "various applications of the useful arts to the service of common life, and practical demonstrations of the principles of science."[61] Such excursions introduce the family to a social world where principles of mechanical philosophy intersect with those of political economy.

Fictional characters in these stories are noticeably divided between wealthier children, who learn mechanical philosophy, and working people, whose movements illustrate mechanical principles. To take one example, *Village Science; or, the Laws of Nature Explained* (1851) by Mrs. E. W. Payne, who wrote science books for the Religious Tract Society, follows Alexander and his mother, Mrs. M—, as they walk through the countryside, playing games and watching people at work. In the first lesson on matter, Alexander races his hoop down a hill, prompting a lesson on Newton's laws of motion. Alexander exclaims, "My hoop obeys nature's laws, dear mama!"[62] Soon they discover some road pavers, who provide an occasion for observing how natural laws make physical labor less demanding. "See my dear!" Mother says, "those men are availing themselves of the laws of nature to lighten their labours." Pointing to their cart filled with stones, Mrs. M— explains that the cart "*rested* on a pivot or axle" until "a *small touch* of the man's hand" rolls out its heavy contents [emphasis mine], a balancing act later compared to Alexander ice-skating. Next a "workman" moves a "heavy block of stone" using "mechanical powers." Mrs. M— advises her son, "Now use your eyes, and you will see the advantage of the lever, a very important mechanical power." As the pavers roll the stones into place using logs, Alexander exclaims, "The man pushing behind it, moves it just as I push my hoop with the stick." At the close of the chapter, Mrs. M— delivers one last lesson about a powerful simple machine: "The screw in your little printing press gives a much greater force than you could command in any other way," a suggestive statement about the power of the press to disseminate knowledge.[63] The choice of such symbolically resonant illustrations is far from accidental. In a single chapter, Alexander progresses from matter in motion to reading and writing, while the family traverses from Roman-era infrastructure to the Gutenberg press. His lessons thus form a racialized recapitulation narrative in which Alexander's development parallels British civilization.[64]

Village Science uses this progress story to represent machines as beneficial aids that advance civilization by making physical labor less strenuous. Used to build infrastructure, machines connect people together rather than divide, and they alleviate the notoriously debilitating labor of paving roads. This lesson with the stonebreakers, in which Mother blithely compares building a road to her son's games, ideologically prepares Alexander to approve machines as civilizing instruments for progress. Consequently, in later chapters, he approves more controversial modern advances, such as the railroad, the steam engine, and factory machines. Despite what Mother says about the pavers, easing hard labor by using mechanical powers did not always improve wages or working conditions. Rather, tasks previously performed by adult men for higher wages were assigned to children, leading to a rise in child low-wage labor during the early Victorian period. In other words, at the same time that Alexander compares his games to work "lightened" by machines, other children entered the manufacturing workforce, where they had less parental supervision and fewer breaks than in agriculture, their tiring work justified as light and playful tasks by those who opposed factory reforms.

Although *Village Science* is not strikingly polemical, the story nevertheless uses mechanical philosophy as an occasion to comment on the machinery question. Even its title, *Village Science*, echoes Hannah More's *Village Politics* (1792), a series of pamphlets created as safe literature for the working classes. And sure enough, in the final chapter, titled "Enough to Spare," Alexander learns about political economy when he observes fish transported inland by rail to feed a manufacturing city. Commenting on the large catch, Mrs. M— praises trade as cooperative (rather than competitive), refutes Malthusian predictions of starvation, and warns that famines are God's punishment. Her final food for thought quotes the Bible, "He that will not work, neither let him eat," spoken without any hint of irony.[65] Self-cultivation through games and country tours must count as work for Alexander and his Mother.

What is most curious about such books is how they manage to communicate Newton's divide between rational and practical mechanics through subtle cues while seeming to avoid the polemical pitfalls of Tom Telescope's excised final chapter. Alexander's education in rational mechanics distinguishes him from the various working-class characters who are introduced in the narrative as illustrative bodies. *Village Science* does not portray the road pavers, themselves, as capable of discussing rational mechanics. They do not speak, and M— explains what they do. Moreover, she compares her son's toys to the workers' tools, emphasizing theoretical similarities between their movements, even though Alexander and his mother clearly do not work in the same way as the pavers. The comparison is made precisely to establish the difference between those who perform hard labor and those who have the leisure and ocular distance to contemplate the laws behind that labor, but also to deny that any meaningful distinction exists for the privileged observer between labor and play. The story praises this division of mental and physical labor, which makes possible the invention of machines that lighten all loads. By learning mechanical philosophy, one day readers might leave behind their toys and invent labor-saving devices. In *Village Science*, mechanical philosophy has an improving effect; it cultivates young minds and relieves the burden of physical labor.

Schools as Factories / Factories as Schools

The belief that machines improve individuals and solve social problems intensified in the early Victorian period into a widespread mythology. A positive association between machines and child development may seem puzzling in the same decades when factory work was blamed for destroying the minds and bodies of child workers. The Parliamentary reports of the 1830s and '40s, detailing poor conditions for children in mines and factories, made work seem incompatible with child health let alone mental growth, while Matthew Arnold, John Ruskin, and William Morris depicted the factory system as antithetical to cultivation and a threat to civilization. A close relationship between cultivation and manufacturing was not uncommon, however, in writings on the factory system. According to Joseph Bizup, apologists for the factory system such as Andrew Ure, William Cooke Taylor, and Edward Baines admired the vitalism of machines as living organisms and used cultivation metaphors to describe the growth of industry.[66] Far from expressing distaste for mechanization, children's mechanics textbooks embrace this same vitalist thinking when they compare human anatomy to machinery, or celebrate the cultivating potential of machines. Mechanics textbooks thus envisioned education as a modernizing force allied with industrialization.

One reason for this enthusiasm was that schools for the poor were celebrated as machines that enabled social progress. Rather than regulate child labor, early Victorians applied the division of labor to the schoolroom, using the Monitorial methods of Andrew Bell and Joseph Lancaster to reduce the cost and time it takes to learn. What Lancaster described as his "new and mechanical system of education," Samuel Taylor Coleridge praised as "this incomparable machine, this vast moral steam-engine," and Henry Brougham named "the steam engine of the moral world." Sir Thomas Bernard, an early advocate of educating the poor, clarified the connection to Adam Smith's writings: "The principle in schools and manufactories is the same. The grand principle of Dr. Bell's System is the division of labour applied to intellectual purposes."[67] And for decades these phrases were echoed in Parliament. If factory machines degraded the mind, then intellectual machines could fix them.

For those who opposed limiting the work hours of children, the association between education and machinery implied, rather conveniently, that children could learn while they work. Once education is portrayed as a machine and steam power associated with child genius, then factories seem like wonderful schools for anyone smart enough to pay attention. Since steam engines relieve workers from heavy manual labor, they leave the mind free for contemplation. Andrew Ure reports, "A mule-spinner told Mr. Tufnell, that in the intervals of labor allowed by his steam-going spindles, he had read through several books. The workmen who superintend the frames . . . seemed to me so much at their ease, that they might study the circle of the sciences [a children's textbook series] in the course of their business."[68] Criticizing Lord Ashley's call to limit how long children work so that they can attend school, Ure suggests that the factory is itself an educational environment. Three-quarters of children "engaged at piecing at the mules," have the free time to study while they work. "When the carriages of these have receded a foot and a half or two feet from the rollers, nothing is to be done, not even attention is required." Ure interprets this interval as an opportunity for self-improvement. The adult spinner and child piecer "stand idle for a time, and in fine spinning particularly, for three-quarters of a minute, or more. Consequently, if a child remains at this business twelve hours daily, he has nine hours of inaction. And though he attends two mules, he has still six hours of non-exertion. Spinners sometimes dedicate these intervals to the perusal of books" or "moving about in a sportive mood." Ure's assertion that factory labor is light work that leaves time for study or "sport" may seem too ludicrous to take seriously. Yet his assessment remains surprisingly consistent with the way Alexander, in *Village Science*, compares the road pavers' work to his childish game while his Mother praises the ease with which they perform their labor assisted by levers and screws. Such ideas appear over and again in Victorian children's books about mechanical philosophy and manufacturing. In Jane Marcet's *Willy's Travels on the Railroad* (1835), seven-year-old Willy comments while watching textile operatives, "Every thing seems alive in the factory, . . . nothing stands still except the people, who are really alive, and they move only when they have threads to tie, or other work to do, whilst the machinery is at work all day long; it works a great deal harder, and does a great deal more, than all the live people."[69] The empowering strategy of learning philosophy through play, used by Tom Telescope and Tom Seymore in their country estates, ultimately feeds into a defense of child factory labor and long work hours for everyone.

Children's biographies greatly contributed to this mythology about the cultivating power of machines by describing exceptional individuals who manage to magically teach themselves reading, writing, and mechanical philosophy through sheer proximity to machines. An 1881 article in the weekly youth magazine *Chatterbox* on David Livingston, a missionary to Africa, claims that "he brought his books to the factory, and placing one of them on the 'jenny,' with the lesson open before him, he divided his attention between the running of the spindles and the rudiments of knowledge."[70] In such stories, working with machines inspires children to learn. An article on the history of abolition in *Boy's Own Paper* notes that "while watching a steam-engine fire in a shipyard," Frederick Douglass "learned to write."[71] According to Douglass's unabridged biography, he also tricked white schoolboys into teaching him letters, but this clever stratagem (omitted from the article) challenges dominant beliefs, where reading the letters on a steam-engine's valves accords with prevailing beliefs that machines improve the mind. Similarly, an 1864 biography of Patrick Bell, who invented the reaping machine, optimistically reflects on the "mental and moral advantage to the farm labourer" of mechanized agriculture: "It has been the fashion to compare the farm labourer with the skilled operative, much to the disadvantage of the former." But now, "the essential knowledge of the engines employed, will quicken into life and activity the mental faculties of the agriculturist, and place him on an equal footing with the miner, the mill-hand, and the artisan" by "employing their minds as well as their hands, and by setting their mental machinery in motion."[72] Such stories are published throughout the century, the artisanal metaphor of self-fashioning coexisting with the cultivating motifs of gardens and village greens commonly associated with late Victorian children's fiction.

In addition to learning their letters, biographical subjects teach themselves mechanical philosophy. In the story of Scottish civil engineer John Rennie, he first learned mechanics by watching the machinery of a mill, fortuitously located halfway between his home and school and operated by Andrew Meikle, inventor of the threshing machine. Soon his detour at the mill became his preferred school, and "every spare hour and all his holidays were sure to find him at his post, examining the various operations in progress." In the evenings, Rennie "constructed the model of a windmill, a pile-engine, and a steam-engine."[73] Rennie's ability to access factories for the purpose of self-improvement requires peculiar luck and privilege; yet lengthy compilations of such stories imply, to the contrary, that worthy individuals find ways to teach themselves. Exacerbated by the deployment of these anecdotes, Rev. George Stringer Bull, an abolitionist Anglican minister who organized children's marches for a ten-hour workday, comments, "The Rev. John Newton, when a sailor, mastered Horace without a Dictionary, or any help, but Castallio's Latin Bible; but this will not be urged as a proof that the cabin of a Guineaman, with such a library, is an efficient Classical Seminary. . . . these cases can never be urged in proof that a sufficient education is afforded to the factory children, or to poor children generally, in Sunday Schools."[74] These inventor biographies helped to make Ure's argument seem plausible, that child workers can easily teach themselves while they work because factory machines leave them little to do, and steam engines are so inspiring.

These ideas were sometimes directed at factory children themselves, chastising them for their ignorance. A lengthy RTS tract entitled *The Young Folks of the Factory; or, Friendly Hints on their Duties and Dangers* (1840) informs children that factory work may "quicken your faculties of observation," but warns them against "being so entirely engrossed with one pursuit, as not to exercise the faculties of observation and common sense upon the various objects that surround us. People of this class are little better than machines."[75] Here is Adam Smith's well-worn fear about the division of labor; but the author believes the factory itself offers a schoolroom to mend the mind: "I can hardly conceive of a young person so stupid as to go day after day to work in a factory and never inquire into the principle of the steam-engine, into the method of obtaining cotton, wool, coal, iron, . . . and through what process they have previously passed, and what is still required to fit them for the consumer."[76] The author assumes that factories supply child workers with an empowering vision of the factory system, failing to consider that only children of leisure, who learn abstractly from books in schoolrooms, benefit from a practical field trip to a factory. In other words, the same progress narrative used in books for wealthier children was leveraged by early Victorians to make child labor and mass education seem compatible, when in fact, education for children and adult workers alike depended on regulating work hours to create the leisure to learn.

Chartists argued this point when they demanded a ten-hour workday and a political education for their children. One children's book on manufacturing, written from a radical artisan's perspective, *The Cotton Fields and Cotton Factories*, which is "*adapted for youth*," by "Henry Brown, artisan" (1840) spends half its pages in reveries on factory machines, and half in virulent denunciation of child labor. This unique volume demonstrates that celebratory language about machines does not always correlate with a laissez-faire stance on the factory question. Brown directly enlists middle-class readers as agents responsible for learning the "full political and moral bearing" of the factory system and criticizes the present state of education that leaves most Englishmen "utterly ignorant of the nature of that policy which regulates their present existence." As fellow children, his young readers should know that the wealth of English manufacturing "has done little more than nothing for that infant population, whose nimble fingers are said to be so essential to the manufacture."[77] Although the 1833 Factory Act required that children attend two hours of school per workday, such attempts to teach children without reducing their work hours are nonsense. "Education! Pardon us that word; it was proposed that the children should be taught to read; but mark! The mill-owners were still determined to relinquish no part of the children's toil. Sunday schools and night schools were to be established for this purpose. Truly, the children must have had but an irksome life; what with their toil of the day and their 'education' at night." One day, Brown envisions, child labor will end, and all children will attend school. Then educated workers will "feel their own consequence, morally and politically" and "command that machinery which has so long and cruelly commanded their parents."[78] Far from objecting to the machinery progress narrative, Brown concludes with the image of working-class children who gain power over themselves and their world by mastering machines.

Tinkering in Victorian Engineer Biographies: Gendering Tech Play

As engineer or "mechanician" gained visibility as possible professions, books about mechanical philosophy that at one time featured girl and boy siblings learning together now favored boy characters almost exclusively, with titles specifying "books for boys." The decline of girl/boy sibling protagonists may reflect a change in intended audiences. When Newbery, Paris, and Marcet wrote about natural philosophy for families from the landed gentry, mercantile, and middle classes, they targeted a lay audience of parents and female educators and their young charges. By comparison, Victorian books are more likely to teach the practical applications of mechanical philosophy to new technologies, writing for a cross-class audience that includes upwardly mobile artisans and professionals, predominantly men seeking employment as factory managers and mechanicians. This change occurs alongside rising respect for an industrial middle class, trained in mechanical philosophy but distinguished from the gentleman's family featured in Paris's novel and from the village artisans he deplores.

The marginalization of both working-class teachers and curious girl characters sends the message that mechanical philosophy belongs to white men of a certain rank. Anticipating this trend, publisher John Harris added to his Little Library a fictional autobiography of a would-be engineer, *Francis Lever, the Young Mechanic: Being Incidents and Lectures Explanatory of the First Principles of Mechanics* (1835), which includes a mechanical philosophy textbook. The story follows Francis, a comfortably middle-class boy with a "mechanical turn," who is subject to "fits of meditation, even when engaged in mere boyish sports." He pursues his adventures alone, occasionally with his brother, while his sister provides a supportive audience. In the opening episode, Frank causes his brother to tumble off a teeter-totter when he steps off to examine how it works, learning an "impressive lesson in the doctrine of consequences." The accident proves an opportunity to chat about levers and gravity with Frank's father. Afterward, Frank declares, "I should like to understand *mechanics*, . . . then I could understand machines and engines. I—I—I think I should like to be—*an Engineer*." His father supports his choice, recollecting that Frank once made "a little hydraulic engine" to play with in streams; he tinkers with old clocks, substituting different pendulums; and he steals the kitchen roasting jack to try lifting things about the garden.[79] Frank is a model troublesome boy, favored by fictional stories like this one, in which endearing accidents and restlessness in school indicate mechanical talents. While this Tom Sawyer type features prominently in Golden Age children's literature, Frank's literary kin read as an update for the boys from *Learning in Sport* or *Village Science*, both gentlemen's sons who claim playful learning as a class-appropriate substitution for physical labor. Instead of separating himself from manual crafts altogether, Frank signals his class privilege by tinkering—that is, by having the leisure to make and break things without regard to practical ends—which distinguishes his middle-class learning practices from those of artisan apprentices or child wage-earners.

The novel sketches out the kind of education best suited to a prospective engineer, making the case for blending together home, work, and school, with experimentation taking place in all locations. Frank first encounters a real engineering problem when a construction crew arrives to jack up the neighboring house to replace its crumbling foundation. Watching the men lift the immense structure, Frank is "impressed with astonishment at the vast results attained by the mechanical powers, and felt a sort of reverence of those who thus enforce them." Unfortunately, their efforts end like the teeter-totter: the workers miscalculate, the house falls, and the windows smash to pieces. These misadventures induce Frank to learn mechanics from an informed teacher, Mr. Brindley (whose namesake is the famed eighteenth-century engineer, James Brindley), who teaches boys on his property, equipped with a playground, plots for "experimental farming," and a proper workshop "supplied with all the tools and materials which ingenuity apart from mischief could require." Where Frank formerly made slow progress learning to read with his mother, he now learns quickly and feels "at home" surrounded by the tools, wires, chains, fireplace, and model engines. In other words, the mother's domestic space presents a problem, and it must be replaced with a boyish space of experimentation. Just as Brindley's school imitates the home, Frank's home transforms into a school when he returns for summer break. His father delivers lectures on mechanical philosophy to the neighborhood families with Frank as his able assistant. "The library is to be the lecture-room," exclaims his sister, "and we have got printed cards, and papa has made large paper drawings, and everybody is to come, and your jack is to be there, and there is to be a great ball—a wooden one, I mean, and forms, and inclined planes, and an electrifying machine, and a skeleton, and a crane, and—oh! such a large pair of compasses!—Come and see!" Frank finds a table "spread with a most interesting assortment of philosophical implements and materials. The walls, too, were hung with diagrams and other scientific delineations." [80] Frank's home has a new "foundation," so to speak, that leverages the boy's destructive impulses into something useful to his community.

Frank's progress from teeter-totter to workshop follows the familiar formula of earlier domestic science books. Lessons proceed spatially outward from domestic settings, where learning is visceral (the teeter-totter), to transitional spaces between home and work (school and workshop), where Frank learns mathematics and complex machines. The novel concludes with Frank and his father modeling metacognitive work for readers through their salon lectures, which include the usual recapitulation narrative. Frank's father praises England as the "mother country of the arts," their engineers as the vanguard of civilization, who "seek to diminish the use of physical labor." Engineers transform work from its historical childhood to its modern intellectual form, just as Frank's childhood "sports" evolve over time into purposeful experiments that illuminate "the laws and properties" of matter.[81] In some ways Francis Lever is another Tom Telescope, but Francis learns engineering rather than science. In this way his story is quite different from Paris's *Philosophy in Sport*, which features a landed gentleman's family, because it provides professional career advice. Like Frank, who finds the house jack episode inspiring, but the workers less competent than his middle-class teacher, these stories tend to depict artisan teachers and female caregivers as necessary but inadequate, reflecting that such children's biographical fiction about engineering as a profession targets middle-class boys.

In such books, the workshop or toolbox takes on symbolic weight as a physical representation of the boy's mind, a space he develops by accumulating tools and projects as material manifestations of the knowledge inside his head. An alternative to the home (coded feminine), the workshop is an indispensable boy's space, appended to the home but beyond the reach of mothers, imitative of an artisan workshop but with more room for experimentation—a place owned by boys where they can tinker without pecuniary ends. The shift away from the domestic science setting in boys' books contrasts with the reality that scientists from the sixteenth through the nineteenth century pursued experiments at home, supported by family members and household servants, who took measurements and produced notes or managed translations and visitors, while a single male householder took public credit for this collective labor.[82] Jacob Abbott begins *The Boy's Own Workshop, or, The Young Carpenters* (1860) with directions for constructing a wooden box

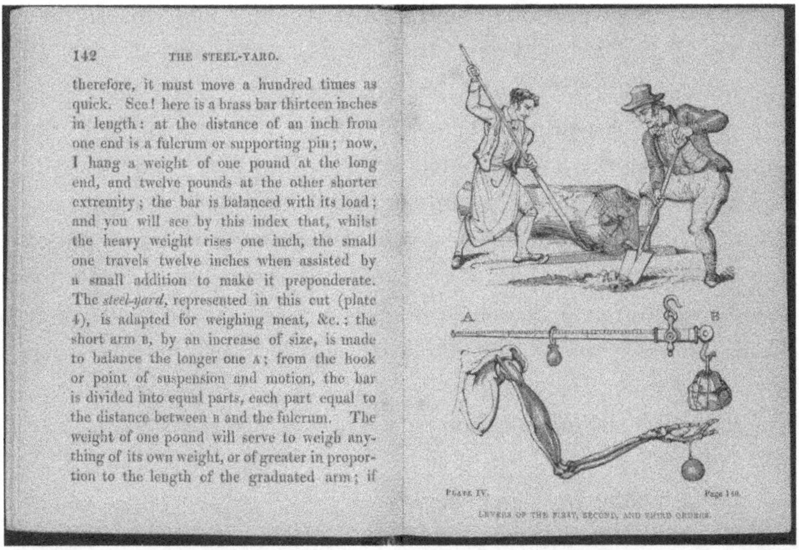
142 THE STEEL-YARD.

therefore, it must move a hundred times as quick. See! here is a brass bar thirteen inches in length: at the distance of an inch from one end is a fulcrum or supporting pin; now, I hang a weight of one pound at the long end, and twelve pounds at the other shorter extremity; the bar is balanced with its load; and you will see by this index that, whilst the heavy weight rises one inch, the small one travels twelve inches when assisted by a small addition to make it preponderate. The *steel-yard*, represented in this cut (plate 4), is adapted for weighing meat, &c.; the short arm B, by an increase of size, is made to balance the longer one A; from the hook or point of suspension and motion, the bar is divided into equal parts, each part equal to the distance between B and the fulcrum. The weight of one pound will serve to weigh anything of its own weight, or of greater in proportion to the length of the graduated arm; if

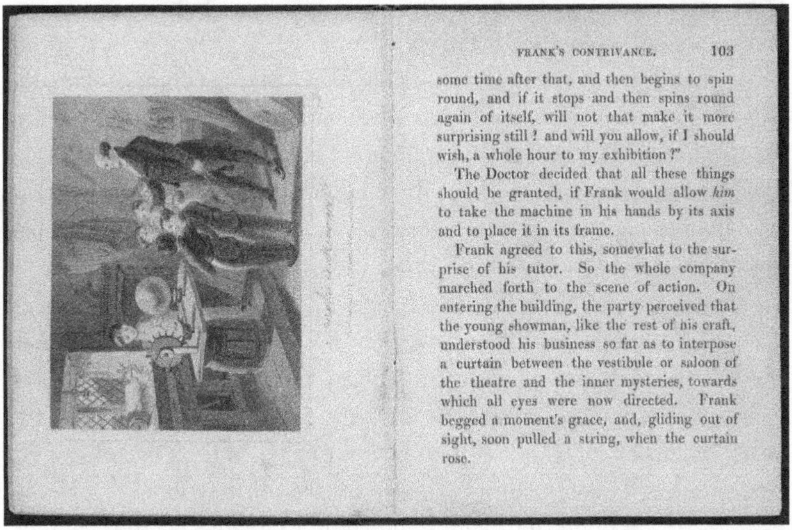
FRANK'S CONTRIVANCE. 103

some time after that, and then begins to spin round, and if it stops and then spins round again of itself, will not that make it more surprising still? and will you allow, if I should wish, a whole hour to my exhibition?"

The Doctor decided that all these things should be granted, if Frank would allow *him* to take the machine in his hands by its axis and to place it in its frame.

Frank agreed to this, somewhat to the surprise of his tutor. So the whole company marched forth to the scene of action. On entering the building, the party perceived that the young showman, like the rest of his craft, understood his business so far as to interpose a curtain between the vestibule or saloon of the theatre and the inner mysteries, towards which all eyes were now directed. Frank begged a moment's grace, and, gliding out of sight, soon pulled a string, when the curtain rose.

FIGURES 21–22. Anonymous, *Francis Lever, the Young Mechanic: Being Incidents and Lectures Explanatory of the First Principles of Mechanics: with Some Account of the Most Celebrated Engines, Ancient and Modern* (London: John Harris, 1835), 103, 142. Cotsen Children's Library. Courtesy of Princeton University Library. Frank demonstrates a machine he built for his classmates (102–3). The principal of the lever demonstrated three ways: a man moving a log while another digs, a "steel-yard" or meat scale, and a human arm (142–43).

for storing tools. Successive chapters expand the box's contents with new tools as the reader collects skills. Readers thus stock their minds and build themselves, as self-made men, just as they build their workspaces. The boy's workshop functions similarly to the collection spaces examined in chapter 1, but in this case knowledge becomes property, owned by the boy, as he owns his tools. By owning skills inside their minds, boys imitate the behavior of exemplary inventors like James Watt, whose "memory," according to one biography, was "vastly capacious and retentive," but as orderly as a toolbox: "Its compartments were all distinctly defined, and each was replenished with its peculiar store of intellectual wealth."[83]

Self-fashioning through tinkering—or building, collecting, owning as learning—runs throughout the "do it yourself" literature of the "amateur work" movement. Victorian middle-class handcraft hobbies are essentially an adult version of what children do when they play at weaving or bricklaying, which became popular when the generation educated this way reached adulthood. Part of the Young Mechanic Series, *The Boy Engineers: What They Did and How They Did It: A Book for Boys* by James Lukin (1878), illuminates the complicated attitudes toward those who held the power to teach mechanical knowledge, including artisans and women writers. A prolific author of boys' craft books, including an automaton toy manual, Lukin ostensibly based *The Boy Engineers* on the childhood diary of a deceased friend, with diary passages alternating with Lukin's discursive commentary. Lukin uses self-deprecating humor to chronicle the perseverance of two brothers, Harry and Tim. What begins as their "boyish hobby" culminates in their establishment as engineers.[84] Along the way, readers learn all they need to cheaply assemble everything from a grinding stone to a lathe, including architectural designs to build their own workshop, and instructions for making an automaton and a steam engine.

The sons of a retired navy captain, Harry and Tim attend the local grammar school, whose classical curriculum the boys supplement by building a workshop from an "old wooden outhouse, adjoining the school" formerly a "fowlhouse." To get permission, they try composing a letter to the schoolmaster in "choicest schoolboy Latin," but give up the effort, because they cannot "find out the Latin for workshop, or fowlhouse, or padlock"—a jibe at their outdated curriculum. The boys learn engineering by painstakingly gleaning know-how from various mentors. The first is a former British army surgeon, who acts as a go-between for other knowledge sources. He tells the boys how an Indian carpenter, whom he observed while posted in India, cleverly assembles a mobile lathe in minutes using minimal materials. The boys learn woodworking from Bill Birch, "a grasping, close-fisted, and churlish old fellow" who whipped his apprentices and who demands payment for instruction, which the boys believe extortionist. Next they find a friend at an iron-works firm who permits them to watch, and they learn "the *theory* of engineering" from an excellent Cambridge student who explains each "mechanical law," illustrated with "a simple experiment."[85]

The boys claim to have earned their specialist knowledge through grease and grit despite their dependence on skills shared through cross-class and cross-cultural mentorship. The story undermines teachers who rank below the middle-class boys, a tendency captured in the very name of Harry's younger brother, Arthur, who goes by "Tim" after his fondness for "Timothy Potter, an itinerant mender of pots, pans, and umbrellas, . . . who supplied solder, and wire, and odds and ends of tin and brass." The narrator remains skeptical of their friendship, noting, "Old Tim beat young Tim sadly at these transactions, and made a very handsome profit," and he suspects "the old tinker sometimes obtained his wares without paying for them at all."[86] The novel is more congenial about learning from middle-class adults, who safely relay knowledge they gain from their worldly interactions, free of charge.

While constructing a mythology of the industrial engineer as self-made man, *The Boy Engineers* ultimately draws attention to the frayed edges of capitalism, where cultural capital determines who "owns" knowledge, defends patents, and earns profits. The boys' first tools are "out of the stock of a bankrupt carpenter," a cautionary premonition repeated in the narrator's final warning against investors. "But our boys will be asking who gets the profit? That depends very much upon circumstances." Scientists are less driven by money, he reflects, leaving them vulnerable to "the manufacturer" who often "reaps the pecuniary reward."[87] Manufacturers are Tim-the-tinker with more money. Such ambivalent attitudes toward capitalists and tinkers alike may reflect the experience of authors like Lukin, who write about making things with their hands, a job that defies Newton's divide between mental and manual labor. Like the British army surgeon, Lukin relays his experiences in amateur crafts so that children do not have to range so far, but, as an author, he is another Timothy Potter, an itinerant salesman who circulates knowledge through texts.

Some positive representations of artisan mentors appear in biographies of famous exemplary geniuses who learned mechanics and gained wealth despite "low" birth and limited education. Reportedly, James Brindley, a civil engineer who built canals, bridges, and shipyards, "was so illiterate as to be scarcely able to read or to write." Possessed of "unrivalled powers of abstraction and memory, he often executed his plans without committing them to paper."[88] Instead of books and technical drawings, Brindley used his mind as a machine for running virtual tests through mental representation: "In his calculations of the powers of any machine, he performed the requisite operation by a mental process."[89] "Machine" takes on, here, its early modern meaning, "to think," rather than its connotation of physical labor. Biographies also highlight moments when young inventors first exhibit mechanical genius through idol play or tinkering, behaviors ordinarily reserved for children of leisure. A neighboring gentleman who visited the home of toddler James Watt, "observed the child bending over a marble hearth, with a piece of coloured chalk," and rebuked his parents for allowing him "to trifle away his time at home." The gentleman notices that Watt "had drawn mathematical lines and circles on the hearth, and was marking, in letters and figures, the result of some calculation," and apologizes, with the remark, "he is no common child." Anecdotally, Watt's inspiration for the steam engine came from a teakettle in the same kitchen (a standard lesson in philosophy-at-home), where he would, "under the very eyes of Aunt Muirhead, take a spoon, gather the steam on it from the kettle-spout, watch it condense, and count the drops." The narrator comments ironically, "So awfully lazy!" Later in life, when Watt sought investors, Dr. Robinson, his partner, assumes he has no knowledge of mechanical philosophy. "I saw a workman, and expected no more," he recalls, "but was surprised to find a philosopher as young as myself, and always ready to instruct me." To contend with these prejudices, Watt reportedly developed storytelling skills that put anyone at ease, and displayed an irreproachable work ethic; "he never allowed his love of reading, or of philosophical research, to interfere with the daily labours on which his living depended."[90] Watt's biography is a favorite in British children's literature and periodicals (one account written by Andrew Ure), possibly because Watt's story deftly navigates the class sensibilities of his contemporaries.

Genius inventors of all stations tinker in family kitchens, yet girl characters seldom play around in workshops. The one female inventor biography I could find, on Barbara Uttman from Saxony, exemplifies this point. Inspired by neither curiosity nor mechanical inclination, Uttman's motivation is saving her family. When the story opens, Uttman's collier husband, laid off work, delivers his last wages to his beloved wife's keeping. After failing to sell muslin veils, she decides to create a new method of lace weaving—but not before she cleans her house and cooks for her children. Then "Barbara shut herself up in the little inner room of her cottage. She had the sticks and cushion with her, and she only entered the outer room when her presence was absolutely necessary for the comfort of her family. . . . On the evening of the fifth day she appeared in the midst of her family, her face beaming with an expression of sublime joy." Instead of a workshop, Uttman finds space to think by retreating into the one interior room in her cottage—technically a room of her own, but the proximity of husband and children, separated by thin wall and locked door, recall the at-home work environment recently enjoyed by quarantined parents. Since the story omits her childhood, Uttman never plays with mechanical models, or tinkers without practical ends; she pursues her task, keenly motivated by starving children. After she saves her family, the narrator praises Uttman, quoting Proverbs 41: "Her children called her blessed, her husband also." Rather than patent her method, Uttman shares her discovery, earning the gratitude of her city, for she had not "concealed the secret of her invention, but had taught all who sought a knowledge of it, receiving from each a moderate remuneration."[91] At her death, hundreds join her funeral, delivering her promised praise at the city gates. Although Uttman's generosity is gendered, her refusal to profit from poor neighbors values community well-being over profit, a perspective largely absent from inventor biographies of men. Noticeably missing, however, is any explanation, delivered by Uttman, about what exactly she did in that room. The chapter closes by quoting paragraphs by George Dodd on the process for making bone lace. While Uttman may charge for teaching her method, she cannot own it.

Instead, a male authority on the factory system records and circulates her method, accompanied by a technical illustration.

By the late nineteenth century, according to Bernard Lightman, women writers were associated with mass culture and the dissemination of science because they wrote many science books for children and lay readers.[92] Yet like Uttman, authors Mary Somerville, Maria Edgeworth, Jane Marcet, and Arabella Buckley struggled to have their science expertise recognized. They wrote accessible science books for wide audiences, then faced backlash for their financial success.[93] To navigate this environment, some women strategically effaced themselves by publishing anonymously, or, as Melanie Keene surveys, used small insects and fairies as their narrative voice.[94] In their small size, fairies or insects also resemble children, with their superior powers of observation. "It is true," says Sarah Stickney Ellis, the popular author of conduct literature for women and girls, "their sphere of observation" is "microscopic," but women possess "an acute vision directed to immediate objects."[95]

These children's science writers participated in a lower-prestige knowledge industry that lay somewhere between manual and intellectual labor, their writing accompanied by the work of raising children. Mary Elizabeth Budden describes what it was like to write as she "superintended the claims of a numerous family":

> The earliest hours of morning, stolen from her pillow, and the seasons of relaxation when her children played around her and she directed their sports, or settled their differences whilst placed at her writing desk; these were the *only* moments she allowed herself to devote to her pen. That under such circumstances she wrote at all may be ground for censure, perhaps for sarcasm; but let the importance of her motives extenuate her from the charge of presumption.[96]

She was not alone. Mary Sherwood wrote over three hundred tracts and stories for children, all the while following her husband, a captain in the military, around the globe, teaching pupils and her own children, and Maria Edgeworth kept her manuscripts between papers while directing numerous siblings. Recalling her struggle to write *Connexion* uninterrupted by her children, Mary Somerville reflects, "A man can always command his time under the plea of business, a woman has no such excuse."[97] These experiences complicate the position of women authors relative to the different classes of characters they represent, because they, too, depended on life experience over formal education, such as teaching children and practicing science in the home, to establish authorial expertise.

The most provocative moments in these children's books on mechanical philosophy thus arise when authors' personal circumstances challenge the division between intellectual and manual labor at the root of mechanical philosophy. Both women and working-class authors used their personal experience as a source of expert authority, as superior to theoretical knowledge or classical learning, a political move that the whole enterprise of learning through daily observation potentially legitimates. In her preface to *Heroes of the Laboratory and the Workshop*, Cecilia Lucy Brightwell relates her experience meeting an artisan in her city who inspired her to write a collection of biographies of men in the "mechanical arts."

> Some months ago, as I was walking in the suburbs of the city in which I live, I met an artisan returning from work, to whom, as he passed, I offered a little book. The man courteously thanked me, and extended his hand to receive the gift. As he did so, I was struck with the strange contrast between his broad, labour-stained palm and my own slight fingers, which nearly touched his, and I experienced a feeling of peculiar and deep interest as I looked upon the working-man, with whom I was thus, for a single instant only, brought in contact.

After the encounter, Brightwell determines to write a book for "working-men," with "the life-histories of men of their own class," who "deserved the respect and gratitude of mankind."[98] Like most inventor biographies, her collection also reached children. The frontispiece shows Robert Stephenson Senior teaching mechanical principles to baby George Stephenson, and a copy at the Baldwin Library passed hands "from Grandmama / To her dear grandson."

Brightwell's experience introduces principles that go against the Newtonian laws that govern this object exchange between the artisan's "labour-stained palm" and the author's "own slight fingers." Their hands are quite distinct in work and appearance, yet "for a single instant only, brought in contact" through the circulation of texts. The acknowledgement of Brightwell's own hand, grasping a book, suggests several

FIGURE 23. C. L. Brightwell, *Heroes of the Laboratory and the Workshop* (London: Routledge, Warnes & Routledge, 1859), frontispiece. Courtesy of Baldwin Library of Historical Children's Literature, George A. Smathers Libraries, University of Florida. Stephenson's father teaching the principles of mechanical philosophy to baby George Stephenson in a workshop, surrounded by books, tools, and a clock. The hatchet at baby's level may puzzle today's parents.

meanings: the charitable gift of literacy that cements vertical loyalty; the metaphor of a country walk, where chance encounters shape the mind; or the hand as a mechanical instrument, joined with a tool, the pen, as an emblem of intellectual and manual labor; or, a living interlocutor gesture, one that points from her book to a working man outside the book, calling attention to the construction of legible objects by many hands.

Conclusion

The science books produced by these authors reveal the class politics of learning by moving around material bodies—whether people, books, hands, pages, specimens, or toys. The study of mechanics makes child readers conscious of how they sense the physical world, originating ideas and generating self-identity. Mechanical philosophy promised children control over the material world and, by extension, over their own bodies, which are jointly governed by the same invariable principles. The concepts of property and literacy imbedded in these books informed material aspects of reading and play, activities described as alternatives to physical labor. By featuring children at play next to people at work, these books reveal how children's play was constructed in relation to wage labor, as a social privilege claimed by child readers who did not have to work for wages. While the elite families portrayed in mechanics books gradually expanded to include middle-class professionals, these movers, traders, and knowledge producers still used playful learning to confidently interpret their subjective experiences as universal facts.

Mechanics textbooks, biographies, and familiar science books were published throughout the Victorian period. However, several new genres and trends appeared mid-century, as middle-class families trained their children for respectable science and engineering professions. By this time, public opinion came round to the position that mass literacy and the dissemination of scientific information, far from threatening public order, posed solutions to social problems, although who exactly should decide curricula remained contested. A bellwether of changing attitudes, children's author and novelist Charlotte Yonge, writing at the height of Chartism, is wary of democratizing science in her novel *Abbeychurch* (1844). The protagonist, Elizabeth Woodbourne, the daughter of a local clergyman who "disapproved of Mechanics' Institutes in general," sneaks out with a tradesman's family to attend an institute event—a serious offence, since (as her sister warns) "Chartists, and Socialists, and horrible people, have been lecturing there!" Appalled by the vulgar lecturer, Elizabeth chastises herself for having "voluntarily meddled with a radical, leveling affair," and begins tutoring poor children to read and write at the local church-run school. But Yonge lived to regret her position, and, like Rev. Twaddleton, she came around to Mr. Seymore's point of view, as reflected in her 1872 reissue of *Abbeychurch*: "I have lived to see that it would have been wiser in the clergyman to have directed rather than obstructed the so-called 'march of intellect.'"[99] By 1870, James Lukin, author of amateur hobby books, could say with confidence, "There never was a time when a taste for practical mechanics was so general among boys as it is now. . . . This probably results from the giant strides which have been made of late years in mechanical enterprise, and the introduction of machinery into every department, as a means of saving labor and facilitating the production of the various necessaries of life."[100] However suspicious of useful knowledge, parents could either teach rational and practical mechanics to their children or let other social classes and institutions corner the knowledge responsible for changing their world. George Eliot's *The Mill on the Floss* (1860) depicts the consequences of such a miscalculation when Mr. Tulliver sends his son, Tom, to learn Latin instead of commerce. Unable to read the laws that govern nature and human development alike, Tom drowns when the flooded Floss breaks its poorly designed dam.

Despite these changes, Victorian boys' books that teach mechanical philosophy through the lives of engineers still used play, recast as tinkering, as a gatekeeping strategy. In their workshops, breaking things is reconfigured as failing up for white middle-class boys. Harry and Tim from *The Boy Engineers* describe their first efforts sharpening their tools as "a long series of failures; for at first we rather blunted than sharpened them, . . . however, we triumphed over this difficulty, as we did over others of a more serious character."[101] Victorian science and engineering books thus created some of the first representations of curious boys learning resilience through failure, a process from which girl characters were largely excluded.

CHAPTER 3

"The Empire of Man over Material Things"

Children's Books on Manufacturing and Trade

During the first half of the nineteenth century, publishers produced a variety of attractive textbooks, fictional stories, periodical articles, travel literature, games, and toys about political economy and manufacturing. These children's industrial media stress the moral and practical urgency of learning these subjects to heal the "two nations" and advance British commerce. George Dodd in *Days at the Factories; or, the Manufacturing Industry of Great Britain Described* (1843), laments children's ignorance about the basic origins of everyday articles. "The bulk of the inhabitants of a great city, such as London, have very indistinct notions of the means whereby the necessaries, the comforts, or the luxuries of life are furnished." The problem, according to Dodd, is that privileged children live geographically sequestered from the families who make their goods, using money to buy things without really knowing the people who make them. "The simple fact, that he who has money can command every variety of exchangeable produce, seems to act as a veil which hides the producer from the consumer." Once children raise the veil, they discover that many of their toys are produced in London by other children: "Could we dive into the alleys and narrow streets at the east end of London, we should probably find many whole families—father, mother, and children—employed in making toys under their own poor roof."[1] He then describes how everyday things are made, using nonfiction articles adapted from *The Penny Magazine* and organized into a series of family daytrips to a Brewery, the London Marble-Works, a Rope and Sail-Cloth Factory, and so forth, which allow child readers to travel virtually into places usually closed from view. The volume is lavishly illustrated with detailed technical drawings used "extensively" in advanced courses at the "Engineering class of King's College."[2] The textbook covers both the macro-level, philosophical knowledge of an economic system and the local, practical knowledge of making things.

Children's books like this one teach mechanical literacy by providing an empowering, comprehensive survey of essential trades, making invisible economic forces seem tangible and easy to navigate. Covering a wide range of industries, *Days at the Factory* offers a panoramic view of the British economy. London serves as a microcosm of global trade while a child sitting at home surrounded by practical examples of the very goods described by the essays can access all of London's industries condensed in its pages, each trade neatly reduced to a single workday's visit. Just as literacy aids could make alphabetical literacy more tangible, the reader's domestic environment could make economic principles more concrete. Children who acquire mechanical literacy—who understand how things are *manufactured, distributed, and exchanged*—elevate themselves from workers in economic systems to active participants who can read trade networks and apply general economic principles across a variety of contexts.

Like mechanical philosophy, political economy is the scientific study of matter in motion. According to Maxine Berg, the subject transformed in the early nineteenth century into a "unified body of theory" with "a consolidated set of principles so systematic in nature as to be called a science," while Eleanor Courtemanche points out that Adam Smith used the phrase "invisible hand," now associated with capitalist markets, in *The History of Astronomy* (1795), if sardonically, to describe the divinely regulated movement of heavenly bodies.[3] As Dodd's publisher, Charles Knight, explains in *Knowledge Is Power* (1855), a textbook on political economy for "*the young*," children should learn "the universal laws which regulate the exchanges of mankind," and they should do so through observation. Knight's preface praises the accessibility of economics, approached "scientifically," and begins by quoting Rousseau: "It requires a great deal of philosophy to observe once what is seen every day."[4] Following convention, Knight opens with an epigram of Francis Bacon: "The empire of man over material things has for its only foundation the sciences and the arts." Although concerned with political economy and manufacturing, Knight and Dodd use the discourse of natural philosophy to create a class divide between economic theory and everyday experience, analogous to the distinction between theoretical and practical mechanics. A philosophical understanding of economic principles provides leisured children with a different kind of mechanical literacy from what is practiced by "whole families" who assemble toys in the "narrow streets" of London. Yet privileged readers depend on those same laboring families as sources of information to construct a macro-level view of the British economy. Accounting for political economy's appeal for working-class readers, R. K. Webb explains that "political economy was put forward as a science" concerned with "the natural laws by which the economy and society operated," laws as unchanging as "the conclusions of Newton." In this science, everyday experiences of poverty could be dismissed as the parochial viewpoints of people who could not understand these laws.[5]

Two class-specific ways of knowing the material world thus come together in these media: the privileged reader's manipulation of domestic objects, including books and toys, and the working person's labor while making these objects. Children's media about manufacturing call attention to the material affordances of print media in order to provide virtual work experience for children who do not work; these media appropriate working-class practical knowledge into middle-class educational forms (books, toys) and spaces (nurseries, classrooms, exhibitions, and homes). In these books and games, working children are overwhelmingly portrayed as sources of authentic knowledge serving as edifying examples of economic principles, technical processes, or affecting moral quandaries. Consequently, the ability to move and manipulate matter—knowledge usually associated with manual laborers, machine operators, or skilled artisans—seemingly belongs to more privileged children, whose education gives them the power to observe, collect, and record knowledge about industry, which could inform government policies or labor-saving inventions. Industrial media socialized wealthier children of leisure to self-identify as agents in economic systems—as consumers who use their purchasing power as leverage and as knowledge-makers who, in Knight's words, expand "the empire of man over material things."

For the purposes of this chapter, I focus on "production stories," or stories of how everyday things are made. Production stories are the most common narrative form in children's industrial media of this era, and one that remains immensely popular today with books by Maud and Miska Petersham, David Macaulay, DK Publishing's picture books, and video series like *How Its Made* and *Some Assembly Required*. I begin with an overview of class, gender, and racial hierarchies in production stories, analyzing how children's agency in production stories depends on emerging beliefs about consumption popularized by abolitionists. Next, I show how the manipulable affordances of children's media—game pieces, pull-tabs, travel maps, indexes, and specimen boxes—enhance a white middle-class reader's sense of control over complex economic networks and technical processes. Through interlocutor gestures that direct readers' attention to commonplace household objects, child readers connect their domestic learning spaces with far-flung geographic locations where work takes place, bringing colonial trade into the home. The second half of the chapter examines the desire for personal, unmediated interactions between consumers and the people who make their goods. Production stories feature formulaic fictional episodes in which wealthy families visit cottages and factories to watch people at work, then exchange gifts and purchases directly with workers. These gifts or purchases bring characters of different classes physically together in mutual aid, but they also reinforce clear social hierarchies between children who make things to earn wages and those who manipulate things to learn. I conclude with a close reading of Jane Marcet's Willy stories, a fiction series that considers the ethical imperative for children to interact personally with people who make the necessities of life.

The Production Story and Child Consumer Agency

Production stories became popular with the rise of consumer culture in the late eighteenth century. Familiar home items used by middle-class children, such as cotton and linen clothing, printed books, porcelain dishes, and silver utensils, were made from globally sourced raw materials, worked in stages by hundreds of people living across multiple continents. In Britain, people of all stations increased their consumption of sugar, tea, coffee, cotton, rum, chocolate, and tobacco, integrating these commodities into daily domestic rituals such as tea-time, which signified female refinement. During the same era, almost three million people were transported to the Americas aboard British or British American ships, roughly half of all enslaved Africans. The West Indies plantation system of slave labor made tropical commodities affordable to consumers, including British children, raising ethical questions about their participation in global economies.[6] While the children's production story promised to explain the origins of everyday household goods, making complex trade networks seem rational and easily grasped, they often detailed processes and technologies without addressing colonial violence and labor exploitation, providing limited information disguised as full disclosure.

The production stories created for children in the nineteenth century typically cover multiple industries in a single volume, or dedicate individual volumes in a series to each commodity's "story" or "progress." The juvenile library of John Wallis produced several commodity biographies of this kind, such as *The Progress of Wool*; *Harvest Home, or the Progress of Wheat*; and *The Progress of the Dairy* (ca. 1805–1820). Another Wallis series on coffee, sugar, and cotton (1820s), delivered in fake-Creole doggerel by "Cuffee," a formerly enslaved Black man, explains agriculture in the British West Indies, with boardgame adaptations of these books available for purchase. Some production stories follow commodities as they travel from far-flung locations to local shops; others do the reverse, following child consumers who leave their homes to visit local artisan workshops or tour industrial regions, where they observe workshops, factories, farms, mines, construction sites, or shipyards. John Harris published several by Rev. Isaac Taylor, a self-educated Dissenting pastor and engraver, and father of poets Ann and Jane Taylor, who wrote "Twinkle Twinkle Little Star." After Taylor's death, Harris began advertising Rev. Taylor's books, *Scenes of British Wealth* (1823), *Scenes of Commerce* (1828), and an it-narrative production story, *The Biography of a Brown Loaf* (1829), as part of his "Little Library for tarry-at-home-travellers," which offered "a familiar introduction to various branches of useful knowledge," and included *The Mine*

(1830), *The Ship* (1830), and *The Forest* by son Jeffreys Taylor, and *The Garden* by Samuel Goodrich.[7] For the youngest children, simple chapbooks display traditional artisans (John and Elizabeth Newbery's *Jack of All Trades*) and picturesque country labor (Mary Elliott's *Rural Employments*), suggesting continuity across generations through comforting depictions of dairymaids, ploughmen, basketweavers, and blacksmiths. For older boys, Victorian illustrated gift volumes, such as *The Boy's Book of Industrial Information* (1859), which boasts 370 engravings by the Dalziel brothers, explain manufacturing professions in great detail, surveying engineering wonders, agriculture, mining, and manufactories.[8]

In its simplest form, the plot arc of a production story follows a commodity's global circulation, from raw material to finished product and

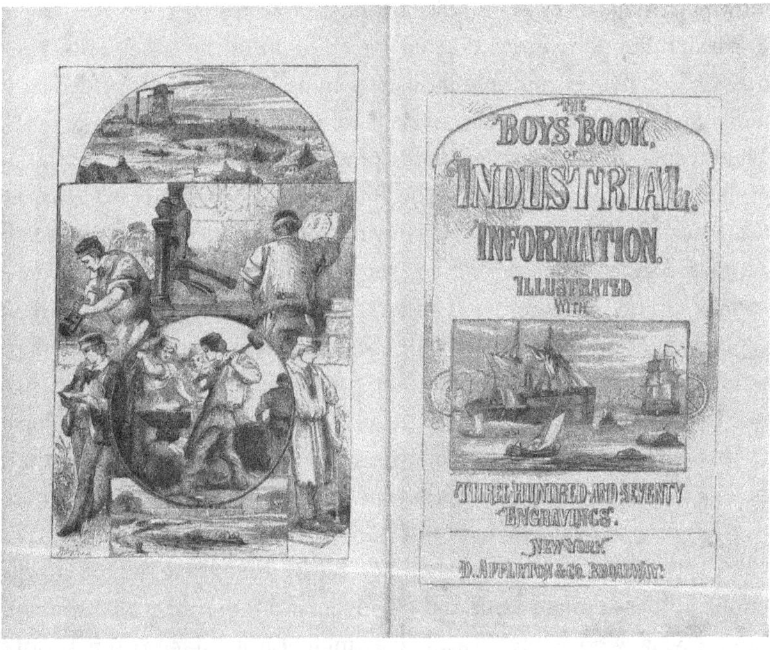

FIGURE 24. Elisha Noyce, *The Boy's Book of Industrial Information* (New York, D. Appleton & Co., 1860). The same illustrations appear on London editions by Ward & Lock from 1858 and 1859. Courtesy of the Baldwin Library of Historical Children's Literature, George A. Smathers Libraries, University of Florida. The frontispiece features twin icons of progress, the printing press and the forge, flanked by a boy reading a book and a navvy wielding a pickaxe, suggesting a partnership between physical and intellectual labor, performed by youth of different classes. On the title page, a steamship navigates between sailing ships, signifying technological progress in trade.

purchase. In this respect, the production story overlaps with nineteenth-century it-narratives, which, according to Lynn Festa, follow the progress of inanimate objects, such as a doll, coin, or pincushion, until that adventuresome object reunites with its first, most worthy owner.[9] Production stories, however, ultimately reward a worthy consumer who eats, wears, uses, and enjoys the thing other people made, incorporating the product into their body. To take one example, *The History of a Pound of Sugar* from William Newman's *Rhymes and Pictures* begins in the West Indies and concludes outside an English sweet shop, where "The Pound of Sugar tarries here, / And waits your purchase, Reader, dear." The child readers' enjoyment of the story, and their vicarious enjoyment of sugary sweets, positions readers as enthusiastic consumers within a global economy. Successive titles (bound as chapters) in Newman's series do the same for bread, cotton, tea, coal, and gold. *The History of a Cup of Tea* begins on a Chinese tea plantation and ends at the reader's table, where "At length we see it here, / Upon our own Tea Table placed," and *The History of a Golden Sovereign* begins "amid Australia's fertile hills" and concludes in the reader's pocket, with a blessing: "May We have ever some to spend, / And some to save or help a friend."[10] This concluding rhyme for Newman's series demonstrates how the genre passes moral judgement on children's consumption, either by naming their complicity in suspect labor practices, or, in this case, by reassuring readers that everyone shares the economic benefits of global commerce.

Through this repetitive formula, British readers living in the imperial metropole discover their unexpected communion with people working around the world, many of them nonwhite colonial subjects, and they conclude by celebrating this connection (mythologized as mutually beneficial), by eating sugar, drinking tea, or spending gold coins. Although repackaged and widely circulated to readers of different ages, races, and economic circumstances, such stories are designed for white children of leisure, who enjoy protection from places where difficult labor occurs. The surprise and satisfaction of the narrative hinges on preserving the reader's ignorance about the work performed in these far-flung locations. The conclusion asks readers to self-identify as the final beneficiaries of these products—as a child who rewards the deserving poor with their purchases. Everything is made for them, to meet their needs, representing an imperialist worldview underwritten by deep anthropocentrism. By comparison, laboring people and the enslaved are put on display alongside the product, yet few production stories provide readers with enough context to question the conditions of labor portrayed in the story. Newman's series, for instance, does not clarify whether the Black workers shown harvesting sugar and cotton are enslaved, since this information might deter readers from joyfully consuming their food and clothing. The result is a practical lesson in applied sciences and political economy that, with notable exceptions, avoids disclosing ecological destruction, labor exploitation, and racial violence.

Encouraging identification with consumers rather than with workers empowers more privileged child readers by subordinating working people, colonial subjects, and the enslaved, whose position as sources of knowledge and labor aligns them with the animated commodities they produce. This identification creates an uncomfortable analogy between consuming goods and cannibalism, widely deployed by abolitionists.[11] Child readers are invited to take the position of Enlightened observers by identifying with child characters representing the intended readers, who tour centers of industry, using broad powers of surveillance similar to those of industrial managers. In one example, the cover illustration for the section on sugar in William Newman's series depicts white English children watching a magic lantern show. Projected by one of the children, the show's title slide introduces Newman's first commodity, "Sugar Cane," as if the book itself were a series of lantern slides. These children's control over the narrative of sugar making (using a visual technology, no less) corresponds to the power of plantation overseers shown in the book. One page spread depicts Black workers planting cane, focalized through the "Planter" in the foreground, who "walks around / With eagle glance, and all controls."[12] Production stories like this one give child readers a "survey" of a manufacturing process using visual strategies to suggest that knowledge implies ownership of land, resources, labor, even human beings. Illustration conventions used to represent Black workers as passive victims by averting their gaze or omitting individuating details, further enhance the reader's sense of power through surveillance.[13] As a result, child readers are invited to identify with the white overseer rather than with the cane harvesters.

Production stories that follow human characters, rather than commodities, focalize events through the eyes of children whose affluence

FIGURES 25–26. William Newman, *Rhymes and Pictures: The History of a Pound of Sugar, A Quartern Loaf, A Cotton Bale, A Cup of Tea, A Shuttle of Coals, and A Golden Sovereign*, (London: Griffith & Farran, successors to J. Newbery, 1860), 1, 3. Courtesy of the Baldwin Library of Historical Children's Literature, George A. Smathers Libraries, University of Florida. The narrative focalization is indicated visually by placing the "Planter" in the foreground.

permits them to travel around, watching people at work, as a form of moral edification and technical instruction. The girls in Charlotte Smith's *Rural Walks* (1795), for instance, learn the mutual dependence between wealthy families and hard-working cottagers when they stop by "a neat cottage" to watch a "decently dressed woman," the wife of a flax-dresser. Asking the exemplary woman to "bring out some flax in its raw state," the book's teacher-mentor, Mrs. Woodfield, "described the process of making it into tow, fit for spinning, and then made each of the girls endeavor to spin a thread." The girls then visit the papermill, where they "saw the whole operation of making several kinds of paper." To conclude, Mrs. Woodfield asks the children to assemble a production story in their minds of the entire process, "from the stalk of the flax they had seen, bearing a blue and simple flower trembling on its slender summit, though all its changes and modifications, till it contributes to make a sheet of paper."[14] *Rural Walks* is typical of how didactic literature integrates a production story into a series of excursions devoted to various rational pursuits, with both technical and moral instruction joined together. The episode teaches about papermaking while transforming Caroline, a dissipated London cousin, into "a rational and thinking being," by teaching her "to think" about fellow "creatures whose feelings and necessities were the same as her own."[15]

This combination of moral didacticism with technical education first appeared in popular French education texts that influenced the British rationalists. Abbé Pluche's eight volume children's encyclopedia, *Le Spectacle de la Nature* (1732–1743), and Stéphanie-Félicité de Genlis's novel of education, *Adèle et Théodore, ou, Lettres sur l'éducation* (1782), both depict fictional children who visit artisan workshops, where they observe skilled labor and try simple tasks, before they return home inspired to build huts and play with carpentry sets. As Cynthia J. Koepp argues of Pluche's *Spectacle*, these workshop visits encouraged wealthy readers to sympathize with artisans and admire their skills, but there is a fine line between valuing workers and appropriating their knowledge.[16] While empowering young readers through child-centered pedagogies, the same episodes casually suggest that readers assume what Simon Schaffer calls the "view of the machine," a managerial surveillance position modeled by French Encyclopedists, who watched, documented, and widely circulated methods that artisans guarded as trade secrets, so that readers might produce labor-saving machines.[17] If their prefaces are any indication, children's authors wrote about workshop visits expecting some child readers would become inventors and managers, who make knowledge about the people who make things.

Children's books enhance the privileged reader's sense of visual access to working bodies by couching child characters as travelers (or rural walkers), who broadly survey entire industries and directly witness their operations. Through a grand tour of industry, they acquire systemic knowledge that distinguishes their own mechanical literacy from the manual skills of people they observe. As Meredith Bak explains, "The power to visually surveil, discern, or scrutinize the social and material world," taught to children through visual technologies, "was one strategy that members of the economically and socially unstable middle class used to fix their own positions."[18] The same lessons designed to teach cross-class sympathy thus teach child readers to assume what Nicholas Mirzoeff calls the "right to look," an unreciprocated privilege to watch and report, used to enforce social categories of race, gender, and class.[19] Workers who appear in production stories are often one-dimensional figures who demonstrate the technical processes and moral principles of the marketplace. Technical drawings provided in these children's books show disembodied hands holding tools, headless torsos manipulating machinery, or small faceless figures populating an endless factory floor. Such visual conventions signal that readers should identify with factory managers who oversee work rather than with the workers themselves. Even fictional stories that integrate production story episodes feature the virtuous poor, like the "decently dressed woman" in *Rural Walks*, whose exemplarity consists of performing their task with skill and pleasure, without ailments or exhaustion, and without any suggestion of pressing personal needs. All of these details empower child readers at the expense of those they watch. Like Mrs. Woodfield's charges, readers can watch other people work as a kind of educational play precisely because they do not have to work.

Slavery and Abolition in Production Stories

The power dynamic between consumer-readers and the workers they watch owes much to antislavery literature. According to Lawrence B.

Glickman, abolitionists depended on a new market-oriented worldview that regarded consumption as the driving force behind global economies. Boycotters of slave-produced goods who self-identified as "conscious consumers" initially demanded pious abstention from tainted foods and fashions, arguing the consumer's addictive, unrestrained appetite for cotton, sugar, rum, and tobacco created the conditions for chattel slavery to flourish. This belief in the power and complicity of consumers is captured by the causal relationship outlined in Thomas Cooper's 1791 abolitionist pamphlet: "If sugar were not consumed it would not be imported—if it were not imported it would not be cultivated, if it were not cultivated there would be an end of the Slave Trade, so that the consumer of sugar is really the prime mover—the grand cause of all the horrible injustice." And likewise, William Fox, founder of the Sunday school movements, contended that slave owners are "virtually the agents of the consumer."[20] Abolitionists, Glickman explains, "identified consumers as perpetrators of far-flung and morally hideous crimes" but also as powerful agents who could "change the world by exerting market power."[21] According to Charlotte Sussman, exerting influence over the market through "consumerist abstention" was "the particular province of women," a strategy made possible by "the globalization of capital."[22]

Several production stories ask child readers to use their purchasing power to end slavery. Priscilla Wakefield's *A Family Tour through the British Empire* (1804) includes a call to boycott sugar following the family's visit to Bristol's sugar distilleries. Fellow Quaker abolitionist Amelia Alderson Opie wrote an antislavery production story, *The Black Man's Lament; or, How to Make Sugar* (1826), which unexpectedly morphs from a factual account of growing cane sugar into an exposé of the slave trade, delivered by a Black man abducted from Africa. Such books addressed children as consumers capable of making ethical selections in the marketplace, encouraging readers to sympathize with people in far-away places and use their purchasing power to intercede, at a distance, on their behalf. By granting consumers greater culpability than slave-owners, abolitionist texts normalized thinking about everyday purchases in moral terms beyond the context of free-labor produce. Since production stories include depictions of labor in multiple industries, performed by free, unfree, and enslaved persons, they readily transposed beliefs about the power of consumption across various labor contexts.

From cane fields to cotton factories, children were complicit in creating the working conditions endured by people they could not see and would never meet. Thus when Willy, the seven-year-old protagonist in Jane Marcet's *The Seasons* (1832–34), discovers the apprenticed chimney sweep hired to clean the kitchen chimney is underfed and unpaid, he gives the boy his breakfast and informs his father, who declares a boycott: "I shall never allow a chimney of this house to be swept by a boy again."[23] Father describes a gadget with long-handled brushes that makes it possible to clean chimneys without employing children. This device was widely advertised by the Society for Superseding the Necessity of Climbing Boys, established in 1803 after the pattern of abolition societies. They called for homeowners to boycott chimney sweeps and offered a reward for "an invention as shall clense Chimnies" with "ease, convenience, and cheapness" but "without having recourse to Climbing Boys, with a view to reduce their numbers."[24] A device invented by "Mr. Smith," matching the one described by the father in *The Seasons*, features prominently on the cover of their circulating pamphlets. This episode resembles strategies that Quaker authors Wakefield and Opie used to elicit participation from children in the sugar boycotts.

While few texts explicitly support boycotts, children's books on manufacturing more often express the moral goodness of trade and the power of children to reward the virtuous poor through their purchases. These positive sentiments agree with conscious consumers who eventually concluded that market participation, rather than abstention, harnessed the capitalist forces of supply and demand to end slavery through competition from free-labor produce. As Mimi Sheller explains, abolitionists bequeathed to fair trade movements their faith in "alternative economic networks" where "both consumers and producers would be pious, prudent, and above all, mutually human in their striving to be humane."[25] In children's production stories, then, exchanging goods is depicted as a form of cross-cultural, cross-class cooperation, made necessary by the division of labor and the dispersion of natural resources across the globe. "Commerce unites men of all countries, and scatters plenty and variety over the earth," explains the Darton's *Jack of All Trades* (1805), an infant's book with rhymes and pictures of printers, basketweavers, smiths, and bakers. The specialization of work creates the perfect balance of interdependence and personal freedom:

> Society resembles a bee-hive, where, in producing a store of sweets, all are employed—all live cheerfully—and whilst each individual works for the general good, the whole community works for him. The baker supplies the bricklayer, the gardener, and the tailor, with breads, and they, in return, provide him with shelter, food, and raiment: thus, though each person is dependent on the other, all are independent."[26]

Here trade seems less about capitalist competition than mutual care, and when this argument is directed toward children it adopts the futuristic optimism of millennialism. Similarly, *A History of Useful Arts and Manufactures* (1822) ascribes ethical outcomes to the division of labor itself as a divine instrument through which different skills and abilities individuate people while knitting them together: "The Almighty has dispensed his blessings over the earth, in order that we might need each other's help, and thus be reminded that we are all of the same family."[27] These references to a human "family" applies a similar discourse as abolitionist literature, but for the innocuous purpose of reassuring readers that they can safely purchase questionably sourced goods and feel good about themselves in the process. Such books teach that everyone is dependent on everyone else, and we offer one another friendly mutual aid through our everyday consumption of goods. As one fictional teacher explains to her pupil, "A piece of cloth passes through one hundred different hands before it is ready for use. I guess, we do not always consider this labour when we put on a new coat, or discard an old one."[28] These reflections acknowledge heightened consumer anxieties over the provenance of goods, but ultimately reassure children that pleasurable consumption is ethical.

Manipulating Trade through Movable Books

While empowering readers to influence events from afar, production stories, in their very function, remind readers of their social and geographical separation from the people who make their basic life necessities. For this very reason, children's production stories dramatize moments of physical intimacy with objects, such as when children touch a product at the store or when they exchange gifts and purchases with working children. This focus on touching goods and meeting workers is one way that production stories tap into experiential learning practices to create an immersive reading experience where the physicality of embodied reading provides a proxy for presence at the actual scene of work. The child reader's paradoxical closeness to work (and protective distance from it) makes the children's production story especially concerned with the manipulable affordances of books. Such books instruct child users how to manipulate them, or they direct readers to objects in their environment in order to overcome the book's limitations as a narrative substitute for life experience. The book's physical presence offers a tangible link with the world of circulating goods and a physical manifestation of invisible market forces.

Child users handle their books or toys as a substitute for direct contact with the locations and people who make things. To give one salient example, *Dean's Dissolving Pictures of Things Worth Knowing: Iron, Diamond, Coal, Slate, Silver, Whale* (1862) represents six natural resources with moveable pull-tab illustrations. Each page first shows a scene familiar to the intended reader, for instance, a boy and his family gathered around the coal-burning fireplace in a fashionable living room, the table set with evening refreshments. Pulling a tab raises the Venetian blind mechanism, revealing a surprising scene initially "hidden" from a privileged child: men at work with pickaxes in an underground coal mine, wearing only pants, while women "hurriers" on their knees pull loaded carts, or "skips," up the rail tracks through narrow shafts. According to Hannah Field, the reveal of these moveable books is intended to recall the dissolving views used in magic lantern shows, in which one slide image slowly fades as the other appears, inviting viewers to conclude a link between the images that depends on commonly held associations.[29] Underneath the coal image, a rhyme pronounces the universal benefits of the industry ("Coals are from mines by manual toil obtained / To all how useful, when their aid we've gained!") and gestures to global trade and conquest (Coals "Create the Steam, that speeds the railway train, / And urge our ships across the pathless main.").[30] With a quick pull, the child user easily summons the miners, collapsing geographical distance between home and mines and between the boy and the colliers. Jacqueline Reid-Walsh compares these dissolving pictures, which provide prescriptive, repetitive revelations, unfavorably against more open-ended moveable books.[31] In this case, the book's limited affordances conscript readers into the class position of consumers, with the pull-tab functioning as a tangible representation of manipulating the economy.

A procession of these pull-tab images reinforces the asymmetrical power of reader-consumers over workers. Each illustration shows a product lavishly enjoyed by fashionably dressed consumers, drawn aside to reveal the difficult physical labor or disturbing violence required for its production: a rail suspension bridge reveals an iron refinery; a school classroom reveals slate mines; a lamplit room reveals whalers spearing a whale; and, finally, the Crown Jewels reveal enslaved diamond miners. This last and most unsettling juxtaposition of extreme wealth with subjugation still implies, rather dubiously, that diamond mining is mutually beneficial, since enslaved minors can earn their freedom: "When one of value great a slave obtains, / His future freedom, as reward, he gains."[32] The source of both this anecdote and the illustration is the British mineralist John Mawe's *Travels in the Interior of Brazil* (1812), a book for adults that provides a longer account of mining along the Jequitinhonha River in Brazil, where he reports over one thousand enslaved persons washed diamonds while bent over troughs from before sunrise until after sunset.

FIGURE 27. *Dean's Dissolving Pictures of Things Worth Knowing: Iron, Diamond, Coal, Slate, Silver, Whale*, (London: Dean & Son, 1865), n.p. Courtesy of the Baldwin Library of Historical Children's Literature, George A. Smathers Libraries, University of Florida.

He describes the disciplinary structures used to force enslaved persons to work and the deformities caused by working bent over, as shown in the engraving copied for *Dissolving Pictures of Things Worth Knowing*. The positive caption in the moveable book, however, discourages readers from considering the tortuous conditions on display, while the pull-tab mechanism deceptively suggests to readers the truthful immediacy of a direct witness account.[33]

The pull-tab is one instance of how moving a book gives readers the sensation of accessing labor in far-away places, but common maps and indexes also provide a physical proxy for trade by encouraging readers to riffle through their books, exploring pages as they might explore objects in their home environment. Mary Elizabeth Budden calls her production story, *Key to Knowledge; or, Things in Common Use* (1814), an "easy dictionary" for "the young pupil" or an aid for parents when children ask questions about household objects, reprinted in expanded editions for decades. Modeling these learning behaviors, Mother invites Helen and Louisa "to learn things" around the fireside, in a "pleasant chit-chat way," before "visiting the several manufactories." Louisa agrees, "That would be charming!"[34] The fireplace provides a point of departure for the family, as furnishings inspire outdoor excursions and the parties reconvene to report their findings. Implicitly, the same kind of exploration could happen for readers, who explore Budden's "easy dictionary" in response to what they see in their home. Likewise, Rev. Taylor's *Scenes of Commerce* (1828), appropriately subtitled, "Where does it come from? / Answered / for the amusement and instruction of tarry-at-home-travelers," depicts siblings who stay at home, where they ask questions about their breakfast table edibles and living room furnishings. The book itself is organized according to a reader's home and daily routine, beginning with "the breakfast" (tea, coffee, sugar), followed by "the withdrawing room" (mahogany, glass, carpets, curtains), and "the wardrobe" (silk, cotton, lace, wool, furs, feathers). Reflecting on her tea and sugar, fourteen-year-old Emma confesses, "I often feel myself quite puzzled, if I try to think, 'where it comes from'" for "almost every thing one sees, or uses." Her mother agrees that such descriptions amount to virtual travel; they might "be carried, as it were, to the countries where these things grow, or are produced by the skill of man." The next morning her father brings a map to breakfast for the children to locate the geographic origins of their edibles. The family demonstrates for readers how to use home objects to reference books and maps, then use these printed texts to "travel" to places of work. Maps and indexes thus function like the pull-tab from *Dissolving Pictures of Things Worth Knowing* by connecting consumers to far-flung locations through the global trade networks legible in everyday domestic objects.

The practice of reading production stories nonlinearly, in response to objects, likely inspired publishers to provide more indexes. Earlier nineteenth-century production stories tend to emphasize a through narrative, such as a traveling family, which encourages front-to-back reading for plot. But a 1798 copy of *A Dialogue between a Lady and Her Pupils, Describing a Journey through England and Wales* contains an index penned into the inner cover by a reader (likely an adult, from the clean script), listing household objects with corresponding page numbers. The amendment proved prescient. Later editions of *A Journey* provide not only a fold-out map but an index of domestic objects. Similarly, Rev. Taylor's *Scenes of British Wealth* (1823), narrated as a family tour of Britain, was republished in an 1826 edition with an index of manufactured items. Such changes suggest that over time, reading practices inspired publishers to add features to make nonlinear browsing easier. Taylor's *Scenes of Commerce* is the logical end of this evolution from travel literature to tarry-at-home travelers, with the book entirely reorganized by room, according to a middle-class home's geography. Such indexing calls readers' attention to their embodied presence, seated at home—presumably, one with reference books, manufactured furnishings, and tropically sourced edibles—all of which children may flip through and move about to facilitate their own lessons on trade.

Books indexed by room position the home itself as a remediated book. The Victorian sitting room is an index of the world, an *Orbis Sensualium Pictus* stocked with furniture, china, books, tea service, and decorative ornaments, which provide tangible representations of places where these objects are manufactured or their materials are sourced. Taking this device to its logical extreme, the aptly named *Things In-doors* (1870) endlessly catalogues "not only those Common Objects of everyday life strictly falling under this head, but all those articles of Food, Industry, Science, and Art, which we talk of and explain to the young round the fire Indoors." The book delivers with 480 small illustrations of chairs, couches, and candelabras, but also of people making wool and linen, or coining

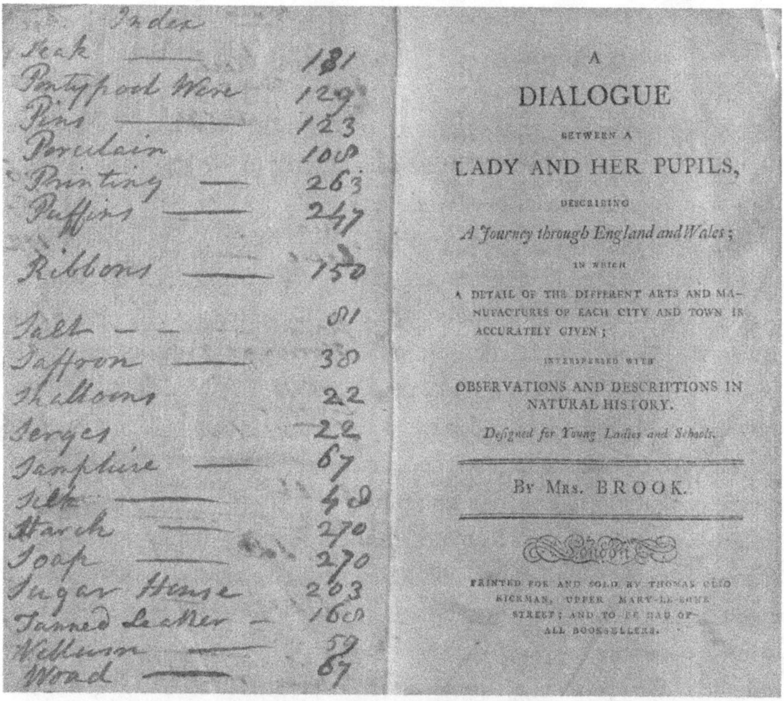
Index
Peak — 181
Pontypool Ware — 129
Pins — 123
Porcelain 100
Printing — 263
Puffins — 247
Ribbons — 750
Salt — — 81
Saffron — 380
Shalloons 22
Serges 22
Samphire — 67
Silk — 40
Starch — 270
Soap — 270
Sugar House 203
Tanned Leather — 160
Wilton — 59
Wood — 67

A
DIALOGUE
BETWEEN A
LADY AND HER PUPILS,
DESCRIBING
A Journey through England and Wales;
IN WHICH
A DETAIL OF THE DIFFERENT ARTS AND MANUFACTURES OF EACH CITY AND TOWN IS ACCURATELY GIVEN;
INTERSPERSED WITH
OBSERVATIONS AND DESCRIPTIONS IN NATURAL HISTORY.
Designed for Young Ladies and Schools.

BY MRS. BROOK.

PRINTED FOR AND SOLD BY THOMAS CLIO RICKMAN, UPPER MARY-LE-BONE STREET; AND TO BE HAD OF ALL BOOKSELLERS.

FIGURE 28. Mrs. Brook, *A Dialogue between a Lady and Her Pupils, Describing a Journey Through England and Wales; in which a Detail of the Different Arts and Manufactures of Each City and Town Is Accurately Given . . . Designed for Young Ladies and Schools* (London: Thomas Clio Rickman, 1798). Courtesy of the Baldwin Library of Historical Children's Literature, George A. Smathers Libraries, University of Florida. One of several flyleaves where a user penned an index for quickly finding information on common household items.

money at the Royal Mint, items arranged in lists with short descriptive passages. If these are not enough, there is, unbelievably, a second volume, *Things Out-of-doors* (ca. 1870). Another version, *Little Ladders to Learning* (1869), with 750 illustrations, provides lists of objects along the tops of the pages, allowing young children to thumb through the book until they find what they want.[35] The indexed production story brings industry close to home, but also mediates access to scenes of commerce through domestic objects. It promises readers at once the attractive authenticity and playfulness of learning directly from things and the authority and protection of learning from texts. Such books bring readers close enough to commerce to engage their interest while shielding children from fully confronting racial violence and class conflict.

CHAPTER 3

Mapping Colonial Violence in the Home

Victorian production stories with girl protagonists who learn around the fireplace from their mothers are especially likely to use the home to teach about commerce. The cultural work performed by these books is the same as industrial fiction by Charlotte Elizabeth Tonna and Francis Trollope, which Susan Zlotnick argues used everyday objects purchased by middle-class women to reimagining the factory as an extension of the home. "By creating a private world either littered with or sustained by objects manufactured in the public world," Tonna and Trollope "lay bare the submerged connections between the factory and the family." As consumers, women are "directly implicated in a system of economic exchange and hence economic exploitation," but their complicity is obscured while the domestic sphere appears protected from and morally superior to the public sphere of market competition. Mimi Sheller describes a similar dynamic in the abolitionist free-produce movement, which located "prime agency" in women consumers, whose domestic purchases signaled their embodied morality.[36] One production story collection for girls, Caroline Amelia Halsted's *Investigation; or Travels in the Boudoir* (ca. 1835), lectures young women to stop yearning for foreign travel and "to secure to themselves those happy homes, which they cannot be too early taught to value," for "there is NOTHING ON THIS EARTH LIKE A HAPPY ENGLISH HOME!" The purpose of the book's lengthy chapters on tapestry, paper hangings, domestic porcelain, foreign porcelain, plumes, and (requiring their own chapter) feathers, is to "prove to young persons of active imaginations" that they can find "pleasant variety and real entertainment" without traveling anywhere.[37] The volume begins with Agnes complaining to her mother about her desire to see the world, which prompts Mamma to suggest exploring objects in their room. Mamma produces quite sophisticated history and science lessons spiced with commentary on British superiority as manifest in its manufactured goods, religion, and personal freedoms. Soon Agnes is a convert to domestic bliss: "To-day we are to examine the inside of the chiffonier," she enthuses, "and I am glad of it; because I have often wondered, dear mamma, why you prize the old-fashioned china within it so highly." In Agnes's house, all furniture is legible, and the storied objects carve memories in the mind, for "examples of such objects," Mamma explains, "are as letters of the alphabet, which lead us to the acquirement of a new language." Agnes's home is full of furniture that provides little memory palaces, from "the contents of a little porcelain box" to a writing desk that discloses the history of "employing signs for well-known and visible things."[38] By including the invention of writing among home industries, *Travels in the Boudoir* is quite deliberate about equating household rooms with the book itself, as two kinds of information technologies, whose indexed, manipulable pages organize objects and illuminate their meanings. Presumably Agnes finishes these lessons equipped to select purchases for her home. Understanding the origins of these objects distinguishes Agnes's consumption practices from the thoughtless rapid accumulation of upward mobility.

There is something contradictory about these domestic production stories, where imagined travel brings colonialism into the home but hides colonial violence by relocating the scene of observation from fields and factories to kitchens and parlors. For readers informed about slavery and colonization, descriptive passages of domestic objects contain traces of erasure. One it-narrative by Samuel Goodrich, *Enterprise, Industry, and Art of Man* (1845), begins with the author's dream vision of living room objects "animated with life, and endowed with the gift of speech." Lumbering forward, the piano forte "informed me that its rosewood covering was violently torn from its birth-place in the forests of Brazil; its massive legs of pine grew in the wilds of Maine; the iron which formed its frame was dug from a mine in Sweden," and, in short, that "the four quarters of the globe had been ransacked for the materials of which to construct this single instrument."[39] Similarly, in the first episode from Annie Carey's *Autobiographies of a Lump of Coal; a Grain of Salt; a Drop of Water; a Bit of Old Iron; a Piece of Flint* (1870), a coal lump interrupts the child about to thump it with a fire poker to tell the history of his removal and processing as a form of violence, by miners who "have broken up the quiet of our resting-places." Coal admits he is "a black and ugly lump," but from an "ancient" and venerable family—possibly alluding to the African slave trade, or to racialized language used by the English to otherize the Welsh, who supplied much of Britain's coal. His removal from the ground commences "the long course of depressing circumstances to which we have been subjected" to render coal fit for "service."[40] In the next story, the "Grain of Salt" declares his former home underground "a true crystal palace" illuminated when "some of your race threw artificial light upon the subject." Though the miners were a "most unwelcome intrusion," the Grain of Salt feels compensated for his displacement by his high status among humankind, as the symbol for the preservation of all good things.[41]

These descriptions of intrusive violence offer a literal account of environmental degradation and a displaced admission of colonial violence, justified by some vague civilizing end—in Salt's case, literally compensated for with enlightened "revelation." Ordinarily silent servants to those who consume them, commodities suddenly find their voice in these autobiographies, a reminder that servant testimonial letters first inspired it-narratives.[42] They confess their painful, self-destructive transformations between different chemical states, which are necessary for the Drop of Water to circumnavigate the globe or the Lump of Coal to power a steam engine. These transformations recall the trauma of diasporic populations globally displaced by slavery and famine. As Maude Hines argues of similar conversations in Victorian botany it-narratives between children and plants in pain, natural history writing contained reform and antislavery messages by giving voice to victim experiences spoken by natural objects. Although Carey uses the earth's materials instead of plants, coal is essentially dead trees agonistically pressurized into fuel. On a different allegorical register, these transformations resemble what children undergo through education or puberty to become adults. As Iron reflects on his harsh treatment in the furnace while being refined into steel, "in judging of the character of a thing or of a person, you should consider not only what they appear to be at the present moment, but what they may be capable by proper treatment of becoming in the future."[43] These stories are, in effect, justifying the furnace (and all that might symbolize in industry and empire) in terms of domestic and educational self-improvement.

This subliminal violence gives a clue to the cultural function of communicating industrial information at home around the fireplace. By diagraming trade onto furniture and china cabinets, children's production stories packaged colonialism and capitalist competition within family conversations and children's play, emphasizing the moral goodness of trade by its association with female domesticity. As Susan Sussman argues, middle-class white women were socialized to regard food and clothing purchases as outward reflections of their intimate moral feelings, while according to Mimi Sheller, white women abolitionists established female moral authority by carefully selecting the commodities that touch their bodies.[44] This moral imperative to know the provenance of goods incorporated into the female body may explain why Dorothea Dix's *Conversations on Common Things* (1824) begins with Mother reproving her daughter for showing so little interest in factories, which she warns will leave her vulnerable to social censure: "Suppose, Sarah, I should ever be asked if I had visited any of our manufactories," and when questioned further, prove ignorant of their "parts" and "principles," would she not "suffer some degree of mortification," when "my friends would have reason to suppose me very stupid and ignorant"?[45] While ignorance of industrial machinery may seem an unlikely source of mortification for a young woman, uninformed consumption negatively reflected on a woman's character because abolitionists, educators, and Evangelical activists had already established that women's duties included circulating relevant moral and religious information. Women abolitionists, for instance, regarded distributing pamphlets or conversing during home visits as feminine activities because they were merely bringing information to people's attention.[46] By comparison, Priscilla Wakefield censures her boy character, Arthur, for preferring consumer aesthetics to curiosity. Instead of investigating the trades carried out in local cottages, like his brother, Arthur neglects his responsibility to support his nation's technological development; he shows "little patience to examine any thing but what was shewy and beautiful" and flits his attention between "glittering toys."[47] Depending on their social position, via race, gender, and class, child characters exhibit different modes of ethical engagement in the marketplace. Girls support the virtues of trade by selecting attractive products to put in their bodies and their homes, while boys prepare themselves to sharpen Britain's competitive edge in a global economy.

While delegating ethical considerations to women consumers, production stories nevertheless limit disclosures of the conditions under which goods are produced. Using the home to map trade thus serves a pedagogical purpose and an ideological one. By describing trade in terms of family care and cooperation, authors countered contemporary arguments against the factory system—that it reduces parental affection by separating children from parents during the workday and reduces the wage-earning power of adult skilled men. Instead of struggling families, children's industrial media could provide healthy family entertainment and stories with loving parent-child dialog taking place around the hearth.

Interlocutor Gestures: From Home, to Classroom, to Exhibition

Production stories use interlocutor gestures to redirect children's attention from the text to domestic objects, and from the home to far-off settings. But these same strategies for binding together domestic objects with reading appear in other industrial media like toys and games, which remediate narrative elements borrowed from production stories. John Wallis produced several trade-themed games that feature temporally and geographically expansive networks of workers, inventors, producers, and consumers. Wallis's Picturesque Round Game of the Produce and Manufactures of the Counties of England and Wales (ca. 1826) illustrates the unique economic contributions of each region with tiny images of people working on the map. A variation on Game of the Goose, game play requires children to answer questions about regional products to advance their token from one place to the next as they spiral toward London. Locations are numbered to help players find information provided in an accompanying booklet, which encourages children to reference the book in a nonlinear fashion. The game play asks children to travel across the map, stopping at different towns, as if the players are acting out a storyline from the travel literature of Wakefield, Mrs. Brook, or Rev. Isaac Taylor. The Picturesque Round Game represents vast systems of production and exchange and allows child players to navigate these systems. Players traverse a metonymic geography of all labor and invention from the comfort of home. Like moveable books, the participatory nature of games enhances the child player's sense of self-directed travel, indicating their control over complex trade networks.

Another Wallis game—Wallis's New Game of Genius, or Compendium of Inventions connected with the Arts, Sciences, and Manufactures (ca. 1835)—provides a sense of mastery over economic networks under the theme of British technological progress. Each space on the game's path is illustrated with fine accomplishments (singing, painting,

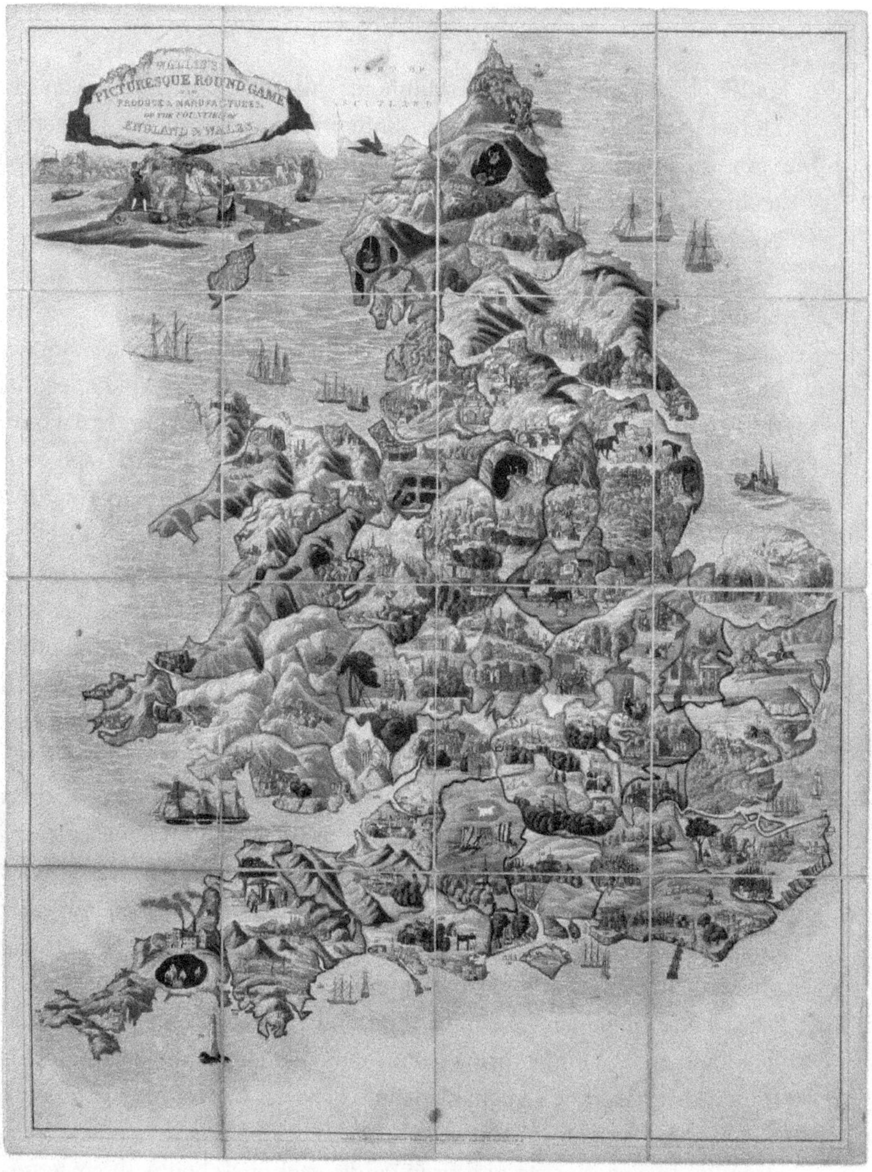

FIGURE 29. Wallis's Picturesque Round Game of the Produce & Manufactures of the Counties of England and Wales (London: Edward Wallis, [between 1826 and 1837]). Courtesy of the Lilly Library, Indiana University, Bloomington, Indiana. This engraved game is printed on paper, hand-colored, and cut into pieces that are glued onto linen to create a foldable, durable board.

and archery), children's entertainments (the kaleidoscope, the magic lantern), and industrial processes both ancient and modern (battering rams, steamboats, and pin-making). Players progress along a road of technologies and activities toward a central illustration of an industrial port city, which celebrates the conquest of time and space through engineering. As the rulebook explains: "At the distance is seen a manufactory worked by steam; on the river a steam-vessel pursues its rapid course, while the stream is crossed by a suspension, or chain-bridge, along which is passing a train, . . . at the almost incredible speed of thirty miles per hour." Using their game pieces, children are virtual travelers who use the train, steamboat, or suspension bridge to trace connections between diverse human accomplishments, participating in a linear path of national intellectual progress. The game threads together technological progress with children's development through forward movement along the game path, offering the game journey as a way to imagine traversing time and space at the speed of steam. Whether through games or books, children used manipulable learning aides to make complex global trade and abstract market forces seem concrete and domestic.

The visual overview of trade offered by these games encourages children to repurpose everyday objects in their environment as learning aids, assembling toys, food, and furnishings as practical examples of economic principles. Games are especially effective at encouraging children to perform the learning practices modeled for them by fictional characters because of the game's liminal status as both text and object. Most educational games simply refer children to accompanying booklets, but some manufacturing games remediate specific books, such as John Passmore's The Laughable Game of What Do you Buy (ca. 1850), a card game roughly derivative of *Little Jack of All Trades* (1805), composed of twelve illustrated artisan cards, each matched with six letterpress cards that represent an item sold by their shop.[48] Games produced by publishers possibly originated with children and parents who played their own games with domestic objects. One children's book from 1838 describes a variant on forfeits, in which children travel an imagined journey to various places following the letters of the alphabet from A to Z (A is for Africa; I went to Alexandria; I saw an amphibious alligator). If they make a mistake, they forfeit an object (a marble), and they earn back their property by working out a brain teaser, dictated by their father, which involves a close investigation of some object in the room (how to open the bellows).[49] In this case, a live-action game integrates children's alphabetical literacy with lessons in geography and natural history while asking players to pause their play intermittently to explore a manufactured item. Victorian children also built or purchased models of industrial machinery, as indicated by youth magazine advertisements for magic lanterns, steam engines, and "Brougham Microscopes," items reportedly quite popular among child readers. One of the most cherished articles in *The Boy's Own Magazine* was a series instructing children how to build their own model steam engine. The correspondence section of the paper for years received repeated requests for information on steam engines—including one child who inquired "how to make a model steam engine and a sponge cake," signed "Crankshaft."[50]

Children from working-class families also encountered production stories through articles published serially in cheap journals, before the same content was repackaged as illustrated compilations, and through infant school wall prints. These differed in predictable ways. Classroom prints supplied to the Home and Colonial Infant School Society by the Darton publishing family included reading cards, maps, natural history, and scriptural lessons—and "Prints Illustrative of Arts, Manufactures, &c," which included *Twelve Pictures and Lessons on Farming* (ca. 1830–1834), *The Progress of Cotton* (ca. 1836–1844), and *The Process of Making Sugar* (ca. 1833–1842). Although exhibiting familiar commodities, both *Cotton* and *Sugar* construct the class position of viewers by omitting any final panel depicting consumption, instead encouraging identification with children shown working, even enlisting viewers to cast moral judgements on their efficiency. "Some of them, you see, have not been working so diligently as the rest," comments one print, showing Black workers holing sugar cane. Referring to boys who stake out cane rows: "It is a sad thing to waste time! Look at those good little boys who are trying to make themselves useful!" *Sugar* explains the abolition of slavery in the British West Indies and the "apprenticeship" system, which required formerly enslaved adults on some islands to provide free labor for up to six years, while describing Black workers as "cheerful" and "grateful." The series at Cotsen Children's Library was printed for "the Ladies' Society for Promoting the Early Education of Negro Children," a reminder that Black children, some living in British colonies, also used these school materials.[51]

Although topically similar, classroom prints served a different purpose from Wallis's games. Cheap prints offered infant and charity schools alternatives to purchasing individual books for pupils. Teachers pasted them onto cloth to post on classroom walls, or on cardboard for display on easels, creating mobile learning stations for student reading and viewing. Children passed around the room from station to station, "visiting" the industries in a metonymic space designed to provide some alternative to the large books and elaborately furnished homes of wealthier children. To fascinate large classes of children, teachers also glued prints together into panorama lesson reels mounted on rollers and cased in a crankable wooden box, creating an attractive visual learning technology reminiscent of street entertainments. The Dartons provided one ready-made, called The Rudiment Box (ca. 1830–1834), complete with a full curriculum that included introductory mechanics, trades, geometry, and manufactures. With mandated elementary education in the late nineteenth century, publishers churned out tremendous quantities of cheap educational prints, including some repackaged scrolls, games, or dissected puzzles.[52] Their appearance in commercial markets by 1830, however, reflects efforts to recover children's minds from the division of labor by providing linear overviews of manufacturing processes while restricting where working children locate themselves in these processes.

Using prints simplified the creation of Pestalozzian object lessons for use at scale, addressing the challenges of setting up classrooms and training teachers in object teaching by offering easily managed substitutes. Influenced by Robert Owen's New Lanark curriculum, Samuel Wilderspin also suggested that infant schools teach the origins of everyday objects through lesson boards with specimens glued to them, such as cotton and its products, various wooden animals, or different kinds of wood; the boards were to be posted on learning station easels.[53] He gives examples of specimens in gradations of processing—"a piece of raw silk, a piece of twisted silk, a piece of woven silk, figured, a piece of white plain silk, and a piece of dyed silk, a piece of ribbon, a piece of silk cord, a piece of silk velvet, &c."—so that children could practice observing the transformation of raw materials. Teachers also used object lesson boxes to provide tangible specimens—bits of cloth, twine, leather, cotton, coal, ore, in various stages of manufacture—a classroom version of the storage boxes for natural history used decades earlier in nurseries.[54] These exercises formed an essential part of the school curriculum for younger children, integrated with learning the alphabet through spelling and letter sounds as suggested by the proliferation of cheap "common things" or "object catechism" books after 1820, advertised in schoolbook end papers and categorized with infant readers. Infant school production stories and object lessons prepared working-class children to become wage earners, most by age ten, by showing the broader context for the repetitive tasks they would perform. Supplied with specimens, the schools substituted for homes, whereas wealthier children could access an entire world of trade in the contents of their larders and china cabinets. Although children from various classes used production stories and specimens, the distinction remains that primary school prints and object lessons did not replace work for children who typically attended school either after their shifts or for short periods interrupted by reentering the workforce. Indeed, Wilderspin advertised infant schools as protective, playful spaces that offered superior alternatives—not to workplaces—but to poor children's barren, inadequate homes, while his school playground replaced the street.

By comparison, the lessons Wilderspin proposes specifically for children from middle-class families provide a broad overview of commerce, typical of children's production stories and games. The first requires painting a nursery floor rug to look like an enormous trade gameboard, or like a book's fold-out map, so that children can run about trading items between various towns. "I would have a floor-cloth in every nursery, painted like a map," and "let the children then be told to proceed from a certain spot, to go through certain counties, towns, &c. and to fetch a piece of cloth from Yorkshire, or a knife from Sheffield, cheese from Cheshire, butter from Dorset, lace from Huntingdonshire, &c. &c." The second live-action game uses a huge water table with little cork islands complete with animals, inhabitants, and "natural products":

> A little boat should then be provided, and a voyage to a given part undertaken; various islands might be touched at, and various commodities taken on board or exchanged, according to the mercantile instruction the children should receive; whilst brief accounts might at first be read or given of the climate productions, and inhabitants of the respective places; till the little

> scholar should be able to conduct the voyage, purchase or exchange commodities, and give an account of the various countries and their inhabitants, &c. by himself.[55]

The classroom itself is the map, navigated by children using game miniatures. The large map on the nursery floor provides a sense of visual dominance over extensive geographies and access to a global workforce. Wilderspin's exercises teach students control over complex systems of production and consumption across vast distances, an important element of mechanical literacy. Unlike the specimen boxes, which teach the stages of manufacturing through samples, the map exercise asks middle-class students to self-identify as capitalists or consumers making purchases. These exercises show the same class divide as production stories between working children who manipulate things for wages and more affluent children who learn to manipulate the principles of commerce.

If educational spaces of the home inspired learning practices in the classroom, classroom practices influenced, in turn, how manufacturing was taught in industrial exhibitions. Most famously, the Crystal Palace that housed the Great Exhibition of 1851 assembled specimens of raw materials, tools, machinery, and finished products from around the world, like an infant-school classroom, so that visitors could walk around and observe these stations. The industrial designer, Henry Cole, who determined the exhibition's organizational schema and advocated for the glass palace design, had previously published over a dozen children's books and two manipulable learning aids under the pseudonym Felix Summerly. The similarity between the exhibition's displays and a Victorian-era production story or classroom would be especially noticeable for the estimated 35,000 school children from 493 schools who visited the Crystal Palace.[56] To facilitate children's learning, the exhibition was supported by educational media that explained to parents and teachers how it could be used for object teaching, with some of these materials written as travel dialogues in the manner of production stories. Anticipating school field trips to the exhibition, the SPCK published *Notes and Sketches of Lessons on Subjects Connected with the Great Exhibition* (1852), with interactive lessons for teachers who bring their students to the exhibition on such exciting topics as maize and porcelain. Another book for home reading, *Fireside Facts from the Great*

Exhibition (1851), advertises "Object Lessons" prominently on the cover, and claims to "cultivate in the reader the powers of observation, comparison, induction, and memory, by the exercise of which the mind is trained to investigate and acquire knowledge for itself," while a spin-off periodical by S. Prout Newcombe, *Pleasant Pages* (1851–53), featuring the same family characters, offers weekly object lessons about common things in the home, authored by former infant school teachers. *The Royal Road to Reading through the Great Exhibition* (1852) uses similar dialogs and illustrations of exhibition objects in "words of one syllable" for beginner readers. Illustrations show each object characters discuss, allowing the dialogs to be used at home with tarry-at-home-travelers, or to prepare parents and children for the conversations they should have during their visit. The Great Exhibition is merely the grandest of learning spaces filled with specimens, texts, and objects about manufacturing, one used for people of all ages and classes.[57] Like production stories or miniature specimen boxes, it created opportunities for redirecting children between books and things, teaching them to browse and "read" them both, as access portals to far-away places of industry.

The Principles of Exchange; or Gifts and Purchases in Production Stories

The materiality of books, toys, and live-action games offered an attractive "feeling" of direct control over economic forces and easy access to plentiful goods. The sensations of controlling trade by manipulating pages or game pieces is also represented in fictional narratives, through frequent scenes in which children of different classes meet one another and pass goods between their hands. These fetishized moments of physical contact between consumers and producers allow readers to imagine direct in-person encounters. Cross-class exchanges are remarkably pervasive and formulaic in longer production stories with fictional characters. Typically, the protagonists are touring children who initially note something they have in common with working children, usually comparing their own play with whatever task they observe. After watching the people work, the child characters exchange gifts or purchases. These exchanges establish mutual aid between classes, but they also reestablish differences between child producers and child consumers. In Priscilla Wakefield's *A Family Tour through the British Empire* (1804), for instance, a mother brings her children to Sir Richard Arkwright's mills, where "our travellers had the satisfaction of seeing here a thousand children employed usefully, and learning an early habit of industry." Noticing her children watch these children work, Mother "encouraged a tender sympathy that she observed in the countenances of her own children with those of the same age, who were compelled, by the necessity of earning their daily bread, to continual labour." Then her children present "small presents" to those working children recommended by an inspector "as best deserving a reward."[58] Here, sympathy across class supports existing social hierarchies by reinforcing vertical loyalty.

One purpose of these exchanges is to make capitalism personal, tangible, and charitable. But they also teach that the laboring poor are dependents of the rich. Curiously, the exact reverse lesson frequently appears in children's moral tales, when an adult mentor rehabilitates a spoiled child by visiting local cottagers who make the necessities of life. In Lucy Peacock's *Visit for a Week* (1794), two spoiled children, Clara and William, take shelter from the rain in Dame Bartlet's cottage while the occupant spins. Clara, "who had never before seen a spinning wheel," "admired" her "dexterity" and "declared she thought it must be a very pretty amusement." As usual, Clara initially mistakes work for play. Her guardian, Mrs. Mills, corrects Clara, explaining that spinning is work—and was at one time "an employment of repute among persons of the first rank," but is now "confined to the lower and middling class of people," hinting that such work is not beneath Clara. After they leave, Clara questions why she bothers visiting a family whose "station in life" is "so much beneath her own," and Mrs. Mill again corrects her charge, explaining that "in the eye of God, we were all equal," and must love our neighbors, whether "he be poor or rich, a mechanic or a gentleman."[59] By no means a radical author, Peacock nevertheless depicts rich children who seek shelter from a cottage woman, placing them at a humbling disadvantage calculated to remind them of their economic dependence on Dame Bartlet, who reciprocates by pouring forth gratitude. Mary Elliott offers the same warning in *Continuation of Rustic Excursions* (1827): "Let us be careful how we conduct ourselves towards the useful classes of society, whose valuable labours heap new obligations upon us town idlers, every year."[60] In these stories, the rich are dependent on the poor.

As the British economy shifted from cottage manufacturing to factories, production stories replaced characters like Dame Bartlett with factory owners and engineers. In an early instance of this, Priscilla Wakefield describes a wealthy family's visit to a cloth factory near Birmingham, where they witness "the vast variety of machines and ingenious contrivances for diminishing the labour of the workmen." Enthralled by these mechanical improvements, rather than the workers themselves, the children admire how work performed with the assistance of the "steam engine" is "done with great ease and dispatch by girls" or "by a few boys" instead of requiring "a great number of powerful men." Because steam power makes work require less raw physical strength, the child tourists describe weaving as leisurely. Unlike Clara's mentor, who corrects her mistake, Wakefield's adults tacitly agree. After dining with the factory proprietor, the family returns to Birmingham impressed, not with the accomplishments of these child operators (who have replaced the jobs of skilled men), but with "admiration of the genius, talents, and virtue of the proprietor."[61] The children feel obligated for their instruction not to the weavers, but to the factory proprietors.

When touring children present gifts to workers or make charitable purchases, they reverse Elliott's warning and make the "useful classes" obliged to the "town idlers." In Rev. Isaac Taylor's *Scenes of British Wealth*, a traveling girl watches how gloves are sewn together, then convinces her mother to buy several pairs from a "young lass" who "appeared," like her merchandise, "to be very delicate too, if not in actual decline."[62] This episode may seem like the usual moral lesson on supporting virtuous tradesfolk, but the charitable purchase serves a different purpose. It distracts readers from the glovemaker's gift of instruction, freely provided to the purchasers, that would otherwise place the touring children in a vulnerable position of obligation. The touring children learn from workers who kindly exhibit their trades to visitors, but this bottom-up gift of knowledge is eclipsed by the top-down charitable purchase. One function of the charitable purchase, therefore, is to manage who legitimately owns "factual" information about manufacturing. Who is knowledgeable enough to write about working conditions? Who testifies to Parliament about what happens in mines and factories?

Whose stories are credible? Whose observations are facts? Although the people performing skilled labor in these factories develop considerable knowledge through their everyday practices, their ways of knowing are delegitimized as a lower kind of mechanical literacy in favor of the observation practices of leisured children.

When production stories deny the expert knowledge of laboring people, they reserve for their readers (and leisure characters) the work of making knowledge. The touring child characters typically journal, write letters, use maps, collect specimens, produce oral reports, and organize their writings and collections, which implicitly suggests that readers try these activities. For instance, Emily and George from Taylor's *Scenes of British Wealth* practice delivering their personal observations as objective evidence through daily reports to their father, who directs them to "give me an account of what you saw" and to ask questions. Meanwhile, Father journals and creates a map, which he appends to the end of the book, "that you," meaning the readers, "may be able to trace him" and "learn both ways." These practices further separate Emily and George from the artisans and operatives they observe. After the first day of watching "woolders" make rope, "The children came home full of the sights they had seen, as well as the good things they had eaten. Both mind and body had had a feast." Then grandfather reveals that the workmen can hardly feed their families, "so the parents rather go short themselves, than give too little to their children." Emily and George's intellectual satiety at the sight of the tired woolders calls attention to the social divide between the children who watch and journal and the hungry families who manufacture things, their work defined by the grandfather as manual labor, "something in which the labour and ingenuity of the hand makes the greatest part of the price." The children's power to observe, granted to them because of their social status and geographic mobility, finds intellectual food in the bodies of manual laborers, and teaches them to distinguish between mental and physical labor. The conclusion of the book passes the authority to manage work and create knowledge to "some child, only old enough now to read this book," when one day, "The love of play may give way to the love of employment."[63] As adults, such expertise grants readers the authority to manage factories, invent machinery, or to speak on behalf of woolders and their families.

While children's production stories strive to heal class conflict, they nevertheless provide elite children with knowledge of economics and technology necessary to consolidate wealth and political power through a combination of alphabetical and mechanical literacies. Conversely, the artisans and operatives portrayed in these materials rarely speak, and if they do, they cannot explain their jobs so well as the fictional parent or tutor, who stands ready to do this job for them. Charitable exchanges thus suggest that wealthy readers as more trustworthy experts on industrial economy than the wage-earners whose livelihoods depend on manufacturing. Instead of promoting cross-class sympathy, gifts and purchases ultimately reestablish class differences between working children who make things and the children who watch them. Class determines whose manufacturing knowledge counts as mechanical literacy.

Returning to Taylor's *Scenes of British Wealth* (1823), we can see how this works in a longer series of production stories about various commodities. The story follows Emily and George on a tour of manufacturing towns, offering a virtual experience for readers to "meet" people with different employments without actually leaving their middle-class domestic spaces. One of the primary ways that Emily and George sympathize with laboring families is by comparing their own children's games to the work performed by other children. The book's frontispiece illustration shows cherub-like infants hammering on an anvil in a shipyard, which frames how readers view these scenes of wealth, as opportunities for playful learning. As they approach one town, Emily mistakenly believes children knitting are playing a game and exclaims,

> "What a number of girls have we seen, each at her cottage door, and in some places in clusters of five or six together! They seem to be playing with little bits of wood: but that cannot do any good, I should think. Is it any game?"—"Playing seldom does any good, unless when work is first done," said the father. "But we are traveling now in Buckinghamshire, where every village is a manufactory, especially about Newport Pagnel, which is the grandmart for lace—for bone lace making at which, all the neighbourhood is greatly occupied."

Curious, the siblings approach one girl knitting (she is not referred to by name), "because the children wished to see how lace was made." The girl is surprised because everyone she knows learns how to knit from

SCENES
OF
BRITISH WEALTH,
IN
PRODUCE, MANUFACTURES, AND
COMMERCE,
FOR THE
Amusement and Instruction
OF
LITTLE TARRY-AT-HOME TRAVELLERS.

By the REV. I. TAYLOR,
AUTHOR OF SCENES IN ENGLAND, EUROPE, ASIA, AFRICA, AND AMERICA.

LONDON:
PRINTED FOR HARRIS AND SON,
ST. PAUL'S CHURCH-YARD.

1823.

FIGURES 30–31. Rev. Isaac Taylor, *Scenes of British Wealth: In Produce, Manufactures, and Commerce, for the Amusement and Instruction of Little Tarry-at-Home Travelers* (London: John Harris, 1823), title page, 25. The Rare Book & Manuscript Library, University of Illinois at Urbana-

Champaign. *Left*: Title page with cherub workers at the shipyard. *Right*: Each chapter provides images of people working, whom the characters visit, allowing readers to share the characters' intimate glimpses into their lives. Here, workers include women and children in their homes.

infancy. She resumes her work with their praise, but Emily and George "could make nothing of it" until they ask questions. Although Emily and George are forced to confront their ignorance, this sense of inferiority is limited to the knitter's dexterous fingers. What follows is a short treatise on "the general principle on which lace is formed," covering geography, trade, and the history of bobbinet—delivered not by the cottage girl, but by Emily and George's father. Taylor is inconsistent, however, with his dialogue quotation marks in these longer essays. As a result, each of the chapters devoted to a different town quickly fades from character dialog to third person essay.[64] This slippage between the touring father's voice and the book's authoritative discourse of nonfiction makes clear that watching people make ropes, lace, gloves, sugar, and so forth, produces knowledge of higher social prestige than the artisanal knowledge necessary to make things. The father's display of mechanical literacy is made possible by his visual position, his ability to write, and his broader systematic view of manufacturing across all of Britain. These scenes show another way that the production story elevates a particular kind of comprehensive knowledge as mechanical literacy while disavowing the importance of what workers learn from their daily experiences.

The chapter closes with a cloyingly dramatic monologue, "The Lace-Maker," whose speaker, a cottage girl, prefers lace-making to the frivolous amusements of "ladies":

> I envy no ladies I ever did see,
> All riding in coaches so gay;
> My cushion, and bobbins, and patterns for me—
> I'd rather be weaving all day.
>
> I've seen them all twist themselves this way and that,
> As angry, fantastic, and vain;
> I twist too—my bobbins—and catch them all pat,
> Nor sigh, nor feel sick, nor complain.

The poem hinges on the difference between leisure and work. The cottage girl may "twist too," but she has no desire to wear lace, while Emily and George are equally unfit for manual labor—as are readers. The narrator warns that knitting point lace for too long can make people blind, with a casual jibe: "we cannot wish any young ladies to do much of it, except such as are idle, and would otherwise read trifling books."[65] The poem hints at a moral message for Emily—that she is responsible, as a woman consumer, for purchasing goods in accordance with ethical principles. She should know how her clothes are made and refrain from frivolous consumption of goods or books.

Jane Marcet's Political Economies

Not all production stories empower readers to create knowledge by silencing working-class characters. The genre formula for production stories creates an opportunity to reveal, alongside the technical process, abuses in the supply chain that consumers ordinarily cannot witness. As shown by Wakefield's and Opie's antislavery sugar stories, and Marcet's chimney sweep boycott, there are instances when authors subvert production story formulas by focusing on the human costs of cheap commodities. In closing, I examine Marcet's Willy books at greater length, as a useful contrast to Taylor's *Scenes of British Wealth*. The daughter of a Swiss banker and chemistry teacher, Anthony Haldiman, Marcet included in her friend circle Thomas Malthus, David Ricardo, Maria Edgeworth, Mary Somerville, and Harriet Martineau.[66] Marcet produced the first political economy textbook for children, *Conversations on Political Economy* (1816), followed by the far less popular *John Hopkin's Notions on Political Economy* (1833) for working-class readers, inspiring Martineau to undertake similar endeavors. Mary Poovey and Hilda Hollis argue that her work defends the new poor law and justifies economic inequality, yet her Willy stories, a popular fictional series for children, creates extensive dialogue between people of different classes.[67] The manual laborers and factory workers Willy meets prove perfectly capable of explaining manufacturing processes and economic forces to an ignorant young gentleman's son. Marcet's willingness to grant her named working-class characters the power of nonfiction's authoritative discourse is a departure from Wallis's *Progress* stories or John Harris's "Tarry-at-home Travelers." Her sustained accounts of children from different classes working together suggests the possible influence of conscious consumer movements on her depictions of trade as a mutually beneficial, collaborative enterprise.

In *Willy's Travels on the Railroad*, published by John Harris in 1835, seven-year-old Willy gains a comprehensive view of trade as an interconnected, global system while traveling from London to his grandmother's farm. Rather than dividing humanity or atomizing individuals, modern industries unite everyone in mutual dependence and necessary cooperation. Touring England by rail, Willy learns that everyone is interdependent because the division of labor requires exchanging goods and services. Willy admires the power of steam when he sees a train for the first time; he learns how people dig tunnels and construct tracks; he meets agricultural workers who bring goods to the market and who explain the economic benefits of railroads; and he tours a Derby factory and a family farm. The railroad lines are a metaphor for personal connections made possible by new markets. Not only is Willy connected to his distant relations, but he connects with other children who share the railroad, with the farmers who trade goods by rail, and with child factory workers who make the cloth he wears. These lessons begin with Willy's family and expand outward to embrace geographically broad communities connected by rail.

The book opens with a familiar stagecoach-as-state metaphor applied to the steam carriage. Willy must imaginatively expand his notion of community beyond his family by making his desires compatible with the happiness of other passengers. At first, Willy tosses a ball with another little girl until their rambunctious play annoys an elderly passenger, who (after a warning) throws the ball out the train window. While the spoiled girl throws a tantrum, demanding they turn around the entire train, Willy controls his temper, and he is rewarded by the annoyed passenger, who allows Willy to look through the bag of toys she bought for her grandchildren. If Willy restrains his pleasures to meet the needs of other passengers, then everyone enjoys the ride.

Like national commerce, the train benefits everyone but distinguishes between three different "stations," with enclosed carriages for first-class passengers, and separate cars for the "second and third classes," which "are cheaper, so that the common people can afford to go in them."[68] As he travels toward Derby, Willy expands his cooperative abilities across classes as he moves, at his request, from his first-class carriage to the third-class open carriages, where he helps Martha, a farmer's daughter, feed and unload her fowl. Later, Willy reencounters the farming family in Derby, where he meets Martha's mother and younger siblings, Johnny and Betsy, who tell Willy about the workings of farms and factories, while he shares what he knows about the operation of water and steam power. They suggest he visit a cotton factory where their uncle works. By chance, Willy's family meet this uncle, who takes them from one room to the next while workers call out to explain their various operations. In a noticeable departure from similar books, Marcet's divisions of labor complicates the divide between intellectual and physical labor. Her characters from different stations all exchange information and all work together to the extent possible in a realist setting.

The grand lesson of *Willy's Travels* is that the division of labor facilitates interpersonal relationships by necessitating collaboration. The degree to which every activity in *Willy's Travels* requires sharing and specialization approaches the absurd. Even picking daisy chains in the arboretum requires a division of labor by gender, since the girls, accustomed to sewing, have the skills to rapidly split stems and assemble the chains, while the boys agree to gather the flowers. As the daisy chains illustrate, dividing any task creates opportunities for teamwork. Thus every object exchanged in *Willy's Travels* prompts an intimate story about human relationships: The stern grandmother shows Willy her beloved purse composed of three pieces sewn by her three granddaughters, and then she, in turn, fills it with toys for them; likewise, Betsy's fowls afford her tea and sugar to comfort her blind mother.[69] By visiting farms, gardens, and factories, Willy learns the interdependence of agriculture and manufacturing, worker and capitalist, consumer and producer.

While praising cooperation, Marcet also reasserts the importance of personal property and free markets by teaching Willy the difference between capitalist and gift economies. At his first visit to an inn, Willy discovers that hospitality is a business, and his parents must pay for food and lodging that supports the Innkeeper's children. "So you see, Willy, she takes money out of her pocket to spend for us, and we put money into her pocket to pay her back again."[70] Willy similarly mistakes a farm for a food charity that makes "bread and meat for poor people's dinners," until the farmer's son, Johnny, explains:

"Father don't give it away . . . he could not afford that; he helps the poor people as much as he can, and pays them wages for their work, but his corn he sells to the baker, who makes it into bread; and his cattle to the butcher, who makes it into meat; and they sell it both to rich and poor, they care not which, so that they do but get paid for it."

"But the poor have no money to pay with," observed Willy.

"Then they must work to earn money; and that they may do either in a farm or a factory. Why, in a factory, as I told you, even little children get paid for their work."

Such conversations are basic lessons in political economy, with a specific focus on how child consumers and producers relate to one another. Marcet's approval of child labor is by no means unusual; the point is that Willy should know why these children work and what they make. Johnny explains that his family must buy clothes produced by these factory workers, and the boys discuss all the different factories that each produce thread, cotton, and wool that are combined to form finished clothes. "Well, how nicely that is contrived!" Willy exclaims, "People all help one another; it is tit for tat, like Betsey and her hens."[71]

Marcet conjoins trade with "help" by depicting generosity as the best protection for personal property. In *Willy's Travels*, amiable business exchanges between strangers universally conclude with gifts between friends, tempering impersonal capitalism. The innkeeper's daughter, for example, picks berries with Willy on the condition that he won't eat any, and Willy's temperance later earns the children an invitation from the innkeeper to eat some of the cherries. On their return home, the innkeeper presents Willy's mother with a basket of fruit, which she reciprocates with a silver pencil case for the daughter. Likewise, Mr. Joseph Strutt, who owns the factory that Willy tours, and "may spend his profits in whatever manner he chooses," builds a beautiful and instructive arboretum, free to the public, and "made for the poor more than for the rich." Because of Strutt's generosity, Derby serves "other factory towns, ever so far off" with its leisure gardens, the same towns and countryside that feed and clothe one another—all joined by the railroad.[72] Because each person respects the property of the other, exchange facilitates friendship, gifts, and charity. In this light, the opening carriage scene in which Willy plays ball depicts an immoral, selfish economy. The ball toss, a metaphor of property exchange, bonds together the two children at the expense of other passengers. As a fit punishment, Willy forfeits his property.

The conclusion of the story reflects on what Willy learns about labor, but also the source of that knowledge. Willy returns to London in a carriage shared with a retired governess (an ambiguous class position of both worker and teacher) who tells him a story, provided to readers as one of the last chapters. Her story is told from the perspective of a washer woman's ten-year-old daughter named Lucy Brown, who accidentally ruins the doll clothes of two wealthy girls through her thoughtless attention while ironing. When she returns the clothes, one spoiled girl yells at Lucy, but her mother interrupts to reprove such treatment. Mother encourages the girls to forgive the mistake and share their cake with Lucy. Like the longer story of Willy's travels, this nested tale depicts sympathy between two sharply divided classes of children, one of whom washes dolls' clothes while the other displays dressed dolls at their tea parties. The tale's reversed point of view, however, invites Willy to sympathize with the washer girl's excitement over her first assignment, her fear of losing her job, and her relief at a kind resolution—notably, the shared consumption of the cake, an inclusive variation on the production story formula. The overall plot of *Willy's Travels* thus follows the class stratification of a train that ventures north toward industrial England and returns home to the south while providing a window into the lived experiences of all stations and occupations.

Willy's Travels offers a panoramic survey of global trade that manages the imposing complexity of Victorian production and consumption. By applying the order of personal narrative, Marcet gives children a comprehensive view of an interconnected, global system. Rather than dividing humanity or atomizing individuals, modern industries unite everyone in mutual dependence. While Victorian nonfiction books about manufacturing communicate the same message, the vision of cooperation through trade promoted by *Willy's Travels* encourages children to work alongside their peers and learn from them, while acknowledging the humanity and expertise of working-class characters. Marcet's storytelling retains many of the same limitations as Rev. Taylor's *Scenes of British Wealth*. The larger narrative is focalized through Willy, the son of a wealthy landed gentleman of leisure who play-acts work while on vacation. Willy's privilege allows him to transform his subjective experience into the scientific principles of political economy. His right to survey workspaces, moving freely from town to town, and entering factories or farms as a welcome visitor, grants Willy the paternalist ability to speak on behalf of those he observes, opening a hierarchical gap between himself, as a privileged viewer, and those he is permitted to watch. Even though Willy's father emphasizes that children perform work for money and not for fun or "charity," Willy nevertheless seems to equate his passing trials at cherry picking or cloth manufacturing with educational fun, at a time when actual child workers struggled to represent their work as grueling and dangerous enough to merit regulation. Nevertheless, Marcet is thoughtful in critically adapting worn genre conventions. She individualizes named working-class characters, and she represents characters of different stations engaged in both physical and intellectual labor. All characters enjoy their time off in Strutt's gardens, including factory workers who picnic with their families on Whitmonday, a traditional day off from work. From Martha's family to the retired governess to Willy himself, all people need time for leisure.

When Marcet wrote *The Seasons*, her first installment of the Willy stories, in 1832 to 1834, Owenite cooperative stores and banks were at their peak, while Chartism was at its peak during her publication of *Willy's Travels*. During the intervening period, thousands of children protested for a ten-hour workday, leading to the 1833 Factory Act, which limited factory children's work hours and mandated some schooling; the radical working-class press resumed prolific publication; and slavery was abolished in the British West Indies. Marcet contends in *Willy's Travels* with the appeal of these reforms by creating a more attractive vision of capitalism, where cooperation is the happy result of the division of labor, a strategy common among her contemporaries. Writing for young readers, Charles Knight called the capitalist division of labor the true "principle of cooperation," while Henry Brougham described mechanics institutes as a place for sharing theoretical and practical knowledge to prevent "the two classes" from conceiving their interests "in opposition to each other."[73] As legislation began protecting children from work, Victorian production stories sometimes reflected these reforms, in Marcet's case, by incorporating some radical ideas into the genre formula.

Conclusion

The children's books and media examined in this chapter are not only a product of the marketplace, but its embodiment. Games, toys, and moveable books about political economy and manufacturing provided children with manipulable, observable representations of invisible forces, and with the ability to feel their consumer agency in the market. In this respect, the science of political economy could be felt in the body in the same way that mechanical philosophy materials taught children to feel centripetal force by sledding or feel the advantage of a pully using model machines. Along with this ability to read and intercede in global trade, children's books and toys provided their users with the skills and confidence to record information about moving bodies, including human ones. As prime movers, girls were responsible for the goods they incorporated into their bodies, whereas boys learned about industries to contribute to national wealth. Longer production stories featured affluent characters who modeled information-gathering for their readers. By imitating these characters, readers validated their opinions as objective facts, their authority as observers instantiated by the tactile, interactive books, prints, and games they manipulated to learn about manufacturing.

While this manifestation of mechanical literacy may seem far removed from alphabet tiles and natural history cabinets, "common things" or village trades were grouped together with alphabets in children's primers and infant lesson materials. When designed for the youngest children, the production story matches early reading instruction for scale and variety of multimedia with everything from wall prints to object lesson boxes, boardgames, live-action games, information books, picture books, maps, exhibition spaces, and fiction. The same holds true of production stories today, with engineering reality shows, picture books on how things are made, and engineering videos on YouTube—suggesting the form thrives on a sense of visual or tactile immediacy. Accustomed to interlocutor gestures from an early age, children who learned to read by moving between books and literacy toys apply these strategies when reading production stories as a hybrid genre that combines texts with the reader's environment.

Throughout the century surveyed here, state support grew for disseminating useful knowledge about manufacturing and trade to upwardly mobile mechanics, men who would gradually have the right to vote as property qualifications were reduced. Victorians remained invested, nevertheless, in maintaining a division between those suited to governance and those who perform physical labor, even if this division shifted down on the social ladder. Dramatizing these social changes, Henry Mayhew in his satirical novel *1851: or, The Adventures of Mr. and Mrs. Sandboys and Family: Who Came up to London to Enjoy Themselves, and to See the Great Exhibition* questions whether mechanical literacy alone can overcome the poverty and disruption caused by industrialization. Interrogating the privileged position of traveling observers, the story follows a country family's London vacation as they fall prey to thieves and charlatans and see very little of the Great Exhibition itself but a great deal of what no one intends them to see. Detained en route in Manchester, the luckless Sandboys family, with son and daughter, tours the city with a local friend, but finds the factories closed while "workers, young and old, had all gone to take their share in England's holiday."[74] Finally, their guide leads the Sandboys family to "the one district where the toil knew no cessation," where "the clicking of the shuttles of the handloom weavers might still be heard." What they see are the "pinched faces and gaunt figures" of impoverished weavers:

> He asked why they were not, like the rest of the town, at the Exhibition of the Industry of all Nations.
> "Ha! Ha! Ha!" laughed out one with a week's beard on his chin—"last week I earnt three and ninepence, and this week I shall have got two and a penny. Exhibition of Industry! Let them as wants to see the use of industry in this country come and see this here exhibition."[75]

Departing from the official tour, the Sandboys family discovers the condition of workers using older technologies whose experience contradicts the Great Exhibition's messaging. Mayhew's expository narrator, as naïve as his protagonists, consistently delivers the official line. The reason "there has been so much more toil and suffering in the world," he explains, is because of the failure to acknowledge "the artistic character of artisanship." The workers do not want "an increase of pay," but to learn science and aesthetics. Even ploughmen can "understand the several subtle laws and forces concerned in the cultivation of every plant," and that ploughing is not "a brute operation, but an intellectual process" that makes "work a pleasure, and the workman a man of thought, dignity, and refinement." Instead, by neglecting education, "our handicraftsmen have remained pure mechanics," who, in ignorance, "merely repeated, mechanically, the series of acts that others had performed before them."[76] While Mayhew's narrator subscribes to this plan to liberate workers' intellects by teaching them middle-class values through mechanical literacy, the reality of weavers left behind in Manchester, their poverty equally the product of modernization, invites reader skepticism toward healing class conflict by inviting artisans and operatives on an improving vacation at the Glass Palace.

CHAPTER 4

Self-Governing Machines

Automata and Autonomy in Maria Edgeworth's Fiction

For over a century, the "Rosamond" stories remained popular with children for their realistic depiction of a spirited, impatient, curious girl, unusual at a time when moral tales preferred "good" and "bad" child foils. Frequently included in anthologies, syllabi, and scholarly studies, including Perry Nodelman's generic analysis of children's literature, *The Hidden Adult*, "The Purple Jar" (1796) has come to exemplify didactic literature of the rational school.[1] The mother's refusal to correct Rosamond's decision to buy a pretty jar over practical shoes, or to relieve its painful consequences, illustrates Maria Edgeworth's parenting philosophy from her *Practical Education* (1798), which values child autonomy, experimentation, even failure, over obedience, best captured when she tells Rosamond, "My dear, I want you to think for yourself."[2]

Not everyone appreciates Rosamond's mother. Sarah Trimmer, a staunch church and king supporter who founded *The Guardian of Education* (1802–1806), the first review periodical devoted to children's literature, objected that if Rosamond had been taught Christian principles, then she would have "acquired beforehand the habit of seeking the advice of her parents, and of submitting to it as a guide for her inexperience." Trimmer advises parents to use "The Purple Jar" to teach children that appearances are deceptive, and children are not to "depend too confidently on their own opinion."[3] Trimmer finds an unlikely ally in fin de siècle authors, who disparage the utilitarian mother, finding something of art for art's sake in Rosamond's attraction to the beautiful jar. In a satirical American children's book from 1902, Rosamond attends a party with other famous children's book characters where she defends her "Mamma," who "wanted to train me to be a Free Moral Agent." Her host, Miss Muffet, responds, "I don't like agents . . . I mean I don't believe in being one till one is more grown up."[4] Twentieth-century scholars have criticized Rosamond's mother for allowing her daughter to suffer, but her command "think for yourself" ultimately formed the centerpiece in Mitzi Myers's recuperative argument defending strong "rational mothers" of women's didactic fiction who take their daughters seriously enough to let them learn through hard experience.[5]

Taking Rosamond as its inspiration, this chapter considers how mechanical literacy makes children into Free Moral Agents. By tinkering with machines, or by observing and ordering objects in the world, child characters gain a new perspective that allows them to act independent of adult authority. Like many British author-educators, Edgeworth is optimistic about what children can learn through their own experiments, but she is equally invested in the socialization of children. Her fictional characters thus learn about themselves, other people, and the material world together using mimetic objects that collate into object assemblages.[6] Approximating socio-economic networks, these objects allow children to see themselves in relation to others, human and nonhuman, as a step toward independent action within complex systems.

The most obvious of these assemblages are the many automata and automated machines her characters observe as models of self-governance. At the time Edgeworth was writing, automata included watches and chronometers, but also impressive machines exhibited for entertainment: small jeweled mice, birds, and insects, or curious humanoids with lifelike movements, but also elaborate grandfather clocks decorated with painted scenes and hundreds of little moving figures.[7] The automaton was a shorthand reference for the universe itself, powered by forces integral to its organization and ruled by God—and for human and animal bodies, governed by the spirit or mind.[8] Observing automata, therefore, teaches children mechanical philosophy; however, the automaton also affords children an opportunity for self-observation. "It is the capital and distinguishing characteristic of our species," explains Catharine Macaulay, in *Letters on Education* (1790), "that we can make ourselves as it were over again," becoming "the carver of [our] own happiness" and fashioning "that artificial being, a social man."[9] Macaulay's sculpted "artificial being" underscores a tendency to externalize development by creating artificial doubles, models for self-reflection that give material substance to a linguistic convention of referring to "ourselves" in the possessive. In automata, children can see their movements modeled by a machine that looks like them, and whose operations they can physically or mentally "grasp." By watching machines, children acquire both mastery over the material world and control over their bodies.

In Edgeworth's fiction, mimetic machines have the same learning affordances as other object assemblages. That is to say, children can learn about the laws governing the universe and acquire self-governance by investigating any objects in their environment to which they assign mimetic properties. Characters who observe automata thus demonstrate Edgeworth's theory of how children, in general, become free moral agents using a socialized material world. Her influential fiction, published over several decades, represents a dominant cultural belief of her era—that children can assert self-governance and independence by tinkering with machines, and they can use that power to reinforce their privileged status, as property owners, over their social inferiors. Once autonomous adults, they have the right to educate others who remain "mechanized," or perceived as lacking rational thought because of their class, race, nationality, gender, or age.

I begin with a brief introduction to automata as Maria Edgeworth likely experienced them—through family and friends who built them, through contemporary automaton shows, and through other literary depictions. Then I examine the various object assemblages and automated machines that Edgeworth's characters observe as models of self-governance, while noting probable sources for each. First, in *Belinda* (1801), Lady Delacour reforms from dissipated lady of fashion to devoted mother-educator after visiting Henri Maillardet's automaton exhibit with her daughter. Several automata exhibited in London and circulating around Britain appear in Edgeworth's fiction, accurately described and credited to famous craftsmen. Second, in the "Rosamond" stories (installments in 1796, 1801, 1814, 1821), Edgeworth's most autobiographical character learns to think for herself through a series of lessons on observing objects, concluding with the jeweled automata of Genevan watchmaker Jean-François Bautte. Jervas, a working-class youth protagonist from *Popular Tales* (1804), proves his ability to ascend the social ladder when he constructs a cabinet machine model of the mines where he worked as a child, then takes his model to India for exhibition. These characters explore automata whose secret inner workings model opaque socio-economy systems, and they gain agency through their ability to command, destroy, build, and own machines.

Automata in the Lives of Maria and Richard Lovell Edgeworth

Maria Edgeworth knew about the life-changing, transformative power of automata from her father and co-author, Richard Lovell Edgeworth, who edited and wrote the preface for many of her books. A self-described "mechanic" and "engineer" who worked in canal and road construction, Richard Lovell claimed that his life changed in the autumn of 1765 when he saw an automaton exhibition of William Bridges's musical grandfather clock, the Microcosm. One of many musical grandfather clocks touring Britain, the Microcosm was created in 1732 and updated in 1741, reaching peak popularity in the 1770s. As its name suggests, the Microcosm is a comprehensive temporal-spatial model of the universe requiring twelve hundred wheels and pinions to regulate its movements. Two clock faces compare the Ptolemaic and Copernican solar systems, with planets revolving to music composed by Handel, complete with a solar eclipse on the proper rotation. The Microcosm grandiosely extends God's ability to understand the universe He created to the mechanical philosophers who build automata. Mirroring the orderly heavenly spheres, its four tiers also represent a social order, with genius elevated over artisan labor. On the top, nine muses play their instruments, while in the middle, a peaceful pastoral scene features wind and rotating water mills, knife grinders, ships, and other trades. The base features Bridges's own trade, carpentry, its humble workshop supporting the world.[10]

Writing his memoires over fifty years later, Richard Lovell identifies this automaton encounter as the turning point of his life. He praises the "neatness and precision" of the Microcosm and pronounced the "movements of the figures, both of men and animals" to be "highly ingenious." At the time, mechanics was a new obsession with Richard Lovell, who passed his days building a watch and an orrery at Hare Hatch, with "frequent visits to smiths, and coachmakers, and workmen of various sorts," but he longed for more "cultivated society" to share his interests. Delighted with the like-minded cosmopolitan exhibitor, Richard Lovell visited the Microcosm so frequently that the exhibitor "let me see the internal structure of the whole machinery." His initiation into the inner workings of the automaton brought him into the orbit of "Dr. Darwin," whom the exhibitor had met when touring in Litchfield, and through Darwin, the Lunar Society members and manufacturers Josiah Wedgwood, Richard Arkwright, James Keir, Matthew Boulton, and James Watt, as well as the chemist and educator Joseph Priestley, master of Warrington Academy. "How little could I then foresee," he reflects, "that my having examined and understood the Microcosm at Chester should lead me to a place, and into an acquaintance, which would otherwise, in all human probability, have never fallen within my reach!"[11]

Following this episode, Richard Lovell constructed a stream of quirky gadgets whose general utility he professed with confidence, including a one-wheeled phaeton for traversing narrow bridges, "a wagon drawn by fire" (a steam-powered train), and a turnip cutting machine.[12] He built over one hundred prototypes of one vehicle, something like a tank, which he hoped could climb walls. His horology projects included "breathing the breath of life into the brazen lungs of a clock," intended as a gift for Erasmus Darwin.[13] Darwin himself constructed a speaking automaton in 1771, capable of calling "mama" and "papa"—one of many contemporary examples of a child automaton designed to acknowledge its maker as its teacher.[14]

Acknowledging the influence of Richard Lovell's automaton encounter on his daughter is tricky, because Maria's contemporaries, as well as her many biographers, have recovered her voice by diminishing their partnership. Her affection for her father bemused some contemporaries, who found Maria, as poet Joanna Baillie describes, a "frank, animated, sensible, and amusing woman, entirely free from affectation of any kind," with a "confiding and affectionate, and friendly disposition," physically small and unassuming, whereas Richard Lovell appeared bombastic, speaking for Maria more than her friends would like.[15] Her Victorian biographers regretted his influence as her gatekeeping editor and coauthor, finding her affectionate deference difficult to reconcile with her feminist voice. More recently, Elizabeth Kowaleski-Wallace argues that Maria Edgeworth's efforts to prove women capable of rational thought, so appealing to modern feminists, shows her complicit "identification with a patriarchal politics," which she uses as "an opportunity for self-definition."[16]

Unfortunately, distaste for her father's influence has concealed the fact that Maria Edgeworth must have known a good deal about mechanics. Ever self-effacing where her father's expertise was concerned, Maria tended to minimize her own knowledge of science. When Sir James Mackintosh visited "Mr., Mrs., and Miss Edgeworth" and their family in May 1813, "under pretence of visiting the new Mint," a machine for printing money that Edgeworth describes in the "Harry and Lucy" stories, he noted "they are all proficients in mechanics."[17] Before publishing fiction, Maria wrote scientific reports of her father's inventions. "My father will allow me to manufacture an essay on the Logograph," she writes to a friend in April 1795, while Richard Lovell worked intensely to perfect an early telegraph signal system, "he furnishing the solid materials and I spinning them."[18] While accompanying Richard Lovell and Frances Edgeworth on their wedding trip, she visited, according to biographer Marilyn Butler, "several factories in the Birmingham area"; "the great ironworks at Ketley Bank"; and, in London, "galleries, museums, and a mechanical exhibition"—quite possibly, given the timing, the Henri Maillardet exhibit she describes in her novel *Belinda*.[19] Following these tours, she produced novels and story collections in quick succession, featuring protagonists who redirect their lives after formative encounters with automata. In effect, Maria experienced her own automaton conversion experience, but she decentered herself from that narrative through her fiction.

Known for her entertaining familiar science books, which depicted children learning from everyday domestic objects, Maria Edgeworth was frequently acknowledged in the introductions of other science writers who praised her work.[20] Surveying the Edgeworths' domestic machines, Joanna Wharton describes Maria Edgeworth's fiction as "repositories of inventions" that also exhibit an "astonishing wealth of 'things,'" including teaching apparatuses and mechanical toys.[21] As a leading education expert, Maria befriended and corresponded with many authors who wrote accessible literature about mechanical philosophy, political economy, and philosophy of mind: Anna Letitia Barbauld; Jane Marcet and Jeremiah Joyce, both prominent science writers for children; Elizabeth Whitbread, wife of Samuel Whitbread, MP, who read the first bill for compulsory primary school in England in 1807 that compared Monitorial education to a machine; English astronomer and polymath Mary Somerville; author and education writer Elizabeth Hamilton, who introduced Pestalozzian object lessons in Britain; and Dugald Stewart, philosopher of mind. All of these friends were directly involved in the advancement of education in ways that embraced mechanical literacy.

In writing about machines, the Edgeworths both relied on and contributed to the widespread cultural mythology about the inspirational power of automata. According to the biographical anecdotes that circulated in popular magazines and children's biographies, countless famous industrialists had formative encounters with automata. Reportedly, James Watt dreamed up his Spinning Jenny when he saw the Mechanical Turk, a chess-playing automaton, and, later, Charles Babbage decided to become an engineer after watching a mechanical doll walk a tightrope. Carving machine models was a favorite pastime of young geniuses. Cecilia Lucy Brightwell describes how Joseph Jacquard, the French silk manufacturer who invented a loom that stored patterns in memory punch cards, was "constantly amusing himself by making little models in wood. He built small houses, towers of churches, and carved miniature furniture," while the Scottish civil engineer John Rennie "constructed the model of a windmill, a pile-engine, and a steam-engine." Like Edgeworth's protagonist Jervas from *Popular Tales*, the watchmaker astronomer George Graham built an exhibition cabinet that "comprised the whole planetary system within the compass of a small cabinet, which invention served as a model for the orreries of the eighteenth century."[22] These formulaic narratives are symptomatic of a cultural mythos about the power of machines to ignite mechanical genius, which shaped how Richard Lovell and Maria understood events in their own lives.

Popular automaton exhibits furthered this mythology by staging the triumph of human will over machines. Showmen first elicit wonder from audiences at their lifelike machines, living matter that moves without a soul, then break the unsettling illusion by exposing their inner mechanisms. The audience then admires the enlightened mechanical genius who built the machine, regarding the automaton as his obedient tool. The French engineer Jacques de Vaucanson, who displayed his automata while seeking royal patronage, used these performance conventions to assert his active, human agency as an engineer over his mechanical flute player and defecating duck. Exhibited on stage at a Paris opera house in 1742, and later in the Opera House, Haymarket, London, in 1746, the flute player began to play with the curtain down while the audience wondered at its precise execution; then the curtain lifted to reveal the mechanical player. His defecating duck exactly replicated the bone and feather structures of its biological original, displayed with its supporting column of mechanical gears exposed to view.[24] These displays reinforce social hierarchies, since showmen are predominantly European men, while automata are shaped like children, small animals, or Orientalized men, who lie open for rational inspection. In literature, automata are usually compared to women, children, or working-class youth, the subjects of education experiments controlled by powerful men. To gain power, then, Edgeworth's youthful characters align themselves with mechanical geniuses who build automata.

Automata and Autonomy in Novels of Education

Automata are especially useful models for child agency because like children, automata occupy a transitional state, halfway between dependence and independence. For instance, building or tinkering with automatous machines is an empowering activity that displays human creativity and control; yet a person described as an automaton is invariably powerless. When used to describe a living human, an automaton is someone controlled by external compulsions, who should be autonomous but upon closer inspection lacks self-direction. This paradox is captured in the very definition of "automaton," which Samuel Johnson's dictionary defines as "a machine that hath the power of motion within itself, and which stands in need of no foreign assistance." Such an ability to act independently also distinguishes adults from children. That is, children begin at one end of the automaton paradox (mechanical obedience) and mature into the other (independence), by becoming "automatous," defined by Johnson as, "that which has the power of motion in itself." Since automata have interior governance, they model human "autonomy," defined as "living according to one's mind and prescription."[25]

The paradoxes embedded in automata are equally present in concepts of autonomy. Beginning in the late eighteenth century, pedagogical writers suggested forming children indirectly through their environment as an alternative to direct physical punishment in order to produce adults with the ability to make independent moral choices. The idea of influencing children indirectly by using the material world to preserve their freedom gained traction in Britain with two influential French pedagogical novels, Rousseau's *Emile* (1862) and Stéphanie-Félicité de Genlis's *Adèle et Théodore, ou, Lettres sur l'éducation* (1782)—the latter Maria translated when she was sixteen. Where John Locke's *Some Thoughts Concerning Education* (1693) advocates replacing physical punishment with shame and praise, Rousseau considers corporeal or psychological incentives equally dangerous, preferring to teach children through "physical obstacles or punishments which stem from the actions themselves." Rather than command Emile to obey, or punish him when he does not, Jean-Jacques changes his environment until Emile voluntarily does as he wishes. "You will not be the child's master," advises Rousseau, "if you are not the master of all that surrounds him."[26] Genlis employs a similar approach. As "governeur des enfants d'Orléans," or "governor" to the three sons of her alleged lover, Louis Philippe II, Duke of Orléans, Genlis had extensive experience teaching children and gave more practical suggestions. Trading Emile's cottage for a wealthy country estate, her novel of education *Adèle et Théodore* features a rational mother who transforms the entire landscape by adding hills for her children to climb, while in her home every wall is papered over with visual learning aides and the furniture embroidered with historical persons.[27]

These novels of education describe for parents how to move the burden of discipline onto inanimate objects, allowing children to freely choose between limited, prefabricated affordances and draw conclusions from their own errors. The end goal is an adult who makes sound decisions informed by personal experience. Some English authors questioned, however, whether such engineered environments promote freedom or produce mechanical subjects. A professed admirer of *Emile*, William Godwin rejects Rousseau's isolationist methods as "generally unhappy, stamped with the impression of artifice, intolerance, and usurpation."[28] In her essay "On Education," Anna Letitia Barbauld criticizes "these mimic experiments of education," insisting, "It is not necessary, with Rousseau or Madame Genlis, . . . to surround him with an artificial world."[29] Natural education unexpectedly requires an artificial, engineered space, and it produces artificial, engineered adults. According to Nancy Yousef, the purpose of Enlightenment isolation thought experiments is to reaffirm, paradoxically, the profound importance of education for subject-formation and the inevitable intersubjectivity of human beings as social animals.[30] The paradox of the automaton neatly translates into the world of education.

A string of French and English novels published from 1740 to 1820 explore the benefits and risks of engineered environments using socially isolated, highly controlled spaces to perform thought experiments in educational and political systems. Whether an island, prison, castle, remote cottage, or country estate, these removed spaces promise to transform pupils by delivering them from the corruptions of society, but they ultimately prove the inevitability of social, political life: Thomas Day's *The History of Sandford and Merton* (1783, 1786, 1789); Charlotte Smith's *Emmeline, The Orphan of the Castle* (1788); Ann Radcliffe's *The Romance of the Forest* (1791); William Godwin's *Things as They Are; or, The Adventures of Caleb Williams* (1794); Jacques-Henri Bernardin de Saint-Pierre's *Paul et Virginie* (1795); Eliza Fenwick's *Secresy; or, The Ruin on the Rock* (1795); Elizabeth Inchbald's *Nature and Art* (1796); Robert Bage's *Hermsprong; or, Man as He Is Not* (1796); Amelia Alderson Opie's *Adeline Mowbray* (1804); and Mary Shelley's *Frankenstein* (1818). Isolation is particularly dangerous for women, whose teachers withhold information about sexuality and economics, leaving the ingénue protagonist desirable, yet vulnerable to predatory men.[31]

These novels, which have much in common with Edgeworth's *Belinda*, are among the first to incorporate artificial life or automata. They do so to suggest that artificial spaces produce mechanized subjects. Frances Burney's ingénue, Evelina, for instance, visits James Cox's London automata exhibit, where she contemplates her status as an object on the marriage market, identifying with yet distinguishing herself from the jeweled curiosities displayed for purchase. Julie Park concludes that such "anthropomorphized" mimetic commodities, such as dolls and automata, reveal "human identity's susceptibility to becoming embodied in inanimate objects."[32] When self-fashioning goes astray, characters are controlled externally; they become soulless automata, their minds subservient to material bodies or crushed under oppressive authority. Burney's animated heroine Camilla is a good example. Subjected to "test" and "experiment" by her lover's tutor, she is drained of all agency, "a fair lifeless machine, whom the music, perforce, put in motion."[33] Camilla is like an automaton because her "power of motion," to use Johnson's dictionary definition, is no longer "within" herself, but "foreign" to her. Tellingly, characters who control others through prisons and castles are called "teachers." Consider Caleb Williams, a promising youth with a "mechanical turn" who makes furniture in prison. Once he escapes, he supports himself as a watchmaker, connecting his freedom with observing automata. He then accuses his antagonist, Falkland, of controlling him through a confining educational environment: "You took me up a raw and inexperienced boy, capable of being moulded to any form you pleased." He adds, with sarcasm, "I may thank you for having taught me a lesson of insurmountable fortitude." Literary characters are empowered by automata, but no one wants to be one.[34]

Automata in novels of education capture the difficulty of fostering child agency through education, given that all knowledge must be gained from external sources through the body's senses. This "new philosophy," as Catharine Macaulay explains, "supposes the human character to be the mere creature of external impressions."[35] From an optimistic perspective, the notion that children are passive clay, empty cabinets, or blank slates, their desires shaped by their surroundings, suggests the potential to mold perfected subjects (or citizens) through socially engineered environments.[36] If, however, the ideal subject is an autonomous one, then the very means of educating children through external impressions challenges the concept of an essential self who originates its own desires, judgments, and actions. To solve the paradox of autonomy through education, Maria Edgeworth suggests participatory systems. Both student and teacher, children build the environment that shapes them. They identify with machine-as-self but also comprehend automaton-as-system. Her theorization of autonomy through mimetic objects illustrates an essential element of mechanical literacy: its self-reflectivity.

Lady Delacour Encounters an Automaton

Her clearest contribution to this literary trend, Maria Edgeworth's *Belinda* (1802) is an education experiment novel whose plot unfolds like an automaton show, as a series of unveiled mechanical wonders. Ostensibly a courtship novel about a young ingénue of limited fortune turned out for display on the marriage market, the novel quickly recenters around the reformation of Belinda's patron, Lady Delacour, a neglectful wife and mother and unhappy slave to fashion. Initially, Lady Delacour wastes her remarkable wit and endearing good heart on false friends who threaten her health and fortune until Belinda's example encourages her to reconcile with Lord Delacour and exchange her corrosive friends for improving company. In a side plot, Belinda's love interest, Clarence Hervey, educates a young woman, Virginia St. Pierre (named after the author of *Paul et Virginie*) on an isolated country estate according to Rousseau's precepts, but she proves an unsuitable wife for him because she is incapable of her own decisions.[37]

Belinda is populated by eye-catching mechanical eccentrics whose antics eclipse its titular heroine. Clíona Ó Gallchoir describes the novel as a visual illusion technology, "a kaleidoscope, in which fashionable images of belles beaux, rakes, fops, servants, conjurers, colonials and émigrés pass before our eyes in sometimes bewildering sequence."[38] Ever predictable, Lord Delacour is set in motion by jealousies and petty power struggles with his wife, and he "must be wound up with half a dozen bottles of champagne, before he can go."[39] Lady Delacour's one-time "masculine" friend, Harrit Freke, performs manual exercises with her rifle, just like a soldier automaton owned by Haddock that toured England in the 1790s.[40] As human automatons that lack interior control, these characters cannot exercise their own judgment. By contrast, Lady Delacour and Clarence Hervey, who ultimately embrace the culture of self-improvement, destroy superficial automata and embrace the educational machinery of self-governance. For instance, Lady Delacour smashes a jeweled watch, crying "Vile bauble!". Clarence Hervey, a "man of genius" who almost drowns himself to please his friends, begins his reform by torching a mechanical snake masquerade costume of "much ingenuity," which he accidentally sets on fire while applying phosphorous to create glowing eyes.[41] Like Lady Delacore, Hervey is vulnerable to mechanization because of his sensitivity: The man of feeling was compared to an automaton because of the "mechanistic physiological processes behind sympathetic sensibility," which Alex Wetmore argues influenced the self-reflexive form of sentimental fiction.[42] Hervey ultimately decides to pursue Belinda over Virginia St. Pierre, favoring a wife who learns autonomy through a socialized environment.

Lady Delacour's transformation begins when she takes her daughter, Helena, whom she has neglected, to see Henri Maillardet's "conjurer and mechanical bird" in Spring Gardens, London. The celebrated automaton show referenced in *Belinda* was a sensation for decades, and, given the timing, this could be the mechanical exhibition that Edgeworth attended in London the year before writing the novel. At the very least, Edgeworth consulted contemporary accounts, since Helena's description of the "little conjuerer" and automaton singing bird are accurate. Maillardet's audience would feed the conjurer tokens printed with different questions (for example, "What is the most universal passion?"). The figure consulted his book, struck his wand, and a door opened to reveal the correct answer (Love).[43] The two Maillardet automata connect thematically with other events in the novel. The mechanical conjurer recalls Lady Delacour's visit with Mrs. Freke and her object of flirtation, Colonel Lawless, to a celebrated fortuneteller, described as "no common conjurer," as well as multiple "magic" tricks Mrs. Freke uses to punish those who earn her displeasure.[44] The mechanical bird automaton, which is built into its cage, recalls Virginia St. Pierre, a woman educated in a cage like a mechanical animal.

The power of this performance to inspire Lady Delacour's reform makes perfect sense, given the clever commentary on education in Maillardet's Covent Garden automaton show. His central attraction were three child-sized automata that executed drawing, penmanship, and musical exercises—all creative accomplishments mastered through repetitive exercise and assigned to schoolchildren. Resembling a young boy of three to four years old, his Draftsman drew six different pictures in pencil, blowing the dust from his paper with bellows-induced breath. His Scribe used a quill to draw pictures and compose poetry, his compositions souvenirs offered for purchase. His "musical lady" bowed to her audience before seating herself at her organ, tapping her foot while she played. She mesmerized audiences with her expressive movements, "the gracefulness" of her "gesture, and lively motion of the eyes," while her "bosom heaves" with the same bellows that animate her instrument.[45] Presiding over the three students was their creator, Maillardet, a headmaster of sorts, who exhibited his own genius through the masterful repetition of his students. Occasionally he would turn to the mechanical dolls and urge them with the commands, "Write! Play! Draw!" As both creator and instructor, he exerts double authority over his students. Yet the child machines are themselves engaged in activities associated with self-improvement and creative autonomy, foreshadowing the day when they will no longer be objects formed by their maker, but self-governing adults. Through these commands and seeming improvisations, Maillardet's performance equivocates between external and internal control, playing with the audience's ideas about autonomy.

Maillardet's child automata capture the paradox of education through the senses. They playfully exhibit how real children build internal memories, enabling consciousness, while mechanical repetition trains the body to form healthy associations and habits, according to the associationism of David Hartley. Moreover, children in Maillardet's audience participate in this same educational process, since automaton shows reportedly spark creative genius. Advertisements for Maillardet's exhibit promised family entertainment that could "entice Youth to an exertion of their mental faculties." Another puff announces, "Future ages may boast of abilities in mechanics, which were first inspired by viewing on a holiday Maillardet's Automatical Exhibition, Spring Gardens."[46] Shortly before Edgeworth wrote *Belinda*, Queen Charlotte and her children visited Maillardet's "Automatical Exhibition," "on which they bestowed the most flattering marks of approbation."[47] Maillardet's child automata were edifying family entertainment, exactly the right combination of high fashion and rational improvement for a mother like Lady Delacour.

Lady Delacour is herself a mechanical mystery of sorts, whose driving mechanisms (like her secret sufferings) are artfully concealed behind decorative exteriors. She reforms by opening her heart to examination—one in a series of enlightened revelations and rationally explained mysteries that conclude the novel. A superstitious Black servant from the West Indies named Juba finds his nightly visions of an Obeah-woman easily dispelled when Belinda demonstrates to him how Mrs. Freke executed the practical joke using phosphorus; Lady Delacour opens her "mysterious boudoir," where she hides her medicines, to Belinda's observation, and confesses her concealed illness to friends and physicians; she opens the locked drawer with her correspondence with Clarence Hervey for the perusal of Lord Delacour to reveal he has no cause for jealousy; and, finally, Lady Delacour's Methodist visions of ghostly visitation prove natural in origin when a gardener's "mantrap" catches the "ghost," Mrs. Freke. In each case, close examination, especially "ocular demonstration," uncovers the illusion through a display-and-explain procedure similar to automaton demonstrations. These revelations indicate that Lady Delacour, who delights in masquerades and locked boudoirs, will pattern her home after Belinda's exemplary friends, the Percivals, in whose rational home "there were not family secrets" or "petty mysteries."[48]

Opening herself to view subjects Lady Delacour's reproductive biology to male medical control, using her renewed motherly affections for Helena to secure her place within a patriarchal family, even if she retains her ostentatious wit and capricious sensibility through the novel's conclusion.[49] In an automaton show, as Lavinia Maddaluno demonstrates, revelation is not necessarily a conservative triumph of reason over the occult, but a way to inspire curiosity, wonder, and an aesthetic appreciation for deception.[50] Automaton showmen cultivated an aura of mystery around their wonderful creations, which they dispelled by opening the mechanism to view. Consider how revelation works in Wolfgang von Kempelen's demonstration of his Mechanical Turk, whose ability to defeat human chess players astounded audiences. A contributor to *Edinburgh Philosophical Journal* in 1821 figured out that the deception is made possible by elaborate disclosures. Kempelen would open all the cabinets and turn back the chess player's clothes while the human player slid around inside to avoid detection. During this procedure, any men of science in the audience were invited to closely examine the automaton while Kempelen pretended to wind his machine at random intervals. Like a magician, Kempelen provides ample opportunity "to explore every corner and recess, which, he well knows, contains nothing that he is desirous of concealing." After Kempelen opens each cabinet door and lifts the Turk's garments, the audience assumes "that the whole was at that time open to inspection," when in fact, "some parts had been entirely withheld from view."[51] Far from atypical, flourishing the magician's toolkit was commonplace in scientific demonstrations from the seventeenth century through the Victorian era, when lecturers relied on optical illusions and slight-of-hand to romanticize science for public consumption.[52] Barbara Maria Stafford argues that automata displays in particular blurred distinctions between quacks and professional scientists.[53] If science plays with the occult to attract interest, then perhaps rational mothers might learn from Lady Delacour's witty performances.

If ostentatious revelation is the best misdirection, what are we to make of the reformed Clarence Hervey and Lady Delacour? At the novel's close, the bizarre revelation that Clarence Hervey secretly experimented on a young lady hidden away in the country can hardly bode well for Belinda's domestic bliss. Lady Delacour paves her way to virtue in smashed machinery and open cabinets, yet continues to exhibit the artistic genius and theatrical skill of an automaton showman. She ends the novel by posing for a domestic tableau, as if aware that domesticity is merely one more performance. If *Belinda* follows the formula of a staged automata show, then, as Mark Sussman argues, elaborate disclosure invites the audience to play along with the performance's conventions. "Again, the trick of the trick is that the spectator knows, and suspends disbelief in, the operation at work."[54] Viewed through these audience expectations, Lady Delacour's revelation is neither sincere nor disingenuous, but an acknowledgement that the culture of self-improvement should embrace mystery and play.

After all, the Edgeworth family loved natural magic, and Richard Lovell engaged in science performances. In his youth, he built a sailboat on wheels and almost ran over a confused shepherd while testing it on the open road. He first entered London society by befriending Sir Francis Delaval, an amateur magician whom he impressed with his own magic performance. He once threw a traveling inn into confusion by disguising himself as the servant to his eccentric traveling companion, Thomas Day, and making outlandish demands on behalf of his master until Erasmus Darwin unexpectedly arrived to unmask his disguise. Another time, he purposefully intercepted "Jack the Darter" on the road to discover how that curious showman accomplished his feat of throwing sticks over a cathedral. He participated enthusiastically in nitrous oxide parties with chemists Thomas Beddoes and Humphry Davy, where participants documented the effects of self-administered laughing gas.[55]

Nor did Maria, who praised Ann Radcliffe's *The Romance of the Forest*, entirely stand apart from these antics. She once humorously described her bizarre domestic life to her Aunt Buxton while surrounded by home chemistry experiments in the form of soaps and perfumes, as her father sifted through mechanics books. Together, the two Edgeworths coauthored a rather gothic play, performed by the family, about an illuminati suitor who secretly performs science experiments on children.[56] This is a family that embraces concealment to anticipate revelation.

This generous reading breathes life into Belinda herself, a heroine whose greatest flaw is her too-perfect control from within. Like Rosamond, she must "think for herself" by questioning marriage advice received from her aunt, from Lady Delacour, and even advice from the perfect Percivals. Yet Belinda's path to autonomy requires a level of discipline and self-control to the point of artificiality. As Toni Wein points out, Belinda conceals her feelings or keeps secrets, easily feigns Lady Delacore's voice, and disguises herself most effectively at the masquerade.[57] Lady Delacour may exhaust herself and her rouge pot trying to convince the world that she is happy, but Belinda requires just as much effort to reason herself out of love with Clarence Hervey when she believes him unavailable. Her free choices are so packaged in rational consideration that when Maria Edgeworth edited *Belinda* for Barbauld's series, The British Novelists (1810/1820), she regarded her with the despair of a coachman facing a wrecked machine: "Mend you! Better make a new one."[58] Her resemblance to a curious machine recalls the paradox of Maillardet's child automata, who hover between repetitive tracing and awakened creative potential.

Lady Delacore's automaton encounter sets the stage for the way object learning functions in Edgeworth's children's fiction. As carefully designed compound-objects, automata are simply the most obvious instantiation of what educational objects do. Edgeworth's child characters acquire autonomy by learning from objects that accumulate into mimetic assemblages. Like watching automata, manipulating these compound-objects grants children mechanical literacy through self-aware participation in systems of production and exchange. Next, I pursue this argument through the life of Rosamond's needle.

Through the Eye of a Needle: Property, Gender, and Class in *Rosamond* and *Emile*

"The Purple Jar" opens in "the streets of London," where seven-year-old Rosamond, overwhelmed by colors and sounds, chooses her monthly purchase: either a purple jar she admires in a chemist's window or new shoes to replace her worn pair. Despite her mother's advice to "see it nearer" and "examine it," Rosamond chooses the purple jar without careful investigation, only to discover it is a clear jar filled with purple liquid. Rosamond must endure painful shoes for a month; she misses family walks and she cannot go with her father and brother to the "glass-house" (a glass manufactory).[59]

Appearing in Edgeworth's first collection of children's literature, *The Parent's Assistant* (1796), "The Purple Jar" was later republished as the first of six "Rosamond" stories in *Early Lessons* (1801), followed by two sequel story collections: *Continuation of Early Lessons* (1814), when she is age nine or ten, and *Rosamond: A Sequel to Early Lessons* (1821), age ten to thirteen.[60] Taken as a whole, the "Rosamond" stories try to answer a fundamental question of educational philosophy: how a moral agent can live freely as part of society. The answer Rousseau provides in *Emile* forms the backdrop for Edgeworth's response. She offers an alternative theorization for Rousseau's "education of things," reimagining specific episodes from *Emile* using a flawed girl protagonist in place of an ideal boy. Where Rousseau favors retreat from society, Edgeworth embraces children's early immersion through objects in economic, social, and political life. The result is an ingenious, philosophically rich, proto-feminist critique of Rousseau, but one that uses Rosamond's privileged class to establish her agency.

When considering all three installments of "Rosamond" stories, the choice between jar and shoes is merely the first in a succession of object encounters designed to exercise Rosamond's cognitive faculties through difficult judgments. The mother's advice, "think for yourself," is far more complicated than it initially appears. Far from acting independently, Rosamond hones over time her ability to read social cues and consult her friends, while overcoming her fear of ridicule and dependence on praise. Each of her choices between objects builds upon previous ones in a spiraling, iterative form, advancing Rosamond from sensations close to her body and concerned with her own happiness to complicated moral quandaries involving the happiness of others.

As Rosamond's choices gain greater stakes, the same objects keep resurfacing throughout the stories, repurposed or assembled into complex machinery. Manipulating objects while young prepares Rosamond to understand the industrial machines, clocks, and automata she observes with increasing frequency as she matures. The objects Rosamond confronts signify inner qualities she might develop or reject through what she purchases, assembles, and exchanges. She thus develops consciousness and practices self-monitoring by using object exploration as a stand-in for self-observation. Her object lessons have a metacognitive dimension; she learns about herself (and herself learning about herself) by investigating objects.

Objects in Rosamond's world have social importance by always belonging to someone; they are property that reveals properties of their owners. Books—those most social of objects—appear early and often. Unlike Emile, who only reads *Robinson Crusoe*, a book whose hero is exactly like himself, Rosamond listens to stories with characters different from her, and by the end of the 1801 collection, she reads her brother's gardening journal for advice. The second installment (1814) begins with Rosamond learning to write and concludes with her cataloging a library—a collection of social objects—to help her brother earn a microscope from their father. Edgeworth therefore integrates reading with observation, since socialized objects cannot entirely circumvent spoken and written authorities.

Edgeworth shares with Rousseau his investment in learning from the material world as the means to independent thought. The purpose of Rousseau's "education of things" is to create an individual who lives in society as a "truly free man," who submits to the material world and natural laws rather than to the capricious wills of powerful men:

> There are two sorts of dependence: dependence on things, which is from nature; dependence on men, which is from society. Dependence on things, since it has no morality, is in no way detrimental to freedom and engenders no vices. Dependence on men, since it is without order, engenders all the vices, and by it, master and slave are mutually corrupted.[61]

Rousseau imagines a society without hierarchical authority, made possible by subjects whose desires, established in isolation, never grow beyond the basic needs they can provide for themselves.[62] For the "education of things" to produce freedom, children must remain unaware that their environment is engineered, or else they might attribute human intention to natural consequences. Children must learn from "things" kept separate from "men"—that is, from things devoid of any social context.

By contrast, Rosamond's autonomy is forged in the marketplace, a social space replete with excessive consumer desires, which Rosamond must learn to navigate—quite the opposite of Rousseau's isolationism, designed to limit Emile's desires. Where Rousseau removes Emile from social pressures, Edgeworth immerses Rosamond in the social context of objects, introducing private property from the earliest age. And where Rousseau considers the division of labor, or satisfying needs through commercial exchange, to be the first step toward servile dependence, Edgeworth uses gifts and purchases to introduce the benefits of interdependence for satisfying human needs.

Rosamond's lessons take the form of gifts or purchases that dramatize ethical quandaries, and she must make decisions in front of judgmental audiences. In "The Purple Jar," her mother advises, "when you are to judge for yourself, you should choose what will make you happiest; and then it would not signify who thought you silly." But the approval of others, she discovers, affects her happiness. The reason she cannot visit the glass manufactory, for instance, is because her father believes her shoddy appearance reflects poorly on his parenting: "No one must walk slip-shod with me" he says, "looking at her shoes with disgust." Her old shoes are not just painful; they are mortifying. "Rosamond coloured and retired." Maybe judging children for dirty shoes is shallow, but as Rosamond's mother says about morning visits (which they both hate), "living in society, there are many little sacrifices we must make to civility."[63]

The gender dimension of these choices refutes Rousseau at every point. Rousseau represents women's education as always already social, performed for an audience of men, in order to produce dependence. A woman's actions are judged by aesthetic appearance rather than substance: "Man says what he knows; woman says what pleases. He needs knowledge to speak; she needs taste. Useful things ought to be his principal object and pleasing things ought to be hers." How fitting that in "The Purple Jar," Rosamond *should* have chosen the useful shoes over the ornamental jar in a straightforward rebuttal to Rousseau's education for girls. The jar is deceptive in precisely the way Rousseau describes women: "flatterers and dissimulators" who "quickly learn to disguise themselves."[64] Under Rosamond's careful examination, Rousseau's dubious compliment proves equivalent to a misogynist reduction of woman to a dirty vessel. The alluring jar filled with disgusting chemicals also recalls Edmund Burke's rhetorical association of chemistry deceptions with French politics in *Reflections on the Revolution in France* (1790), as well as radical chemists Joseph Priestley, Humphry Davy, and Thomas Beddoes (Maria Edgeworth's brother-in-law), who largely inspired the association of chemistry with seductive revolutionary politics in the political cartoons of the 1790s.[65] Replacing Rosamond's worn shoes offers reform as a viable alternative to revolution, and, by extension, suggests incremental reform in women's education.[66]

A second deceptive purple object appears in the next story, "The Two Plums," in which Rosamond exercises her judgment choosing between two plums, identical from a distance. Remembering the purple jar, she looks, touches, and smells the plums, and finds that one is a painted stone. While she eats the real plum, her mother places a housewife (a pouch for storing needles) next to the stone plum and asks her to choose one. Aware that she keeps losing her needles, Rosamond considers, "the plum is the prettiest certainly" but "the housewife would be the most useful." The color purple triggers Rosamond's memory in a visual and auditory way: "Rosamond, as she pronounced the words *purple jar*, turned her eyes from the stone plum and fixed them upon the housewife." In each story where Rosamond makes a choice, Rosamond tries to secure advice or praise from her mother, who redirects her to her own thoughts and feelings. "Don't consult my eyes, Rosamond," her mother tells her, in a later story—notably using sight interchangeably with rational thought—"Use your own understanding, because you will not always have my eyes to see with." When Rosamond asks, "Are you pleased with my choice, mamma?" she replies, "I hope *you* will be pleased with it; for it is your affair, and not mine." Like jar and shoes, housewife and needle are multidimensional symbols connected with Rosamond's cognition. In Rosamond's case, her brother asks to borrow a needle, which she produces safely from her housewife, and as a reward her father invites Rosamond to join them while they do "several experiments with her needle and a magnet"—making a compass by floating a needle on water, a common domestic science experiment.[67] Whereas Rosamond previously missed the trip to the glasshouse, now she can join in her brother's scientific education and build her own moral compass. This analogy between instrument-making and free moral agency is a favorite for Rousseau, whose Emile also makes a compass, an experiment I will return to in a moment.[68]

The initial "Rosamond" stories from *Early Lessons* (1801) build toward complex choices that affect others. Its final story, "The Rabbit," begins with Rosamond overwhelmed by plentiful, mutually exclusive choices in another marketplace, as she decides which seeds to plant in her garden plot. Unfortunately, her "industry and perseverance" are thwarted by a hungry rabbit who eats her laburnums, forcing Rosamond to consider her "property" against the rabbit's natural right to subsistence.[69] "The Rabbit" reworks an episode from Rousseau's *Emile*, in which Jean-Jacques invites Emile to plant beans, mixing his labor with his soil to create property after Locke's concept of possessive individualism. After several weeks tending the beans, Emile discovers his crop plowed under by a farmer who claims that Emile dug up melons that he planted previously. Because the farmer intended to share the melons with him, Emile immediately understands the farmer's plight because he shares the same grievance.[70] As a child, Emile is never expected to sympathize with others who are different from him, since he should not yet realize other wills might conflict with his own. As usual in *Emile*, Jean-Jacques confesses that he carefully orchestrated the entire event by hiring the farmer to play his part.

In the chapter "On Truth" from *Practical Education* (1798), Maria Edgeworth singles out Rousseau's bean garden lesson as an example of how parents "teach truth by falsehood" by creating an engineered environment. "The privilege of using contrivance, and ingenious deceptions, has been uniformly reserved for preceptors; and the pupils, by moral delusions, and the theatric effect of circumstances treacherously arranged, are to be duped, surprised, and cheated, into virtue."[71] By taking the farmer under his employ, Jean-Jacques artificially removes social conflict from his property lesson, making ownership a relation between things instead of people.[72] In response, Edgeworth depicts conflict between multiple parties with mutually exclusive property claims over limited resources. The rabbit and Rosamond cannot both have what they want. To solve the quandary, the sibling must contend with political questions of Edgeworth's day: slavery, enclosure of common lands, poaching laws, factory conditions, restraint in women's domestic education, and vegetarianism.[73]

Ultimately, the "The Rabbit" concludes the initial "Rosamond" stories in *Early Lessons* where it begins, with a lesson about the marketplace. Rosamond learns the rabbit belongs to Anne, the daughter of a poor city dressmaker. A close proxy for a caged rabbit, Anne's mother is dangerously ill from working long hours in a restrictive urban setting. In a mutual exchange that mirrors Emile's resolution with beans and melons, Anne offers to free her rabbit in a far-off warren, while Rosamond gives the family hyacinths to brighten their new city apartment, grown from the roots she previously chose and cultivated over the past year, thus investing her own labor into her gift.[74] If Rosamond wants to defend her own property, then she must respect the property of others, regardless of their station.

Taken together, the 1801 installment of "Rosamond" stories is about insides and outsides—about jars with icky insides and clear outsides, needles encased in wax, and fruits with stones inside and stones next to them—or about the process by which children internalize judgment through external stimuli. The objects Rosamond selects consistently represent her mind as a house or container, or, to borrow Locke's phrase, an "empty cabinet" furnished by the senses.[75] Knowledge appears substantiated as property, owned and organized by Rosamond, and nurtured by her labor. Tinkering not only teaches Rosamond about the world but asserts ownership over herself and her property.

These owned objects adhere together into machines, beginning with needle and magnet, a scientific instrument with a legacy of literary symbolism. In his longest and most elaborate object lesson, Emile also builds a compass. His first experience of social integration is attending a fair, where a magician attracts a floating wax duck with bread in his hand. Jean-Jacques and Emile recreate the trick at home by shaping a wax duck around a needle, floating it in a tub of water, and attracting the duck with a magnet hidden in a piece of bread. The next day

Emile attends the same show, armed with his bread and magnet, where he embarrasses the magician by replicating his trick, to the delights of onlookers. Seduced by praise, Emile accepts the magician's invitation to come again the next day, but the magician hides a boy with a stronger magnet beneath the tub. This time the audience jeers when Emile fails, proving that praise has no relation to merit. The next morning, the magician complains of Emile's attempt to ruin him.[76] Although the magician seems to command nature itself, he is a warning against servile dependence. He serves his audience's pleasure in order to eat bread, like a duck, from their hands.

Emile's social debut is contained within an object lesson about building your own navigation instrument. At the story's close, Emile discovers the floating duck and needle always point north. Like his compass, Emile is pliable wax under his tutor's hand, formed around a needle-center that responds to natural laws. Children who make their own scientific instruments, says Rousseau, avoid becoming "a machine in others' hands," easily controlled by "a visionary, an alchemist, a charlatan, a cheat."[77] Emile is his compass, but potentially could have become the magician's entertainment apparatus, turning toward whomever holds the strongest magnet. Any straightforward reading of the compass object lesson is challenged, however, by the obvious similarity between the magician and his master magician doubles, Jean-Jacques, the ever-present tutor who masterfully controls his passive student through deception, and Rousseau, the author, a virtuoso intellectual performer.[78]

Here is where the paradox of autonomy and the automaton enter Rousseau's education experiment. The doubling of Jean-Jacques as both master magician and self-effacing guide for Emile's explorations gives credence to critics of Rousseau's political philosophy, from Edmund Burke and William Godwin to J. L. Talmon and Hannah Arendt, who question whether absolute submission to civil law as a sign of self-governance is actually consistent with moral autonomy.[79] Isolating Emile from other human influences merely secures Jean-Jacques's power over Emile. In the state of nature, Emile is free to do as he chooses, but the desires that guide his choices are determined by his tutor's micromanaged environment. "There is no subjection so perfect as that which keeps the appearance of freedom. Thus the will itself is made captive. The poor child . . . Do you not dispose, with respect to him, of everything which surrounds him?" Rousseau compares Emile to Condillac's "moving statue," who comes to life as an adult, "a perfect imbecile, an automaton, an immovable and almost insensible statue." Emile must refrain from coming to life too soon before his mind is ready to govern his body. "But where will we put this child to raise him like a being without sensation, like an automaton?" he asks. "Will we keep him away from all human beings?"[80] Yes, we will. In an already socialized world, such an environment must be artificial. In short, Rousseau's child of nature is an automaton living in a lab.

Frustrated with Rousseau's byzantine, impractical lessons, the Edgeworths dispute the importance of abstract freedom for children, who just want "the liberty of doing certain specific things which they have found to be agreeable."[81] The "Rosamond" stories offer a different kind of freedom—limited and provisional, but transparent and practical—a product of a social, material world, where people judge and exchange objects according to their cultural signification. To cultivate children's freedom, Edgeworth extends the mimetic qualities of machine or compass to other object assemblages, which her characters encounter by chance rather than design. Rosamond's objects encompass one another, forming new instruments: Liquid in a purple jar, needle in the housewife, rabbit in a cage, plum eaten, seeds buried in the earth.

These come to fruition in the later installment of Rosamond tales, when she observes no less than six automated machines that represent her development. These machines all trace their way back to Mrs. Egerton, Rosamond's reading companion and mentor, who fits the mold of the "rational mother-figure" or "rational dame," usually a character double for a work's female author, who teaches children reading and moral sentiments. Mrs. Egerton embodies the lesson of the purple jar, but with a deep sense of love and family history. She permanently damaged her hand while saving her granddaughter from a fire, making her inside more beautiful than her outside. Her loving sacrifice recalls Maria Edgeworth's grandmother, an adherent to Locke's education methods, who lost the use of one arm after giving birth to Richard Lovell.[82] Valuing hidden virtues over appearances, Rosamond befriends Mrs. Egerton in *Continuation of Early Lessons* (1814), and together they explore the natural wonders carefully wrapped and organized in her curiosity cabinet. Each item contains vessels within vessels: a nautilus shell formed with "partitions, or distinct cells"; coral made of "innumerable small cells"; and "a set of Chinese toys," or figures rowing boats, drawing water, and tumbling, "set in motion by touching or winding up some machinery inside, which was concealed from view." The nautilus and coral compartments are built by living creatures. They are both architecture and organism, mirroring that most complex hidden organic compartment built by Rosamond: her mind. "Mamma," she remarks, as she locks Mrs. Egerton's curio drawer with her own key, "there is a sort of pleasure, in commanding oneself," better "than seeing Chinese tumblers, or anything else."[83]

However playful, these Chinese automata have instructional uses. Ornate automata were associated with China because they were commissioned as expensive items to trade for Chinese luxury goods, then collected and displayed in James Cox's London museum. And indeed, the jeweled automata, as Rosamond herself declares, are entertaining but impractical—except as predecessors to another British effort at global textile production. Father explains the "*power* or *force* which set the figures in motion" to his little "mechanics," preparing his children to visit a cotton mill. The factory is described in the same terms as the marketplace, where two years ago Rosamond gripped "her mother's hand," as she saw "a great variety of different sorts of things, of which she did not know the use, or even the names." Now ten, she tucks her arm under her older brother's, "almost deafened by the noise, and dizzy from the sight of a multitude of wheels spinning around." Afterward, she puzzles through the purpose of the cotton gin, carding machine, and spinning jenny, comparing these with workers who thresh grain and spin wool by hand, "only better and faster." But she cannot grasp their source of power: "How were they moved—there is the thing I don't know, papa!" Her confusion correlates with her own struggle at this stage to grasp what moral principles should move her. Once her purple jar, or her compass needle, now Rosamond is a thousand needles—a "*spinning jenny*" moved by mechanical principals that she must understand to refashion herself.[84] From curious toy to useful machine, Rosamond builds herself into the very definition, in Johnson's dictionary, of an automatous object: "having the power of motion in itself."

In the final installment, *Rosamond: A Sequel to Early Lessons* (1821), the pre-teen heroine builds a decorative display case for Mrs. Egerton's watch. Once owned by Charles II, and "one of the first watches that ever was made in England" it still keeps perfect time.[85] Godfrey teasingly calls it a "huge, clumsy, warming pan of a watch," but finds it reproachfully staring down from the mantle when the two siblings visit the Egertons. During their trip, they meet a traveling salesman, who presents a "box of curiosities" (another curiosity cabinet), filled with ornamental automata by M. Bautte: a mouse so lifelike the cat tries to eat it; a bird who breathes and warbles; a caterpillar who walks by "drawing ring within ring"; and a beautiful "bracelet of memory," equipped with a hidden watch alarm mechanism that pricks the wearer with an invisible pin. Jean-François Bautte was an actual person, a celebrated watchmaker and jeweler described by illustrious shop visitors like Alexandre Dumas, Honoré de Balzac, and John Ruskin. He produced jeweled automata and watches from an unassuming workshop in Geneva, a workshop Edgeworth may have seen herself when she visited Geneva the previous year.[86] Rosamond's parents give her sixty guineas and let her choose between purchasing a horse or the bracelet.

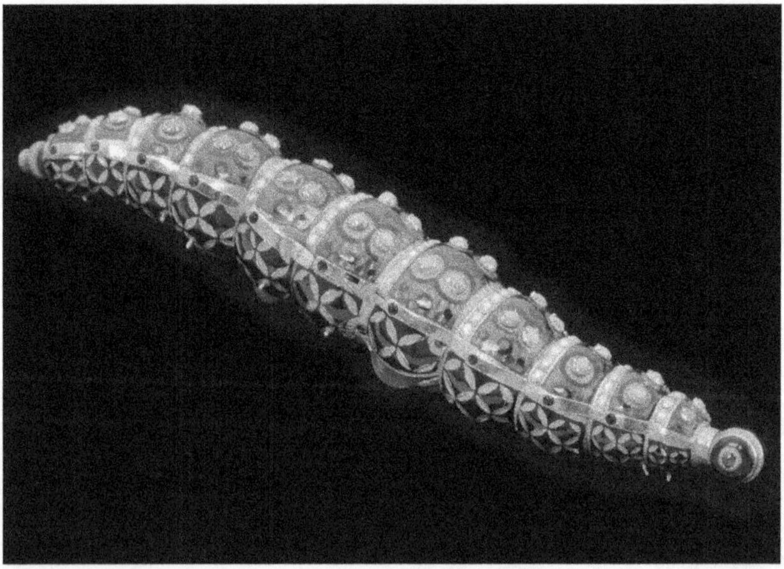

FIGURE 32. Chenille automate (Caterpillar automaton), ca. 1790s, photo by Renaud Sterchi. © Musée d'horlogerie du Locle—Château des Monts, Le Locle, Switzerland. One of several surviving caterpillar automata conventionally attributed to Henri Maillardet, who displayed them in London. The mechanical catepillar also matches the description of M. Bautte's work from "The Bracelet of Memory."

As with jar and shoes, Rosamond chooses between ornament and mobility, but with larger stakes and greater ambiguity. Like housewife and needles, the bracelet is another pin-based "moral compass." They jokingly call it the "bracelet of conscience" for its ability to "prick" Rosamond into punctuality. Deciding for the horse, Rosamond explains that she would grow indifferent to the watch's prick. (According to David Hartley and others, people grow insensitive to repeated sensations.) Again, the choice occurs before a family audience, testing her independence. Her brother, Godfrey, remarks, "What a pretty sort of judgment a person must have who cannot decide when others are standing by."[87] Situated near the conclusion of Rosamond's education, "The Bracelet of Memory"—itself an automaton replica of the human body—depicts Rosamond's successful internalization of her mother's prudence. Rosamond refuses to risk losing a skill developed from habituated discipline—her ability to keep track of time—by re-tooling her internal clock. By refusing the bracelet for the horse, Rosamond affirms her ability to self-regulate, and in the horse, she chooses a means of leaving the home, to go with her shoes.

But the hidden pin makes one last jab. Each of the three Rosamond installments conclude with a social choice in which Rosamond must sacrifice her personal property for the well-being of another person. Just as she gave her hyacinths to the dressmaker's daughter, Rosamond gives up the horse to pay for a surgical procedure in London for "Blind Kate," a kind girl her own age who lost her sight while recovering a flock of sheep in a snowstorm. As mentor to Kate, Rosamond uses the same pedagogical principles as her parents, respecting Kate's autonomy. Kate must think for herself. "We will not force you to do any thing, even for your good, against your will," she tells her. "Only hear me first, then do as you please."[88] She calmly describes an experimental procedure performed by Dr. Jean-Pierre Maunoir, "the celebrated Genevese oculist," and recounted in his *Memoires sur l'organisation de l'iris et l'operation de la pupille artificielle* (1812). The surgery creates an "artificial pupil" with a pin-sized incision, a fitting application of Rosamond's needle.[89]

Rosamond literally gives the gift of observation to the poor. Funded by the money Rosamond received for her horse, this final generous act asserts that private property is essential for both object learning and benevolent action. Moreover, the surgery is a particularly visceral representation of opening the eyes, an ableist trope used to represent curiosity, judgment, and understanding. As Rosamond's mother once told her in "The Two Plums," "Use your own understanding, because you will not always have my eyes to see with." The "Rosamond" stories offer an effective critique of Rousseau, with a clever theory of socialized objects as a source of child agency, yet it depends on cultural amnesia concerning the working-class origins of experiential education. Like Edgeworth, Rosamond learns from visiting workshops and factories, but she easily perceives herself, by virtue of her privileged social position, as the observer, owner, and originator of this knowledge and, therefore, as a fit educator to engineer another human subject. Next, I will explore this ambiguity between gift and cultural theft in "Lame Jervas," the first story from Edgeworth's collection *Popular Tales*.

The Education of Mechanics and the Mechanics of Education in *Popular Tales*

During roughly the same years that Maria Edgeworth wrote her major children's literature series, she published *Popular Tales* (1804), written, as Richard Lovell's preface declares, for those "eighty thousand readers," who are neither "nobility, clergy, or gentlemen of the learned professions," and who rarely see themselves represented in fiction.[90] The opening story of *Popular Tales*, "Lame Jervas," which I focus on here, is a fictional working-class autobiography, one that adapts the same lessons on property and machines from Rosamond to a working-class youth. But where Rosamond's story depicts a girl's progress toward autonomy through rational education, Jervas depicts the rise of the working classes through alphabetical and mechanical literacies.

Educational and industrial machinery come together in Edgeworth's protagonist, William Jervas, who makes his fortune by building a machine model of the Cornish tin mines where he worked as a child. After touring Britain with his model, Jervas captures the attention of an East India Company agent, who employs him as an assistant for Rev. Dr. Bell in his Madras school. Jervas then travels to Mysore, where he assists Tipu Sultan in reforming his diamond mines, before returning to England a rich man. Describing "Lame Jervas" as a "story of self-help which looks back to Dick Whittington and forward to Samuel Smiles," Alan Richardson rightly identifies Jervas "as a prototype of the self-educated technician and self-made inventor and entrepreneur who would constitute the ideal (if hardly the actual) reader of *The Mechanics' Magazine* and the *Library of Useful Knowledge*." But Jervas is equal parts inventor, teacher, and imperialist.[91] He embodies a peculiar moment in education history when teachers could be compared, enthusiastically, to automaton makers, while machines evidenced Britain's potential for global economic dominance. With "Lame Jervas," Edgeworth's approach to learning from objects passes from country estate, to Cornish mines, to the diamond mines and royal courts of India. The story defends expanded access to education for the poor as necessary for England's emergence as an imperial power.

When *Popular Tales* first appeared during the reactionary period following the Reign of Terror in France (1793–74), the Irish Rebellion of 1798, and the 1801 Act of Union, writing anything for plebian readers was a fraught enterprise. While some elites favored reducing access to reading and writing, others, including Edgeworth, sought to create viable alternatives to radical literature aimed at working-class readers. The political significance of *Popular Tales* is obvious to the *Edinburgh Review*, which praises its sympathetic representation of everyday experiences turned to didactic purpose, and finds the collection "superior in genius" and "utility" to Thomas Paine's literature of "disaffection and infidelity" or the poetry of "Messrs. Wirdsworth & Co." The reviewer anticipates that *Popular Tales* will find favor among "the great and respectable multitude of English tradesmen, yeomen, and manufacturers" who compose "the well-educated in the lower and middling orders of the people."[92] Unlike Hannah More's *Cheap Repository Tracts* (1795–98), which were priced to compete with radical literature, *Popular Tales* cost more than what some readers could afford, but when successful, such works could be reprinted and distributed in cheaper editions.[93]

With *Popular Tales*, Edgeworth takes a nuanced position in the debate over whether expanding mass literacy would quiet or enflame political unrest. At the time, Edgeworth corresponded with the English tract writer Mary Leadbeater and the Scottish novelist Elizabeth Hamilton, who volunteered at local schools and promoted the spread of literacy. Confident in the power of rational political didacticism, Edgeworth refutes anti-Jacobin fear mongering directed at the reading public and imagines a kind of popular literature where "one of the dramatis personae is not produced to harangue, and domineer, and the other to ask questions, and be refuted."[94] Her contribution to these ends bears remarkable similarity to *The Cottagers of Glenburnie* (1808), published four years later by Elizabeth Hamilton, which was first conceived as "separate pieces" in "form and size resembling" More's tracts, but ultimately published for general audiences.[95] Both Edgeworth and Hamilton begin with the story of rags-to-riches protagonists (Edgeworth's Jervas, Hamilton's Mrs. Mason) who gain literacy through a benevolent patron, repay their education with gratitude, and become the center of moral authority within their communities as school teachers to the poor. Both story collections also promote Monitorial schools, a new method of co-instruction that promised to make government-funded mass education feasible in England and Ireland by applying the division of labor to classrooms.[96]

As an exploration of autonomy and automata, "Lame Jervis" differs from Edgeworth's *Belinda* or *Rosamond* because it represents mimetic machines in the context of popular education. The story quotes from a recently published pamphlet on the monitorial method by Rev. Dr. Andrew Bell, head of a charity school in Madras where he taught "the orphan and distressed male children of the European military." Bell used a method of co-teaching he observed among Indian youth in the Malabar region who taught one another to write by tracing letters "on the ground," before he published a pamphlet on his "Madras Method" titled *An Experiment in Education Made at the Male Asylum: Suggesting a System by which a School or Family May Teach Itself under the Superintendence of the Master or Parent* (1797).[97] Before long, educators grasped the potential of the Monitorial "machine" for scaling cheap literacy instruction in Britain and Ireland. Instead of expensive books and paper, children traced letters in sand on a board. By repeating lessons in pairs simultaneously instead of each reporting to the teacher, pupils efficiently covered the material, requiring children to absent themselves from work for a shorter period, an advantage in poor families that depended on child wages.

The machine analogy for Monitorial schools was widespread among Edgeworth's contemporaries, who praised co-instruction for applying the division of labor to organizing students.[98] Bell's friend and supporter Samuel Taylor Coleridge, whose organic metaphors for children's minds have come to epitomize Romanticism, personally lectured in support of Bell, pronouncing monitorial education a "vast moral steam-engine" that should be "adopted and in free motion throughout the Empire."[99] In two pamphlets supporting education for poor children, Sir Thomas Bernard, president of the Royal Institute and its parent organization, the Society for Bettering the Condition and Increasing the Comforts of the Poor, blithely compares the wonders of industrial machinery, which "simplified and facilitated the most irksome and labourious operation," with what "Dr. Bell has done to *intellectual* operations. It is the division of labour in his schools, that leaves the master the easy task of directing the movements of the whole machine," and "the principle in manufactories, and in schools, is the same."[100] But far from degrading the mind, as Adam Smith warns, the machinery of Monitorial schools improves the intellect of workers by forming "the habit of using and exercising his own faculties," producing subjects capable of reasoned consent to their governance.[101]

Taking the factory schoolroom to its logical extreme, the Dissenting Quaker schoolteacher Joseph Lancaster published a more detailed account of what he called, in widely circulating advertisements, his "new and mechanical system of education," titled *Improvements in Education, as It Respects the Industrious Classes of the Community* (1803), which boasted the monitorial education of "one thousand poor children" at his Southwark institution.[102] Fueled by religious sectarian rivalry, Bell and Lancaster schools opened across England, rapidly expanding access to affordable schools over the next decades, and directly leading in 1807 to the first bill proposing (unsuccessfully) a national system of primary education for England, read by Samuel Whitbread, MP (whose wife, Elizabeth Whitbread, was a friend of Maria Edgeworth and Jane Marcet); and Richard Lovell read another unsuccessful bill, composed with assistance from Maria, shortly before the dissolution of Ireland's Parliament.[103] This "approved system of mechanical education," as Whitbread called it, offered a poetic solution, in which the division of labor, after degrading minds in precisely the way predicted by Adam Smith, emerged once again on the side of "civilization" when implemented in the classroom.[104] If factory machines injured the mind, then intellectual machines could fix them. Like the "Rosamond" stories, then, *Popular Tales* comfortably links industrial and educational machines as twin engines for progress.

In defense of popular education, "Lame Jervas" begins with the unsettling appearance of the alphabet in a mine—the haunting sign of unregulated education. Pointing "to some letters that were carved on the rock," a gentleman touring a Cornish mine asks his guide, "Whose name was written there?" The guide pronounces, "William Jervas," and recounts Jervas's disappearance long ago and the rumors that his ghost haunts the mine. The ladies and gentlemen touring the mine laugh at the guide's quaint superstitions, and "words" almost come "to blows," before the inquiring gentleman "put an end to the dispute" by revealing, to everyone's astonishment, that he is William Jervas. The miner-turned-gentleman visits the mine's proprietor, Mr. R—, and the miners accept a general invitation to dine outside in tents with their employer, where Jervas appears "dressed in his miner's old jacket and cap" to tell his story for the entire audience of miners and traveling tourists.[105]

The real ghost in the Cornish mines is the disturbing presence of writing itself, in a community regarded as a hotbed of radical unrest. The audience assembled by Jervas for his dinnertime biography symbolizes the rapprochement between classes advocated by Edgeworth's collection, with its economically diverse target audience. Because he prevents violence from erupting between the miners and the touring gentlemen, Jervas is a double for Maria Edgeworth, an Anglo-Irish landlord who "cloaks" herself as a Cornish miner to write stories for turbulent times. Recognizing her ventriloquism, *The Annual Review and History of Literature* praises Edgeworth's "simple art, of talking on paper, in the very style really employed by such characters as those that she so naturally represents."[106]

Echoing events from Rosamond's property lesson in "The Rabbit," Jervas gains access to education through repeated demonstrations of his respect for property. At the beginning of the story, Jervas is the tool of the worst men in the mine. But while recovering from his broken leg under the mine proprietor's care, Jervas observes those "better sort" of miners who visit his sick bed. Like them, he wants "a little garden, and property of my own, for which I knew I must work hard."[107] Rebounding with a new appreciation for personal property, Jervas next protects his master's property by informing on several miners who hide their discovery of "Cornish diamonds" and secretly steal the load for themselves. After building his automaton model, Jervas gains the confidence of his next master, a traveling science lecturer, by speaking up when he accidentally pays Jervas with a guinea covered with quicksilver (from a chemical demonstration) in place of a shilling. Thereafter, the suspicious instructor trusts Jervas with his property, allowing him to read from his library of books and to help produce his lectures. Once in India, the reports of Jervas's honesty impress Tipu Sultan, who employs him to tutor his son and improve his diamond mines. Jervas advances from mentee to mentor, and from miner to proprietor. As Julia Wright observes, each stage in Jervas's advancement requires passing "a test" that "proves his usefulness to his masters," but each test also demonstrates his respect for his masters' property, which is rewarded with access to a quality education.[108]

Respect for property, it is worth noting, is the prerequisite for education in all of Edgeworth's stories. Rosamond's education begins with a purchase and ends with a gift, while the "Frank" stories, intended for younger readers, seems entirely preoccupied with what belongs to Frank and what does not, a distinction necessary before Frank can safely pick things up and explore. Because Frank does not grab things without asking, a gardener allows Frank to visit whenever he likes, but he shuts the gate to another boy who steals his fruit. Likewise, the first two installments of the "Harry and Lucy" stories revolve around the children's efforts to restore a brickmaker's property that Harry carelessly destroys. The brickmaker tells Harry he must pay for the bricks, for "I am a poor man," and "I shall have less bread if I have a smaller number of bricks to sell." His father simplifies the lesson for him: "You must not meddle with what does not belong to you."[109] Respect for property ensures that children only meddle with the right stuff, and if they do, they are rewarded with access to more things, and eventually books. Alphabetical and mechanical literacies are outgrowths of property, while literacy is also the property of children, earned through labor.

Popular Tales offers the same bargain to a poor protagonist who also respects property, then enjoys object lessons, then access to books. He receives his first education from a benevolent teacher, Dr. Y—, a practitioner of Edgeworth's methods, who protects Jervas after his life is threatened in the mines as an informant. When Jervas first joins Dr. Y—'s household, the doctor has his "children about him" engaged in active investigations, "one little chap on his knee, another climbing on the arm of his chair." The doctor invites Jervas to join his children's lessons, and he connects reading with mining, praising Jervas when he asks a "sensible question":

> He saw that I gazed, with vast curiosity, at several objects in the room, which were new to me: and, pointing to the glass tube, which he had been showing the boys when I first came in, he asked me if they had such things as that in our mines; and if I knew the use of it? I told him I had seen something like it in our overseer's hands; but that I had never known its use. It was a thermometer. Mr. Y— took great pains to show me how, and on what occasions, this instrument might be useful.

Jervas readily participates in the kind of domestic scene described in *Practical Education*, in which adults converse rationally with children, teaching by letting the children explore the objects surrounding them. Mr. Y— follows a number of Edgeworthian best practices: he lets Jervas's curiosity determine what lessons he teaches; he connects new knowledge with older, concrete knowledge from Jervas's own experience; he invites Jervas to ask questions; and he permits Jervas to explore the thermometer with his hands.

Objects lead naturally to reading. Through handling the thermometer, the doctor discovers that Jervas cannot read and, once again guided by Jervas's desires, offers to pay for a writing master "as I wished to learn." The relationship between handling the thermometer and learning to read is the first indication that Jervas's education plaits together mechanical literacy with other forms of literacy. Significantly, Jervas associates the thermometer with a position of authority. It belongs in the "overseer's hands" and Jervas "had never known its use." By learning its use, Jervas takes the place reserved for the overseer, holding his symbol of authority. Notably, the thermometer is an instrument of measurement, but also a vessel for knowledge, like Rosamond's housewife and compass. Learning to read and use instruments allows Jervas to build a model of the mines where he worked, using the reward money from his master to hire a craftsman to help. The project requires Jervas to revisit the mines at night, risking his life to "make it exact." "I measured and minuted down every thing with the most cautious accuracy," he recalls.[110] As an observer of the mines, Jervas now resembles the proprietor who holds the themometer: He returns to the mines to measure them.

Jervas's automaton miners communicate order, improvement, and control, through both education and industrial machines. Once he builds the sophisticated automaton model of the mines, Jervas conducts demonstrations for the local children of middle-class families. His mechanical figures are superior to living miners because they submit to his corrective tools. Jervas adjusts "one stiff old fellow" and "an obstinate old woman, who would . . . but curtsey, when I wanted her to kneel down and to do her work." He describes his power over the figures using managerial language: "At last we got our wooden miners to obey us, and to perform their several tasks at the word of command; that is to say, at the pulling of certain strings and wires, which we fastened to their legs, arms, heads, and shoulders: which wires, being slender and black, were at a little distance invisible to the spectators."[111] Jervas's transition from puppet to puppet-master is typical of the mystique surrounding automaton makers and engineers, whose intellect places them above the machines that do their bidding.

In modeling the mines, Jervas places himself in a God-like visual position, able to see the entire mining process at once and comprehend it as his own creation. With his newfound perspective, Jervas distances himself from mechanical labor and views the mines as a system, achieving what Simon Schaffer describes as the industrial manager's "view of the machine." To understand the class significance of this move, consider how Andrew Ure (decades later) defends the "factory system" as a mysterious whole, incomprehensible to the common laborer: "Of the amount of the injury resulting from the violation of the rules of automatic labour, he [the laborer] can hardly ever be a proper judge; just as mankind at large can never fully estimate the evils consequent upon an infraction of God's moral law."[112] The perspectival change that Jervas undergoes shows the kind of power over production achieved by learning the general laws or principles behind mechanical work. As the final step, Jervas adds a glass viewing window to his automaton, creating the visual effect of a peep show, in which figures appear realistic and life-sized, enabling him to share his empowering perspective with audiences.

Stories about the ascension of a working-class youth through mechanical savvy are a favorite of nineteenth-century biographies for children. One anecdote, republished in several children's books, is so similar to Jervas that it seems like a possible source for Edgeworth's story. A seventeen-year-old "self-taught mechanist" named John Young, a weaver's son, gained "notice" among scientists for building a sort of automaton called the Jack of All Trades. Using only a pocket knife, the youth created "a box, about three feet long by two broad, and six or eight inches deep," replete with artisans "two or three inches high" hard at work, "employed in those trades and sciences with which the boy is familiar," which he displayed around his neighborhood.[113] Jervas is thus an instance of a type portrayed in inventor biographies of the poor, clever youth who tinkers with clocks until he finds sponsorship from a wealthy gentleman, achieves success through hard work, and ultimately teaches mechanics to other children. James Ferguson, the first member voted to the Royal Society with his dues paid, spent his youth "making models of mills, spinning-wheels," and later built a "wooden clock." A local minister, like Dr. Y—, lent Ferguson star maps and "often took the threshing-flail out of my hands and worked himself, while I sat by him in the barn busy with my compasses, ruler, and pen." Ferguson later became an educator, writing lectures on "the various branches of physical science" to "render them accessible" to lay readers.[114] The story finds its fullest Victorian substantiation in George Stephenson, a favorite for children's biographies, who invented the steam locomotive and was known to teach his fellow navvies. He first worked as a cow-keeper in "marshy country-side" where "he erected numerous little mills and fashioned engines out of clay, employing hemlocks to represent their tubes and pipes."[115] The children's biographies of Helen C. Knight illustrate young Stevenson, surrounded by neighboring children who eagerly observe while he fixes clocks outside his home. Once a celebrated engineer, Stevenson shaped men and machines: "He employed in his collieries upwards of a thousand men, and his attention to their physical and mental improvement is said to have been unremitting. . . . He had made in babyhood clay engines, and now in his manhood he built them of stouter material."[116] Whether biography or fiction, these books show a consistent pattern. Building model machines sparks a youth's social mobility yet confirms the social order through paternalist mentorship. Both mechanic and teacher, Jervas can narrate his own story, yet his ability to read and understand science is portrayed, nevertheless, as a charitable gift from Dr. Y—, who opens the understanding of a deserving poor boy, much as Rosamond gives blind Kate her sight, a gift Jervas repays by teaching what he knows about mining to wealthier children across England and serving as a civilizing influence on the Cornish miners.

In the second half of the story, Jervas plays the same role in India, where he secures a position with Rev. Dr. Andrew Bell's school and tutors Tipu Sultan's son, Prince Abdul Calie. He then persuades the Sultan to free the slaves who work his diamond mines, and instead creates a system that rewards miners with a portion of what they find. A jealous, corrupt merchant betrays him, however, and he narrowly escapes with his life. His wages are, thankfully, invested safely in a bank, and he also sells a diamond ring given to him by the Prince, returning to England a wealthy man. By locating abusive working conditions in India, the story implies that English miners are comparatively well off as "free" laborers in a capitalist system that rewards hard work and honesty, whereas Tipu betrays his unfitness for rule, as a childish, petulant enslaver. In short, Edgeworth projects British injustices onto Tipu, since at the time Britain led the world in transporting enslaved Africans.

India is where Jervas can test his full power by sharing his experimental apparatuses and automaton model with his pupils at Bell's Madras Asylum and with Tipu's son, just as Mr. Y– – once shared his lab with him. Giving instruction proves Jervas to be a rational adult, just as Rosamond proves herself by gifting sight to Blind Kate. In both stories, several intersectional identities—gender, disability, race, class, and nationality—allow Edgeworth's protagonists to learn from more privileged characters (coded rational), then to regift sight, mobility, and observation to those younger or socially below them. Since Jervas begins life as a miner, he must travel abroad to find a fitting young protégé for himself, one ranked above him but portrayed as his cultural inferior. As is usual in Edgeworth's fiction, Jervas's Indian adventures incorporate real life details, but in this case, the real historical persons, texts, and objects that she references tell a very different story from the one she invents.[117] A closer look at the real events that inspired "Lame Jervas" exposes Edgeworth's complicity in erasing cultural theft in India by inventing a story about paternalist mentorship and respect for property.

The episodes at Bell's school and Tipu's court closely follow details from Bell's pamphlet on the Monitorial method, with passages quoted verbatim in the footnotes. Curiously, by citing Bell as her source, Edgeworth gestures to the Indian influence on English Monitorial schools even though her story intends to claim cultural superiority for Englishmen. Despite the Indian origins of Bell's co-teaching practices, there was a heated pamphlet debate over whether Rev. Dr. Bell, an Anglican, or Lancaster, a Quaker, first invented the Monitorial method, fueled by a sectarian contest over whether schools should remain tied to the Anglican church. After devoting an entire book to the question, the poet Robert Southey, who later wrote a three-volume biography of Andrew Bell, acknowledged that some people believe neither Englishman deserves credit, since "the new system is merely the Hindoo system imported into England." In the end, however, Southey credits Bell after considering what constitutes a discovery and who can claim to own it, a question equally contentious for any technology: "The person who first introduced into a school the principle, as a principle, of conducting it by means of the scholars themselves, is as much the discoverer of that principle, as Franklin of electricity or Jenner of vaccination. The facts were known before them, but in an insulated and unproductive form; they systematized them, and thus communicated to us a new power."[118] Southey's language compares pedagogical methods to the physical sciences and ultimately assigns ownership to those with Jervas's comprehensive vision, who, like mechanical philosophers, comprehend "principles" and "systemized" classrooms. Since India's independence, Bell's and Lancaster's claim has been challenged by historians of Indian education, who more recently have called attention to the creation of hybrid institutional models that combined parochial Indian and European methods.[119] Edgeworth, however, displays the same logic as Southey by giving Bell credit for generously helping Indian children rather than reciprocally learning with them.

These same assumptions apply to scientific knowledge in Tipu's court, which Edgeworth portrays as the gift of European emissaries to an ungrateful despot. As Ian Haywood argues, Jervas is "an ambassador of technological modernization," while as Julia Wright notes, Tipu "is painted in overwrought orientalist colours."[120] In Edgeworth's story, Tipu Sultan is infantilized, "intent upon displaying his small stock of mechanical knowledge," and he treats Jervas "as a species of mechanic juggler, who was fit only to exhibit for the amusement of his court." When Jervas uses instruments to demonstrate scientific principles, the Sultan demands the objects as gifts "with the eagerness of a child who has begged and obtained a new plaything."[121] Instead of finding practical applications for the principles of science, Tipu tries to steal the exhibit equipment and relishes mere entertainment.

Tipu Sultan's incompetence contrasts with the curious, respectful bearing of his son, who received a British education. In real life, two of Tipu's children became the hostages of Lord General Cornwallis in 1792 at the close of the Third Anglo-Mysore War, ensuring Tipu's compliance with an unfavorable treaty that seized half his lands and a large portion of his wealth. Although armed conflicts are noticeably absent from "Lame Jervas," the story must take place after the heirs' return to Tipu's court. Edgeworth's depiction of the Mysore royal family is consistent with other representations of the hostage transfer circulating at the time, which Catherine E. Anderson argues Europeanize Tipu's sons and portray General Cornwallis as a safe, paternal figure, while Tipu appears "a poor father, to his subjects and to his sons." These depictions portray "the East India Company" as "a better parent to India than its own native rulers."[122] Edgeworth corroborates these images of colonial paternalism by portraying education as a European gift, bestowed through Bell's charity school and Jervas's mentorship, in the same decade when, in fact, English schools adapted co-teaching practices of the Malabar region for their classrooms, practices they celebrated as a high-tech "moral machine" for their empire.

In addition to giving education, Jervas arrives in Tipu's court as a European scientist, ready to give his industrial knowledge to improve what Edgeworth portrays as a backward economy. This representation also differs from Edgeworth's source. Jervas's experiences in India are based on the historical account of William Smith, provided in an appendix to Bell's monitorial pamphlet. The real William Smith was a seventeen-year-old military clerk and former pupil of Rev. Dr. Bell whose accomplishments Bell details to document his school's achievements and to combat reservations about educating the biracial children of British officers.[123] Monitorial schools in India exclusively hired "native" Indian teachers, not Cornish miners. Alumni like William Smith were supposed to aid "downward filtration" of British cultural knowledge, including the gospel, but also physical astronomy, calculated to displace Indian cosmologies. Their hybrid cultural identities were leveraged for a social technology (the Monitorial school), created to transform poor colonial and metropole subjects alike through mutual student surveillance.[124] Likely the son of a British military officer and an Indian woman, Smith accompanied the British embassy "when the hostage princes were restored, and went through a course of experiments in natural philosophy in the presence of the Sultaun," using equipment given by the "government of Madras," most of which Tipu Sultan already understood. Some of Tipu's inquiries, recorded by Bell, suggest concern for military applications. This account is consistent with the cautious respect that British officials afforded Tipu, who was a divisive and formidable opponent waging war in the region using advanced rocket technology unknown to Europeans.[125] Tipu's scientific acumen is absent in Edgeworth's adaptation of this source material. As retold in "Lame Jervas," these events become a heroic drama in which a white Cornish miner arrives in India, equipped with his educational and industrial machinery to teach an ignorant court that fails to appreciate his gift.[126]

Edgeworth's nationalist retelling legitimates the recent British invasion of Tipu's fortress at Seringapatam on May 4, 1799, when troops killed Tipu, stole a jeweled ring from his body, and looted the city, an event so violent that it would later inspire the opening sequence about the mythical gem stolen in Wilkie Collins's 1868 detective novel *The Moonstone*. While Edgeworth wrote "Lame Jervas," newspapers recounted the fall of Seringapatam during the months preceding October 1799, along with reports of Tipu's unparalleled library, seized and shipped to England, in yet another instance of stolen knowledge.[127] By September, popular panoramas in London included "The Storming of Seringapatam" with "new scenery and machinery," while the Tower of London displayed two cheetahs and Tipu's gold throne alongside an automaton seized from Tipu's palace.[128] Now exhibited at the Victoria and Albert Museum, Tipu's Tiger was a sensation, its appearance dramatically advertised in the *Weekly Entertainer* as a "mechanism representing a tiger in the act of devouring a prostrate European" that produces "the cries of a person in distress, intermixed with the roars of a tiger," while "the hand of the European is often lifted up to express his helpless and deplorable condition."[129] A figurine of Tipu's Tiger titled "The Death of Monroe" (the man believed depicted) became one of the most popular chimney-piece decorations in British households, reducing Tipu's royal symbol to a decorative toy.[130] As with Monitorial education, Tipu's tiger indicates that social and scientific technologies circulated in both directions between Europe and India against a backdrop of colonial war, which resulted in theoretical education systems supposedly capable of executing a civilizing mission in any locale, whether the city of London or Madras.

Retelling this history as the adventures of a heroic English machine-builder accords with emergent beliefs among Edgeworth's readers about Britain's coming global preeminence through industrial technology. Michael Adas describes a new mode of Eurocentric cultural assessment at the close of the eighteenth century, when "European observers came to view science and especially technology as the most objective and unassailable measures of their own civilization's past achievement and present worth."[131] Jervas's adventures cover one episode in the slow erosion of India's considerable craft expertise and economic power through colonial violence followed by collective amnesia as Britain asserted global supremacy by right of its newfound technological expertise. By 1832 Charles Babbage could celebrate the "tools and machines" that "distinguishes our country" above all others: "The cotton of India is conveyed by British ships round half our planet, to be woven by British skill in the factories of Lancashire" and "repurchased by the lords of the soil which gave it birth."[132]

There was no place in this new nationalist vision for acknowledging the science expertise of Tipu's court and its renowned library, the influence of Indian education practices on British schools, the achievements of a biracial teacher and emissary like William Smith, or the transcontinental collaboration between French and Indian craftsmen who produced Tipu's Tiger. Over time, British policymakers grew to recognize the advantages of popular education for extending colonial power, since sustaining technological supremacy required expanding access to education. In a pamphlet from 1805, Andrew Irvine, personal chaplain to the Marquis Cornwallis (Cornwallis served as military governor in India during the Third Anglo-Mysore War of 1790 to 1792, then in Ireland during the unification), supports Monitorial schools for poor children, "by whose skilful exertions the resources of our national prosperity will be extended, and Britain's superiority over other nations maintained upon the most noble and commanding grounds." Monitorial schools would make poor children into soldiers and bureaucrats for the Empire.[133]

Let us pause to tally the layers of amnesia at work in both the "Rosamond" stories and "Lame Jervas." The "Rosamond" stories represent wealthy families as generous mentors who bequeath their pedagogical methods to illiterate factory children and open the eyes of Blind Kate; *Popular Tales* credits Andrew Bell with inventing co-education in the Madras school for boys and a Cornish miner with bringing automata to Mysore. In both cases, a gift overwrites an appropriation that at best can be generously described as cross-class and cross-national collaboration, creating a false paternalist narrative of top-down instruction. What educators did, then, was assert educational expertise by systematizing practices used by workers, both locally and globally, producing generalizable theories with universalist claims, which could be re-exported through institutions that serve those same communities. This practice places the curriculum goals and content firmly in the hands of those invested in maintaining a stable, stratified society. To this point, a half-century later "Lame Jervas" was reprinted with a new title, "The Reward of Honesty" (1849), as part of the *Encyclopaedia Bengalensis*, edited by Krishna Mohan Banerji "for young readers in Bengal," a collection of "European history and physics" selected for "combating aberrations in the minds of the common people of Bengal."[134]

Conclusion

These three texts by Maria Edgeworth, written for distinct audiences and with protagonists of different ages and stations, all emphasize the importance of observing and manipulating the material world to establish human agency and capacity for rational thought. Rosamond, Jervas, and Lady Delacour each begin from a position of exclusion, as less-than-capable individuals because of their gender, class, age, disability, or misbehavior, and must prove themselves through their object choices before they are welcomed into a circle of rational science educators. As a science writer familiar with engineering, Edgeworth uses automata to establish each character's governance of themselves and their world, always in relation other characters who remain automated, grouped with the object assemblages Rosamond manipulates. In this respect, Edgeworth's fiction captures how mechanical literacy in general produces the sensation of autonomy by equipping some children with knowledge of political economy or natural philosophy, which they use to establish their "empire" over the material world. This concept of autonomy reduces the material world to passive property, underwriting colonial conquest and environmental degradation while leaving intact the active/passive binary between object and subject that is so easily deployed to justify domination of some humans over others through objectification. Even though Edgeworth presents the path to autonomy as universally accessible, her emphasis on property ownership favors those who have a lot of stuff. Moreover, these stories imply that systematic education systems designed in one place are easily exported in the service of Britain's civilizing mission with its vision of top-down knowledge dissemination.

When Rosamond visits the textile mill with her family, for instance, she strongly identifies with another girl her own age, a worker leaving the factory surrounded by children. Ellen is a favorite because she worked extra hours for the littlest ones who could not stay awake at their machines so that they could each purchase subscriptions under their own names, the money going toward a silver cup, a parting gift for a clergyman who taught the factory children "to read and write." "They had no money; nothing of their own to give, but their labour," explains Rosamond's father.[135] The same may be true of Rosamond, but she is allowed to survey the industrial process, the hundreds of moving needles, top-down from that window. In the next chapter, I examine the politics of learning with the senses from the ground up, with radical author-educators active in the cooperative movement who challenge the exclusion of working-class people from political representation by valuing knowledge acquired through manual labor.

CHAPTER 5

"Knowledge Which Shall Be Power in Their Hands"

Radical Grammars for Working-Class Readers

While tutoring in composition at the Strand in London, George Mudie developed a seemingly uncontroversial method for teaching the first elements of grammar, which he published as *The Grammar of the English Language Truly Made Easy and Amusing; By the Invention of Three Hundred Moveable Parts of Speech* (1840). Constructed as a book/toy hybrid, the learning aid consists of a lesson book fused to a latched case that contains words printed on small pieces of paper color-coded by parts of speech, with the nouns illustrated by "sensible signs" (small pictures). Associating the grammar with other instructive toys, reviewers described the aid's success in teaching through play and recommended its use in schools or home nurseries. One reviewer from *The Spectator* reported the *Grammar* "set a party of children in a roar of laughter in the attempt to test the efficacy of its instruction," while another from *The New Satirist* predicts the "excessively ingenious" system "will be almost universally adopted in primary schools," as the method is "as diverting as a puzzle or a moveable map."[1]

At first glance, Mudie's *Grammar* uses a familiar metaphor of knowledge-as-property, stored in the mind-as-container. By moving about the slips of paper, children "grasp" grammar as something concrete, then they safeguard their paper words back in the box, just as the child's mind learns (or stores) grammatical concepts. However, Mudie was also a radical journalist who wrote extensively about property, and his views are quite different from those of Maria Edgeworth or Jane Marcet. Twenty

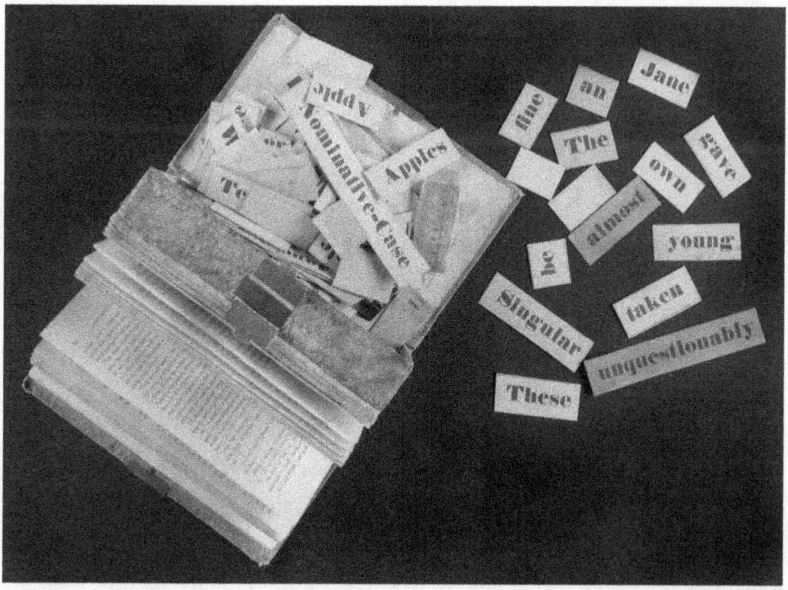

FIGURE 33. George Mudie, *The Grammar of the English Language Truly Made Easy and Amusing; By the Invention of Three Hundred Moveable Parts of Speech* (London: John Cleave, 1840). This copy does not have "sensible signs," or small images of objects, which appear on the noun papers of the Bodleian Library's copy.

years earlier, Mudie founded a Co-operative and Economical Society at Spa Fields based on the ideas of Robert Owen. The first of its kind, the society consisted of 250 families who "eat, live, work, and educate children together"; and from their offices he published the first cooperative periodical *The Economist* (1821–1822).[2] Mudie attacked classical economists such as David Ricardo, who argued that land is the source of all wealth by contending that labor generates the nation's wealth and workers should own all that they produce.[3] He built a reputation as an ardent opponent of Thomas Malthus, whose notion of limited resources and fatalistic attitude toward mass starvation Mudie equated with infanticide.[4] The reason that industrious people starve, Mudie countered, is that "surplus wealth" has never been "equitably distributed." Despite the great wealth of his nation, whose scientific advances enabled the production of more goods and food than ever before, "millions of her own people" remained "entirely destitute" of the "necessities and comforts of life."[5] As his writings on political economy indicate, Mudie had different ideas about property from the vast majority of middle-class authors who wrote for children—and he was not alone.

As I explore in this chapter, Mudie was one of several prominent activist-educators, many connected with the cooperative movement, who designed radical grammar textbooks for teaching working-class youth. Understanding the principles governing how material objects are created, exchanged, and distributed—what I define as mechanical literacy—could be described as the heart of the cooperative movement, which began in the 1820s to support the fair distribution of knowledge and goods through democratically operated schools, stores, and businesses. In the first half of the chapter, I define radical grammars and explain their emergence during a period of economic distress after 1815, when authors began combining playful pedagogical strategies used in instructional books for middle-class children with the satirical play that characterized working-class print culture.[6] While mainstream children's authors used the material affordances of books and learning aids to associate literacy with property ownership, radicals used similar teaching techniques to emphasize shared governance and economic justice.[7] In the second part, I analyze grammars published by two cooperators during the 1840s, at the height of the Chartist and cooperative movements: *Grammar of the English Language* by George Mudie (ca. 1840) and *Practical Grammar; or, Composition Divested of Difficulties* (1844), by George Jacob Holyoake. Grammar textbooks are a useful focus because they helped to establish a cannon of radical authors by collecting exemplary passages of political literature for emulation. Grammars also reveal intersections between women authors of children's books and working-class writers, despite their distinct social circles, genders, and political affiliations, particularly among cooperators, whom Anna Clark characterizes as more inclusive of women and feminist ideas.[8] Notably, George Mudie lived at the cooperative community at Orbiston, where Catherine Whitwell, after departing New Lanark, became "superintendent of the schools." Delivering lectures on history, chronology, and geography, she created a "chronological and historical chart to teach the children," along with other visual aids, including terrestrial and celestial globes (see chapter 1).[9] Putting these traditions into conversation highlights their indebtedness to one another while placing in sharp relief the divergent concepts of property imbedded in their teaching materials.[10]

Mudie and Holyoake were both teachers who wrote extensively on cooperative political economy. After editing several cooperative periodicals, Mudie worked as a schoolteacher and tutor before publishing *The Illuminated Temple of Letters*, an alphabet learning aid. He announced plans to write "The Philosophy of Grammar," likely an advanced work for youth and adults, although there is no indication he completed that project.[11] Of these projects, only his *Grammar* survives. Although Mudie remains mostly a footnote in histories of radical journalism, Holyoake is one of the cooperative movement's most prominent leaders. At age eighteen, Holyoake experienced a political awakening while reading Robert Owen's works and subsequently pursued a career as educator, cooperator, proponent of free speech, and historian of the cooperative movement. Holyoake edited several radical papers, including the cooperative paper *The English Leader* (1864–67), and co-founded the Rochdale Society of Equitable Pioneers, a cooperative society in Manchester whose success in creating affordable housing, food, and education served as a national model. In his textbooks, Holyoake subverts traditional hierarchies of knowledge by offering a theory of language in which everyday observation provides the foundation for grammar instruction.

Mudie and Holyoake used manipulatives and scientific observation to challenge the hierarchical divide between physical and intellectual labor. Instead of connecting the manipulation of matter with children's play, they connect it with physical labor. In doing so, they push back against deficit models that considered mechanical labor intellectually degrading by insisting that the manipulation of matter, through work, prepares youth to analyze political systems and suggest new governing laws. Radical instructors remind their students that by working with their hands they learn more about the world around them, making them astute observers with privileged access to practical knowledge. People who work with their hands easily perceive that society needs tinkering to put it to rights. To propose alternative systems of government, however, the people must "get knowledge," that is, learn the kind of systematic thinking about the economic "laws" and "principles" leveraged against them and master the advanced rhetorical skills needed to convince others.[12] In other words, they need mechanical literacy. In cooperative writings, the laws and principles governing how things move are analogous to grammatical laws; thus, physical labor leads to writing, which leads to political power.

In addition to books for children, Mudie and Holyoake drew inspiration from other radical working-class writers who for decades supported worker-organized mutual instruction and self-study to prepare the people for political action. "Knowledge Is Power" announced the banner at the top of Henry Hetherington and Bronterre O'Brien's paper *The Poor Man's Guardian* (1831–35), a quote from Francis Bacon, who was credited with formulating inductive reasoning. "Very true," commented the newly elected William Cobbett, MP, shortly after the Reform Act of 1832 fell far short of universal male suffrage, "but it must BE knowledge," not mere "Heddekashun," calculated "to bend the minds of children towards passive obedience and slavery," when they need "knowledge which shall be power in their hands."[13] The orator Henry Hunt agreed that the people must control their own institutions if they want an empowering education for their children, proclaiming himself "a warm advocate for the Education of the people; but he wished the people to be well remunerated for their labour," that they might "educate their own children in their own way, and not by charity (tremendous cheering)."[14] Working-class writers refer, instead, to the "knowledge of men and things"—an embodied, empowering knowledge, distinct from "education," a word with Latin roots that radical publications printed in ironic quotations.[15] Thus William Lovett and John Collins in *Chartism* (1840) deride that "word-teaching, rote-learning, memory-loading system" called "education," which teaches "mere barren symbols of realitics." Instead, "Real knowledge must be conveyed by *realities*; the *thing* itself must be made evident to one or more of the senses," so that students may use "*reflective powers*" to judge "the *why* and *wherefore*" of what they observe.[16] Using their own style, working-class authors praised teaching with "things," weaving experiential education into a radical materialist tradition of plain speaking and common sense, popularized by that loadstone of radical infidels, Thomas Paine.[17] "Knowledge must consist of observations made on mankind, and on whatever else exists within the scope of your observation," spoke Eliza Sharples at the Rotunda Theatre, "Books will aid you, but you must not make an authority of books, or of that which is written" but "prove all things."[18] The radical working-class press deployed mainstream pedagogical discourse with its skepticism of book learning to recuperate infantilizing and paternalist language used by middle-class educators who wished to bestow upon them a quantity of knowledge. The result was a lively, ironic teaching rhetoric, playful in its own way, that commends the working classes for their material mindedness, so often compared to childish understanding, and criticizes the rich and powerful as ignorant children, distracted from reality by the clanging nonsense of classical learning. They mobilized this radical language in the struggle for universal suffrage and legislative reforms curtailing work hours so that children could have more time to learn.

Defining the Radical Grammar

Once considered one of the "higher subjects" along with geography, advanced mathematics, and history, grammar was the prerequisite for studying rhetoric and included standard spelling and aesthetic style. With the rise of mass literacy and basic schooling in the late eighteenth century, grammar replaced the bare ability to read as a class marker, igniting enthusiasm among the upwardly mobile for acquiring the speech and writing styles of their social superiors through grammar instruction. English grammar was previously taught mostly to boys from wealthy families who studied classical languages. Designed for these elite students, grammar schoolbooks relied on complex philosophical ideas and technical terms, with ill-fitting rules borrowed from Latin and imposed onto vernacular English. During the late eighteenth century, publishers began producing grammar books for different kinds of readers, including young children, working-class youth, and girls.[19] The most popular of these was Lindley Murray's *English Grammar, Adapted to the Different Classes of Learners* (1795), an inexpensive schoolbook with simplified terminology, originally written at the request of a Quaker girls' school in York. Soon ubiquitous, Murray's *English Grammar* reached over three hundred editions in England and the United States by 1850, with various abridgements for plebian readers; it was published in Ireland, India, Germany, Portugal, France, and Japan. By the mid-nineteenth century, readers could choose from several hundred similar competing works.[20]

Despite the affordability of cheap grammars patterned after Murray, learning advanced grammar remained difficult for British working-class students. During the 1830s, the century's lowest decade of literacy rates in England, most working-class children entered the workforce full-time by age ten, with as little as two or three years of frequently interrupted schooling, so that with the exception of upwardly mobile families, youth had few opportunities to learn grammar or mathematics through formal education.[21] The various schools for the poor, such as Sunday schools, dame schools, Monitorial schools, or charity schools, generally taught "passive literacy," or reading lessons with, at most, limited writing instruction. As one man explained at a meeting of the British Association for Promoting Co-operative Knowledge, the problem with "the poorer classes being 'educated' as it was called by the rich or their underlings" is that "they were taught just as much as would suit the purposes of the latter."[22] Schools deliberately produced students whose level of literacy marked their social status, and, in circular fashion, pointed to their writing as evidence that they lacked the intelligence necessary to comprehend their own political interests.[23]

Inexpensive grammars held out the promise of self-study, but they retained vestiges of classical learning and required extensive time dedicated to memorization. One teacher of working-class adults and children, William Hill, laments that all grammars published during the past eighty years are written by "persons of a College Education—whose lives have been spent in poring over the Greek and Latin Languages, and whose heads are, consequently, so full of the laborious mechanism of those Languages, that the very simplicity of the English Language is a stumbling block to them." They give an "alarming catalogue of unmeaning names" and "useless, or mischievous, rules." Aggravating these difficulties, teachers command students to memorize and repeat a portion of the book as a "task" and "thus the mechanical revolution goes on," the pupil forgetting the beginning of the book before the end, especially if they only learn on Sundays. Whether for children, youth, or adults, "this method of teaching Grammar is absurd, inefficient, and totally useless," because lessons fail to engage the "understanding."[24] Rather than memorizing word lists and rules, students need to understand why grammar works the way that it does and exercise their own judgment in their compositions.

To address these limitations, radical grammars motivated students by promising political empowerment while taking seriously the challenges of learning while working. These needs determined several shared features of radical grammars. First, they use everyday activities and physical labor, instead of Latin, as a framework for teaching alphabetical literacy.[25] Especially when sustained through advanced lessons, this mechanical framework disrupts the binary between physical and mental labor that underlies the classist structure of education. Respect for physical labor is woven into lessons through frequent reminders that people who cannot read or write may be highly intelligent. Authors question the value of the "education of words," a phrase used to encapsulate classical education for the rich and obedience for the poor. Second, these grammars incorporate working-class authors and reading practices. For advanced grammars, this means using excerpts from popular radical authors and orators, which infuses grammar lessons with political information and confirms that authors with humble upbringings are worthy of stylistic imitation.[26] Third, instead of limiting literacy instruction to the bare minimum useful in the workplace, they teach active literacy that combines elements of reading, writing, and printing together. The goal of these three features is to teach youth to see themselves as knowledge consumers *and producers* from a young age. Instead of learning that some forms of literacy are the sole property of an elite class, they embrace all forms of knowledge as power in their hands.

Such grammars were published during the resurgence of the radical press after the end of the Napoleonic Wars in 1815, a period of famine, high employment, and crippling taxes, when large protest gatherings heightened elites' anxieties about the ability of everyday people to write and circulate their ideas in cheap periodicals. Radical textbooks for self-study also served the concurrent rise of educational organizations run by workers themselves—without government or Anglican church financial support—which included Chartist and cooperative schools that offered lectures and curricula inclusive of higher subjects.[27] Reporting on their free evening school, the Co-operative School Association of Manchester boasted that three times a week "many ragged little boys, barefooted and barelegged" are "absorbed in the study of geometry and algebra," while they offer "experiments in electricity and aerostatics for working men," their students seeking higher wages "and something better besides."[28] As part of this movement for broader curriculum, designed for and by the people, radical grammars challenged prevailing notions about not only what working-class children should learn, but also what their education was for—whether in addition to preparing children for work, all children should be equipped for political participation.

Playful Grammars for Young Children and Girls

The rising popularity of grammar instruction in the late eighteenth century also stimulated demand for grammars designed for young children and middle-class girls. Vernacular grammars like James Gough's 1754 schoolbook written for "the Use of Youth, designed for mechanick and mercantile Arts, who have no Occasion for Latin" were also for "the Service of young Women." Since female education also favored modern vernaculars, these grammars introduced playful strategies that working-class teachers found quite useful. Grammars such as those by schoolmistresses Ann Fisher (ca. 1745), the first woman to publish a grammar, and Ellin Devis (1775), the first to address her grammar to women, prepared more affluent mothers to teach their children letters, vocabulary, spelling, and parts of speech before they entered formal schooling.[29] Surviving examples of home learning aids, such as the extensive alphabet, lesson, and story cards created by Jane Johnson (1708–1759) for teaching her four children, resemble those sold in bookstores, while Sara Coleridge published *Pretty Lessons in Verse for Good Children* (1834) using the mnemonic rhymes from the flash cards she made for her children.[30] The commercialization of home literacies by mothers and teachers spurred the creation of the first grammars for young children by Ellenor Fenn, mother of two adopted children and author of over sixty children's books, including *Cobwebs to Catch Flies* (ca. 1783) and *The Rational Dame* (1886). Under the pseudonyms Mrs. Lovechild and Mrs. Teachwell, Fenn designed literacy teaching aids that resemble a ready-made box kit for mothers. *The Teacher's Assistant, in the Art of Teaching Grammar in Sport* (1809) contained three smaller boxes on spelling, arithmetic, and grammar. Fenn later produced several spelling and grammar textbooks written as family conversations between mothers and their young children. Her immensely successful *Child's*

Grammar initially sold 10,000 copies, with reprints numbering 200,000 by 1830, and *The Mother's Grammar* (1796) was continually reprinted for over a century.[31]

Fenn's approach to language through conversation and games inspired a steady stream of playful children's grammars and conversational textbooks. Following a suggestion from Fenn's *Art of Teaching Grammar in Sport* (1809) that parts of speech "may be marked by colours," Eliza Fenwick, an experienced schoolteacher, governess, and novelist, produced *Rays from the Rainbow: Being an Easy Method for Perfecting Children in the First Principles of Grammar, without the Smallest Trouble to the Instructor* (1811), which introduced color-coded underscores for parts of speech in sample passages—an antecedent to Mudie's colored pieces of paper. The instructions suggest that children first read consulting the colors, then try to identify parts of speech independently.[32] Other grammars for young children, such as *The Paths of Learning Strewed with Flowers: or English Grammar Illustrated* (1820), teach using attractive illustrations, or in the case of *The Infant's Grammar, or a Pic-nic Party of the Parts of Speech* (1822), through humorous personifications. In addition to books, publishers like John Wallis produced learning aids, such as A Picturesque Grammar of the English Language (ca. 1820), a dissected puzzle that illustrates the parts of speech through children at play, as well as an English Grammar game (ca. 1820) sold in a box with a sliding lid.[33] These playful introductory grammars for young children are far simpler than anything patterned after Murray's *English Grammar*, and they employ everyday objects or domestic scenes familiar to their youngest readers to make abstract grammatical concepts available to the senses.

Whether for women, young children, or plebian readers, cheap grammar books enabled a broader cross-section of the population to publish writing that stylistically resembled that of their social superiors. Some grammars acknowledge this challenge to sociolinguistic norms by incorporating political commentary on the gendered and class ideology of language into instructional passages. In a lesson on active and passive verbs from Jane Marcet's *Mary's Grammar* (1835), a conversational textbook, the young protagonist challenges traditional feminine virtues, such as patience and forbearance: "'I think passive verbs are very disagreeable,' said Mary; 'one has nothing to do but remain quiet, and suffer something to be done to you.'" Acknowledging her point, her mother notes that a person may "struggle to get free" and yet "*be caught*," but she counters with several positive passive verbs, "*To be admired, to be praised, to be caressed*." These are all phrases used to objectify women as passive recipients of male attention, which may explain why Mary rejoins, "I like the active verbs the best, mamma, because I have something to do myself." In another lesson, the indefatigable Mary announces, "I like the indicative mode much the best, for there you positively do ride, or have ridden, or shall ride, without so many *ifs* to stop you."[34] Grammar lessons provide an opportunity for teaching girls that although language can limit the range of possible actions they imagine for themselves, understanding the rules of grammar increases their agency and mobility.

Playful grammars like this one empower girls and mothers, but they imply class limitations on who can learn grammar by linking instruction to property. From the very beginning, Mary learns that nouns are anything she can see around her, as well as the places and containers that hold these things, "so *room* is a place to sit in, and *stable* a place to keep horses in," she reflects. Confirming her reasoning, mother provides another example, "Certainly, this little box is a place to hold sugar plums, therefore box is a noun; and the key-hole of the door is a place to put the key in, so key-hole is a noun." Mary continues this thought by considering that her "drawer is a noun" because she keeps her toys in it, while mother clarifies that some things are also places, "especially if they are made for the purpose of keeping the things they hold in safety." This observation leads Mary to consider "her father's desk, and a tea chest," which "is a very pretty thing, and a very safe place; for you know you always keep it locked."[35] The logical progression is quite plain: from objects to places, then to ways of securing property in locked boxes. Marcet's readers might expect such commentary from a personal friend of classical economists Adam Smith and David Ricardo, whose ideas she put into plain language in her popular economics textbook for children. Indeed, her name was so firmly associated with economics in the public consciousness that when Robert Torrens attacked Robert Owen's proposal to create villages of cooperation in the *Edinburgh Review*, he condescendingly accused Owen of ignorance on a subject "rendered familiar to every school girl by an admirable little book, entitled, *Conversations on Political Economy*."[36]

For Marcet, grammar is not only bound up with economics, but is itself a kind of property, held secure and tidy in the educated mind. At one point, Mother suggests that Mary name the different drawers she would need for different kinds of words, to help her "class them in regular order in your memory."

> "Yes," said Mary, "I must put them in order in my head, as I do my doll's clothes in her chest of drawers." . . . . "How droll," said Mary, laughing, "that my head should be like a chest of drawers!"
>
> "I hope it is like a tidy chest of drawers, Mary: I have known some little girls whose drawers are in such confusion, that when they want any thing in them, they do not know in which drawer to look for it."[37]

Marcet's conversational approach allows Mary to initiate clever observations in collaboration with Mother, but Mary's creative agency remains connected to her father's locked desk and tea chest as emblems of inherited class privilege. This metaphor of mind-as-box, or knowledge-as-property would be reinforced for readers who purchase the Game of Grammar (1842), which comes with a Book of Conversations "in a varnished box," according to an advertisement in the endpapers, so that readers can effectively store grammar in their own box.[38] To reinforce this connection between grammar and property, Mary practices her grammar on a story, also provided for the reader's practice, about the children of a poor fisherman who find a gentleman's lost purse. They return it, and the gentleman rewards the family by paying for the children to attend school, where they learn to read.[39] The implication is clear: For the poor, learning to read is a gift from those who own literacy in exchange for accepting class stratification. Nothing is said about whether the poor man's children learn grammar.

Radical Grammars and Satirical Play

Whereas books by women authors like Fenn or Marcet accommodated children's playful bodies, radical grammars accommodate youth's working bodies. This substitution of work for play reflects a working-class childhood defined by wage labor, with limited leisure hours for self-education. Successive acts of Parliament only raised the legal age when factory children entered the workforce to ten in 1844, instigating half-days for those under fourteen in 1878 to accommodate primary school. Youth ages fourteen and older worked full time, six days a week, through the end of Queen Victoria's reign. A day's labor was much longer in practice, since factories manipulated clocks and excluded meals and machine maintenance when calculating work time.[40] In winter months, workers left their homes and returned in the dark, which meant that youth studied by the luxury of candle, rush, or stove light, possibly exhausted and hungry, in apartments shared with large families, or in public gathering spaces such as taverns, coffeehouses, or reading rooms, where likeminded radicals pooled their resources to provide periodical subscriptions.[41]

These material conditions are reflected in textbook prefaces, which speak earnestly to young readers themselves, presenting arguments about the usefulness of grammar not only as the means for economic advancement, but for political liberation. Working-class youth recount in their autobiographies a common experience of political awakening during adolescence (the period of time when they would study grammar), a "secularized conversion" when they first encountered "a highly-motivated and wide-ranging program of reading," made available through social relationships with other politically informed readers.[42] They joined debate societies and reading societies, paid one workmate to read while the others worked, passed around newspapers until they fell to pieces, accessed radical papers in public houses and coffeeshops, borrowed books from employers, and collaborated to purchase small book collections.[43] This cultural community of readers sustained youth in pursuing their studies, but this world of working-class print culture was not represented in schoolbooks.

The first popular grammar to do so is William Cobbett's *A Grammar of the English Language: In a Series of Letters, for the Use of Schools and of Young Persons in General; but, More Especially for the Use of Soldiers, Sailors, Apprentices and Plough-boys* (1818). Addressed as a series of letters to "My Dear Little James," or James Paul Cobbett, his fourteen-year-old son (notably the age when youth contracted their own labor), the book targets youth who want to improve their writing after hours, as Cobbett once did as a soldier.[44] Cobbett wrote his grammar after fleeing to the United States to avoid imprisonment for his journalism—cheap "two-penny trash" editions of his *Weekly Political Register* (1802–35; cheap editions 1816–19), which he adapted into pamphlets to avoid the four-pence stamp on political periodicals, known as the "taxes on knowledge," designed to drive the radical press out of business.[45]

In his grammar, Cobbett expresses skepticism of book learning and destigmatizes illiteracy. Whereas books by Fenn, Barbauld, Marcet, or Edgeworth regularly compare young reading children favorably against speechless domestic pets, a strategy that dehumanizes people who cannot read, Cobbett constantly reminds his readers to respect the intelligence required for manual labor and the practical knowledge of experience, for "a comparatively small part of useful knowledge comes from books" and those who cannot read are not ignorant. He compares the poor who cannot read favorably against the ignorant rich, who, like birds, acquire the "endowments" of "a parrot or a bull-finch" through classroom memorization. "It is this mode of teaching, which is practiced in the great schools, that assists very much in making dunces of Lords and Country Squires. They 'get their lesson;' that is to say, they repeat the words of it; but as to its sense and meaning, they seldom have any understanding." Cobbett concludes his grammar by warning his son against "the using of many words to say little," advising him to seek "the substance" of his argument and guard against "figurative language."[46]

Seething with the fury of a political exile, Cobbett's grammar weaves politics into the fabric of language instruction.[47] The best use of literacy is to gain political information by reading the "history of those Laws of England, by which the freedom of the people has been secured," for in these histories, "tyranny has no enemy so formidable as the pen." To participate in politics, a person must learn to write precisely what he means to say, an ability that grants workers the advantage over a gentleman—for as Cobbett remarks, in an example purporting to illustrate different uses of the word "there/their," "There are many men, who have been at Latin-Schools for years, and who, at last, cannot write six sentences in English correctly." Such encouraging examples must have been a constant source of delight for readers, already exhausted from a full day's labor, motivated by an awareness that grammar or spelling mistakes were used to dismiss poor authors as ignorant. To teach commas, Cobbett writes a sentence about the protests that would culminate in the Peterloo Massacre in 1819, when soldiers fired upon peacefully assembled families who gathered in Manchester: "There were, in the year 1817, petitions from a million and a half of men, who, as they distinctly alleged, were suffering the greatest possible hardships." In a lesson on conjugation, Cobbett suggests that radical agitators will ignore legal persecution: "Evans defies the tyrants; Evans defied the tyrants; Evans will defy the tyrants." In another lesson, he shows how to express "great force" through "exclamation": "What! Rob us of our right of suffrage, and, then, when we pray to have our right restored to us, shut us in dungeons!"[48] Finally, in the practice section, Cobbett invites students, after a practice introduced by Ann Fisher, to correct false grammar in a speech delivered by the prince regent.[49] One appalled reviewer, who devoted an entire pamphlet to reviling Cobbett's *Grammar*, estimates its sales at 8,000 to 10,000 copies in the first month alone. He laments that "with such a book in our schools, we might hereafter have reason to say to him, in the language of Shakespeare: 'Thou hast most traitorously corrupted the youth of this realm.'" Rev. William Lisle Bowles, chaplain to the prince regent, agreed, "Its object is to pervert and corrupt the youthful mind in its first and earliest avidity of knowledge."[50]

Cobbett's *Grammar* exhibits radical ideas about property, play, and work. In grammars by Marcet or Fenn, young children use leisure play to acquire language, which empowers them to claim ownership over their toys and their writing. In Cobbett's *Grammar*, youth or adults use literacy to defend work as their property. A section on verb conjugation uses the word "to work" and suggests that labor is capital owned by the poor that deserves legal protection. "To say I work, or I worked, or I will work: these will not answer my purpose. No: I must call in the help of the verb to have, . . . for, when I say 'I have worked,' my words amount to this; that the act of working is not in my possession. It is completed. It is a thing I own, and, therefore, I say, I have it."[51] Calling attention to work as a poor man's property protected by the English constitution exposes the unequal legal protections offered to capitalists and workers. Successive Combination Acts (1799, 1800, 1825) limited the ways that workers could organize to raise wages or demand reforms, but these laws were not used against employers who coordinated to reduce wages. Similarly, child heirs, while still minors, were protected from adult coercion to sign away their inheritance before the age of twenty-one, yet working children could independently contract their labor by age fourteen, when they became "free agents." In this context, a children's moral tale about returning a gentleman's wallet is nonsense because, as Holyoake succinctly puts it, "We live in a society of thieves, whom competition licenses to plunder."[52] Whether it is the trucking system, or docking wages, or enclosing common lands, or the corn laws, or the taxes on knowledge—the rich have legal permission to steal from the poor.

While emphasizing work, Cobbett's *Grammar* is playful in its own way, through its carnivalesque pleasure in defying social and linguistic boundaries. Although Cobbett's *Grammar* became an indispensable reference for later textbook authors, he was not a schoolteacher, although his practical cottage guides earned him the epithet of "public instructor."[53] The author-teachers who followed after Cobbett, however, show familiarity with women-authored commercialized home literacies and grammars, which taught using simplicity, play, conversation, observation, and everyday objects. They used these strategies to teach working-class students, but instead of nursery play and domestic objects, they reference carpentry and metallurgy. One book recommended by Holyoake, William Hill's *Fifteen Lessons on the Analogy and Syntax of the English Language* (1833), dispenses with Latin (preferring "*Name*" to "the Anglo-Latinism, NOUN"), simplifies the parts of speech to five, and opens the first lesson with this reassuring analogy between grammar and artisan work:

> You are aware that the mechanic in his regular employment, has occasion to make use of various materials, such as Wood, Stone, Iron, Steel, Copper and Brass—and it is necessary, in order to his becoming a good workman, that he should know these things asunder—that he should be in no danger of mistaking the Steel for the Iron or the Brass for the Copper—and, . . . that he should understand, thoroughly, all the various particulars, relative to each of these articles, separately considered—and, lastly, that he should know how to fit and join them together . . . . Just so it is with Language, which is the expression of our ideas. All Speech or Language is made up of FIVE different kinds of words, which from their fitting, and joining together, so as to form Speech, have been, appropriately, called the PARTS of SPEECH."[54]

Language is no different from joining together different materials in a workshop. With notable exceptions, the political slant of Hill's grammar is inflected through his frustration with other grammarians, whom he castigates for their needless confusion. Notably, he quotes from Cobbett on active verb, "to work" ("a working man is more worthy of honour than a titled plunderer who lives in idleness"), and his exercises for conjugating verbs suggest that students try "to walk, to carry, to labour, to reason, to raise, and to work," a suggestive combination of intellectual progress with bodily movement.[55] Although focused on labor, Hill's approach actually uses a strategy introduced by women authors of children's books: making abstractions concrete through cultural references specific to one's audience—mothers, young children, and girls—or in Hill's case, artisans. A handloom weaver in his youth, Hill gained extensive classroom and tutoring experience, eventually founding a school near Huddersfield, before preaching as a Swedenborgian minister "the principles of social benevolence and justice, of civic equality and of political right," while editor from 1837 to 1843 of Furgus O'Connor's *Northern Star*, the leading Chartist periodical.[56] Known for his public demonstrations with schoolchildren of his "system of educational mneumonics," Hill created subsequent grammars that targeted different ages, using words that represent "tangible objects to the minds of children, which they can see, hear, or feel." Language instruction should be based on "facts and things"[57]; or, students must "FATHOM THE THING in his mind."[58]

These commonplace phrases are straight from mainstream pedagogy, but in the context of radical print culture, Hill could be interpreted as supporting an observation-based science curriculum unmoored from the Anglican church. His frequent praise for associationism, his disdain for Latin, and his caution against words that "do not give children ideas" and are "so much empty sound"[59] are all positions expressed more provocatively by Richard Carlile, editor of *The Republican* (1819–26), whose biography Holyoake wrote. While in Dorchester Gaol for reprinting Paine's *Age of Reason*, Carlile outlined in 1821 a secular curriculum of modern subjects for all, arguing that children should "at an early period of life form correct notions of organized and inert matter." In place of dead languages, they should learn "knowledge of Nature and her laws," and avoid classical study that "fills the mind with useless jargon" and "unmeaning trash—words of sound, to which it would be difficult to attach an idea."[60] They should learn, not by "repetition," but through "every thing both in the animal and vegetable world, which comes under the every day observation of the child, or even the grown person." With such an education, a child can make the world his classroom and "read a useful lesson in every object that came within his view."[61] By embracing rational science and simple language, James Epstein claims, radical atheists could "cast themselves in the roles of plebeian 'philosophers.'" Carlile embraced natural philosophy, pursuing Bacon's quest for a rational language purified of Latinate jargon and archaic mysteries, "I test history by physics, religions by physics, gods by physics and morals by physics."[62] As working-class radicals organized schools and debated public education, they infused mainstream pedagogical discourse into their own rhetorical traditions. Strategies for teaching with the body, activating the senses, and learning with everyday things easily merged with the longstanding materialist thread of Thomas Paine's common sense. This fusion of two materialist traditions created unstable meanings for schoolbooks, depending on a reader's political frame of reference, as in the case of George Mudie's *Grammar*.

George Mudie's *Grammar of the English Language*

Despite its introductory level, George Mudie's *Grammar* illustrates all three of the features of radical working-class grammars introduced by William Cobbett and William Hill while incorporating the playful learning techniques of women authors like Ellenor Fenn, Eliza Fenwick, and Jane Marcet. Contemporary reviews thus anticipate a crossover audience for this grammar in age, gender, and class. Identifying these multiple readers, *The New Satirist* reports the "work" is "adapted for the use of schools of private families" but also for "adults whose knowledge of grammar may be defective: these may speedily become self-instructed." Its playful, anti-theoretical approach is associated with teaching children, with their "playful and material minds, for all children are materialists, and love handling and touching, and noise and bustle, and motion and change," instead of the "abstract and metaphysical system of schools." Imagining a younger audience, *The Penny Satirist* recommends that "governesses and mothers" in charge of "early education," may "amuse her children in a very profitable manner with this box of parts of speech, and even improve herself whilst amusing her offspring." Yet a reviewer from *The Northern Star*, likely its editor, William Hill (the same who published grammars), immediately identifies these choices as politically radical and mentions using similar manipulatives in lecture circuits to teach working-class adults. In an article nestled next to the latest installment of *The Fleet Papers*, the review praises Mudie's grammar for dispelling "the mystery hanging over the whole matter in ordinary books," which discourages ordinary people from learning the subject, but recommends, with linguistic anarchy, that Mudie should have dispensed with grammatical terms entirely.[63]

Although the political inflection of Mudie's *Grammar* may seem less obvious than Cobbett's, its publisher, John Cleave, was a cooperator and radical journalist whose writings criticized the Anglican church as a corrupt monopoly. To begin with, the preface for teachers criticizes the common practice of using Latin grammar terms to teach English grammar. He mocks grammar teachers at length, as "luminous expositors of palpability, and most methodical creators of confusion" who mystify students with "unintelligible terms and pompous enunciations." He lists a befuddling array of grammatical terms, calculated to make students "relinquish in despair." Why all of these words, he asks, when students comprehend very well what is right in front of them? "Instead of abstract Rules" teachers should use "practical *realities* of Grammar."[64] Mudie's over-the-top language uses the rhetorical style of the working-class press, the parodic, ironic double-speak that repeats mainstream sentiments at a slant. While rejecting Latin grammar terms, for instance, he humorously overuses Latinate English words (luminous) in order to satirize the unnecessarily ornate language of the so-called well-educated governing class. Although easily mistaken for childish playfulness, the significance of this satirical style would be obvious to readers versed in radical working-class print culture, in which prolific Latinate words targeted out-of-touch elites.[65]

In Latin's place, Mudie substitutes new grammatical terms derived from the physical sciences, which associate writing with labor. "GRAMMATICAL LAWS" like nature's mathematical laws, act upon matter. His lessons draw analogies between simple grammatical terms and familiar objects by appealing to practical mechanics. A conjunction, for instance, is a "Grammatical Joint or HINGE," words defined together in standard mechanics textbooks. He invites his students to "examine the hinges or joints of the door of this room" and see how each joins together two things.[66] Mudie celebrates the materiality of language as something children see and hear, taking advantage of their ability to easily understand what they learn through the senses. "Students PRACTICALLY observe the divisions and distinctions themselves, though they can neither see through nor comprehend the clouds and mystery with which the School Grammarians have surrounded them," he argues. "They already know the THINGS themselves." Therefore, teachers should avail themselves "of Sensible Signs and Representations, and of Movable Pieces of the Parts of Speech and even of Colours." With these learning aids,

> The laws of Grammar are thus practically exemplified, . . . before the eyes of the Students, who thus readily perceive and easily comprehend. . . . I show them the PARTS OF SPEECH themselves, and the GRAMMATICAL LAWS actually WORKING upon and amongst the Parts of Speech sensibly moving and changing, controlling and governing the latter . . . . before the eyes of the delighted, the attentive, and the rapidly improving Learners, who thus quickly obtain the very SUBSTANCE of the Grammatical Knowledge with which it is sought to imbue them.[67]

Sounding like an unholy combination of Bill Nye and Thomas Gradgrind, Mudie implies a number of fascinating claims about the privileged epistemological position of children. They "know the THINGS themselves" precisely because they have not yet been mystified by language. Yet language properly taught can have substance ("SUBSTANCE"!) because words, like things, are subject to "LAWS" and can be manipulated "sensibly" by the same principles "governing" matter. Like William Hill, Mudie compares grammar with artisanal mechanics, describing how it reduces language to its simple "parts" acting on one another.

By poking fun at the style-markers of classically educated authors, Mudie undercuts grammar's gatekeeping function and calls into question the need to imitate styles of social elites. This approach captures an irony at the heart of all radical grammars. Teaching grammar threatens to demystify distinguishing class markers, such as spelling, speech, or stylistic elegance as a rhetorical performance, easily imitated by anyone with the right insider knowledge. Paradoxically, the more readers follow the rules, the more they expose how class is socially constructed through language. Radical grammars teach about words while lifting up the superior knowledge of "men and things," hard earned through toil and life experience, offering a twist on mechanical literacy in which the working poor are superior observers, better suited to governance.

Mudie's deployment of experiential education and object-teaching terminology is surprisingly typical within the cooperative movement. Cooperative periodicals regularly published essays on philosophical determinism, and they describe public lectures where teachers use maps, globes, manipulatives, and natural history specimens. An 1826 article series from *The Co-operative Magazine and Monthly Herald* insists, for example, that students at mechanics institutes should be "taught a real knowledge of *things* acquired by the evidence of the senses, instead of the *words* of dead languages, scarcely ever taught so as to be known, to be spoken, written, or even read!" (italics in the original) Instead, schools must make abstract concepts available to the senses by using "the *sensible signs* (where you cannot get the objects themselves) of the things to be taught—maps, models, prints, machines, apparatus, books, &c." Professors should have "a knowledge of all the objects of nature," rather than theoretical knowledge only. "The old plan of instruction was to teach by words and books," cultivating the "memory," while "in the new system, words and books are mere instruments towards the elucidation of things themselves, or of their representatives, submitted to your senses."[68] Such diatribes against book learning, this one likely written by William Thompson, show that Mudie's language resembles the education discourse of the cooperative movement, including his reference to "sensible signs."

The prevalence of these pedagogies in the cooperative press can be traced to the movement's initial leader, Robert Owen, a paternalist factory owner who later founded British socialism. Owen argued in *A New View of Society* (1813–14) that children are "universally plastic"; they have their character formed for them by their environment, in a manner not of their choosing. The current mode of government, however, is based on a mistaken belief that "each individual forms his own character" and "is accountable for all his sentiments and habits."[69] His infant school and Institute for the Formation of Character, now a World Heritage site, used Pestalozzian object teaching and creative visual aids to teach dance, geography, reading, writing, and mathematics to the children of his New Lanark cotton factory workers in a curriculum that Karl Marx described as uniting "productive labour with instruction and gymnastics" for the purpose of "producing fully developed human beings."[70] Owen encourages other capitalists to educate "your living machines" and improve "their curious mechanism" and "self-adjusting powers," just as inventors improve industrial equipment.[71] Such frequent mechanistic descriptions of human beings reflect Owen's belief in philosophical determinism, an idea supported by William Godwin and Joseph Priestley that the human mind is made of the same material and subject to the same physical laws as other objects. Determinism implies that human behavior follows predictable patterns, meaning that crime or poverty are not the result of individual moral choices, but of environmental influences, such as government and early education.[72] The cooperative movement joins together mechanical philosophy with reading and writing in their educational efforts, using these to transform children's minds and society at large. These mechanical theories also explain why Mudie invokes language from the physical sciences in the way that he does as part of a politically informed effort to reconceive of language as reflecting the body's mechanical movements in the physical world.

At Robert Owen's direction, Mudie first developed his playful multisensory teaching methods to promote cooperative economic theories. Twenty years earlier, Mudie published a prospectus containing his cooperative approach to political economy that formed the leading January 1823 issue of his short-lived periodical *The Political Economist and Universal Philanthropist*. Around that time, Mudie gave oral lectures to working-class audiences based on the prospectus, using visual aids and manipulatives. In a letter dated January 2, 1823, Mudie tells Robert Owen about his "conversion of numerous persons" to cooperative views by speaking at Lunt's Coffeehouse in Clerkenwell Green, an established underground gathering place for the British Forum, a radical debate society: "I lecture every Monday evening, using sensible signs for the demonstration of Political Economy. It is by Political Economy that your system must triumph. The world must be convinced that it will be productive of increased wealth, as well as increased intelligence." The pedagogical term "sensible signs," refers to pictures of objects, used to engage the senses when things themselves are unavailable—as when Mudie's

Grammar uses "sensible signs and Representations" (pictures of nouns) to represent "THINGS themselves." Mudie found these visual aids essential for swaying his audience: "By the use of the sensible signs, we can now convince every person who sees them of the prodigious pecuniary advantages derivable from your system," he tells Owen. "I use square pieces of wood in my lectures."[73] Mudie's economic learning aids seem to involve both images and wooden manipulatives, likely square counters of the kind Owen himself used, who stacking them in pyramids in his lectures to visually demonstrate how the lowest-paid laborers shouldered the nation's economy, based on statistics from Patrick Colquhoun's *A Treatise on the Wealth, Power, and Resources of the British Empire* (1814).[74] Witnessing the efficacy of these manipulatives for teaching economics, Mudie invented a similar strategy for teaching grammar.

The parallels between Mudie's early cooperative journalism and his grammar are remarkable. The teaching instructions provided in his *Grammar* liberally use all-caps or italics, as do his cooperative periodicals and his letters to Owen. Although typographical variation also appeared in mainstream grammar textbooks to differentiate parts of speech, including *Murray's Grammar,* Mudie employs these visual techniques to emphasize certain concepts and keywords. This kind of typographical variation is a feature of working-class newspapers, which use visual signals to aid people in reading papers out loud at work or in public gathering places, a practice that accommodates varying abilities to read.[75] Likewise, the mechanical metaphors in Mudie's grammar are typical of his early journalism, showing frequent extended metaphors drawn from physical labor to explain abstract ideas, such as mining layers of strata to discover economic truths. Mudie uses the same pedagogical approach for both political economy and grammar because in both cases he overturns abstract theoretical knowledge in favor of everyday observation. Whereas Latin or political philosophy are knowledge areas secured by a select few, primarily those with extraordinary resources of time and money, everyone has the power to observe the world using their bodies, and workers in particular understand the practical mechanics of manipulating matter and feel the consequences of fluctuations in the economy. Associating bodily work with writing is part of Mudie's effort to reorder society on a large scale, to reflect that labor is the source of wealth *and* the source of knowledge.

George Jacob Holyoake's Cooperative Grammars

During the height of the Chartist movement, Holyoake began his career as a teacher and lecturer, first in Worcester at the English Socialists' Hall of Science while also teaching mathematics (under a pseudonym) at a women's school, before accepting a position at Sheffield, where he established a Pestalozzian day school for girls and boys, while writing the first of many textbooks covering subjects as diverse as public speaking and Euclidian geometry.[76] Holyoake's textbooks show a sensitive awareness of the stigmatization of physical labor that many working-class students internalize, which he counters by firmly asserting that mechanical work prepares people to think. Holyoake worked with his father, a Birmingham whitesmith, from the age of nine, which no doubt informed his dedication to teaching "young thinkers" of "the artisan class," who are "engaged in a double battle against Want and Error." As he assures readers in *A Logic of Facts: or, Plain Hints on Reasoning* (1848), "those who stand at the anvil and the loom, and who never had the benefits of scholastic education, and who never will" can become "a shrewd master of plain facts."[77] There is a parallel between hammering iron and logical arguments; both work matter into new forms, requiring an uncompromising grasp of the raw material. He describes education as a life-long endeavor that begins with early schooling and progresses through community practices. As he reassures his pupils, "upon the learning of the Schools is engrafted the learning of life—the Literature of the streets and of trade—the Logic of the newspaper and the platform—which should enable the reader to acquire a public spirit."[78] Literacy enables civic participation, which is nevertheless grounded on practical, situated knowledge.

Although observation as the source of all knowledge is a basic tenant of educational theory after John Locke, Holyoake writes within a long tradition of radical working-class materialism and rational skepticism. Since the 1790s pamphlet wars following the French Revolution, radical authors appealed to evidence from the senses to insist upon the undeniable reality of "things as they are," while imagining a utopian future of "things as they might be."[79] Thomas Wooler, for instance, cautions that "managers of charities" cunningly "render the education they bestow subservient to the purpose of perpetuating *'things as they are*.'"[80] An education for all "sentient rational beings," William Thompson expounds, should teach them "to form right judgements, to see things as they really are, the real qualities and relations of physical objects, real facts and the real consequences of actions."[81] In the decades after Paine's *The Age of Reason* (1794–1807), Richard Carlile and William Thompson promoted a curriculum based on scientific rationalism free of church control, and Holyoake continued this work.[82] Convinced that "observation of nature is the only source of truth," Holyoake founded and edited an atheist paper, *The Reasoner* (1846–61), and created children's alphabet books that taught reading without religious instruction.[83] The founder of several rationalist organizations, he coined the word "secularism" and served six months in jail for blasphemy for his response to a question about whether utopian communities would have chapels, following his 1842 Cheltenham Mechanics' Institute lecture, during which he recommended that while poverty persisted, God should go on "half-wages."[84] His editorial work provided youth with access to polemical literature through excerpts gathered in textbooks, his freethought bookstore (1850s), and his library series, The Cabinet of Reason: A Library of Free Thought, Politics, and Culture, which included books ordinarily neglected by "Publishers of Information for the People, and devisers of popular Libraries," who wish "to take a neutral course."[85] Since young people were so often denied access to political information, learning grammar, or any subject, could not be politically neutral.

Holyoake's energetic career as a free thinker and cooperator informs his theorization of language as a system of signs for representing what we observe. His secular reading books for young children tie language to scientific observation using "the simple language of children—the ideas are the ideas of things."[86] Whereas typical first reading lessons scaffold from learning the letters of the alphabet to reading two-letter syllables (ba, be, bi) to words of one, two, and three syllables, Holyoake omits any short syllables that are not meaningful. "Each word stands for some idea which can be brought home to the child's understanding." Among the short passages provided for practice reading is this one, which offers a philosophy of language for infants:

> If mama wanted to tell her little child about the stars and the sea, she would be obliged to wait till a clear night came when she could show him the star-light sky, and wait till she could take him to see the ocean. But, by the use of the words *star* and *sea*, mama can talk about these things without waiting every time to take her little child to see them.[87]

Using the world itself to establish language lays an early foundation for reasoned thought and argumentation, which Holyoake valued as a religious skeptic. Moreover, this child's first nouns, "*star* and *sea*," cannot be locked in a tea chest; they are held in common by everyone on earth, just as written language is common property that gives voice to all.

An advanced explanation of this philosophy of language appears in Holyoake's *Practical Grammar; or, Composition Divested of Difficulties* (1844), which defines grammar as a "doctrine of signs" for representing the world readers have observed since childhood. The fifth edition is subtitled, "Intended for the Use of Those Who Have Little Time for Study" (1847), since his students pursue education while working long hours. According to the preface, the natural sciences, learned intuitively through the senses, form the first foundation of grammar:

> Before people commence the study of grammar, it is very requisite to call their attention to the general system of the world, to life and society, as far as these have been the subjects of their own observations, thoughts and actions. The most ignorant persons know something of the sky, the earth, and natural objects. All people have seen the sun, moon, and stars rise and set, they have seen rivers and seas swell and flow. . . . he can recognize nothing but MATTER and MOTION, cause and effect, real or imaginary. . . . the most ignorant individual can know grammar in its *primitive state*; for all that he sees, hears, and understands, all that we have been speaking of, is grammar in its original state.[88]

"MATTER and MOTION, cause and effect"—here is mechanical knowledge supporting language. Ever concrete, Holyoake denies the existence of abstract nouns, since "there are no abstractions—we cannot escape from nature or ourselves. All ideas are of material origin, as the philosophy of Locke has long established." To study grammar, then, students must begin with all that they see, hear, and understand, just as educators theorized that infants build a foundation for words and letters with their earliest sensations. But where Maria Edgeworth or

Elizabeth Hamilton—using a deficit model—attribute difficulties with reading among poor children to their lack of exposure to varied objects, Holyoake assumes that knowledge of the material world is precisely where his readers have the advantage. All that remains for them to learn is the grammatical rules governing how people represent their world with words:

> The secondary state of grammar, which is all that is usually treated of by grammarians, is the reading, speaking, and writing of all this matter and motion, this cause and effect. Grammar is therefore a picture, a copy, a system of marks, a set of signs—a grammarian is nothing but a drawing-master, a painter, and imitator of nature.[89]

The concept of a "secondary state of grammar" creates an analogy between writing and creating a government, suggesting that working-class writers exit the state of nature through self-education. At that moment (according to contract theory), they acquire a new set of governing laws created by humans—the laws of grammar, used to describe what we see every day. Grammatical laws are a human creation and, once equipped with this knowledge, his readers might change other manmade laws.

Like the laws of nations, grammatical laws are created. Grammar, in this analogy, is Thomas Hobbes's Leviathan, a mechanical man, a technology invented by humans that reflects human prejudices. Government and writing—two interdependent technologies kept from the working classes—are nothing to fear; they can be demystified for everyone to learn. Holyoake draws support from eighteenth-century grammarians: Joseph Priestley's *A Course of Lectures on the Theory of Language, and Universal Grammar* (1762) explains that in the "early ages of the world" humans "invent and apply" names for what "first occur to their observation"; Samuel Johnson states that "words are the children of men—things the sons of heaven—meaning that things *are*, that words are human inventions whereby to designate them." As a tool for shaping the world, grammar is "*indispensable*" and a "glorious advantage." Holyoake thus encourages the "young grammarian" to persist and "take courage" by questioning the supposedly superior style of social superiors. He also corrects the "complicated, unintelligible, feeble, ill-arranged, long-drawn sentences" of a pamphlet on Christianity by Christopher Wordsworth, master of Trinity College, Cambridge. "The wealthy and educated daily triumph over the ignorant and poor. Grammar is defensive, and gives a man more useful arms than those which Magna Charta permits him to carry. The battle of liberty is now fought with the tongue and the pen, and he puts in the strongest claim to freedom, who is able to explain and defend it."[90] A contributing letter to Holyoake's *The Reasoner* from a reader using the *Practical Grammar* testifies to the inadequate education offered to working-class children, and the strong desire among youth to gain the knowledge of writing denied to them:

> Sire, I confess that I am not able to write a letter at all creditable. My grammar is very bad, and my spelling is not likely to be much better. But when I tell you that I received my education in the Cannon-street Sunday school, you will not be surprised. They did not teach the art of writing or reading correctly. They taught me to read the Bible indifferently, and made me a present of it. . . . I hope to write correctly yet. I feel very acutely the remarks you make in Practical Grammar.[91]

This contributor knows very well that his school disingenuously gave him a Bible while limiting his training in reading and writing to disqualify him for publication, and he is determined to learn what they would not teach.

The political orientation of Holyoake's grammar was legible to contemporary reviewers, one of whom calls it, "A series of smart remarks in the conjoint style of *Punch*, and an Ultra Radical, setting the world to rights."[92] Although the intended audience for Holyoake's *Practical Grammar* includes all ages, Holyoake created a companion exercise book for children, *The Hand-book of Grammar: For the Use of Teachers and Learners* (1846), that maintains Holyoake's political edge for younger audiences. In one striking instance, Holyoake invites pupils to change from first to third person while reading Brutus's soliloquy defending king-killing in Shakespeare's *Julius Caesar*. He also includes, among his exercises on punctuation, precepts by radical authors supporting free universal education, independent of the church:

> "The grand doctrine, that every human being should have the means of self-culture, of progress in knowledge and virtue, of health, comfort, and happiness, of exercising the powers and affections of a man—is slowly taking its place as the highest social truth."—*Channing*.

> "It is better to fast on ignorance than feed on error."—*Bentham.*
>
> "Universal education will make power, like water, find its level."—*Mrs. Leman Gillies.*
>
> "The storehouse of nature is open to all and the only fee demanded for inspection is attention."—*Detroisier.*[93]

As these examples suggest, Holyoake excelled at creating what education scholar Gloria Ladson-Billings calls "culturally relevant pedagogy," an approach to teaching that equips students to critique social inequalities while recognizing students' home cultures as assets for academic success.[94] Holyoake's grammar books acknowledge his students' expertise by citing those writers most familiar to working-class readers. He praises Carlyle and Cobbett for their personal style; refers to radical grammar books by Cobbett, William Hill, and Joseph Priestley; quotes Thomas Paine and William Hazlitt; and often mentions Lord Jeffery, a founding editor of the *Edinburgh Review*. For those readers eager to contribute articles in newspapers, Holyoake recommends consulting the composition advice offered in *The Northern Star*, a leading Chartist periodical edited by William Hill.

One of the essential components of mechanical literacy is using knowledge gained through observation and tinkering to support metacognitive thinking. Awareness of how one's own mind and body develop was a foundational goal of Owenite cooperative education. By studying their self-development, children preserve their natural benevolence, becoming aware of how competition corrupts interpersonal relationships and realizing how environment shapes personal choices. Holyoake's exercises often lead students from observation to language to metacognitive thought. For instance, his *Practical Grammar* conjugates three verbs in succession: "to be," "to write," and "to think." These verbs announce readers' undeniable humanity and their right to education—I am, I write, I think—a progression from mere existence to affirming one's intellectual potential. Similarly, the *Hand-book of Grammar* helps children reflect on their mental development through suggested composition topics, beginning with the student's first moment of consciousness: "Reflect on the beginning of your life, and describe your sensations and situation, the first moment that you were sensible of existence." A later topic supports political consciousness by proposing that youth write about a favorite newspaper: "*Why* is it so? How long has it been established, and who is its Editor? Describe its character, whether chiefly political, literary, or commercial. Specify its circulation, and give your opinion upon its claims to public support."[95] These composition topics boost students' confidence by building on literacy practices specific to working-class culture, such as writing autobiographies and reading newspapers. Holyoake then scaffolds these practices to draw his readers from reflection about their own body sensations to an outward-facing consciousness of their politically active reading community. His infant alphabet book *The Child's Second Letter-Book* (1853) follows a similar progression. Instead of teaching letters alphabetically, he explains, they begin with the letter "I," a single line meaning the "self," and end with "O," the circle, which is the cooperative symbol for community.[96]

Holyoake also applied cooperative principles to classroom relationships. An advertisement for Holyoake's lectures on "grammar, logic, and rhetoric," offered to any age and gender, promised an equal relationship with students, where "no superiority is affected, no infallibility is arrogated. Teacher and student stand on the same level—thus a common ground is established, from which mutual inquiry can start." Although Holyoake created traditional cheap textbooks rather than learning aids, his lectures evidently took a multisensory approach. The equality in Holyoake's teaching follows a similar logic to cooperation, which Holyoake describes as a "partnership" between workers and consumers.[97] The subjects covered are modern, made relevant to pupil's lives. The goal is "to realize a *distinct* individual" who is "capable of usefully influencing [world] affairs." His teaching techniques "combine the realities of Pestalozzi with the famous repetitions of Jacotot," referencing the French mechanical engineer Joseph Jacotot, who taught himself to read—meaning Holyoake used a combination of learning aids, manipulatives, and repeated exercises.[98] The equality between teacher and student is supported by Holyoake's appeal to the physical world as the source of knowledge familiar to his students.

Holyoake extended this same principle of cooperation to other subjects, creating radical teaching materials for precisely those varieties of mechanical knowledge I have analyzed. His education materials on the physical sciences, philosophy, manufacturing, and political economy, form a coherent resistance to concepts of property ownership imbedded across disciplines. At the Great Exhibition of 1851, Holyoake even questioned the production story formula in his pamphlet *The Workman and the International Exhibition*, distributed free to exhibit attendees and government officials connected with the exhibit, which critiqued the wonderous display of beautiful goods as a calculated distraction from the misery of the impoverished working families who made them. Again, in *Mathematics No Mystery, or the Beauties and Uses of Euclid* (1847), Holyoake not only teaches mathematics to artisans, but complicates the distinction between theoretical and practical geometry, which textbook authors traditionally used to hierarchize mechanical knowledge along class and gender lines. "Euclid's Elements are considered pure Mathematics," he explains, because "No instruments, nor compass, nor rule, are used, and the results arrived at are all abstract and unapplied," whereas, "Practical Geometry" is "the application of Geometry to the arts of life." He insists that each is founded on the other—the only "difference" is that in "Practical Geometry the rule and compass are in the *hands*, in pure Geometry only in the thoughts."[99] Whether they admit it or not, boys at Eton studying Euclid are tool-wielding artisans. This perspective reflects Holyoake's experience learning mathematics in evening courses before constructing his own compasses in 1838 from scrap sheet iron lying around his workshop. Using these instruments, Holyoake won an exhibition prize at the Mechanics' Institute for "correct diagrams to the six books of Euclid"—and the same diagrams compose the letters of Euclid's name on his textbook's cover, a fit emblem of mechanical literacy.[100]

Conclusion

The grammar textbooks and learning aids designed by Fenn, Cobbett, Hill, Mudie, Marcet, and Holyoake display the multiple contested conceptualizations of mechanical literacy in circulation after 1815. As reading and writing became closely connected with manual manipulation, authors with competing ideologies used similar techniques to make literacy, mathematics, and the sciences more entertaining and accessible. These similarities between educators espousing divergent economic philosophies reflect their shared assumptions about early childhood—that children learn through the senses, that early life environments irrevocably shape children's minds, and that children should be educated in developmentally appropriate ways. These author-educators disagreed, however, over whether economic inequality and competition are part of the natural order of things. According to Owenite cooperators, some people cannot access the basic necessities of life because of an economic system so against human nature that it can only be maintained by falsely educating children to suppress their tendencies toward mutual aid. Improving individual children thus requires changing society itself, a belief that defines the radical education tradition. Using manipulatives to demonstrate both the laws of grammar and the inequitable distribution of wealth, radical grammarians taught young people to think about the social construction of language and its role in creating the laws governing their physical world. Whereas grammars produced by Ellenor Fenn and Jane Marcet used the material affordances of print and toys to socialize children into accepting tiered access to literacy skills and to naturalize associations between literacy and property ownership, radical educators used playful manipulatives and haptic learning to design widely accessible lessons for people of varied reading levels. Making things, moving things around—moving toys and letters—embodied the radical work of reordering matter and reforming government.

Embodied learning thus holds a different meaning for these radical educators, for whom moving around letters or parts of speech in a self-reflexive, conscious, purposeful way not only prepares young people to persuade others through writing, but prepares them to shape the government that shapes its citizens. Unlike many elites who associated embodied learning with childhood, radical educators enthusiastically embraced the similarity between haptic or experiential learning and the skilled physical work of making things. These contested notions of mechanical literacy also reflect competing epistemologies. Whereas Adam Smith suggested disseminating a little mechanical philosophy to guard against the mental and social disorder caused by the division of labor, radical educators who valued working-class ways of knowing reframed everyday work as the foundation for inductive reasoning. By learning to express themselves clearly in writing, working-class youth could systematize and distribute the knowledge produced by their labor. Radical grammarians thus offered a more inclusive vision of who creates and circulates knowledge.

CONCLUSION

William Lovett's Case of Moveable Types

The intersection of playful learning and child labor is the subject of two familiar industrial novels that offer strikingly differently critiques of recreational and experiential learning. Frances Trollope's *The Life and Adventures of Michael Armstrong, the Factory Boy* (1840) criticizes playful teaching methods that cultivate children who are conveniently ignorant about their privilege, while Charles Dickens's *Hard Times: For These Times* (1854) equates object lessons with soul-killing materialism. Despite this stark opposition, both novels consider how exploring the material world teaches children about social class in an economy altered by new technologies. A visit to the home learning environments described in these familiar novels to observe their educational playthings may help us resituate science books, production stories, learning aids, and grammars as part of the history of imaginative youth literature.

Trollope's novel musters a superb defense of learning from experience. At the beginning of *Michael Armstrong*, the antagonist Sir Matthew Dowling, factory owner and father of a family large enough for Malthusian hypocrisy, adopts (or abducts) young Michael, the only healthy wage-earner for his widowed mother, as a charity publicity stunt. Yet soon tired of a boy who cannot perform affecting gratitude on cue, Sir Matthew packs him off as apprentice to a secluded mill, where Michael languishes half-starved until rescued by the novel's heroine, Mary Brotherton, an independent heiress. Mary's trajectory follows her re-education from a complacent beneficiary of her father's wealth, accumulated by employing parish poorhouse apprentices, to an inquiring mind investigating the factory system. She unlearns her education through real-life experience, and, in doing so, she questions what kind of education is really possible within the protective confines of the home.

Fiction and hearsay compete against observation in the opening third of Trollope's novel, which culminates in a "masque" praising Sir Matthew's virtues that is performed by his family—notably in the Dowling Place schoolroom. The amateur theatrical recounts Michael's heroics while "rescuing" Sir Matthew and Lady Clarissa (a silly, middle-aged aristocrat of declining family) from a harmless cow, which under Sir Matthew's embellishment becomes a vicious monster. Mere propaganda masquerading as high art, the masque opens with an ironic "Shakespearean Prologue" that commands Sir Matthew's neighbors to use their senses: "Open your ears! For which of you will stop / The seat of hearing, when rumour speaks?"[1] What Mary hears, however, as she steps backstage at the play's conclusion, is Sir Matthew beating Michael for forgetting his lines, the noise obscured from the audience out front by the many "accomplished" Dowling children banging their "tambourines and triangles." By setting this revelatory scene in a private schoolroom, "dedicated to the reception of globes, slates, guitars, dumb bells, dictionaries, embroidering-frames, and sundry other miscellanies connected with an enlarged system of education," Trollope critiques middle-class education as a performance of learning, or "masque," that preserves ignorance.[2] Like the musical instruments that drown out Sir Matthew's abuse, the schoolroom's "enlarged system of education" is mere noise, an education of words—literally, the clanging symbol of false charity.

An elaborately stocked, elite nursery also miseducates Gradgrind's children in Charles Dickens's *Hard Times*, through an eviscerated form of object learning. Like the Dowling's nursery, the Gradgrind's home is a state-of-the-art child environment, equipped with every instructional technology that "heart could desire":

> Everything? Well, I suppose so. The little Gradgrinds had cabinets in various departments of science too. They had a little conchological cabinet, and a little metallurgical cabinet, and a little mineralogical cabinet; and the specimens were all arranged and labelled, and the bits of stone and ore looked as though they might have been broken from the parent substances by those tremendously hard instruments their own names; and, to paraphrase the idle legend of Peter Piper, who had never found his way into their nursery, If the greedy little Gradgrinds grasped at more than this, what was it for good gracious goodness' sake, that the greedy little Gradgrinds grasped at!

In the decades before *Hard Times*, children's magazines regularly advertised new and used specimen cabinets like these as the ideal improving nursery toys. But in Dickens's view, family affection or imagination cannot be "grasped at" through objects. Teaching children though the senses accomplishes the very opposite of what it intends because children are not stuck in a material state but forced into one. Instead of transitioning materially minded children into abstract thinkers, rational cabinets deprive children of the room for creating mental images of things unseen. Thus when Louisa, broken by marriage and seduction, returns to her father, she wishes she could not see: "If I had been stone blind; if I had groped my way by my sense of touch, and had been free, while I knew the shapes and surfaces of things, to exercise my fancy somewhat in regard to them; I should have been a million times wiser, happier, more loving, more contented, more innocent and human in all good respects, than I am with the eyes I have." Substituting groping for grasping, Louisa describes blind man's bluff as a parody of Pestalozzian object lessons, responsible for the "deadened state of my mind." Although Dickens undervalues a pedagogical tradition that undoubtedly inspired many young people, *Hard Times* also questions, rightly so, whether learning about manufacturing processes constitutes a sympathetic engagement with the working people who make things. The "improving party" that attend Louisa's wedding "knew what everything they had to eat and drink was made of, and how it was imported or exported, and in what quantities, and in what bottom, whether native or foreign, and all about it," yet the event marks an affectionless marriage that bodes ill for national unity.[3]

Trollope and Dickens may criticize children's industrial media, but they nevertheless share its gendered division of labor, where women are the prime movers responsible for conscientious teaching and consumption. Both novels feature children miseducated by fathers, with absent mothers. Sir Matthew not only protects his children's ignorance, he prefers an illiterate workforce that cannot read their own contracts, leaving them dependent on his motherly advice. Likewise, in *Hard Times*, Gradgrind strays by taking parenting advice from Bounderby, a manufacturer who fraudulently represents himself as a bootstrapping autodidact, "a commercial wonder more admirable than Venus, who had risen out of the mud instead of the sea." The unlikely comparison with Venus hints that Bounderby seizes the mother's role in transmitting literacy, first denying the instruction provided by his own mother, then supplanting Mrs. Gradgrind in Tom and Louisa's family. We first meet Bounderby in the Gradgrind kitchen, boasting that he learned his letters and numbers by studying chance objects encountered in his environment: "Josiah Bounderby of Coketown learnt his letters from the outsides of the shops, Mrs. Gradgrind, and was first able to tell the time upon a dial-plate, from studying the steeple clock of St. Giles's Church, London, under the direction of a drunken cripple, who was a convicted thief, and an incorrigible vagrant." *Hard Times* pulls hope from its despairing pages by restoring the mother-teacher, with "Sissy's happy children loving her; all children loving her."[4] Sissy's disinterest in observing things, however, equates imagination (or ignorance) with child liberation, vilifying the women authors Percy Muir called "that monstrous regiment," whose defense of women's rational thought in didactic books empowered girl readers.[5] In her investigation of Victorian fairytale science books, Melanie Keene opens with *Hard Times* to question whether facts and fairies are antithetical, given how often these two unite in women's science writing.[6] To appreciate object lessons and experiential learning, we must turn back to Trollope, whose nursery critique calls for more facts. Trollope's novel positions Mary Brotherton as a model for how readers should question what they are taught, and "woe to those who supinely sit in contented ignorance of the facts." Trollope's readers, like Mary, must visit industrial districts "to see and judge for ourselves."[7] Readers should not tarry-at-home.

Looking back at the didactic literature that flourished before the Golden Age, each of these industrial novels presents an important critique still relevant today. Often children's literature and media, like the Dowling schoolroom, are more concerned with protecting the ignorance of young people privileged by their race, class, gender, or citizenship than providing meaningful stories from the perspectives of those experiencing hardship or trauma. Yet children also need imaginative stories that envision inclusive futures where all children experience joy, validation, love, and creative play. As we pursue these two imperatives—that children's media should more accurately reflect our world and all its children, and that it should foster creativity through its otherworldly possibilities—it may prove useful to think about the relationship between imaginative play, didacticism, and labor in new ways.

Since theories and practices for learning through play were created to exclude labor, it is difficult to recover how children learned from everyday experience using theories of play alone. The concept of mechanical literacy helps consider play and labor as sources of knowledge about the world, which together informed how children learned to read and write during the first century of British children's literature publishing. The affordances of children's materials often asked children to switch learning modalities and take actions in the world—to purchase or gift domestic goods, construct toolboxes, build model steam engines, conduct experiments, tour factories, write letters, and organize cabinet specimens. Through these learning activities, children created tangible representations of ideas accumulated and organized in their minds, thereby developing and displaying the rational self-governance and moral feelings associated with political life.

The manipulation of material objects and texts meant something different, however, for radical educators, who approached literacy instruction with an awareness of the unequal distribution of knowledge and property, and who embedded this knowledge in their education designs. This kind of political agency is less prominent within the history of children's literature and material culture. Compared with imaginative literature or playful toys, the polemical messages of radical teachers and their texts may seem too factual, controlling, or indoctrinating. Nevertheless, a book whose design and contents seem adult-oriented or didactic may enhance children's agency, not by offering opportunities for interactivity or imaginative play, but by equipping children with the plain knowledge they need to challenge economic and political systems.

In the middle of William Lovett and John Collins's *Chartism* (1840), written while in Warwick jail, Lovett, a schoolteacher and cabinet-maker, pauses to describe a classroom learning aid of his own design, which creates "*a closer connection of words and things.*" A microcosm of his political vision, the Case of Moveable Types resembles a typesetter's printing press block, stored in a wooden box, which can be posted on classroom "reading stands." The specifications provided by Lovett enable anyone to build the Case inexpensively and integrate its use into existing classrooms, where young children gathered around learning stations to share lesson visual aids, including object lessons stored in a drawer. In surprising detail, Lovett specifies gluing printed letters onto small wooden blocks, so that children spell out words in lines on the box's lid, like setting real moveable type. The Case is also used for "*grammar* and *composition*" lessons with older children. His drawing of the Case shows examples that spell "Tin is heavy" and "Wax is soft," which connect lessons on perceiving these manufacturing materials with learning to write.[8]

By integrating reading with writing and typesetting, Lovett's Case guards against teaching children to read to make them good workers without teaching them to write. Warning against schools that teach passive literacy and apolitical knowledge, Lovett, who wrote the "six points" presented to the Crown that became the People's Charter in 1838, asks his readers, "How can they trust the sincerity of those persons who would mould them into more tractable and ingenious machines for the production of wealth, but would deny them any political power to determine how that wealth should be distributed?" Convinced that such schools governed by the church or wealthy patrons would never teach workers their "political rights and obligations," Lovett argues that workers must "mainly rely on our own energies to effect our own freedom." Therefore, Lovett's Case is one part of a practical plan for educating the people, to secure "*equality of political rights*" through evening lectures and practical training, circulating libraries, prizes for best essays, a printing press, and staff devoted to disseminating the ideas and texts produced by the association. This larger plan explains some curious features of his literacy aid, such as using printed letters rather than handwritten ones. Children operating the Case self-identify as radical journalists who print and circulate their ideas; they learn to read printed typefaces before handwriting so that letters "in print" do not "appear" to them like "Greek or Hebrew characters."[9] This method ensures that working children who attend school for short, intermittent periods nevertheless learn the typographical vernacular of political knowledge.

Learning aids like Lovett's Case teach mechanical and alphabetical literacies in ways that reflect the working-class culture of mutual improvement and political activism. The alignment of Lovett's design with his ideological position could be critiqued for enforcing an adult agenda over children's creative process, but this objection ignores the "education of government," the insensible power relations that educate children. Lovett calls attention to this broader context when he describes the "franchise" itself as shaping children's minds by teaching their "political equality with other classes."[10] This history helps us understand why, currently in the United States, fiction and learning materials designed to represent and empower historically marginalized groups, or math textbooks that motivate students through practical life applications, are being removed from classrooms and libraries in the name of protecting children from indoctrination. In the field of childhood studies, political novels and information books can be undervalued in favor of imaginative literature, which presents challenges for including texts written for marginalized communities within established historical narratives.

In his global overview of literacy, Martyn Lyons describes how wealthy elites, colonizers, enslavers, husbands, and parents restricted or withheld literacy to maintain docile and economically dependent populations.[11] As manipulation and observation of the material world became a valuable category of knowledge, elites applied similar gatekeeping measures to claim some portion of this new knowledge about the world as their property. Unlike reading and writing, practical knowledge of the physical world is shared widely by everyone, yet the close association between mechanical and alphabetical literacies permitted exclusionary thinking around reading and writing to envelop other skillsets in the sciences, manufacturing, and political economy. Many children's books and materials in these subject areas constructed physical labor as detrimental for governing oneself and others; likewise, children's fiction and educational toys often suggested that some ways of using the body to learn about the world support higher cognitive and spiritual awareness, but physical labor does not. To draw another contemporary comparison, the recognition and exclusion of different ways of making continues today in the digital humanities and in maker cultures where, as Jentery Sayers points out, "knowledge of circuitry is often conflated with (superheroic) command over people, situations, and things." Providing historical context for the separation of doing and thinking at the root of this problem, Julie Thompson Klein argues that "the relationship of humanities and new technologies was confronted from the beginning by the higher status of interpretation, analysis, and abstraction over fabrication, application, and production."[12] As I have argued in this book, the boundary work Klein describes was performed two centuries ago, by the instructional materials children used to learn mechanical philosophy, political economy, and reading and writing.

Acknowledging the class politics of play challenges the grand historical narrative of children's books as a transition from instruction to delight. In literacy studies, Brian Street critiques the "autonomous model" of literacy, a form of technological determinism that credits literacy with enabling rational thought, which he contrasts with an ideological model that recognizes literacy as culturally situated. Similarly, an ideological model of play can explain why mechanical literacy and the embodied learning practices used to teach it at times empowered some children while excluding others. Although children's leisure is idealized and equated with freedom, play is not a class- or race-neutral activity, but a scarce resource once deployed in debates over slavery and child labor. Play offered wealthy families a respectable alternative to learning from labor, then it offered upwardly mobile middle-class families a way to distinguish their own labor as intellectually superior. Learning through experience, observation, and play supported parents who celebrated pedagogical strategies traditionally pursued in cottages and workshops as their own original methods. Manual manipulation or experiential learning could be called play, while nevertheless relying on its similarity to labor to support the analogy of intellectual property and deny the intellectual life of working-class people. Given the way play can be used to falsely claim the educational value or voluntary nature of work performed under coercion, determining whether an activity is education, leisure, or work is a politically significantly act.

Besides rethinking play, there are several practical applications of mechanical literacy for teaching through making things, but also for the stories we tell about making. How we should represent consumption and production remains a practical question for people creating engineering videos or designing museum exhibits, which may explain technology while omitting human labor. While conducting research at the Cooperative Archive in 2019, I visited the Science and Industry

Museum of Manchester, which was exhibiting Stephenson's Rocket, on a day when the museum floor around his steam train prototype was alive with schoolchildren visiting for a maker-space event. The kinds of technologies included in maker events depend on what organizers expect children will find engaging, but also what work we hope they might do, and the gendering, classing, and racialization of that labor. Thus, despite the museum's impressive floor of cotton machinery, where staff expertly delivered demonstrations of Victorian manufacturing, the maker event enthralled children with building playsets and the first stored-program electronic digital computer created at the University of Manchester affectionately called the "Baby," but not sewing machines.[13] Gallery wall spaces overlooking the textile machinery displayed cotton's "progress" from seed to cloth, with half the steps removed for renovation as the museum revised its materials to acknowledge Manchester's complicity in slave labor through the cotton industry. Such displays are so commonplace that the Field Museum in Chicago, which I visited with my daughter in 2020, was also displaying production stories for cotton and linen alongside other plant-based products with natural specimens.

Cotton and linen are the materials of children's books. Jacqueline Reid-Walsh considers the pertinence of these same textiles to children's book design, speculating that the material affordances of rag linen paper allowed book flaps, used for harlequinades, to stay in place when users move them, possibly explaining the turn-up book's popularity during the period when England began using linen paper for cheap publications. Using the history of papermaking, she compares Dean and Son's indestructible rag books, printed on woven cotton in the Victorian era, with other durable cotton papers selected for movables, which, like modern board books, anticipate heavy use by young people.[14] Such lessons on the materiality of children's books are a frequent subject of nineteenth-century production stories, and they are part of the history of colonization, global trade, slavery, and child labor. Considering the full life cycle of children's books continues to illuminate hidden aspects of making these objects—such as logging, toxicity of materials, or cotton harvesting—that we little think of as part of reading because we are conditioned by the very genre patterns examined in this book. Such histories address urgent environmental issues affecting the survival of children and animals on a planet too often treated as a passive object.

Although these concerns over the anthropocentrism of early children's books about science and technology lie outside the scope of this book, they have shaped the writing of it. When we thoughtfully consider how play and work informs what we make, whether the creation of digital archives, or selection of public humanities projects, or the design of hands-on experiential projects in our classrooms, we become readers and writers who take action in a shared world.

Notes

Since there are many different texts and artifacts mentioned in this book, I included publication dates in the text after titles to help readers place each item in history as they read. These dates reflect the earliest edition according to WorldCat, often verified by scholarship. Dates in the endnote citations below reflect the edition(s) I consulted when quoting or describing contents. Where copies of books contain unique markings referenced in my argument, or where surviving copies of miniature libraries, games, and other realia may differ, endnote citations include the institution where I viewed the item, using dates from their catalog.

BALDWIN: Baldwin Library of Historical Children's Literature, George A. Smathers Libraries, University of Florida
COTSEN: Cotsen Children's Library, Princeton University Library
LILLY: Lilly Library, Indiana University, Bloomington, Indiana

INTRODUCTION

1. Elizabeth Hamilton, *Letters on the Elementary Principles of Education*, 3rd ed., 2 vols. (Bath: R. Cruttwell; London: C. & J. Robinson, 1803), 2:79–80.
2. Hamilton, *Elementary Principles*, 2:81, 1:297, 2:114.
3. Barbara Maria Stafford, *Artful Science: Enlightenment Entertainment and the Eclipse of Visual Education* (Cambridge, MA: MIT Press, 1994). Stafford greatly influenced my thinking on the connections between science, automata, and educational aids. Jessica Riskin, *Science in the Age of Sensibility: The Sentimental Empiricists of the French Enlightenment* (Chicago: University of Chicago Press, 2002). Riskin explains, for eighteenth-century empiricists, all sense impressions are united in the *sensorium commune* where the brain meets the soul (25). Touch teaches where the self ends and the world begins, engaging the "sixth sense" or "common sense" that allows a unified conscious self (44–47). For British educators, touching passive objects precedes visual tasks like reading, as touch is unmediated and intuitive.
4. Jill Shefrin, *The Dartons: Publishers of Educational Aids, Pastimes & Juvenile Ephemera, 1787–1876* (Princeton: Cotsen Occasional Press, 2010); Megan A. Norcia, *X Marks the Spot: Women Writers Map the Empire for British Children, 1790–1895* (Athens: Ohio University Press, 2010); Sarah Anne Carter, *Object Lessons: How Nineteenth-Century Americans Learned to Make Sense of the Material World* (Oxford: Oxford University Press, 2018), 93–116.

5. Robin Bernstein, "Toys Are Good for Us: Why We Should Embrace the Historical Integration of Children's Literature, Material Culture, and Play," *Children's Literature Association Quarterly* 39, no. 4 (winter 2013): 459.
6. Seth Lerer, *Children's Literature: A Reader's History, from Aesop to Harry Potter* (Chicago: University of Chicago Press, 2008), 105.
7. Lissa Paul, *The Children's Book Business: Lessons from the Long Eighteenth Century* (New York and London: Routledge, 2011), 28.
8. Lerer, *Children's Literature*, 89–90.
9. Meredith Bak, *Playful Visions: Optical Toys and the Emergence of Children's Media Culture* (Cambridge, MA: MIT Press, 2020), 22. See also Beverly Lyon Clark and Margaret R. Higonnet, eds., *Girls, Boys, Books, Toys: Gender in Children's Literature and Culture* (Baltimore: Johns Hopkins University Press, 1999).
10. Bernstein, "Toys," 459.
11. Jacqueline Reid-Walsh, *Interactive Books: Playful Media before Pop-Ups* (London: Routledge, Taylor & Francis Group, 2018), xx.
12. M. O. Grenby, *The Child Reader, 1700–1840* (New York: Cambridge University Press, 2011), 9.
13. Marah Gubar, "On Not Defining Children's Literature," *PMLA* 126, no. 1 (2011): 209–16; Andrew O'Malley, "Acting out Crusoe: Pedagogy and Performance in Eighteenth-Century Children's Literature," *The Lion and the Unicorn* 33, no. 2 (April 2009): 131–45; Alisa Clapp-Itnyre, *British Hymn Books for Children, 1800–1900: Re-Tuning the History of Childhood* (Abingdon: Routledge, 2016); Robin Bernstein, *Racial Innocence: Performing American Childhood from Slavery to Civil Rights* (New York: New York University Press, 2011).
14. Andrew O'Malley, *Making of the Modern Child* (New York: Routledge, 2003), 2–6.
15. Michelle Beissel Heath, *Nineteenth-Century Fictions of Childhood and the Politics of Play* (London: Routledge, Taylor & Francis Group, 2018), 4.
16. Christopher Parkes, *Children's Literature and Capitalism: Fictions of Social Mobility in Britain, 1850–1914* (New York: Palgrave Macmillan, 2012), 6–7.
17. Karen Sanchez-Eppler, "Playing at Class," *ELH* 67, no. 3 (Fall 2000): 820.
18. Pamela Horn, *Children's Work and Welfare, 1780–1890* (Cambridge: Cambridge University Press, 1994), 22.
19. Bill Brown, ed., *Things* (Chicago: University of Chicago Press, 2004); Lorraine Daston, ed., *Things That Talk: Object Lessons from Art and Science* (New York: Zone Books, 2004).
20. Arjun Appadurai, ed., *The Social Life of Things: Commodities in Cultural Perspective* (New York: Cambridge University Press, 1986), 34.
21. George Levine, *Dying to Know: Scientific Epistemology and Narrative in Victorian England* (Chicago: University of Chicago Press, 2002); Barbara Herrnstein Smith, *Scandalous Knowledge: Science, Truth, and the Human* (Durham, NC: Duke University Press, 2006); Lorraine Daston and Peter Galison, *Objectivity* (New York: Zone Books, 2007); Mary Poovey, *The History of the Modern Fact: Problems of Knowledge in the Sciences of Wealth and Society* (Chicago: University of Chicago Press, 1998).
22. Mrs. Lovechild [Ellenor Fenn], *The Art of Teaching in Sport* (London: John Marshall, 1785), 19–20. I viewed the editions and *The Spelling Box* (London. John Marshall, [ca 1790]), Cotsen.
23. For a description of this version of forfeits, see *The Gaping Wide-Mouthed Waddling Frog, a New Game of Questions* (London: E. Wallis, J. Wallis, ca. 1817); for long story

about a family playing forfeits, see Mrs. Bourne, *The Game of Forfeits* (London: Houlston & Co., 1838).

24. Shefin, *Dartons*, 60; M. O. Grenby, "Delightful Instruction? Assessing Children's Use of Educational Books in the Long Eighteenth Century," in *Educating the Child in Enlightenment Britain: Beliefs Cultures, Practices*, ed. Mary Hilton and Jill Shefrin (Burlington: Ashgate, 2009).
25. John Locke, *Essay Concerning Human Understanding*, ed. Peter H. Nidditch (Oxford: Clarendon Press Oxford, 1795), 2.1.3–4.
26. An anonymous 1815 British treatise on Pestalozzi credits both Germaine de Staël and Elizabeth Hamilton: *A Biographical Sketch of the Struggles of Pestalozzi, to Establish His System of Education* (Dublin: William Folds, 1815), vi. Contemporaries often credit Elizabeth Hamilton: see William Shepherd, Jeremiah Joyce, and Lant Carpenter, *Systematic Education* (London: Longman, Hurst, Rees, Orme, and Brown, 1815); Andrew Irvine, *Reflections on the Education of the Poor* (London: Edmund Lloyd, 1815), 50; David Davidson recommends pedagogies "of Pestalozzi, Hamilton, and Jacotot" as "the most prominent" and enjoyable in *Remarks on the Best Means of School Education* (London: W. Hughes, 1833), 4.
27. *Hints Addressed to the Patrons and Directors of Schools* (London: Longman, Hurst, Rees, Orme, and Brown, 1815), 59, 40, 82.
28. Harvey Graff, *The Legacies of Literacy: Continuities and Contradictions in Western Culture and Society* (Bloomington: University of Indiana Press, 1987); Brian Street, *Literacy in Theory and Practice* (Cambridge: Cambridge University Press, 1984); Patricia Crain, "New Histories of Literacy," in *A Companion to the History of the Book*, ed. Simon Eliot and Jonathan Rose, 2nd ed. (Hoboken: Wiley Press, 2019), 959–85; Leah Price, "Reading: The State of the Discipline," *Book History* 7 (2004): 303–20; James Collins and Richard K. Blot, *Literacy and Literacies: Texts, Power, and Identity* (New York: Cambridge University Press, 2003).
29. Deborah Brandt, "Sponsors of Literacy" *College Composition and Communication* 40 (1998): 165–85.
30. Jeanne D. Petit, *The Men and Women We Want: Gender, Race, and the Progressive Era Literacy Test Debate* (Rochester, NY: University of Rochester Press, 2010), 1–37, 135–38.
31. Patricia Crain contrasts legal prohibitions against teaching the enslaved to read, which prevented enslaved persons from signaling their self-ownership, with extending literature to Indigenous peoples, "acculturating them to white property customs," to steal their land. See *Reading Children: Literacy, Property, and the Dilemmas of Childhood in Nineteenth-Century America* (Philadelphia: University of Pennsylvania Press, 2016), 6. On personal and resistant uses of literacy by Indigenous readers, see Bernadette A. Lear, "Libraries and Reading Culture at the Carlisle Indian Industrial School, 1879–1918," *Book History* 18 (2015): 166–96; Hilary Wyss, *Writing Indians: Literacy, Christianity and Native Community in Early America* (Amherst: University of Massachusetts Press, 2000).
32. Dana Nelson Salvino, "The Word in Black and White: Ideologies of Race and Literacy in Antebellum America," in *Reading in America: Literature and Social History*, ed. Cathy N. Davidson (Baltimore: Johns Hopkins University Press, 1989), 140–56.
33. Crain, *Reading Children*, 6.
34. Pamela Horn, *Children's Work and Welfare, 1780–1890* (Cambridge: Cambridge University Press, 1994), 22–42; Jane Humphries, *Childhood and Child Labour in*

the British Industrial Revolution (Cambridge: Cambridge University Press, 2010), 21, 207–14.

35. Jonathan Rose, *The Intellectual Life of the British Working Classes*, 2nd ed. (New Haven: Yale University Press, 2010).
36. Lucy Wilson, *A Visit to Grove Cottage* (London: Harris and Son, 1823), 22.
37. Lucille M. Schultz, "Pestalozzi's Mark on Nineteenth-Century Composition Instruction: Ideas Not in Words, but in Things," *Rhetoric Review* 14, no. 1 (Autumn 1995): 25–29; Margaret Crawford Maloney, *English Illustrated Books for Children: A Descriptive Companion to a Selection from the Osborne Collection* (Tokyo: Holp Shuppan, 1981), 57.
38. Nicholas Bohny, *The New Picture Book: Being Pictorial Lessons on Form, Comparison and Number, for Children under Seven Years of Age* (Edinburgh: Edmonston and Douglas, 1858), preface, n.p.
39. Carter, *Object Lessons*, 1–64.
40. Bohny, *New Picture Book*, 1, 9.
41. *Biographical Sketch*, 192–93.
42. Jean-Jacques Rousseau, *Emile; or, On Education*, trans. Allan Bloom (United States: Basic Books, 1979), 89.
43. Rousseau, *Emile*, 86, 92.
44. Courtney Weikle-Mills explains the political theory behind Rousseau's *Emile*, which imagines the child as both a natural citizen, born free, and a fashioned citizen, made through education. The "education of things" attempts to reconcile these two child models of citizenship by hiding the social meaning of things that shape Emile. See *Imaginary Citizens, Child Readers and the Limits of American Independence, 1640–1868* (Baltimore: Johns Hopkins University Press, 2013), 168–205.
45. Jonathan Lamb, *The Things Things Say* (Princeton: Princeton University Press, 2011); Mark Blackwell, *The Secret Life of Things* (Cranbury: Bucknell University Press, 2007); Elaine Freedgood, *The Ideas in Things: Fugitive Meaning in the Victorian Novel* (Chicago: University of Chicago Press, 2006); John Plotz, *Portable Property: Victorian Property on the Move* (Princeton: Princeton University Press, 2008); Blackwell, *Secret Life of Things*; Cynthia Sundberg Wall, *The Prose of Things: Transformations of Description in the Eighteenth Century* (Chicago: University of Chicago Press, 2006); Lynn Festa, *Fiction without Humanity: Person, Animal, Thing in Early Enlightenment Literature and Culture* (Philadelphia: University of Pennsylvania Press, 2019).
46. Rousseau, *Emile*, 118.
47. Stéphanie-Félicité de Genlis, *Adelaide and Theodore*, ed. Gillian Dow (London: Pickering and Chatto, 2007).
48. Reid-Walsh, *Interactive Books*, 53.
49. James Mill, *James Mill on Education*, ed. W. H. Burston (London: Cambridge, 1969), 41–42.
50. Mill, *James Mill on Education*, 95.
51. David Hartley, *Observations on Man, His Frame, His Duty, and His Expectations*, 3 vols., engravings by William Blake (London: Joseph Johnson, 1791), 1:27.
52. David Hume, *A Treatise of Human Nature*, ed. L. A. Selby-Bigge and P. H. Nidditch, 2nd ed. (Oxford: Clarendon Press Oxford, 1978), 12.
53. Joanna Wharton, *Material Englightenment: Women Writers and the Science of Mind, 1770–1830* (Woodbridge, UK: Boydell Press, 2018). Wharton's study forms

an interesting companion with my own. She is more concerned with the Romantic tradition, but she groups together the same associationist women authors treated in this book for their formulation of mechanical literacy, suggesting that the philosophy of mind she explores underpins the fusion of children's science and technology education with reading and writing. Wharton argues that Barbauld, Honoria and Maria Edgeworth, Elizabeth Hamilton, and Hannah More participated in the development of philosophy of mind through their writings on domestic education. Carefully researching each author, Wharton ties them together through their shared investment in Hartley's associationism and Locke's rejection of innate ideas. While not as radical as the Hays, Wollstonecraft, Godwin circle, these women used materialist philosophy of mind to create practical teaching techniques and education materials.

54. Anna Letitia Barbauld, *Anna Letitia Barbauld: Selected Poetry and Prose*, ed. William McCarthy and Elizabeth Kraft (Petersborough, ON: Broadview, 2002), 324, 307–8. Like Mill, Barbauld defines education as "a thing of great scope and extent," that includes "the whole process by which a human being is formed to be what he is, in habits, principles, and cultivation of every kind," 306.
55. Barbauld, *Selected Poetry and Prose*, 319.
56. Claude-Adrien Helvétius, William Godwin, and John Aiken all tell some version of "Eyes, and No Eyes; or, the Art of Seeing," in which two boys report opposite experiences of a country walk: the first boy gets bored and walks straight home, while the second collects curious specimens on a meandering ramble, presents his findings to his father, and learns by asking him questions. Thus even the same experiences educate people differently through small occurrences. Donelle Ruwe has a wonderful overview of this analogy for education. See *British Children's Poetry in the Romantic Era: Verse, Riddle and Rhyme* (Houndmills: Palgrave Macmillan, 2014), 108–20.
57. William Godwin, *Enquiry Concerning Political Justice and Its Influence on Morals and Happiness*, 2 vols., 3rd ed. (London: G. G. and J. Robinson, 1798), 1:111, 114.
58. Carter, *Object Lessons*, 1–92.
59. "The Value of Iron: The Mariner's Compass," *The Crisis* (Sept. 22, 1832): 115; "The Gold Watch," *The Crisis*, (Sept. 1, 1832): 101; "Silver Shovel, Tongs, and Poker," *The Crisis* (Sept. 15, 1832): 109. Likely, the articles are titled "fables" despite the object lesson format because fables were some of the first fiction in radical journals, and cooperative journals adapted fables to teach lessons. See Paul Thomas Murphy, *Toward a Working-Class Canon: Literary Criticism in British Working-Class Periodicals, 1816–1825* (Columbus: Ohio State University Press, 1994), 88–94.

CHAPTER 1: WHAT CHILDREN GRASP

1. Honoria Edgeworth and Richard Lovell Edgeworth, *Practical Education: or, The History of Harry and Lucy*, vol. 2 (Lichfield: J. Jackson; J. Johnson, 1780), Cotsen; Anne Markey, "Honora Sneyd Edgeworth's 'Harry and Lucy,'" *Eighteenth-Century Ireland* no. 34 (2019), 50–65. Using the Edgeworth papers to untangle family coauthorship, Markey establishes that Honoria Edgeworth wrote the 1780 "Harry and Lucy" story and Richard Lovell Edgeworth wrote the glossary. Maria Edgeworth with Richard Lovell Edgeworth and advice from Joseph Priestley later revised this "Harry and Lucy" episode for inclusion in *Early Lessons* (1801), with an expanded glossary. Maria Edgeworth collaborated with Richard Lovell Edgeworth on "Harry

and Lucy" stories about performing home science experiments and touring industrial sites, which appear in *Continuation of Early Lessons* (1814) and *Harry and Lucy Concluded* (1825). On surviving editions, see Bertha Coolidge Slade, *Maria Edgeworth, 1767–1849: A Bibliographical Tribute* (London, Constable, 1937), 3–7.

2. H. Edgeworth and R. Edgeworth, *Practical Education*, 122, 104–40.
3. A scientist, educator, and theologian, Joseph Priestly published sections of *Hartley's Theory of the Human Mind* in 1775 and 1790 with his own essay comments. Joseph Johnson reprinted the entirety of Hartley's *Observations on Man* in 1791, which contains Hartley's chapter, "A View of the Doctrine of Philosophical Necessity." These ideas influenced educators. See Robert E. Schofield, *The Enlightened Joseph Priestley: A Study of His Life and Work from 1773 to 1804* (University Park: Pennsylvania State University Press, 2004).
4. In many contemporary stories a single day or year in a child protagonist's life recapitulates human history, with the advent of literacy marking child consciousness. Such stories share common assumptions with Jack Goody and Ian Watts's widely critiqued argument in "The Consequences of Literacy" that the introduction of reading and writing in Ancient Greece divided Western society from its prehistorical oral traditions. See *Comparative Studies in Society and History* 5, no. 3 (April 1963): 304–45.
5. *A History of British Birds, Vol. I*, 6th ed. (1797, Newcastle: Edw. Walker, 1826), iii.
6. In Early Modern art, the interlocutor figure looks at the audience and points to something further *inside* the painting. In children's materials, the gesture can be textual or visual (or both). Whether the gesture points into or outside the text can vary, because the toy or book mirrors the child user's world. Illustrations on toys may show a parent who points to an everyday item inside the painting, or an image of the book/toy in question, inviting the adult/child using the book/toy together to investigate that same object or scene in real life. Art historian Lisa Rosenthal kindly advised on this term. See also Elizabeth Massa Hoiem, "A Child-Centered Universe: Growth and Development in Nineteenth-Century Children's Nonfiction," *A Companion to Children's Literature*, ed. Karen Coats, Deborah Stevenson, and Vivian Yenika-Agbaw (Hoboken, NJ: Wiley Press, 2022), 58–59.
7. David Vincent, *Literacy and Popular Culture: England 1750–1914* (Cambridge: Cambridge University Press, 1989), 24. Patricia Crain quotes Vincent and others to note a common "self-reflexive and self-conscious strain" in definitions of literacy. See "New Histories of Literacy," in *A Companion to the History of the Book*, ed. Simon Eliot and Jonathan Rose, 2nd ed. (Hoboken, NJ: Wiley Press, 2019), 145.
8. Children's stories about toys and dolls instruct children to project themselves onto material things in their care, using objects to negotiate adult models of child subjectivity through children's play. See Lois Kuznets, *When Toys Come Alive* (New Haven: Yale University Press, 1994). Susan Honeyman's fascinating argument explores the implications for child agency of identifying with objects that go limp when touched, implying that children subordinate themselves to adults through affective labor. See "Manufactured Agency and the Playthings Who Dream It for Us," *Children's Literature Association Quarterly* 31, no. 2 (Summer 2006): 109–31.
9. Spelling in Play, [England, ca. 1830], Cotsen; The Elegant and Instructive Game of Useful Knowledge (London: William Darton, ca. 1819), Cotsen and Lilly; The Infant's Cabinet of Trades (London: J. Marshall, 1802), Cotsen, described in Brian Alderson, "Miniature Libraries for the Young," *Private Library* 3rd series, vol. 6, no. 1 (Spring 1983), 4, Cotsen.

10. On mothers as source of letters, see Mitzi Myers, "The Erotics of Pedagogy: Historical Intervention, Literary Representation, the 'Gift of Education,' and the Agency of Children," *Children's Literature* 23 (1995): 1–30; Mary Hilton, *Women and the Shaping of the Nation's Young: Education and Public Doctrine in Britain, 1750–1850* (Aldershot, UK: Ashgate, 2007); Julia Briggs, "'Delightful Task!': Women, Children and Reading in the Mid-Eighteenth Century," in *Culturing the Child, 1690–1914*, ed. Donelle Ruwe and Mitzi Myers (Lanham, MD: Scarecrow Press, 2005); Rebecca Davies, *Written Maternal Authority and Eighteenth-Century Education in Britain: Educating by the Book* (Farnham, UK: Ashgate Publishing Limited, 2014). For Myers, the surrogate mother figure in books, represents the female author, who aids mothers by offering her literature. Mary Hilton analyzes the way women used the rational mother figure to participate in the public sphere through their traditional role as family instructors; Rebecca Davies investigates authors who establish authority writing about mothers' work of caring for and teaching children.
11. This series was published in London in the 1830s, but I describe the Harper frontispieces, held at Baldwin, because they offer an exceptional example of interlocutor frontispieces. Jacob Abbott's "The Little Learner" series, published in New York by Harper & Bros., includes: *Learning to Read* (1856), *Learning to Talk* (1855), *Learning to Think* (1856), *Learning about Common Things* (1857), and *Learning about Right and Wrong* (1857).
12. Katherine Pandora, "The Children's Republic of Science in the Antebellum Literature of Samuel Griswold Goodrich and Jacob Abbott," *Osiris* 24, no. 1 (2009): 75–98. Pandora argues that Abbott's working-class characters learn science, while British audiences often found Abbott's style too casual, expecting wealthier science families.
13. Patricia Crain, *The Story of A: The Alphabetization of America from "The New England Primer" to "The Scarlet Letter"* (Stanford: Stanford University Press, 2000), 93.
14. Shefrin, *Dartons*, 52–54.
15. Joseph Lancaster, *The British System of Education* (London: J. Lancaster, 1810).
16. Catharine Macaulay, *Letters on Education with Observations on Religious and Metaphysical Subjects* (Dublin: Printed for H. Chamberlaine and Rice, L. White, W. McKenzie, J. Moore, Grueber and McAllister, W. Jones, and R. White, 1790), i–ii; on Macaulay's determinist philosophy of education, see Hilton, *Women*, 63–75.
17. Garrett Stewart, *The Look of Reading: Book, Painting, Text* (Chicago: University of Chicago Press, 2006). In analyzing paintings of readers as a genre, Stewart notes the prominence during this period of readers positioned indoors in relation to visually accessible outdoors.
18. William Martin, *The Parlour Book, Or, Familiar Conversations on Science and the Arts: For the Use of Schools and Families* (London: Darton and Clark, 1839).
19. H. Edgeworth and R. Edgeworth, *Practical Education*, iii–xv.
20. J. G. Wood, *The Common Objects of the Country*, new ed. (London: G. Routledge & Co., 1858), 2.
21. Priscilla Wakefield, *Mental Improvement: or the Beauties and Wonders of Nature and Art*, new ed., rev. by Edward Emerson (1794, London: George Bingley, 1840), 3, iii–iv.

22. Isaac Watts, *The Improvement of the Mind, or, a Supplement to the Art of Logic* (London: J. Buckland and T. Longman, 1787), 31–34; Wakefield, *Mental Improvement*, iii–iv.
23. Wakefield, *Improvement of the Mind,* 10.
24. John Locke, *Essay Concerning Human Understanding*, ed. Peter H. Nidditch (Oxford: Clarendon Press Oxford, 1795), 2.1.5.
25. Leah Price, *How to Do Things with Books in Victorian Britain* (Princeton: Princeton University Press, 2012), 7–15; Jacqueline Reid-Walsh, *Interactive Books: Playful Media before Pop-Ups* (London: Routledge, 2018), 25.
26. Literacy toys with family-added scrapbooking are common in collections, such as a "Jacob's ladder decorated with cut-out engraved images" [ca. 1770–1799], Cotsen, with lotto prints pasted onto the wooden pieces; and The Alphabet in Verse (London: W. Darton and J. Harvey, 1800), Lilly, a set of alphabet cards reinforced by users with scrap hand-colored prints.
27. Exactly how much assembly was required for reading a children's book is connected to the book's price. While one family might purchase a hand-colored chapbook with pages cut and bound, another family might purchase the same book uncolored or unfolded as a single printed sheet. Other families worked at home by painting the illustrations of children's books around a table, each child adding a color before passing the toy or book to their neighbor. See Leonard de Vries, *A Treasury of Illustrated Children's Books: Early Nineteenth-Century Classics from the Osborne Collection* (New York: Abbeville Press, 1989), 29; Hannah Field, *Playing with the Book: Victorian Movable Picture Books and the Child Reader* (Minneapolis: University of Minnesota Press, 2019), 15. More affluent children also painted their books for fun, or made beautiful hand-crafted cards or books for their loved ones.
28. Blair Whitton, *Paper Toys of the World* (Cumberland: Hobby House Press, 1986); Shefrin, *Dartons*; Barbara Maria Stafford, *Artful Science: Enlightenment Entertainment and the Eclipse of Visual Education* (Cambridge, MA: MIT Press, 1994).
29. M. O. Grenby, *The Child Reader, 1700–1840* (New York: Cambridge University Press, 2011), 41–43.
30. Heather Klemann, "The Matter of Moral Education: Locke, Newbery, and the Didactic Book Toy Hybrid," *Eighteenth-Century Studies* 44, no. 2 (Winter 2011): 223–44.
31. Benjamin Collins, *Directions for Playing with a Set of Squares, Newly Invented for the Use of Children* (London. J. Newbery [between June. 1743 and March 1744]), Cotsen. This item's catalog record at Cotsen explains the relationship between this alphabet game, which Collins published first, before Newbery published the same game the following year. Then Newbery incorporated the letter game into his *Pocket-Book*. The order of events reveals a game later made part of a book, with the expectation that children could cut it up to make a game.
32. Scholars of moveable books and learning aids remark on their experiences accessing book-toy hybrids in archives that may not categorize them as books, see Reid-Walsh, *Interactive Books*, 1–23; Field, *Playing*, 17.
33. [Thomas and Mary Cooper], *The Child's New Play-thing*, 8th ed. (London: T. Cooper, 1763), 4, Cotsen; Sheffin, *Dartons*, 17–18. There are several editions at Cotsen, beginning with 1842, all with child marginalia and drawings.
34. Wooden jumping jack with inlaid ivory plaque incised with an alphabet of capital Roman letters (England?: 1810), Cotsen.

35. Lissa Paul and Michael Joseph use "handmade literacies" to refer to lovingly hand-constructed books created for home teaching, "Editor's Introduction: Praise for Handmade Literacies in an Age of the Standardized Kind," *Lion and the Unicorn* 29 (2005): v–vii.
36. Richard Altick, *The Shows of London* (Cambridge: Belknap Press of Harvard University Press, 1978), 198–99.
37. Crain, *Story of A*, 83–91.
38. *The Universal Shuttlecock* (London: John Marshall, ca. 1790), 45, Lilly.
39. Macaulay, *Letters on Education*, 47.
40. Macaulay, *Letters on Education*, 45.
41. Macaulay, *Letters on Education*, 45–46.
42. Anna Letitia Barbauld, *Lessons for Children from Two to Three Years Old* (London: J. Johnson, 1787), 5–9. William McCarthy, "Mother of All Discourses: Anna Barbauld's Lessons for Children," in *Culturing the Child, 1690–1914*, ed. Donelle Ruwe and Mitzi Myers (Lanham, MD: Scarecrow Press, 2005), 261–76; and William McCarthy, "Performance, Pedagogy, and Politics: Mrs. Thrale, Mrs. Barbauld, Monsieur Itard," *Childhood and Children's Books in Early Modern Europe*, ed. Andrea Immel and Michael Witmore (New York: Routledge, 2006), 261–76. On Barbauld's lessons as a model for other middle-class mothers, see Sarah Robbins, "Lessons for Children and Teaching Mothers: Mrs. Barbauld's Primer for the Textual Construction of Middle-Class Domestic Pedagogy," *The Lion and the Unicorn* 17, no. 2 (1993): 135–51. On Barbauld's and Maria Edgeworth's materialist pedagogies and observation of things, see Joanna Wharton, *Material Enlightenment: Women Writers and the Science of Mind, 1770–1830* (Woodbridge: The Boydell Press, 2018), 31–112, 197–230.
43. Louise M. Rosenblatt, "Transactional Theory of Reading and Writing," in *Theoretical Models and Processes of Reading*, ed. Robert B. Ruddell, Harry Singer, and Martha Rapp Ruddell, 4th ed. (Newark, DE: International Reading Association, 1994), 1057–1092. For a cognitive approach, see Natalie M. Phillips, *Distraction: Problems of Attention in Eighteenth-Century Literature* (Baltimore: Johns Hopkins University Press, 2016).
44. William Wordsworth, *The Prelude, Book V* (Oxford and New York: Woodstock Books, 1993), lines 349–59. Wordsworth describes educators who approach teaching as engineering, using association to perfect humanity: "These mighty workmen of our later age, . . . they who have the skill / To manage books, and things, and make them act / On infant minds as surely as the sun / Deals with a flower." These educators "confine us down, / Like engines." I do not share this ungenerous interpretation of such theories.
45. Donelle Ruwe points out that many early children's readers, including Aiken and Barbauld's *Evenings at Home*, are sold as the home literacies of fictional characters. See "The British Reception of Genlis's *Adèle et Théodore*, Perceptive Fiction and the Professionalization of Handmade Literacies," *Women's Writing* 25, no. 1 (2018): 14–16; Shirley Brice Heath, "Child's Play or Finding the Ephemera of Home," *Opening the Nursery Door: Reading, Writing and Childhood 1600–1900*, ed. Mary Hilton, Morag Styles, and Victor Watson (London: Routledge, 1997), 91–103.
46. "Book 4," *The Infant's Library* (London: John Marshall, 1800–1801), 5, 17, copy 1, Lilly. I viewed about a dozen miniature libraries from the Lilly Library collections. Copies with the same title usually have different, individually crafted cabinets, and the volumes may vary if replaced by successive owners. In general, the sliding lid illustrations feature the split bookshelves with cabinet on bottom, or an illustration of children reading and/or using other learning aids.

47. Alderson, "Miniature Libraries," 2–38; Evelyn Arizpe, Morag Styles, with Shirley Brice Heath, eds., *Reading Lessons from the Eighteenth Century: Mothers, Children and Texts* (Lichfield, EN: Pied Piper Publishing, 2006); Lissa Paul, *The Children's Book Business: Lessons from the Long Eighteenth Century* (New York and London: Routledge, 2011), 26–17; Grenby, *Child Reader*, 211–15. These authors all describe and provide images of miniature libraries. According to Katherine Wakely-Mulroney, an aesthetics of miniaturization suffuses eighteenth-century children's books designed for readers with small bodies and limited understanding, see "Nuts, Flies, Thimbles, and Thumbs" in *Eighteenth-Century Children's Literature and Scale*, ed. Chloe Wigston Smith and Beth Fowkes Tobin (Cambridge: Cambridge University Press, 2022), 31–46.
48. *The Infant's Library* (London: John Marshall, 1801–1802), copy 3, Lilly.
49. This description relies on the collection of John Marshall's infant cabinets that I viewed at Lilly and Cotsen.
50. Donelle Ruwe, *British Children's Poetry in the Romantic Era: Verse, Riddle and Rhyme* (New York: Palgrave Macmillan, 2014), 108–20. Please also see Introduction, n. 56, this volume. Jane Gardiner, *An Excursion from London to Dover* (London: Longman, Hurst, Rees, and Orme, 1806). Mary Ellen Bamford, *The Look-About Club, and the Curious Live Things They Found* (Boston: D. Lothrop & Company, 1887).
51. E. W. Payne, *Earth's Riches; or, Underground Stores* (London: Religious Tract Society, ca. 1850), 11, 25.
52. Lucy Wilson [Sarah Atkins], *The India Cabinet Opened*, 2nd ed. (London: Harris and Son, 1823), 39, 23, 268. On organizing botanical specimens to encourage children's moral development, see Judith Page and Elise L. Smith, *Women, Literature, and the Domesticated Landscape: England's Disciples of Flora, 1780–1870* (Cambridge: Cambridge University Press, 2014), 15–78.
53. Sean Silver, *The Mind Is a Collection: Case Studies in Eighteenth-Century Thought* (Philadelphia: University of Pennsylvania Press, 2015), 1–20. See also Stafford, *Artful Science*, 225–64.
54. Anke Te Heesen, *The World in a Box: The Story of an Eighteenth-Century Picture Encyclopedia* (Chicago: University of Chicago Press, 2002).
55. Anne Secord, "Containers and Collections," in *Worlds of Natural History*, ed. H. A. Curry, Nicholas Jardine, James A. Secord, and E. C. Spary (Cambridge, UK: Cambridge University Press, 2018), 298.
56. Wilson, *India Cabinet*, 169.
57. Jeffrey A. Auerbach, *The Great Exhibition of 1851: A Nation on Display* (New Haven and London: Yale University Press, 1999), 106–7. See also Jeffrey A. Auerbach and Peter H. Hoffenberg, eds., *Britain, the Empire, and the World at the Great Exhibition of 1851* (Burlington, VT: Ashgate, 2008).
58. Felix Summerly, *An Alphabet of Quadrupeds* (London: Joseph Cundall, 1844).
59. Harvey Darton, *Children's Books in England*, 3rd ed., revised by Brian Alderson (Cambridge: Cambridge University Press, 1982), 233–35; Geoffrey Summerfield, "The Making of the Home Treasury," *Children's Literature* 8 (1980): 35; Ezra Shales, "Toying with Design Reform: Henry Cole and Instructive Play for Children," *Journal of Design History* 22, no. 1 (March 2009): 3–26. Cole's experience writing London tour books may have inspired the way his books and toys reference real-world places. Guides for London visitors are among the earliest children's travel literature, and there are several children's games that come with similar guidebooks, which players reference to learn trivia needed to advance on the board composed of London attractions. Such

games include: The Panorama of London, or, A Day's Journey Round the Metropolis (London: J. Harris, 1809), Lilly; The British Tourist: A New Game (London: E. Wallis [between 1830 and 1850]), Lilly.

60. *The Illustrated Girl's Own Treasury, Specially Designed for the Entertainment of Girls, and the Development of the Best Faculties of the Female Mind* (London: Ward and Lock, 1861), xvii, Baldwin.
61. Richard Edgeworth and Maria Edgeworth, *Essays on Practical Education,* 2 vols. (London: J. Johnson, 1798): 1:1–2, 1:10.
62. R. Edgeworth and M. Edgeworth, *Practical Education,* 1:9.
63. Locke, *Human Understanding,* 1.2.15; 2.1.2–4.
64. R. Edgeworth and M. Edgeworth, *Practical Education,* 1:11, 1:24.
65. Locke, *Human Understanding,* 1.2.15; 2.1.2–4; 2.1.22.
66. Advertisement for *Wilson's Catechisms on Common Things*; see Mary Elliott, *Tales for Girls* (London: Darton and Co., ca. 1845), endpapers.
67. R. Edgeworth and M. Edgeworth, *Practical Education,* 1:69, 1:72, 1:64.
68. John Locke, *Two Treatises of Government and A Letter Concerning Toleration,* ed. with an introduction by Ian Shapiro (New Haven, CT: Yale University Press, 2003), 5.27–28.
69. Watts, *Improvement of the Mind,* 35.
70. Locke, *Two Treatises,* 2.4–6.
71. Quoted in Cynthia J. Koepp, "Curiosity, Science, and Experiential Learning," in *Childhood and Children's Books in Early Modern Europe, 1550–1800,* ed. Andrea Immel and Michael Witmore (New York and London: Routledge, 2006), 176, 166; Stafford, *Artful Science,* 217–20, 233–37.
72. Simon Schaffer explains the analogy between God as Creator, who knows all His creation, and an engineer who knows his machine. See "Enlightened Automata," in *The Sciences in Enlightened Europe,* ed. William Clarke, Jan Golinski, and Simon Schaffer (Chicago: University of Chicago Press, 1999), 145–47. Jonathan R. Topham explores how children learned to observe the world as God's book through the Bridgewater Treatises, integrating science into Christian religious beliefs. See Topham, *Reading the Book of Nature: How Eight Best Sellers Reconnected Christianity and the Sciences on the Eve of the Victorian Age* (Chicago: University of Chicago Press, 2022).
73. E. Burrows, *The Triumphs of Steam* (London: Griffith and Farran, 1859), 18–19, 16–17.
74. Silver, *Mind Is a Collection,* 246.
75. Ian McKay, "A Half-Century of Possessive Individualism: C. B. Macpherson and the Twenty-First-Century Prospects of Liberalism," *Journal of the Canadian Historical Association / Revue de la Société historique du Canada* 25, no. 1 (2014): https://doi.org/10.7202/1032806ar.
76. Locke, *Two Treatises,* VI.57.
77. Adam Walker, *A System of Familiar Philosophy,* 2 vols. (1799, London: Walker, 1802), 1:x.
78. Early British Pestalozzian manuals for teaching "numbers" contain charts with squares divided into sections, which show teachers how to direct students on dividing up their slates into regular pieces. Such exercises convey that all quantities are part of a whole and provide children with an intuitive grasp of fractions prior to their symbolic representation with numbers, much as the "pure forms" lead to letters.
79. E. Biber, *Dr. Henry Pestalozzi, and His Plan of Education* (London: John Souter, School Library, 1831), 388, 389.

80. [Synge], *A Biographical Sketch of the Struggles of Pestalozzi, to Establish His System of Education* (Dublin: William Folds, 1815), 14.
81. Pestalozzi, *Biographical Sketch*, 16.
82. Sarah Anne Carter, "On an Object Lesson, or Don't Eat the Evidence," *Journal of the History of Childhood and Youth* 3, no. 1 (2010): 8.
83. Biber, *Pestalozzi*, 244, 170–71.
84. Locke, *Human Understanding*, 3.9.23.
85. *The Keepsake, or, Poems and Pictures for Childhood and Youth* (London: Darton, Harvey, and Darton, 1818), 3–5, 40–42.
86. Samuel Wilderspin, *Infant Education: or, Practical Remarks on the Importance of Educating the Infant Poor* (London: Simpkin and Marshall, 1829), 171.
87. Wilderspin, *Infant Education*, 169–70.
88. Horace Grant, *Exercises for the Improvement of the Senses: For Young Children* (London: Darton and Co., 1848), 1–55. Teachers begin with the "actual experience of the child," using "real objects" for "examination," training "the physical senses" to "accurate perception, and the understanding is gradually led to generalize and classify." Rev. Charles Mayo, *Memoirs of Pestalozzi* (London: J. A. Hessey, 1828), 26–27.
89. Biber, *Pestalozzi*, 173.
90. Shefrin, *Dartons*, 7–14.
91. Brad Sullivan, "Cultivating a 'Dissenting Frame of Mind,'" *Romanticism on the Net* 45 (February 2007), https://ronjournal.org/s/1145; Felicity James and Ian Inkster, eds., *Religious Dissent and the Aikin-Barbauld Circle, 1740–1860* (Cambridge: Cambridge University Press, 2012). For more on the dominance of mercantile and professional class Dissenting Protestants among children's writers and publishers, see Issac Kramnick, *Bourgeois Individualism*; Andrew O'Malley, *Making of the Modern Child* (New York: Routledge, 2003), 1–17; Hilton, *Women*, 87–107.
92. John Bunyan, *Divine Emblems: or, Temporal Things Spiritualized* (London: C. Dilly, 1790), ii–v. The 1686 preface also includes these lines.
93. Illustrated information books often refer to *Orbis Pictus* as the pedagogical inspiration for teaching with images of worldly things (Shefrin, *Dartons*, 66–71; Sarah Ann Carter, *Object Lessons: How Nineteenth-Century Americans Learned to Make Sense of the Material World* (Oxford: Oxford University Press, 2018), 65–92.
94. Watts, *Improvement of the Mind*, 196.
95. John Aiken and Anna Letitia Barbauld, *Evenings at Home; or the Juvenile Budget Opened*, 6 vols. (London: J. Johnson, 1792), 5:136.
96. Aiken and Barbauld, *Evenings at Home*, 5:141–42.
97. Paul Olson, *The Kingdom of Science: Literary Utopianism and British Education, 1612–1870* (Lincoln: University of Nebraska Press, 2002), 56–57.
98. Thomas Hodgson, "Preface," *A Curious Hieroglyphick Bible*, 20th ed. (London: J. Barker, 1812), n.p. Despite reservations about adapting the Bible, Sarah Trimmer also produced a series of historical prints for school or nursery walls depicting biblical scenes.
99. The word "God" is replaced with the sun, containing the Hebrew letters "Yud Hey Vav Hey" or Yehovah—a substitution that recalls an anecdote of Pricilla Wakefield, whose children learned to pause when reading scriptures aloud rather than speak the Deity's name (Darton, *Children's Books*, 168). Where rebus parlour games use images as sounds (a picture of an "awl" replaces part of "always"), the *Hieroglyphick Bible* refuses to make the Word an empty sound. Thank you to Guy Tal for assistance with Hebrew letters.

100. Peter Borsay, "Children, Adolescents and Fashionable Urban Society," in *Fashioning Childhood in the Eighteenth Century: Age and Identity*, ed. Anja Muller (Burlington, VT: Ashgate, 2006), 63–80; Paul, *Children's Book Business*, 1–66; Laurence Talairach, *Animals, Museum Culture and Children's Literature in Nineteenth-Century Britain: Curious Beasties* (Basingstoke: Palgrave Macmillan, 2021). Talairach shows the relationship between museum culture and children's natural history books through home practices like collection. Leonore Davidoff and Catherine Hall, *Family Fortunes: Men and Women of the English Middle Class, 1780–1850* (Chicago: University of Chicago Press, 1987), 235.
101. [Richard Johnson], *The Toy-shop, or, Sentimental Preceptor* (London: E. Newbery, 1791), 26–27. The 1805 John Harris edition is "by Miss Nancy Meanwell."
102. Arnaud Berquin, *The Looking-Glass for the Mind; or, Intellectual Mirror*, 8th ed. (London: J. Crowder; E Newbery, 1800), preface; [Johnson], *Toy-shop*, 87, 118.
103. Patricia Crown, "Visual Culture of Consumption," in *Fashioning Childhood*, ed. Muller, 63–73.
104. *The Toy-shop* became *more* self-reflective about legible objects when adapted for children. When Robert Dodsley wrote the satirical one-act play in 1735 that Richard Johnson adapted into *The Toy-shop*, he confined the action to a single visit by adults to a curiosity shop where the shopkeeper corrects the follies of customers. Johnson's 1787 adaptation added referencs to Newbery's shop and wares along with a frontispiece showing children entering a toy shop adjoining a bookshop. In the 1830 edition, revised by E. H. Barker, the toy shop contains the publisher's name "F. Skill" over the door, reinforcing references to the reader's experience in the world.
105. [Richard Johnson], *Toy-shop; or, Sentimental Preceptor*, rev. by E. H. Barker (Swaffham, UK: F. Skill, 1830), vi.
106. Megan Norcia, "The London Shopscape: Educating the Child Consumer in the Stories of Mary Wollstonecraft, Maria Edgeworth, and Mary Martha Sherwood," *Children's Literature* 41 (2013): 28–56, 31–39. Maria Edgeworth's "Purple Jar" is another morally legible marketplace. See my chapter 4.
107. Blair Whitton, *Paper Toys of the World* (Cumberland: Hobby House Press, 1986).
108. [Charles Tilt], *Figures of Fun*, 2 parts (London: Charles Tilt, 1833), Lilly; James A. Secord, "Scrapbook Science: Composite Caricatures in Late Georgian England," in *Figuring It Out : Science, Gender, and Visual Culture*, ed. Ann B. Shteir and Bernard V. Lightman (Hanover, NH: Dartmouth College Press, 2006), 183, 181.
109. The Newberys produced a nonsense miscellany that pokes fun at the comparison of marketplaces to reading in didactic fiction. As its preface proclaims, *The Fairing; or, A Golden Toy* (London: Printed for Newbery and Carnan, 1768), Lilly, is a collection of tales much like a fair is a collection of goods: "I understand the Matter . . . A Metaphor is a kind of Simile, and a Simile a Kind of Description, and a Description a Kind of Picture; and as all of them are intended to convey to the Mind an Image of the Things they represent, what they represent must be like themselves; and as this Book is a Metaphor, or Simile, or Description, or a Picture of a Fair, it must be like a Fair, and like nothing else; that is, it must be one entire whole, but a whole Heap of Confusion" (v).
110. Steven Shapin and Barry Barnes, "Head and Hand: Rhetorical Resources in British Pedagogical Writing, 1770–1850," *Oxford Review of Education* 2, no. 3 (1976): 231–54.
111. Locke, *Human Understanding*, 2.1.7.
112. Anonymous, *The Rational Exhibition for Children* (London: Darton and Harvey, 1800 and 1824), Lilly; Margaret Spufford, "Women Teaching Reading to Poor Children in

the Sixteenth and Seventeenth Centuries," in *Opening the Nursery Door*, ed. Hilton, Styles, and Watson.

113. The conceit resembles Lady Ellenor Fenn's strategy of styling herself a "rational dame" after the village woman who teaches children reading and mending in her kitchen.
114. Brian Simon, *The Radical Education Tradition in Britain* (London: Lawrence and Wishart, 1972), 19.
115. Ian Donnachie, "'We Must Give Them an Education, Large, Liberal and Comprehensive': Catherine Vale Whitwell: Teacher, Artist, Author, Feminist and Owenite Communitarian," *Women's History Review* 28, no. 4 (2019): 552–65.
116. Robert Owen, *The Life of Robert Owen* (London: E. Wilson, 1857), 60.
117. Robert Dale Owen, *An Outline of the System of Education at New Lanark* (Glasgow: Wardlaw & Cunninghame; Edinburgh: Bell & Bradfute; London: Longman, Nurst, Rees, Orme, Brown, & Green, 1824), 29.
118. Catherine Whitwell, *The Material and Intellectual Universe, from Which the Object and End of Education May be Deduced*, 2nd ed. (London: Wertheim and Mackintosh, 1849), 62, 29, 81.
119. Catherine Whitwell, *Her Education, An Address to Mothers in the British Empire* (London: G. Wilson, 1819), 7, 38.
120. Catherine Whitwell, *An Astronomical Catechism* (London: G. Wilson, 1818), 2, 314.
121. Whitwell, *Her Education*, 27, 29; Whitwell shares Isaac Newton's theological and scientific belief in a unifying, simple set of natural laws that God uses to govern the material universe. Whitwell mentions "simplicity" as God's guiding principle, a reference to the first law in the *Principia*, and "benevolence" as that simple rule of human nature.
122. Robert Owen, *A New View of Society*, 2nd ed. (London: Longman, Hurst, Rees, Orme, and Brown, 1816), 39.
123. Whitwell, *Her Education*, 2–5.
124. Animal, vegetable, and mineral are not discrete categories, and many specimens would belong to multiple categories, a possibility Owen mentions when describing natural history lessons at New Lanark. Whitwell mentions that students can devise their own categories.
125. Whitwell, *Her Education*, 39.
126. Whitwell, *Her Education*, plates 1 and 3, pages 38, 56, 57.
127. R. D. Owen, *Outline*, 34, 35, 36.
128. R. D. Owen, *Outline*, 23.

CHAPTER 2: MOVING BODIES

1. Newton calls any artisan who strays from mathematical precision an "imperfect mechanic," while the man capable of perfect lines and circles "would be the most perfect mechanic of all." *The Mathematical Principles of Natural Philosophy*, trans. Andrew Motte, with "A Short Comment on, and Defense of, the 'Principia,'" by William Emerson, 3 vols. (London: Sherwood, Neely, and Jones, 1819), 1:ix–x. On Motte's translation, see I. Bernard Cohen's introductory guide in *The Principia: Mathematical Principles of Natural Philosophy*, trans. I. Bernard Cohen and Anne Whitman, assisted by Julia Budenz (Berkley: University of California Press, 1999), 26–42. Seemingly referencing this passage of *Principia*, John Ruskin's "The Nature of the Gothic" recognizes that the practical/rational divide undervalues the intelligence needed for physical labor: "We prize and honour [men] in their imperfection

above the best and most perfect manual skill. And this is what we have to do with all our labourers; to look for the *thoughtful* part of them." *Unto This Last and Other Writings*, introduction and notes by Clive Wilmer (London: Penguin Books, 1997), 84.

2. William Emerson, *The Principles of Mechanics* (London: W. Innys, J. Richardson, 1754), ix.
3. Emerson, *Principles of Mechanics*, i–vi.
4. John Aiken and Anna Letitia Barbauld, *Evenings at Home; or the Juvenile Budget Opened*, 6 vols. (London: J. Johnson, 1792), 2:101.
5. Samuel Goodrich, *A Glance at the Physical Sciences* (New York: John Allen, 1844), 5.
6. James Ferguson, *Lectures on Select Subjects in Mechanics, Hydrostatics, Hydraulics Pneumatics, and Optics* (London, W. Strahan, 1776), 1. Science disciplines changed considerably from 1760 to 1860, and children's textbooks use terms inconsistently, according to the convenience of teachers and booksellers. "Natural philosophy" was used interchangeably with "physics" in the eighteenth century until physics and chemistry became separate disciplines. Anatomy is part of mechanics but treated separately in medicine. Mechanics can refer to general principles expressed mathematically that underlie all sciences. Yet in children's textbooks, "mechanics" may be the first chapter of natural philosophy, covering matter, motion, and simple machines, followed by advanced concepts like sound, hydraulics, astronomy, and optics. See Mary Jo Nye, *From Chemical Philosophy to Theoretical Chemistry: Dynamics of Matter and Dynamics of Disciplines, 1800–1950* (Berkeley: University of California Press, 1993), 34–55.
7. James C. Ungureanu, "Newton Deified and Defied: The Many 'Newtons' of the Enlightenment," *Perspectives on Science and Christian Faith* 72, no. 4 (December 2020): 232. See also Joan L. Richards, "God, Truth, and Mathematics in Nineteenth Century England," in *The Invention of Physical Science*, ed. Mary Jo Nye, Joan L. Richards, and Roger H. Stuewer (Dordrecht: Springer Netherlands, 1992); P. M. Heimann, "The 'Unseen Universe': Physics and the Philosophy of Nature in Victorian Britain," *British Journal for the History of Science* 6, no. 1 (1972): 73–79.
8. J. H. Plumb, "The First Flourishing of Children's Books," in *Early Children's Books and Their Illustration*, ed. Gerald Gottlieb (London: Oxford University Press; New York: Pierpont Morgan Library, 1975), xxii.
9. James Secord, "Newton in the Nursery," *History of Science* 23 (1985): 127–51.
10. Aileen Fyfe notes that Marcet, Joyce, and so on were pricier books at 14–15 shillings, while the Religious Tract Society produced cheaper books at 2 shillings, with tracts and journals available for less. See "Science for Children in the Nineteenth Century," in *Popular Children's Literature in Britain*, ed. Julia Briggs, Dennis Butts, and M. O. Grenby (Aldershot, UK: Ashgate, 2008), 215.
11. For an overview of women writers of children's physics books, see M. T. Brück, *Agnes Mary Clerke and the Rise of Astrophysics* (Cambridge: Cambridge University Press, 2002); Le-May Sheffield, *Women and Science: Social Impact and Interaction* (Santa Barbara, CA: ABC-CLIO, 2004); Aileen Fyfe, *Science for Children* (Bristol: Thoemmes, 2003); Dometa Wiegand Brothers, *The Romantic Imagination and Astronomy: On All Sides Infinity* (New York: Palgrave, 2015). The prominence of women authors is more obvious in natural history books: Sarah Trimmer, Charlotte Smith, L. M. Budgen, Maria Hack, Margaret Gatty, and Jane Webb Loudon. For an essential bibliography of women science writers, see Suzan Alteri, J. Prussing, and A. Warwick,

Guiding Science: Publications by Women in the Romantic and Victorian Ages, ed. A. Rauch and D. Van Kleeck, *Baldwin Library of Historical Children's Literature*, https://www.uflib.ufl.edu/guidingscience/index.html. See also Barbara T. Gates and Ann B. Shteir, eds., *Natural Eloquence: Women Reinscribe Science* (Madison: University of Wisconsin Press, 1997); Barbara T. Gates, *In Nature's Name: An Anthology of Women's Writing and Illustration, 1780–1930* (Chicago: University of Chicago Press, 2002); Le-May Sheffield, *Revealing New Worlds: Three Victorian Women Naturalists* (London: Routledge, 2001).

12. Melanie Keene, "Domestic Science: Making Chemistry Your Cup of Tea," *Endeavor* 32 (2008): 16–19; Marion Amies, "Amusing and Instructive Conversations: The Literary Genre and Its Relevance to Home Education," *History Education* 14, no. 2 (June 1985): 87–99; Jonathan R. Topham, "'Popular Science' in Early Nineteenth-Century Britain," in *Science in the Marketplace: Nineteenth-Century Sites and Experiences*, ed. Aileen Fyfe and Bernard Lightman (Chicago: University of Chicago Press, 2007), 135–68.
13. Greg Myers, "Science for Women and Children: The Dialogue of Popular Science in the Nineteenth Century," in *Nature Transfigured: Science and Literature, 1700–1900*, ed. John Christie and Sally Shuttleworth (Manchester: Manchester University Press, 1989), 171–80. Myers relies on Shapin and Schaffer's argument in *Leviathan and the Air-Pump* that Boyle's experiments are written dialogs circulated to create consensus. "Boyle shifted the terms of scientific proof from actual witnessing of an experiment to reading about it" (172). Ann B. Shteir describes teaching through family dialog the "familiar format" in *Cultivating Women, Cultivating Science* (Baltimore, MD: Johns Hopkins University Press, 1996), 83. Julia V. Douthwaite connects written experiments with education experiment novels in *The Wild Girl, the Natural Man, and the Monster: Dangerous Experiments in the Age of Enlightenment* (Chicago: University of Chicago Press, 2002). Thus, educationalists replicated their experiments on child learning through the circulation of conversational literature modeled on Enlightenment science practices.
14. Alan Rauch, *Useful Knowledge: The Victorians, Morality, and the March of Intellect* (Durham, NC: Duke University Press, 2001), 40–46; Aileen Fyfe, *Science and Salvation: Evangelical Popular Science Publishing in Victorian Britain* (Chicago: University of Chicago Press, 2004).
15. Adam Walker, *A System of Familiar Philosophy*, 2 vols. (London: Walker, 1802), vi–vii.
16. John Ayrton Paris, *Philosophy in Sport Made Science in Earnest*, 3 vols. (London: Longman, Rees, Orme, Brown, and Gren. London: 1827), title page.
17. Jacob Abbott, *The Little Philosopher for Schools and Families* (London: T. Allman, 1835), 6.
18. Abbott, *Little Philosopher*, 8.
19. Abbot, *Little Philosopher*, 17, 14, 17.
20. Richard Edgeworth and Maria Edgeworth, *Essays on Practical Education*, 2 vols. (London: J. Johnson, 1798), 2:596. On the child as unprejudiced observer, see Susan Manly, "Maria Edgeworth and 'the Light of Nature': Artifice, Autonomy, and Anti-Sectarianism in *Practical Education* (1798)," in *Repossessing the Romantic Past*, ed. Heather Glen and Paul Hamilton (New York: Cambridge University Press, 2006), 146; Hilton, *Women*, 26–30.
21. R. Edgeworth and M. Edgeworth, *Practical Education*, 2:276.
22. Paris, *Philosophy in Sport*, 1:xii, 1:61, 1:69; 1:vi.

23. Meredith Bak, *Playful Visions: Optical Toys and the Emergence of Children's Media Culture* (Cambridge, MA: MIT Press, 2020), 64. Bak also analyzes Paris's *Philosophy in Sport* as an early instance of the commercialization of recreational learning and concomitant skepticism toward public schooling for its association with upending social order (46–54).
24. Paris, *Philosophy in Sport*, 1:25. American John Hunt's abridgment, *Sports and Amusements for the Juvenile Philosopher* (Middletown, CN: E. Hunt, 1836), covers additional experiments but omits disparaging artisans for pursuing education, presumably unrelatable to US readers.
25. Isaac Kramnick, *Republicanism and Bourgeois Radicalism: Political Ideology in Late Eighteenth-Century England and America* (Ithaca: Cornell University Press, 1990), 44–45.
26. Paris, *Philosophy in Sport*, 1:7–8, 1:20, 1:7–8, 1:20, 1:46. The Gradgrind children in Charles Dickens's *Hard Times* are also named Tom and Louisa.
27. Paris, *Philosophy in Sport*, 1:27, 1:40.
28. Paris, *Philosophy in Sport*, 1:28, 1:26, 1:40, 3:73.
29. Bernard V. Lightman, *Victorian Popularizers of Science, Designing Nature for New Audiences* (Chicago: University of Chicago Press, 2007), 18–29. Lightman notes Murry's Family Library and Longman's 133-volume Cabinet Cyclopedia of introductory science books.
30. See Rauch, *Useful Knowledge*. Examples of RTS productions on mechanics include natural theology books by Mrs. E. W. Payne, which connect mechanical wonders with God's animal kingdom, *Village Science* (1851), *Nature's Wonders* (1850), *Earth's Riches* (ca. 1850), and *Wayside Fragments* (1852), and Cecilia Lucy Brightwell's inventor biographies, *Lives of Labor* (1875), *Annals of Industry and Genius* (1863), and *Heroes of the Laboratory and the Workshop* (1859).
31. Bak, *Playful Visions*, 61, 81.
32. Priscilla Wakefield, *Mental Improvement: or the Beauties and Wonders of Nature and Art*, new ed., rev. by Edward Emerson (1794, London: George Bingley, 1840), iii.
33. Adam Smith, *The Wealth of Nations*, ed. Edwin Cannan, with an introduction by Robert Reich (New York: The Modern Library, 2000), 841.
34. John Locke, *Essay Concerning Human Understanding*, ed. Peter H. Nidditch (Oxford: Clarendon Press Oxford, 1795), 2.1.7.
35. Smith, *Wealth of Nations*, 843.
36. Philip Connelly, *Romanticism, Economics, and the Question of "Culture"* (New York: Oxford University Press, 2001), 63–92. Connelly examines Adam Smith and political economists on education in greater depth, showing their fears that the division of labor will destroy workers' minds without paternalist intervention through support for mass education. He explains how James Mill's associationism attempts to create ideas through an intellectual process analogous to the division of labor, recovering degraded minds through the study of mechanics and political economy.
37. James Mill, *James Mill on Education*, ed. W. H. Burston (London: Cambridge, 1969), 89–90.
38. Rowland Detrosier, *An Address, Delivered to the Members of the New Mechanics Institution, Manchester, on Friday Evening, March 25, 1831, on the Necessity of an Extension of Moral and Political Instruction among the Working Classes* (London: W. Strange, 1831), 6–7, 14, 10.
39. Whig MP Henry Brougham co-established the first mechanics institute and advanced bills for a nationally funded education system. See Claire Brock, "The

Public Worth of Mary Somerville," *British Society for the History of Science* 39, no. 2 (2006): 255–72.

40. Mary Somerville, *On the Connexion of the Physical Sciences*, revised by Arabella B. Buckley, 10th ed. (London: John Murray, 1877), 3.
41. Lightman, *Victorian Popularizers of Science*, 95–165; E. C. Patterson, *Mary Somerville and the Cultivation of the Sciences* (Dordrecht, NL: Springer, 1983), 147–77; Robyn Arianrhod, *Seduced by Logic: Émilie du Châtelet, Mary Somerville, and the Newtonian Revolution* (New York: Oxford University Press, 2012), 177–79; see also, Kathryn Neeley, *Mary Somerville: Science, Illumination, and the Female Mind* (Cambridge: Cambridge University Press, 2001).
42. James Secord, *Visions of Science: Books and Readers at the Dawn of the Victorian Age* (Chicago: University of Chicago Press, 2014), 107–38.
43. While writing *Mechanism* and *Connexion*, Somerville received peer advisory from famous scientists like John Herschel, Charles Babbage, Michael Faraday, and Charles Lyell. A year later she became the first woman (along with her friend Carolina Herschel) appointed a member of the Royal Astronomical Society. Arianrhod, *Seduced by Logic*, 129–35, 177.
44. Patterson, *Mary Somerville*, 129.
45. Walker, *A System of Familiar Philosophy*, x.
46. Joan L. Richards explains how spiritual knowledge of God has the same certainty as mathematics, but derives from conclusions drawn from personal experience. For nineteenth-century Britains, the profoundly individual and "experiential" quality of spiritual knowledge makes it difficult to share with others and different from the social mechanisms for establishing scientific facts. "God, Truth, and Mathematics in Nineteenth Century England," in *The Invention of Physical Science*, ed. Mary Jo Nye, Joan L. Richards, and Roger H. Stuewer (Dordrecht: Springer Netherlands, 1992), 54. Somerville's correspondents, William Herschel and William Whewell, also explored how science leads to spiritual truths. On faith and popular science, see Secord, *Visions of Science*, 80–138; James A. Secord, *Victorian Sensation: The Extraordinary Publication, Reception, and Secret Authorship of Vestiges of the Natural History of Creation* (Chicago: University of Chicago Press, 2000); Bernard Lightman, "Constructing Victorian Heavens: Agnes Clerke and the 'New Astronomy,'" in *Natural Eloquence: Women Reinscribe Science*, ed. Barbara T. Gates and Ann B. Shteir (Madison: University of Wisconsin Press, 1997), 61–78; Alan Rauch, "A World of Faith on a Foundation of Science: Science and Religion in British Children's Literature: 1761–1878," *Children's Literature Association Quarterly* 14, no. 1 (1989): 13–19; Fyfe, *Science and Salvation*; Jonathan R. Topham, *Reading the Book of Nature: How Eight Best Sellers Reconnected Christianity and the Sciences on the Eve of the Victorian Age* (Chicago: University of Chicago Press, 2022).
47. Sally Shuttleworth, *The Mind of the Child: Child Development in Literature, Science, and Medicine, 1840–1900* (Oxford: Oxford University Press), 2010.
48. Margaret Bryan, *Lectures on Natural Philosophy* (London: George Kearsley and Jordan Hookham, 1806), 48. Bryan supported teaching science to girls and dedicated her work to ten-year-old Princess Charlotte.
49. William Pinnock, *A Catechism of Anatomy: For the Instruction of Youth in the First Principles of that Science* (London: G. B. Whittaker, 1825), A1.
50. Pinnock, *Anatomy*, 71. Secord lists Locke's outline with chapter VI, "Of the five Senses of Man, and of his Understanding." "Newton in the Nursery," *History of Science* 23 (1985): 132.

51. Rev. Charles Williams, *Art in Nature and Science Anticipated* (London: Frederick Westley and A. H. Davis, 1833), 13–15; W. Payne, *Village Science; or, The Laws of Nature Explained* (London: Religious Tract Society), 40–42.
52. Anne Bullar, *Every-Day Wonders of Bodily Life* (London: Jarrold & Sons, [1862]).
53. On the closing gap between mind and brain, or thinking and feeling, in Romantic-era adult literature: Sharon Ruston, *Shelley and Vitality* (Houndmills, Basingstoke, Hampshire: Palgrave Macmillan, 2005); Noel Jackson, *Science and Sensation in Romantic Poetry* (New York: Cambridge University Press, 2008); Alan Richardson, *British Romanticism and the Science of the Mind* (New York: Cambridge University Press, 2001). For relevant Victorian-era writings on the mind, matter, and sensation, see Jenny Taylor and Sally Shuttleworth, eds., *Embodied Selves: An Anthology of Psychological Texts, 1830–1890* (Oxford: Clarendon Press, 1998).
54. Anonymous, *Francis Lever, the Young Mechanic* (London: John Harris, 1835), 117.
55. Mary A. Swift, *First Lessons on Natural Philosophy for Children: Part Second* (Hartford: Belknap and Hamersley, 1837), 30–31.
56. Douthwaite, *Wild Girl*, 70–92. See also Paul De Man, "Self (Pygmalion)," *Allegories of Reading: Figural Language in Rousseau, Nietzsche, Rilke, and Proust* (New Haven: Yale University Press, 1979) 163–65.
57. Johnathan Smith, *Fact and Feeling: Baconian Science and the Nineteenth-Century Literary Imagination* (Madison: University of Wisconsin Press, 1994), 55; Jessica Riskin, *Science in the Age of Sensibility: The Sentimental Empiricists of the French Enlightenment* (Chicago: University of Chicago Press, 2002).
58. R. Edgeworth and M. Egeworth, Practical Education, 2:302–3, plate CCCCLXX; "Amusements of Science. Sect. XI. Recreations and Contrivances Relating to Mechanics," *Encyclopedia Britannica: or, a Dictionary of Arts, Sciences, and Miscellaneous Literature; Enlarged and Improved*, 6th ed., vol. 28 (Edinburgh: Archibald Constable, 1823), 443–50, 563–66. William Leybourn also invented a different astronomical instrument the called the Panorganon in 1672, which likely inspired this term.
59. Jeremiah Joyce, *Scientific Dialogues*, vol. 1, "Of Mechanics" (Printed for J. Johnson, 1800), 1:10.
60. Jane Marcet, *Conversations on Natural Philosophy* (London: Printed for Longman, Hurst, Rees, Orme, and Brown, 1819), 1–4; Rauch, *Useful Knowledge*, 46–57.
61. William Martin, *The Parlour Book* (London: Darton and Clark, Holborn Hill, 1839), preface, 227. Textbooks vary on which subjects offer accessible, concrete first lessons in physical sciences. Some introduce mechanics with astronomy, e.g., Anonymous, *Wonders of the World in Earth, Sea, and Sky* (London: Ward and Lock, 1863). Although children cannot touch the stars, most can see them. Astronomy correlates with balls and slings, toys children can hold, leading to matter, bodies, and motion.
62. Payne, *Village Science*, 24. Aileen Fyfe notes that Payne wrote fourteen tracts for the RTS. Her husband was a technical chemist. See Fyfe, "Science for Children," in *Popular*, ed. Briggs, Butts, and Grenby, 218.
63. Payne, *Village Science*, 32, 34, 35, 40.
64. Patricia Fara explains Somerville's mythology of spreading British science as civilization through print, empire, and global trade, "Mary Somerville: A Scientist and her Ship," *Endeavour* 32, no. 3 (September 2008).
65. Payne, *Village Science*, 223.
66. Joseph Bizup, *Manufacturing Culture: Vindications of Early Victorian Industry* (Charlottesville: University of Virginia Press, 2003), 18–30, 1–5. Bizup argues that Arnold fights this entrenched belief in manufacturing as civilizing force by

constructing "culture" in opposition to industry.

67. Lancaster's advertisements refer to his "new and mechanical system of education." Robert Southey quotes these lines in *The Origin, Nature, and Object of the New System of Education* (London: John Murray, 1812), 128; Samuel Taylor Coleridge, *The Statesman's Manual, Lay Sermons*, ed. R. J. White, *S. T. Coleridge Collected Works* (London: Routledge and K. Paul, 1969–2002), 6:41; Sir Thomas Bernard, *Of the Education of the Poor* (London: W. Bulmer and J. Hatchard, 1809), 35; Sir Thomas Bernard, *The New School: Being an Attempt to Illustrate its Principles, Detail, and Advantages* (London: W. Bulmer and Co., 1809), 17–18.
68. Andrew Ure, *The Philosophy of Manufactures* (New York: A. M. Kelly, 1967), 371.
69. Ure, *Philosophy of Manufactures*, 310–11; Jane Marcet, *Willy's Travels on the Railroad* (London: Longman, Brown, Green, and Longmans, 1850), 156–57.
70. "A Glasgow Factory Boy," *Chatterbox*, April 23, 1881, 175.
71. "Slavery as It Was and Is: The Heroes of Abolition," *The Boy's Own Paper*, January 27, 1883, 187.
72. Anonymous, *Great Inventors: The Sources of Their Usefulness, and the Results of Their Efforts* (London: Ward and Lock, 1864), 224.
73. C. L. Brightwell, *Heroes of the Laboratory and the Workshop* (London: Routledge, Warnes, & Routledge, 1859), 126–27.
74. George Stringer Bull, *A Respectful and Faithful Appeal to the Inhabitants of the Parish of Bradford, on the Behalf of the Factory Children* (Bradford: T. Inkersley, 1832), 8–9.
75. Anonymous, *The Young Folks of the Factory; or, Friendly Hints on their Duties and Dangers* (London: Religious Tract Society, 1840), 310.
76. *Young Folks*, 312–13.
77. Henry Brown (artisan), *The Cotton Fields and Cotton Factories* (London: Darton and Clark, Holborn Hill, ca. 1840), 2, 138.
78. Brown, *Cotton Fields*, 121, 166. Placing "education" in quotations suggests a radical author familiar with working-class journalism.
79. *Francis Lever*, 2–4, 11.
80. *Francis Lever*, 32, 49, 50, 113–14.
81. *Francis Lever*, 66, 118.
82. History of women's science requires recovering contributions by servants, wives, and children. For an overview, see Donald L. Opitz, Staffan Bergwik, and Brigitte Van Tiggelen, eds., *Domesticity in the Making of Modern Science* (Houndmills: Palgrave Macmillan, 2016).
83. Anonymous, *Great Inventors*, 54.
84. James Lukin, *The Boy Engineers* (London: Trubner & Co, 1878), 198.
85. Lukin, *Boy Engineers*, 4, 54, 147–48.
86. Lukin, *Boy Engineers*, A, 2.
87. Lukin, *Boy Engineers*, 31, 311.
88. Anonymous, *Invention and Discovery* (Edinburgh: W. P. Nimmo, 1868), 43–44; Eric S. Hintz argues for the importance of these children's biographies for understanding popular perceptions of invention in "Heroes of the Laboratory and the Workshop: Invention and Technology in Books for Children, 1850–1990," in *Enterprising Youth: Social Values and Acculturation in Nineteenth-Century American Children's Literature*, ed. Monika Elbert (New York: Routledge, 2008), 197–211.
89. Brightwell, *Heroes*, 24.
90. Anonymous, *Perseverance Under Difficulties* (London: Society for Promoting Christian Knowledge, 1868), 170, 174–75; Anonymous, *Great Inventors*, 37.

91. Anonymous, *Great Inventors*, 173–74.
92. Lightman, *Victorian Popularizers of Science*, 100–46; Barbara T. Gates and Ann B. Shteir, eds., *Natural Eloquence: Women Reinscribe Science* (Madison: University of Wisconsin Press, 1997), 3–17.
93. Norma Clarke, "'The Cursed Barbauld Crew': Women Writers and Writing for Children in the Late Eighteenth Century," in *Opening the Nursery Door: Reading, Writing and Childhood 1600–1900*, ed. Mary Hilton, Morag Styles, and Victor Watson (London: Routledge, 1997), 91–103; Megan A. Norcia, *X Marks the Spot: Women Writers Map the Empire for British Children, 1790–1895* (Athens: Ohio University Press, 2010), 7–10.
94. Melanie Keene, *Science in Wonderland: The Scientific Fairy Tales of Victorian Britain* (Oxford: Oxford University Press, 2015), 54–82. Insect authors include Mary Ward, L. M. Budgen, Mary Howitt, and Margaret Gatty.
95. Sarah Stickney Ellis, *Women of England* (London: Fisher, Son & Co., 1839), 11–12.
96. Mary Elizabeth Budden, *Right and Wrong: Exhibited in the History of Rosa and Agnes* (London: J. Harris and Son, 1822), preface. This story centers around marketplace object lessons, similar to Maria Edgeworth's "Rosamond" stories, but with two "good" and "bad" sisters.
97. Quoted in Arianrhod, *Seduced by Logic*, 193.
98. Brightwell, *Heroes*, v–vi, Baldwin.
99. Charlotte Yonge, *Abbeychurch*, 2nd ed. (London: J. & C. Mozley, 1872), 110, 111, 153, 3.
100. James Lukin, *The Young Mechanic: A Book for Boys, Containing Directions for the Use of All Kinds of Tools and for the Construction of Steam Engines and Mechanical Models* (London: Trübner & Co., 1871), 1.
101. Lukin, *Boy Engineers*, 114.

CHAPTER 3: "THE EMPIRE OF MAN OVER MATERIAL THINGS"

1. George Dodd, *Days at the Factories* (London: Charles Knight, 1843), 1, 11.
2. Dodd, *Days at the Factories*, 16.
3. Maxine Berg, *The Machinery Question and the Making of Political Economy* (Cambridge: Cambridge University Press, 1980), 42. On natural sciences and political economy, see Margaret Schabas and Neil De Marchi, eds., *Oeconomies in the Age of Newton* (Durham, NH: Duke University Press, 2003); Eleanor Courtemanche, *The "Invisible Hand" and British Fiction, 1818–1860: Adam Smith, Political Economy, and the Genre of Realism* (Houndmills and New York: Palgrave Macmillan, 2011), 5–6, 44–52.
4. Charles Knight, *Knowledge Is Power* (London: J. Murray, 1855), 2–5. After the SDUK closed in 1846 Knight republished *The Results of Machinery* (1831) and *The Rights of Industry* (1831)—initially written to persuade working-class readers that new machinery would improve their lives—into a treatise for "*the young*," retitled *Knowledge Is Power*.
5. R. K. Webb, *The British Working Class Reader, 1790–1848: Literacy and Social Tension* (London: George Allen & Unwin, 1955), 99.
6. Clare Midgley, "Slave Sugar Boycotts, Female Activism and the Domestic Base of British Anti-Slavery Culture," *Slavery and Abolition* 17, no. 3 (1996): 137–39; Marcus Rediker, *The Slave Ship: A Human History* (New York: Penguin Group, 2007), 5; Richard S. Dunn, *Sugar and Slaves: The Rise of the Planter Class in the English West Indies, 1624–1713* (Chapel Hill: University of North Carolina Press, 1972), 188–263;

James Walvin, *Black Ivory: Slavery in the British Empire*, 2nd ed. (Malden, MA: Blackwell, 2001), 3–9.

7. Anonymous, *Francis Lever, the Young Mechanic* (London: John Harris, 1835), endpapers.
8. Elizabeth Massa Hoiem, "The Progress of Sugar: Consumption as Complicity in Children's Books about Slavery and Manufacturing, 1790–2015," *Children's Literature in Education* 52, no. 2 (June 2021): 162–82. For a media studies approach, see Salomé Aguilera Skvirsky, *The Process Genre: Cinema and the Aesthetic of Labor* (Durham, NH: Duke University Press, 2020). Eugenia Gonzalez deftly explores "production narratives" and it-narratives about dolls using thing theory, noting these stories report to middle-class children that doll makers are impoverished children who come to hate the dolls they make. See "'What Remains? An Empty Doll-Case': Deconstruction and Imagination in Victorian Narratives of Doll Production," *Journal of Victorian Culture* 18, no. 3 (2013): 335–49.
9. Lynn Festa, "The Moral Ends of Eighteenth- and Nineteenth-Century Object Narratives," in *The Secret Lives of Things: Animals, Objects, and It-Narratives in Eighteenth-Century England*, ed. Mark Blackwell (Lewisburg, PA: Bucknell University Press, 2006): 309–28. See also, Lynn Festa, *Fiction Without Humanity: Person, Animal, Thing in Early Enlightenment Literature and Culture* (Philadelphia: University of Pennsylvania Press, 2019).
10. William Newman, *Rhymes and Pictures: The History of a Pound of Sugar, Rhymes and Pictures* (London: Griffith & Farran, 1860), 12 (sugar), 11 (tea), 2, 12 (gold). Other titles in the Rhymes and Pictures series include "A Quartern Loaf," "A Cotton Bale," "A Cup of Tea," "A Shuttle of Coals," and "A Golden Sovereign." These commodity chapters are individually paginated and bound together but also sold individually.
11. Kyla Wazana Tompkins, *Racial Indigestion: Eating Bodies in the Nineteenth Century* (New York: New York University Press, 2012); Vincent Woodard, *The Delectable Negro: Human Consumption and Homoeroticism within U.S. Slave Culture*, ed. Justin A. Joyce and Dwight A. McBridge, with a foreword by E. Patrick Johnson (New York: New York University Press, 2014).
12. Newman, *Rhymes and Pictures*, 3 (sugar). Production stories often describe Black people working without specifying whether they are enslaved. Without knowing when and where the work takes place, much is left to reader interpretation on this important distinction.
13. Martha Cutter, *The Illustrated Slave: Empathy, Graphic Narrative, and the Visual Culture of the Transatlantic Abolition Movement, 1800–1852* (Athens: University of Georgia Press, 2017), 81–83.
14. Charlotte Smith, *Rural Walks* (London: T. Cadell Jun. and W. Davies, 1795), 95–96.
15. Smith, *Rural Walks*, 59, 24. Single episode production stories in moral tales are commonplace. In Francis T. Jamieson's *The Young Travellers, Or, a Visit to the Grandmother* (London: M. J. Godwin, 1816), the four eldest Longman children visit poor cottagers and make a curiosity cabinet. Using their mineralogical specimens, Father describes how miners work around the world. Similar manufacturing visits occur in Lucy Peacock, *Visit for a Week* (1796); Jane Loudon, *Glimpses of Nature and Objects of Interest Described, During a Visit to the Isle of Wight* (1848); Charlotte Smith, *Rambles Farther* (1796); and Lucy Wilson, *A Visit to Grove Cottage* (1823).
16. Cynthia J. Koepp, "Advocating for Artisans: The Abbé Pluche's *Spectacle de la nature (1732–51)*," in *The Idea of Work in Europe from Antiquity to Modern Times*, eds. Josef Ehmer and Catharina Lis (Farnham, England: Ashgate, 2009), 245–75.

17. Simon Schaffer, "Enlightened Automata," in *The Sciences in Enlightened Europe*, eds. William Clarke, Jan Golinski, and Simon Schaffer (Chicago: University of Chicago Press, 1999), 130.
18. Meredith Bak, *Playful Visions: Optical Toys and the Emergence of Children's Media Culture* (Cambridge, MA: MIT Press, 2020), 13.
19. Nicholas Mirzoeff, *The Right to Look: A Counterhistory of Visuality* (Durham, NC: Duke University Press, 2011).
20. William Fox, *An Address to the People of Great Britain on the Propriety of Abstaining from West Indian Sugar and Rum*, 7th ed. (London: M. Gurney, T. Knott, and C. Forster, 1791), 2.
21. Laurence B. Glickman, "'Buy for the Sake of the Slave': Abolitionism and the Origins of American Consumer Activism," *American Quarterly* 56, no. 4 (2004): 889–912.
22. Charlotte Sussman, *Consuming Anxieties: Consumer Protest, Gender, and British Slavery, 1713–1833* (Stanford: Stanford University Press, 2002), 190–91; Clare Midgley, "Slave Sugar Boycotts, Female Activism and the Domestic Base of British Anti-Slavery Culture," *Slavery and Abolition* 17, no. 3 (1996): 143–44.
23. Jane Marcet, *The Seasons, Stories for Very Young Children*, 4 vols., 8th ed. (London: Longman, Green, Longman, Roberts, & Green, 1865), 1:156–57.
24. *Society for Superseding the Necessity of Climbing Boys, by Encouraging a New Method of Sweeping Chimneys* (London: M. and S. Brooke, 1803).
25. Mimi Sheller, "Bleeding Humanity and Gendered Embodiments: From Antislavery Sugar Boycotts to Ethical Consumers, *Humanity* 2, no. 2 (2011): 182.
26. *Jack of All Trades*, Part 1 (London: Darton, Harvey, and Darton, 1814), 4.
27. *A History of Useful Arts and Manufactures* (Dublin: A. O'Neil, 1822), 47–48.
28. Mary Elliott, *Rural Employments, Or, a Peep into Village Concerns* (London: William Darton, 1820), 14.
29. Hannah Field, *Playing with the Book: Victorian Movable Picture Books and the Child Reader* (Minneapolis: University of Minnesota Press, 2019), 146–54.
30. *Dean's Dissolving Pictures of Things Worth Knowing: Iron, Diamond, Coal, Slate, Silver, Whale* (London: Dean & Son, 1865), n.p, Baldwin.
31. Jacqueline Reid-Walsh, "Activity and Agency in Historical 'Playable Media,'" *Journal of Children and Media* 6, no. 2 (2012): 164–81. On independent play and Dean's dissolving images, see Bak, *Playful Visions*, 119–29.
32. *Dean's Dissolving Pictures*, n.p.
33. John Mawe, *Travels in the Interior of Brazil* (London: Longman, Hurst, Rees, Orme, and Brown, 1812), 219–28. Passages from *Travels* appear in four children's production stories, shortening Mawe's account while retaining this proslavery anecdote, e.g. Isaac Taylor's *The Mine* (London: John Harris, 1829). *A History of Useful Arts and Manufactures* claims that enslaved miners who find large diamonds are "crowned with a wreath of flowers, and carried in procession to the administrator, who gives him his freedom, by paying his owner for it," yet they prevent "negroes from stealing the diamonds," (168). By focusing on the supposed generosity of enslavers, this projects the theft of mining lands onto the enslaved, implying slavery justly rewards hard work from duplicitous Africans.
34. Maria Elizabeth Budden, *Key to Knowledge*, 11th ed. (London: John Harris, 1841), 9. The 1814 edition is considerably shorter.
35. *Things In-doors* (London: George Routledge and Sons; R. Clay, Sons, and Taylor, 1870); *Little Ladders to Learning* (London: George Routledge and Sons, 1869).
36. Susan Zlotnick, *Women, Writing, and the Industrial Revolution* (Baltimore: John Hopkins University Press, 1998), 130; Sheller, "Bleeding Humanity," 182–86.

37. Caroline Amelia Halsted, *Investigation; or Travels in the Boudoir* (London: Smith, Elder and Co., 1837), vii–xi.
38. Halsted, *Investigation*, 160, 182-83, 211.
39. Samuel Goodrich, *Enterprise, Industry, and Art of Man* (Boston: Bradbury, Soden, and Co., 1845), iii–iv.
40. Annie Carey, *Autobiographies of A Lump of Coal; A Grain of Salt; A Drop of Water; A Bit of Old Iron; A Piece of Flint* (London: Cassell, Petter, and Galpin, Belle Sauvage Works, 1870), 18. Geologist J. E. Taylor also wrote rock autobiographies in *Geological Stories* (1873).
41. Carey, *Autobiographies*, 27.
42. Tess Cosslett, *Talking Animals in British Children's Fiction, 1786–1914* (Aldershot, UK: Ashgate, 2006), 84–85. Cosslett expands on work by Carolyn Steedman, "Enforced Narratives: Stories of Another Self," in *Feminism and Autobiography*, ed. Tess Cosslett, Celia Lury, and Penny Summerfield (London: Routledge, 2000), 28–31.
43. Carey, *Autobiographies*, 95. Maude Hines, "'He Made Us Very Much Like the Flowers': Human/Nature in Nineteenth-Century Anglo-American Children's Literature," Wild Things: Children's Culture and Ecocriticism, ed. Sidney I. Dobrin, Kenneth B. Kidd (Detroit: Wayne State University Press, 2004), 18–22.
44. Commodities touching the body, like sugar and cotton, symbolized white femininity while signaling a woman's proslavery or antislavery stance. For women abolitionists, ingesting slave goods taints the body's purity. See Tompkins, *Racial Indigestion*; Mimi Sheller, *Consuming the Caribbean: From Arawaks to Zombies* (London: Routledge, 2003), 71–104; Sheller, "Bleeding Humanity," 171–92; Sussman, *Consuming Anxieties*, 6–14; Karen Sanchez-Eppler, *Touching Liberty: Abolition, Feminism, and the Politics of the Body* (Berkeley: University of California Press, 1993).
45. Dorothia Dix, *Conversations on Common Things* (Boston: Munrow and Francis, 1835), 13–14, Baldwin.
46. Sussman, *Consuming Anxieties*, 130–47, 190.
47. Priscilla Wakefield, *A Family Tour through the British Empire* (London: Harvey and Darton, 1804), 30.
48. Professor Punch, The Laughable Game of What D'Ye Buy (London: J. Passmore, ca. 1850), Lilly and Cotsen. The suggested game play seems close to Mad Libs. A "conductor" tells a story, while players (each assigned an artisan) play down cards with goods sold at their shop to complete the story. Games about consumption also include A Fancy Bazaar; or, Aristocratic Traders: A Comic Game (London: ca. 1862), Lilly, in which players compete selling their goods at a charity bazaar to raise funds for satirical enterprises of dubious public good.
49. Jane Bourne, *The Game of Forfeits* (London: Houlston & Co., 1838).
50. "Correspondence," *Boy's Own Paper*, November 8, 1879, 96.
51. Olwyn Mary Blouet, "Slavery and Freedom in the British West Indies, 1823–33: The Role of Education," *History of Education Quarterly* 30, no. 4 (Winter, 1990): 625–43. Blouet describes charities sending these materials to the British West Indies.
52. Shefrin, *Dartons*, 57, 214, 344, 107–9. *Cotton* and *Sugar* quotations are from materials reproduced here.
53. Analysis of a surviving lesson board. See Sarah Anne Carter, "On an Object Lesson, or Don't Eat the Evidence," *Journal of the History of Childhood and Youth* 3, no. 1 (2010): 7–12; Carter provides several images of object lesson boxes and cards filled with specimens. See Sarah Anne Carter, *Object Lessons: How Nineteenth-Century Americans Learned to Make Sense of the Material World* (Oxford: Oxford University

Press, 2018).

54. Samuel Wilderspin, *Infant Education: or, Practical Remarks on the Importance of Educating the Infant Poor, from the Age of Eighteen Months to Seven Years* (London: Simpkind and Marshall, 1829), 238, 257.
55. Wilderspin, *Infant Education*, 288–89.
56. Jeffrey A. Auerbach, *The Great Exhibition of 1851: A Nation on Display* (New Haven and London: Yale University Press, 1999), 106–7.
57. *Notes and Sketches of Lessons* (London: SPCK, 1852); Anonymous, *Fireside Facts from the Great Exhibition* (London: [1851]); S. Prout Newcombe, *Pleasant Pages for the Young*, 6 vols. (London: Houlston and Stoneman, [1851]); S. Prout Newcombe, *Royal Road to Reading, Through the Great Exhibition* (London: Houlston and Stoneman, 1852). Newcombe wrote several additional children's exhibition titles.
58. Wakefield, *Family Tour*, 40.
59. Lucy Peacock, *Visit for a Week* (London: Hookham and Carpenter, 1794), 24–25.
60. Mary Elliott, *Continuation of Rustic Excursions* (London: William Darton, 1827), 33.
61. Wakefield, *Family Tour*, 31, 33.
62. Isaac Taylor, *Scenes of British Wealth: In Produce, Manufactures, and Commerce, for the Amusement and Instruction of Little Tarry-at-Home Travelers* (London: John Harris, 1823), 39.
63. Taylor, *Scenes of British Wealth*, 14–19, 301.
64. Taylor, *Scenes of British Wealth*, 25–27.
65. Taylor, *Scenes of British Wealth*, 30.
66. Alison Comish Thorne, "Jane Marcet and Harriet Martineau," in *Women of Value: Feminist Essays on the History of Women in Economics*, ed. Robert W. Dimand, Evelyn L. Forget, and Mary Ann Dimand (Aldershot, UK: Edward Elgar, 1995). 71–81; Bette Polkinghorn, *Jane Marcet, An Uncommon Woman* (Aldermaston, UK: Forestwood, 1993); Bette Polkinghorn and Dorothy Lampen Thomson, *Adam Smith's Daughters: Eight Prominent Women Economists from the Eighteenth Century to the Present* (Cheltenham, UK: Edward Elgar, 1998), 1–29; Willie Henderson, *Economics as Literature* (London and New York: Routledge, 1995), 43–60.
67. Hilda Hollis, "The Rhetoric of Jane Marcet's Popularizing Political Economy," *Nineteenth-Century Contexts* 24, no. 4 (2002): 379–96.
68. Jane Marcet, *Willy's Travels on the Railroad* (London: Printed for Longman, Brown, Green, and Longmans, 1850), 11.
69. Betsy's mother travels by train to access a medical procedure to return her sight. Compare with Maria Edgeworth's Rosamond, who helps a blind girl restore her damaged sight through an operation (see chapter 4). Restoring a working-class character's sight is a metaphor for sharing the ability to observe the world.
70. Marcet, *Willy's Travels*, 71.
71. Marcet, *Willy's Travels*, 131–33.
72. Marcet, *Willy's Travels*, 66, 110.
73. Knight, *Knowledge Is Power*, 433; Henry Brougham, *Practical Observations upon the Education of the People* (London: Richard Taylor, 1825), 5.
74. Henry Mayhew, *The World's Show, 1851; or, The Adventures of Mr. and Mrs. Sandboys and Family*, illustrated by George Cruikshank (London: David Bogue, 1851), 54.
75. Mayhew, *World's Show*, 36.
76. Mayhew, *World's Show*, 129–31.

CHAPTER 4: SELF-GOVERNING MACHINES

1. Perry Nodelman, *The Hidden Adult: Defining Children's Literature* (Baltimore, MD: Johns Hopkins University Press, 2008), 1–80.
2. Maria Edgeworth, *Early Lessons* (London: R. Hunter; Baldwin, Cradock, and Joy, 1815), 2:9 Rosamond first appears in "The Purple Jar" and "The Birthday Present" in Maria Edgeworth's first collection of children's literature, *The Parent's Assistant* (1796). "The Purple Jar" was republished as a series of Rosamond tales in *Early Lessons* (1801) that included "The Two Plums" and "The Rabbit," among other additions, dropping "The Birthday Present," which creates a neat developmental sequence of object choices. *Early Lessons* also includes"Frank" and "Harry and Lucy." Later prefaces to her works advise reading in order of difficulty. Young children begin with *Frank*, followed by *Harry and Lucy*, and conclude with *Rosamond*. Edgeworth returns to each of these characters in *Continuation of Early Lessons* (1814), then concludes them separately in the 1820s with *Rosamond: A Sequel to Early Lessons* (1821), *Frank: A Sequel* (1821), and *Harry and Lucy Concluded* (1825), all published after her father's death, as she finished his memoirs (1820). Edgeworth's publisher was Joseph Johnson (and his successor, R. Hunter), who also published many Radical Dissenters, including Mary Wollstonecraft. Because these tales were frequently reprinted, many surviving editions combine stories from these four major collections under various titles. For editions, see Bertha Coolidge Slade, *Maria Edgeworth, 1767–1849: A Bibliographical Tribute* (London: Constable, 1937).
3. Sarah Trimmer, *The Guardian of Education: A Periodical Work*, 5 vols., introduction by Matthew Grenby (Bristol: Thoemmes; Tokyo: Edition Synapse, 2002), 2:235–37.
4. Samuel McChord Crothers, *Miss Muffet's Christmas Party* (Boston and New York: Houghton, Mifflin, 1902), 66.
5. My argument on child agency and rational mothers relies on Mitzi Myers's indispensable scholarship: "Socializing Rosamond: Educational Ideology and Fictional Form," *Children's Literature Association Quarterly* 14, no. 2 (1989): 52–58; "Impeccable Governesses, Rational Dames, and Moral Mothers: Mary Wollstonecraft and the Female Tradition in Georgian Children's Books," *Children's Literature* 14 (1986): 31–58; "'A Taste for Truth and Realities': Early Advice to Mothers on Books for Girls," *Children's Literature Association Quarterly* 12, no. 3 (1987): 118–24.
6. Joanna Wharton, *Material Enlightenment: Women Writers and the Science of Mind, 1770–1830* (Woodbridge: Boydell Press, 2018), 198.
7. Richard Altick, *The Shows of London* (Cambridge: Belknap Press of Harvard University Press, 1978), 58.
8. Otto Mayr, *Liberty, Authority, and Automatic Machinery in Early Modern Europe* (Baltimore: Johns Hopkins University Press, 1986).
9. Catharine Macaulay, *Letters on Education with Observations on Religious and Metaphysical Subjects* (Dublin: H. Chamberlaine and Rice, L. White, W. McKenzie, J. Moore, Grueber and McAllister, W. Jones, and R. White, 1790), 9, vi. Macaulay attributes to Lord Monboddo.
10. Barb Drummond, *Mr. Bridges' Enlightenment Machine: Forty Years on Tour in Georgian Britain* (self-pub., 2018), 1–16. Paul E. Sampson analyzes these tiered classes and explains why audiences may have objected to its social order in "Lost and Found: The Cosmos in a Cabinet: Performance, Politics, and Mechanical Philosophy in Henry Bridges' 'Microcosm,'" *Endeavor* 43 (2019): 25–31.

11. Richard Lovell Edgeworth, *Memoirs of Richard Lovell Edgeworth, Esq.*, ed. Maria Edgeworth, 2 vols. (London: R. Hunter; Baldwin, Cradock, and Joy, 1820), 1:109–11; 1:119; 1:110–11; 1:165.
12. Robert E. Schofield, *The Lunar Society of Birmingham: A Social History of Provincial Science and Industry in Eighteenth-Century England* (Oxford: Clarendon Press, 1963), 72.
13. Marilyn Butler, *Maria Edgeworth: A Literary Biography* (Oxford: Clarendon Press, 1972), 34–45; Augustus J. C. Hare, *The Life and Letters of Maria Edgeworth*, 2 vols. (London: Edward Arnold, 1894), 1:21.
14. Jessica Riskin, "Eighteenth-Century Wetware," *Representations* 83, no. 1 (Summer 2003): 105–6.
15. Emily Lawless, *English Men of Letters: Maria Edgeworth* (New York: MacMillan, 1905), 125.
16. Elizabeth Kowaleski-Wallace, *Their Fathers' Daughters: Hannah More, Maria Edgeworth, and Patriarchal Complicity* (New York: Oxford University Press, 1991), 98.
17. Lawless, *English Men of Letters*, 123; Kathryn Scantlebury and Collette Murphy, "Maria Edgeworth: Nineteenth Century Irish Female Pioneer of Science Education," *Irish Educational Studies* 28, no. 1 (2009): 103.
18. Hare, *Life and Letters*, 1:40–41. Wharton explains that Mara Edgeworth worked on the language used for the telegraph, while her brothers assisted Rochard Lovell with testing it, *Material Enlightenment*, 205–8.
19. Butler, *Maria Edgeworth*, 141. Although Butler does not specify which mechanical exhibits they attended, the Edgeworths were in London when Maillardet's show was popular. Butler relies on the letters of Frances Edgeworth, Maria's stepmother, who describes visits to manufactories. Few letters by Maria Edgeworth survive from this period.
20. Elleanor Anne Peters, "Observation, Experiment or Autonomy in the Domestic Sphere? Women's Familiar Science Writing in Britain, 1790–1830," *Notes and Records of the Royal Society of London* 71, no. 1 (March 2017): 71–90.
21. Wharton, *Material Enlightenment*, 198, 230.
22. C. L. Brightwell, *Heroes of the Laboratory and the Workshop* (London: Routledge, Warnes, & Routledge, 1859), 81, 125.
23. Brightwell, *Heroes*, 65.
24. Jessica Riskin, "The Defecating Duck, or, the Ambiguous Origins of Artificial Life," *Critical Inquiry* 29, no. 4 (Summer 2003): 599–633; Altick, *Shows of London*, 64–66; Barbara Maria Stafford, *Artful Science: Enlightenment Entertainment and the Eclipse of Visual Education* (Cambridge, MA: MIT Press, 1994), 198–204.
25. Samuel Johnson, *A Dictionary of the English Language*, 5 vols. (London: Longman, Rees, Orme, and Brown, 1818). Earlier editions also specify self-movement, or power located within the machine.
26. Jean-Jacques Rousseau, *Emile, or, On Education*, trans. Allan Bloom (New York: Basic Books, 1979), 86, 95.
27. François Bessire and Martine Reid, eds., *Madame de Genlis: Littérature et education* (Publications des Universités de Rouen et du Havre, 2008), 41–49, 241–265.
28. William Godwin, *Enquiry Concerning Political Justice and Its Influence on Morals and Happiness*, 2 vols., 3rd ed. (London: G. G. and J. Robinson, 1798), 1:50.
29. Anna Letitia Barbauld, *Anna Letitia Barbauld: Selected Poetry and Prose*, ed. William McCarthy and Elizabeth Kraft (Petersborough, ON: Broadview, 2002), 317.
30. Nancy Yousef, *Isolated Cases: The Anxieties of Autonomy in Enlightenment*

Philosophy and Romantic Literature (Ithaca, NY: Cornell University Press, 2004), 1–26, 96–114.

31. Elizabeth Massa Hoiem, "From Philosophical Experiment to Adventure Fiction: English Adaptations of French Robinsonades and the Politics of Genre," *Children's Literature* 46 (2018): 1–29.
32. Julie Park, *The Self and It: Novel Objects in Eighteenth-Century England* (Stanford, CA: Stanford University Press, 2010), xiii, xv; Julie Park, "Pains and Pleasures of the Automaton: Francis Burney's Mechanics of Coming Out," *Eighteenth-Century Studies* 40, no. 1 (2006): 23–49.
33. Francis Burney, *Camilla; or, A Picture of Youth*, ed. Edward A. Bloom and Lillian D. Bloom (Oxford: Oxford University Press, 1999), 653, 670, 714. See Andrea Haslanger, "From Man-Machine to Woman-Machine: Automata, Fiction, and Femininity in Dibdin's *Hannah Hewit* and Burney's *Camilla*," *Modern Philology* 111, no. 4 (May 2014): 808–17. These metaphors continue throughout the nineteenth century, e.g., Charles Maturin's tortured monk, Monçada the Spaniard from *Melmoth the Wanderer* (1820), who is forced in his youth to take monastic vows, declares, "I am a clock that has struck the same minutes and hours for sixty years. Is it not time for the machine to long for its winding up?" (Oxford: Oxford University Press, 2008), 110. Dorian Gray, a compulsive collector, has an irresistible attraction to "sin." Such people "lose the freedom of their will. They move to their terrible end as automatons move. Choice is taken from them." Oscar Wilde, *The Picture of Dorian Gray*, ed. Michael Patrick Gillespie (New York: Norton, 2007), 158. For comprehensive historical studies of automata in European literature, see Minsoo Kang, *Sublime Dreams of Living Machines: The Automaton in the European Imagination* (Cambridge, MA: Harvard University Press, 2011); Jessica Riskin, *Restless Clock: A History of the Centuries-Long Argument over What Makes Living Things Tick* (Chicago: University of Chicago Press, 2016); Gaby Wood, *A Magical History of the Quest for Mechanical Life* (New York: A. A. Knopf, 2002). For a descriptive catalog, see Alfred Chapuis and Edmond Droz, *Automata: A Historical and Technological Study*, trans. Alec Reid (Neuchatel, CH: Editions du Griffon; New York: Central Book Company, 1958).
34. William Godwin, *Caleb Williams*, ed. Gary Handwek and A. A. Markley (Petersborough, ON: Broadview, 2000), 384–85. Whereas Caleb challenges his educator for control, women rarely exhibit a mechanical mastery, except the tech-savvy shipwrecked heroine of Charles Dibdin's *Hannah Hewit; or, the Female Crusoe*, who patches together a speaking automaton that declares "I love you, Hannah," accompanied by hourly amorous sighs. See Haslanger, "Man-Machine," 795–808.
35. Macaulay, *Letters on Education*, 23.
36. Colleen E. Terrell, "'Republican Machines': Franklin, Rush, and the Manufacture of Civic Virtue in the Early American Republic," *Early American Studies* 1, no. 2 (Fall 2003): 100–32.
37. Julia V. Douthwaite, *The Wild Girl, the Natural Man, and the Monster: Dangerous Experiments in the Age of Enlightenment* (Chicago: University of Chicago Press, 2002), 115–63.
38. Clíona Ó Gallchoir, Maria Edgeworth, *Women, Enlightenment and Nation* (Dublin: Univeristy College Dublin Press, 2005), 38.
39. Maria Edgeworth, *Belinda*, ed. Kathryn J. Kirkpatrick (Oxford and New York: Oxford University Press, 1994), 12.
40. Altick, *Shows of London*, 67.

41. M. Edgeworth, *Belinda*, 206, 23. Hervey's snake costume is based on Fuseli's 1802 painting. Jeffrey Cass, "Fuseli's Milton Gallery: *Satan's First Address to Eve* as a Source for Maria Edgeworth's *Belinda*," *ANQ* 14, no. 2 (Spring 2001): 15–23. Such automaton costumes made appearances in London masquerades through a mutual friend of Richard Edgeworth and Fanny Burney, the eccentric inventor John Joseph Merlin, a former partner of automaton collector and exhibitor James Cox. Merlin appeared at the Prince of Wales' masquerade inside Fortune's Wheel and at the Pantheon masquerade as a sick man in a wheelchair invented by himself, and he crashed other soirées as Cupid and Vulcan "forging his own darts." Altick, *Shows of London*, 72–75.
42. "Sympathy Machines: Men of Feeling and the Automaton," *Eighteenth-Century Studies* 41, no. 1 (2009): 38.
43. Altick, *Shows of London*, 66–67. Opening with the arrival of Swiss clockmaker Jacquet-Droz from Paris in 1776, the exhibit continued under his partner, Maillardet, after the London branch's liquidation in 1790 until 1820. The two automata Edgeworth mentions feature in the cover illustration of two pamphlets that provide scientific explanations for uncanny phenomena: Philip Astley, *Natural Magic: or, Physical Amusements Revealed* (London: printed for the author, 1785); Henri Decremps, *The Conjurer Unmasked* (London: T. Denton, 1785).
44. M. Edgeworth, *Belinda*, 47.
45. Quoted in Altick, *Shows of London*, 66.
46. "Public Office, Bow-Street," *Morning Chronicle*, June 27, 1798; "Public Office, Bow-Street," *Morning Chronicle*, July 13, 1798, 90–91.
47. "The Queen accompanied by Princess Elizabeth" and "Impromptu, written in the room, on Seeing Maillardet's Mechanical Exhibition, Covent Garden," *Observer* no. 339, June 10, 1798. For a poetic puff piece, see "Maillardet's Automatical Exhibition," *True Briton*, April 1798.
48. M. Edgeworth, *Belinda*, 133, 57.
49. Kowaleski-Wallace, *Fathers' Daughters*, 101–8.
50. Lavinia Maddaluno, "Unveiling Nature: Wonder and Deception in Eighteenth-Century London Shows and Exhibitions," *Nuncius* 27 (2012): 56–80.
51. Anonymous, "An Attempt to Analyse," *Edinburgh Philosophical Journal* (April 1821): 396. See also Tom Standage, *The Turk: The Life and Times of the Famous Eighteenth-Century Chess-Playing Machine* (New York: Walker and Company, 2002).
52. Iwan Rhys Morus, "'More the Aspect of Magic than Anything Natural': The Philosophy of Demonstration," *Science in the Marketplace: Nineteenth-Century Sites and Experiences*, ed. Eileen Fyfe and Bernard Lightman (Chicago: University of Chicago Press, 2007), 337.
53. Stafford, *Artful Science*, 121–30.
54. Mark Sussman, "Performing the Intelligent Machine: Deception and Enchantment in the Life of the Automaton Chess Player," *The Drama Review* 43, no. 3 (1999): 9.
55. Jan Golinski, *Science as Public Culture: Chemistry and Enlightenment in Britain, 1760–1820* (Cambridge: Cambridge University Press, 1992), 153–76.
56. Hare, *Life and Letters*, 1:35, 1:64.
57. Toni Wein, "'Dear Prudence': The Art of Management and the Management of Art in Edgeworth's *Belinda*," *Women's Studies* 31, no. 3 (May/June, 2002): 315.
58. Hare, *Life and Letters*, 1:169.
59. M. Edgeworth, *Early Lessons*, 2:1–17.
60. Maria Edgeworth, *Rosamond: A Sequel to Early Lessons* (London: R. Hunter; Baldwin, Cradock, and Joy, 1821), 1:iii.

61. Rousseau, *Emile*, 84, 85.
62. For an in-depth exploration of Rousseau's education of things, see Julia Simon, "Natural Freedom and Moral Autonomy, Emile as Parent, Teacher, and Citizen," *History of Political Thought* 16, no. 1 (1995): 21–36. Simon argues that relations between things fail to teach Emile social relations, leaving him morally dependent on his tutor as an adult.
63. M. Edgeworth, *Early Lessons*, 2:9–10, 2:16; M. Edgeworth, *Rosamond: A Sequel*, 2:99.
64. Rousseau, *Emile*, 376, 369.
65. Golinski, *Science as Public Culture*, 176–86. See also Sharon Alker, "Explosive Potential: Radicals and Chemistry in Maria Edgeworth's Fiction," *European Romantic Review* 23, no. 1 (2011): 1–18.
66. Iain Topliss, "Mary Wollstonecraft and Maria Edgeworth's Modern Ladies," *Etudes Irelandaises* 6 (1981): 13–31. Harriot Freke functions as an extreme position that makes Edgeworth's own feminist ideas seem moderate and rational.
67. M. Edgeworth, *Early Lessons*, 2:27, 2:29, 2:113, 2:114, 2:31.
68. There are several additional needle appearances: Rosamond next uses her needle for a utilitarian moral comparison, choosing between letting her mother remove a thorn from her finger with a needle (an immediate but momentary pain), or leaving the thorn to fester (a greater pain in the future).
69. M. Edgeworth, *Early Lessons*, 2:30, 2:141.
70. Rousseau, *Emile*, 98–99.
71. Richard Edgeworth and Maria Edgeworth, *Essays on Practical Education*, 2 vols. (London: J. Johnson, 1798): 1:286.
72. Simon, "Natural Freedom," 29–32.
73. M. Edgeworth, *Early Lessons*, 2:141–50. Rosamond's desire to keep the rabbit as a pet "against his will," or fence in her garden and deprive him of food, suggests that personal property, unchecked, can threaten personal liberty and food rights, 2:140. The siblings debate what is best for the rabbit, and whether they have the right to decide for the animal, demonstrating a sophisticated awareness of the abusive potential of claiming to know what is best for another.
74. M. Edgeworth, *Early Lessons*, 2:150–67.
75. Sean Silver, *The Mind Is a Collection: Case Studies in Eighteenth-Century Thought* (Philadelphia: University of Pennsylvania Press, 2015).
76. Rousseau, *Emile*, 174. Richard Edgeworth enjoyed popular "deceptions" in shows that used magnets, mentioning the "celebrated Comus," who "exhibited a variety of scientific deceptions in London," and his friend, Matthew Boulton, the business partner of James Watt, "made a large number of magnets for exportation." Edgeworth, *Memoirs*, 1.120, 1.168).
77. Rousseau, *Emile*, 178.
78. Douthwaite, *Wild Girl*, 93–115.
79. Critics object that under Rousseau's social contract, a citizen who disagrees with the general must be forced to submit to it for his own good. For critics, the *forcer d'être libre* provision of Rousseau's social contract is a stepping stone to totalitarian democracy, wherein the government claims to know better than its citizens how to make them free. J. L. Talmon, *Origins of Totalitarian Democracy* (New York: Praeger, 1960), 38–50; cf. Mark Evans, "Freedom in Modern Society: Rousseau's Challenge," *Inquiry* 38, no. 3 (September 1995): 245–46. Rousseau was likewise targeted in Isaiah Berlin's influential essay "Two Concepts of Liberty" for suggesting that freedom requires both self-government and rationality, such that forces outside

the self (other people, or the state), might step in and "second guess" a person's true desires, justifying coercion. Since women are incapable of self-government, and children are incapable of reason, their interests would always be represented indirectly, by adult male citizens. See Nancy J. Hirschmann, *The Subject of Liberty: Toward a Feminist Theory of Freedom* (Princeton, NJ: Princeton University Press, 2003), 4–39.

80. Rousseau, *Emile*, 120, 94. On the relationship between sensation and discovering the existence of a free, essential self, see Richard Noble, *Language, Subjectivity, and Freedom in Rousseau's Moral Philosophy* (New York: Garland, 1991), 133–70. By machine or automaton, Rousseau means the child's body, distinct from functions of the soul, e.g., "accustom the operations of the machine and those of judgement always to work harmoniously." Rousseau, *Emile*, 141.
81. R. Edgeworth and M. Edgeworth, *Practical Education*, 1:264.
82. Maria Edgeworth, *Continuation of Early Lessons* (London: R. Hunter; Baldwin, Cradock, and Joy, 1816), 1:212; Edgeworth, *Memoirs*, 1:21, 1:108.
83. M. Edgeworth, *Continuation of Early Lessons*, 1:218, 1:235, 1:237, 1:240. Wharton argues that the object lesson in the "India Cabinet" show the imperial connections of the Lunar Society's technological innovations, Material Enlightenment, 219–26.
84. M. Edgeworth, *Continuation of Early Lessons*, 1:245; *Early Lessons*, 2:1; *Continuation of Early Lessons*, 2:256, 2:272, 2:271.
85. M. Edgeworth, *Rosamond: A Sequel*, 153.
86. Maria Edgeworth visited Geneva in 1820 with the Marcets. See Hare, *Life and Letters*, 1:320. According to John Ruskin, any English visitor in Geneva inevitably "went to Mt. Bautte's with awe, and of necessity" to purchase one of his pieces. John Ruskin, "Praeterita," in *The Genius of John Ruskin: Selections from His Writings*, ed. John D. Rosenberg (Charlottesville: University of Virginia Press, 1998), 531–32. The mechanical caterpillar image also appears in a museum catelog with other watches and wonders by Bautte. Caroline Junier Clerc, Claude-Alain Künzi, and Nicole Bosshart, eds., *Automates & merveilles: une exposition, 3 villes, 3 musées*, 3 vols. (Neuchâtel: Éditions Alphil, 2012) 1:36.
87. M. Edgeworth, *Rosamond: A Sequel*, 143, 166.
88. M. Edgeworth, *Rosamond: A Sequel*, 189. In the Edgeworth household, the phrase "good against her will," which appears in "The Rabbit" and "Blind Kate," is one Richard Edgeworth used to defend Irish sovereignty, speaking against unification in Irish Parliament: "the Union would be advantageous to all the parties concerned, but that England has not any right to do to Ireland *good against her will*." Hare, *Life and Letters*, 69.
89. Jean-Pierre Maunoir describes several such operations in his pamphlet *Organisation de L'Iris et L'Opération de la Pupile Artificielle* (Paris: J. J. Paschoud, 1812).
90. Maria Edgeworth, *Popular Tales*, 3 vols. (London: R. Hunter; Baldwin, Cradock, and Joy, 1823), 1:iv–v. I suspect Richard Edgeworth's 80,000 readers come from *Proposals for Peace with the Regicide Directory of France* (London: J. Owen, 1796), in which Burke estimates the informed British public at "four hundred thousand political citizens, . . . about eighty thousand" of whom are "pure Jacobins" (67).
91. Alan Richardson, *Literature, Education, and Romanticism: Reading as Social Practice, 1780–1832* (Cambridge: Cambridge University Press, 1994), 226.
92. "Miss Edgeworth's Popular Tales," *Edinburgh Review* 4, no. 8 (July 1804): 330.
93. One way to combat Radical literature was cheap, entertaining, loyalist alternatives: "If the British elite learned one thing from the suppression of publications in the wake of Thomas Paine's *Rights of Man*, which sold 200,000 copies in one year, it was that

artisans, tradesmen, and common laborers would read literature. As Hazlitt recalled, 'It was impossible to prevent our reading something.'" Richard Altick, *The English Common Reader: A Social History of the Mass Reading Public, 1800–1900* (Chicago: University of Chicago Press, 1957), 73, 69–70. While Edgeworth's *Popular Tales* was too expensive, Sir James Mackintosh hoped to republish an Irish translation for distribution to cottagers. Ian Haywood, *Revolution in Popular Literature: Print, Politics, and the People, 1790–1860* (Cambridge: Cambridge University Press, 2004), 11–25; Slade, *Maria Edgeworth*, 103.

94. Mary Leadbeater, *Cottage Dialogues among the Irish Peasantry, . . . with Notes and a Preface by Maria Edgeworth*, 2 vols. (London: J. Johnson, 1811), 1:iv.
95. Elizabeth Hamilton, *Cottagers of Glenburnie; A Tale for the Farmer's Ingle-nook*, 3rd ed., 2 vols. (Edinburgh: James Ballantyne, 1808), 1:iv. Edgeworth recommended Hamilton's The *Cottagers* of *Glenburnie* to her aunt Margaret Ruxton on February 2, 1809: "I think it will do a vast deal of good in Ireland." Hare, *Life and Letters*, 1:160. Contemporaries pair *Popular Tales* with *Cottagers*. See letters in Agnes Porter, *A Governess in the Time of Jane Austen: The Journals and Letters of Agnes Porter*, ed. Joanna Martin (London: Hambledon Press, 1998), 292.
96. Hamilton's *Cottagers* concludes with Mrs. Mason's recommendations on school management, informed by Irish monitorial educator David Manson, adding Joseph Lancaster in later editions (2.373–74). Lancastrian methods were used in Ireland, supported by the Kildare Place Society (founded 1811). See *Dublin Reading Book* (Dublin: P. Dixon Hardy, 1830).
97. Rev. Dr. Andrew Bell, *An Experiment in Education, Made at the Male Asylum of Madras* (London: Cadell and Davies, 1797), 11.
98. Patricia Crain, *Reading Children: Literacy, Property, and the Dilemmas of Childhood in Nineteenth-Century America* (Philadelphia: University of Pennsylvania Press, 2016), 64–66. Patricia Crain examines the technologies used in these classrooms to teach Indigenous students in the United States. Her work builds on the similarity between manufacturing and teaching in US Monitorial schools by Carl Kaestle and Colleen Terrell. In Britain, comparisons between education and machinery were not limited to Monitorial schools. Machine metaphors for schools conflictingly connoted freedom, conformity, and efficiency, while mixing metaphors with cultivation was common.
99. Samuel Taylor Coleridge, *The Statesman's Manual*, in *Lay Sermons*, ed. R. J. White, *S. T. Coleridge Collected Works*, 16 vols. (London: Routledge and K. Paul, 1969–2002), 6:41.
100. Bernard repeats the same passage about the division of labor in two essays: Sir Thomas Bernard, Esq., *Of the Education of the Poor* (London: W. Bulmer and J. Hatchard, 1809), 35; Thomas Bernard, *The New School* (London: W. Bulmer and Co.; Society for Bettering the Condition of the Poor), 17–18.
101. Bernard, *New School*, 38, 47.
102. Quoted in Robert Southey, *The Origin, Nature, and Object of the New System of Education* (London: John Murray, 1812), 128.
103. Edward F. Burton, "Richard Lovell Edgeworth's Education Bill of 1799: A Missing Chapter in the History of Irish Education," *Irish Journal of Education / Iris Eireannach an Oideachais* 13, no. 1 (1979): 29–30; Donald H. Akenson, *The Irish Education Experiment: The National System of Education in the Nineteenth Century* (Abington: Routledge, 2011); Wharton notes that the bill is written in the handwriting of Maria and Frances Anne Beaufort Edgeworth (Richard Lovell's fourth wife), Material Enlightenment, 209–12.

104. 9 Parl. Deb. (1st ser.) (April 1807) col. 550.
105. M. Edgeworth, *Popular Tales*, 1:6–7. Featuring a Cornish miner may reflect low literacy rates among child miners, or fear that Thomas Paine's *Rights of Man* circulated in the "Cornish tin-mines." See Haywood, *Revolution*, 21.
106. "Popular Tales," *Annual Review and History of Literature* 3 (January 1804): 461.
107. M. Edgeworth, *Popular Tales*, 1:114.
108. Julia Wright, *Ireland, India, and Nationalism in Nineteenth-Century Literature* (Cambridge: Cambridge University Press, 2007), 74; Julia Wright, "Courting Public Opinion: Handling Informers in the 1790s," *Éire-Ireland: A Journal of Irish Studies* 33, no. 1–2 (1998): 149.
109. M. Edgeworth, *Early Lessons*, 2:187–88.
110. M. Edgeworth, *Popular Tales*, 1:31–32, 1:39.
111. M. Edgeworth, *Popular Tales*, 1:41–43.
112. Andrew Ure, *The Philosophy of Manufactures* (New York: A. M. Kelly, 1967), 279.
113. A full description of the boy "in 1819 resided at Neton-on-Ayr," who made a box with "wooden figures, about two or three inches high," of people in "trades and sciences," moved by organ crank: "A weaver upon his loom, with a fly-shuttle, uses his hands and feet, and keeps his eye upon the shuttle, as it passes across the web. A soldier, sitting with a sailor at a public-house table, fills a glass, drinks it off, then knocks upon the table, upon which an old woman opens a door, makes her appearance, and they retire. Two shoemakers upon their stools are seen, the one beating leather, and the other stitching a shoe. A cloth-dresser, a stone-cutter, a cooper, a tailor, a woman churning, and one teasing wool, are all at work. There is also a carpenter sawing a piece of wood, and two blacksmiths beating a piece of iron, the one using a sledge, and the other a small hammer; a boy turning a grindstone, while a man grinds an instrument upon it; and a barber shaving a man, whom he holds fast by the nose with one hand," Anonymous, *Invention and Discovery* (Edinburgh: W. P. Nimmo, 1868), 149–50. The same passage appears in earlier books, suggesting a boy like him as Edgeworth's inspiration.
114. C. L. Brightwell, *Annals of Industry and Genius* (London: Nelson and Sons, 1863), 161, 264, 258.
115. W. H. D. Adams, *Steady Aim* (London: James Jogg and Sons, 1863), 21.
116. Anonymous *Great Inventors: The Sources of Their Usefulness, and the Results of Their Efforts* (London: Ward and Lock, 1864), 131, 133.
117. Afras Sial, "The Oriental Despot: Cultural Mischaracterization in Maria Edeworth's *Lame Jervas*," *Utraque Unum* 9, no. 1 (Spring 2016): 62–66. Sial reviews the political context for the M. Edgeworth's portrayal of Tipu Sultan.
118. Southey, *Origin*, 180–84.
119. Jana Tschurenev, "Diffusing Useful Knowledge: The Monitorial System of Education in Madras, London and Bengal, 1789–1840," *Paedagogica Historica: International Journal of the History of Education* 44, no. 3 (June 2008): 259–62.
120. Wright, *Ireland*, 75; Haywood, *Revolution*, 85.
121. M. Edgeworth, *Popular Tales*, 175–76.
122. C. E. Anderson, "Tipu Sultan's Sons and Images of Paternalism in Late Eighteenth-Century British Art," in *Romanticism and Parenting: Image, Institution, Ideology*, ed. Carolyn Weber (Cambridge: Cambridge Scholars Publishing, 2007), 20, 27.
123. Bell agrees with stereotypes of multiracial Indian children's "inferiority in the talents of the head, the qualities of the mind, and the virtues of the heart," which he attributes to education: "I think I see, in the very first maxims which the mothers

of these children instill into their infant minds, the source of every corrupt practice, and an infallible mode of forming a degenerate race." Bell, *Experiment in Education*, 7. Blaming mothers creates the supposed need for his schools.

124. Tschurenev, "Diffusing Useful Knowledge," 256–62.
125. Bell, *Experiment in Education*, 46–48.
126. Edgeworth's fiction contains paternalistic representations of slavery in "The Grateful Negro" from *Popular Tales*.
127. Hare, *Life and Letters*, 1:69; "Memoires of Tippoo Sultaun, Late Sovereign of Mysore," *European Magazine and London Review* 37 (June 1800): 419–24; "Address from the Comissioner at Seringapatam, Dated June 30, 1799," *Times*, December 1799; "Half-Yearly Retrospect of Domestic Literature," *Monthly Magazine*, January 1801, 585.
128. "Extraordinary Novelty," *Times*, September 30, 1799, 1. Moving mechanical panoramas with military battles or raised cities were popular street entertainments. See Altick, *Shows of London*, 198–220. By February 1800, the Seringapatam panorama was exhibited alongside humanoid automata. "Harlequin Magician," *Times*, February 18, 1800, 1.
129. "A Description of the Magnificent Throne of the Late Tippoo Sultaun, in the Laul Mahaul of Seringapatam, His Capital," *Weekly Entertainer*, December 1800. See also, "Capture of Seringapatam," *General Evening Post*, April 1800.
130. Thanks to Alan Rauch, who brought these popular porcelain figurines to my attention.
131. Michael Adas, *Machines as the Measure of Men: Science, Technology, and Ideologies of Western Dominance* (Ithaca: Cornell University Press, 1989), 134.
132. Charles Babbage, *On the Economy of Machinery and Manufactures* (London: C. Knight, 1832), 3–4.
133. Andrew Irvine, *Reflections on the Education of the Poor* (London: Edmund Lloyd, 1815), 22.
134. *Moral Tales*, volume X of the *Encyclopaedia Bengalensis/Vidyakalpadrum*, ed. Krishna Mohan Banerji, scholar and editor of *The Inquirer* (1831) and *Hindu Youth* (1831), includes "Lame Jervas" retitled as "The Reward of Honesty" by Maria Edgeworth. The volume was printed in three editions: a diglot edition (in English and Bengali), a Bengali edition, and a cheap edition for Indian students. Slade, *Maria Edgeworth*, 114. Incidentally, the first volume in Banerji's series is Isaac Watts's education treatise *The Improvement of the Mind*. In his preface, Banerji states that "translation of studies on European history and physics in Bengali is an effective means of combating aberrations in the minds of the common people of Bengal." Quoted in *Encyclopaedia of Indian Literature*, vol. 2, ed. Amaresh Datta (New Delhi: Sahitya Akademi, 1988, 2005), 1162.
135. M. Edgeworth, *Continuation of Early Lessons*, 1:275–76.

CHAPTER 5: "KNOWLEDGE WHICH SHALL BE POWER IN THEIR HANDS"

1. George Mudie, *The Grammar of the English Language Truly Made Easy and Amusing* (London: John Cleave, 1840), Cotsen; *New Satirist; or Censor of the Times*, no. 2 (November 28, 1841): 7; *The Spectator*, April 10, 1841.
2. *Economist* 1, no. 1 (1821): 11–12.
3. *Political Economist* 1, no. 1 (1821): 11–12.

4. Andrew Bennett, *The Hidden Oak: The Life and Works of George Mudie, Pioneer Co-operator* (self-pub., open access, 2016), 144–46.
5. *Economist* 1, no. 1 (1821): 6.
6. Marcus Wood identifies satirical play as a defining feature of radical working-class print culture in *Radical Satire and Print Culture, 1790–1822* (Oxford: Clarendon Press, Oxford University Press, 1994). On satirical play, see also Joss Marsh, *Word Crimes: Blasphemy, Culture, and Literature in Nineteenth-Century England* (Chicago: University of Chicago Press, 1998); Jon P. Klancher, *The Making of English Reading Audiences, 1790–1832* (Madison: University of Wisconsin Press, 1987); Ben Wilson, *The Laughter of Triumph: William Hone and the Fight for the Free Press* (London: Faber, 2005).
7. I use "radicalism" to refer to the nineteenth-century British political movement that supported constitutional reform, criminal justice reform, tax reform, redistribution of wealth, access to education, working-class management of public institutions, protective labor laws, a free press, and universal suffrage. I define a "working-class text" as one "that is self-consciously directed toward the working class and that clearly reflects working-class interests," following Paul Thomas Murphy's definition in *Toward a Working-Class Canon: Literary Criticism in British Working-Class Periodicals, 1816–1858* (Columbus: Ohio State University Press, 1994), 31. I consider children's working-class texts as those directed to younger children under age fourteen, and youth working-class texts as those targeting under age twenty-one, which reflects the ages that working-class activists requested for legal protection for their children.
8. Anna Clark, *The Struggle for the Breeches: Gender and the Making of the British Working Class* (Berkley: University of California Press, 1995), 196–203.
9. "Orbiston," *Cooperative Magazine and Monthly Herald* 1, no. 12 (December 1826): 389; "Orbiston," *Cooperative Magazine and Monthly Herald* 2, no. 4 (April 1827): 170.
10. On the overlap of children's literature with radical satire, see Wood, *Radical Satire*, 215–63; Donelle Ruwe, "Satirical Birds and Natural Bugs," in *The Satiric Eye: Forms of Satire in the Romantic Period*, ed. Steven E. Jones (New York: Palgrave Macmillan, 2003), 130–32; Wilson, *Laughter of Triumph*.
11. Bennett, *Hidden Oak*, 148–50. The *Satirist* review states Mudie was known for *Temple of Letters*, suggesting its publication.
12. The phrase "get knowledge" is an exhortation in the working-class press, which David Vincent glosses as getting "book knowledge" that brings "freedom." *Bread, Knowledge and Freedom: A Study of Nineteenth-Century Working Class Autobiography* (London: Europa Publications, 1981), 109. The phrase derives from Proverbs 4:7, often quoted as, "Wisdom is the principle thing: Get Wisdom, and with all thy getting, get understanding." Quoted in Paracelsus [Emma Leslie], *Seed and Fruit, Or, Young People Who Have Become Famous* (London: Religious Tract Society, 1876), 127. I find "knowledge"—as opposed to "education"—means empowering political knowledge from books and life experience. For example, the minutes for a meeting of the "National Union of the Working Classes," published July 16, 1831, in *The Poor Man's Guardian* records a petition to Parliament objecting to taxing the poor "for the education of the rich." Mr. Warden (attending) "exhorted the Working Classes to bestir themselves and get knowledge" to "show them (mob and rabble as we are) that we are capable of doing our business in that house [Parliament], better than it has ever yet been done for us."

13. William Cobbett, "Education and 'Heddekashun,'" *Cobbett's Weekly Political Register*, December 7, 1833. Cobbett's "Heddicashun" is another way of exploring the education of words vs. things. Cobbett protested that government-funded or charity-supported education is properly called "headikashon" because it teaches empty words devoid of political and economic power: "Scrawling upon paper with a pen, and gabbling over words printed upon paper; it signifying nothing what sort of scrawling it is, or what are the words which are printed upon paper; whether the scrawling be legible or not whether the right letters be put into the words that are intended to be made, or whether the gabbling be of a Magdalen Hymn, or of a smutty ballad: still it is all 'headikashon.'" "Education," *Cobbett's Weekly Political Register*, October 12, 1833. By failing to teach children to understand the meaning behind words, headikashon levels all speech, sacred and profane. The word "headikashon" is spelled many ways, satirizing the indifferent literacy bestowed by rote-learning. Moreover, its pronunciation by regional English or London Cockney speakers would drop the "H," pronouncing "edication" for a pun on "edification," while mocking the learned superfluous "H" pronunciation as a class marker.
14. "Mr. Hunt at Blackburn and Padiham," *Poor Man's Guardian*, December 8, 1832.
15. E.g., An article from Thomas Wooler's *The Black Dwarf* distinguishes between the "knowledge of words" and a "knowledge of things" or "men and things," meaning a rational scientific education separate from the church: Although clergymen have the "general learning and acquirements" of their rank, "In practical and useful knowledge, they are, for the most part, lamentably deficient. Ignorant alike of men and things, and employed for the most part in the study of the language and history of a barbarous age and people, . . . In the business of education, therefore, if we make any distinction between a knowledge of mere words and a knowledge of things, between truth and fiction, we must allow that, in this respect, the Clergy . . . have done more harm than good, by impeding the progress of natural and scientific knowledge." A. H., "Character of the Clergy," *Black Dwarf*, March 24, 1824, 382–84.
16. William Lovett, Cabinet-marker and John Collins, Tool-maker, *Chartism; A New Organization of the People: Embracing a Plan for the Education and Improvement of the People, Politically and Socially* (London: J. Watson, H. Hetherington, J. Cleave, 1840), 81–82.
17. Contemporaries described Thomas Paine's style as direct and unembellished, and radicals aspired to imitate this plain speaking. Thomas Jefferson praised his "ease and familiarity" and his "simple and unassuming language" (Quoted in Marsh, *Word Crimes*, 62). Marsh argues that Paine's style resulted in the English words "plain," "course," "common," and "vulgar" gaining their current "pejorative meaning" through frequent iteration of these descriptives in blasphemy court cases (74). Plainly written critique of religion or nation was both a grammatical stylistic violation and a legal one.
18. Eliza Sharples, *The Isis* 1, no. 1, February 11, 1832. Dressed as Isis, Goddess of Wisdom, Eliza Sharples gave lectures at the Rotunda Theatre, a radical venue managed by her common-law husband, Richard Carlile, that "attracted a significant number of women" when "other radical venues were less inclusive." Government spy reports record that some children attended events. Christina Parolin, *Radical Spaces: Venues of Popular Politics in London, 1790–1845* (Canberra, AU: ANU Press, 2010), 247. Sharples expressed a desire to open a school, which she probably pursued, as later in life she requested schoolbooks in a letter to Holyoake, held at

The Co-operative Archive. On women radicals and Owenites, see Barbara Taylor, *Eve and the New Jerusalem: Socialism and Feminism in the Nineteenth Century* (London: Virago, 1983), 83–118; Helen Rogers investigates women radical teachers, including Eliza Sharples and Mary Smith, in *Women and the People: Authority, Authorship and the Radical Tradition in Nineteenth-Century England* (Aldershot, UK: Ashgate, 2000).

19. On the history of English grammars, see Ian Michael, *The Teaching of English, from the Sixteenth Century to 1870* (Cambridge: Cambridge University Press, 1987); Ian Michael, "More than Enough English Grammars," in *English Traditional Grammars: An International Perspective*, ed. Gerhard Leitner (Amsterdam: J. Benjamins, 1991), 11–26; Ingrid Tieken-Boon van Ostade, ed., *Grammars, Grammarians and Grammar-Writing* (Berlin: Mouton de Gruyter, 2008); Beth Barton Schweiger, "A Social History of English Grammar in the Early United States," *Journal of the Early Republic* 30, no. 4 (2010): 536–41; Andrew Elfenbein, *Romanticism and the Rise of English* (Stanford: Stanford University Press, 2009).
20. Schweiger, "Social History," 540; Ingrid Tieken-Boon van Ostade, ed., *Two Hundred Years of Lindley Murray* (Munster, DE: Nodus Publikationen, 1996).
21. Jane Humphries, *Childhood and Child Labour in the British Industrial Revolution* (Cambridge: Cambridge University Press, 2010) 21, 207–14. Similarly, in the United States, grammar "marked out a color line of singular significance," so that Boston schoolmasters who taught Black children to read and write refused to teach grammar because they regarded the subject as "the center of all higher learning." Schweiger, "Social History," 534.
22. "Taxes on Knowledge," *Poor Man's Guardian*, Issue 7, August 20, 1831.
23. On the class politics of radical grammars, see Olivia Smith, *The Politics of Language, 1791–1819* (Oxford: Clarendon Press, 1984); Robert Pattison, *On Literacy: The Politics of the Word, from Homer to the Age of Rock* (New York: Oxford University Press, 1982); William F. Woods, "Evolution of Nineteenth-Century Grammar Teaching," *Rhetoric Review* 5 (Fall 1986): 4–20; Ingrid Tieken-Boon van Ostade, "The Grammatical Margins of Class," in *Standardising English: Norms and Margins in the History of the English Language*, ed. Linda Pillière, Wilfred Andrieu, Valérie Kerfelec, and Diana Lewis (Cambridge, UK: Cambridge University Press, 2018).
24. William Hill, *The Grammatical Text Book, for the Use of Schools* (Leeds: Joshua Hobson, 1839), vi.
25. Lauren Ann Schachter explores Romantic-era grammars that embrace rules particular to English over Latin to create a flexible language that, for Priestley and Barbauld, accommodates Dissenting beliefs. See "Fixing Words: English Grammar and the Literary Imagination in Britain, 1760–1832," order no. 22584552, University of Chicago, 2019. https://www.proquest.com/dissertations-theses/fixing-words-english-grammar-literary-imagination/docview/2311073048/se-2.
26. Paul Gillory, "Canon," *Critical Terms for Literary Study*, ed. Frank Lentricchia and Thomas McLaughlin, 2nd ed. (Chicago: University of Chicago Press, 1995), 241–43; Cassie LeGette, *Remaking Romanticism: The Radical Politics of the Excerpt* (Cham, CH: Palgrave Macmillan, 2017), 1–15. Gillory argues that excerpted passages in grammars create canons by identifying styles for emulation. Excerpts in radical grammars also function similarly to republication in radical periodicals, which LeGette describes as the creative process of claiming literature for radical purposes.
27. Malcolm Chase, "'Resolved in Defiance of Fool and Knave'?: Chartism, Children and

Conflict," in *Conflict and Difference in Nineteenth-Century Literature*, ed. Ninah Birch and Mark Llewellyn (New York: Palgrave Macmillan, 2010), 126–40.

28. "Congress of Co-operative and Trades' Union Delegates," *Poor Man's Guardian*, October 19, 1833.
29. Quoted in Tieken-Boon van Ostade, "Female Grammarians of the Eighteenth Century," *Historical Sociolinguistics and Sociohistorical Linguistics* (August 2000), http://www.let.leidenuniv.nl/hsl_shl/femgram.htm. On women authors of grammars, see also Carol Percy, "Women's Grammars," in *Eighteenth-Century English: Ideology and Change*, ed. Raymond Hickey (Cambridge: Cambridge University Press, 2010), 38–58; Andrea Immel, "Eighteenth-Century Teacher-Grammarians and the Education of 'Proper' Women," in *Grammars, Grammarians and Grammar-Writing in Eighteenth-Century England*, ed. Ingrid Tieken-Boon van Ostade (Berlin and New York: Mouton De Gruyter, 2008), 191–222.
30. Shirley Brice Heath, "Child's Play, or Finding the Ephemera of Home," in *Opening the Nursery Door: Reading, Writing and Childhood, 1600–1900*, ed. Mary Hilton, Morag Styles, and Victor Watson (London: Routledge, 1997), 91–103; Evelyn Arizpe, Morag Styles, and Shirley Brice Heath, eds., *Reading Lessons from the Eighteenth Century: Mothers, Children and Texts* (Lichfield, EN: Pied Piper Publishing, 2006).
31. On Ellenor Fenn's toys and grammars, see Carmen Gallego-Sturla and Lidia Taillefer, "An Analysis of Ellenor Fenn's Work: Influence on Nineteenth Century English Linguistics," *International Journal of Interdisciplinary Educational Studies* 16, no. 1 (2021): 107–20; Andrea Immel, "'Mistress of Infantine Language': Lady Ellenor Fenn, Her *Set of Toys*, and the 'Education of Each Moment,'" *Children's Literature* 25 (1997): 215–28; Karlijn Navest, "Reading Lessons for 'Baby Grammarians': Lady Ellenor Fenn and the Teaching of English Grammar," in *Acts of Reading: Teachers, Texts, and Childhood*, ed. Morag Styles and Evelyn Arizpe (Stoke-on-Trent, UK: Trentham Books Ltd., 2009), 73–86; David Stoker, "Ellenor Fenn as 'Mrs. Teachwell' and 'Mrs. Lovechild': A Pioneer Late Eighteenth Century Children's Writer, Educator and Philanthropist," *Princeton Library Chronicle* 68 (2007): 816–48.
32. Lissa Paul, *Eliza Fenwick: Early Modern Feminist* (Newark: University of Delaware Press, 2019), 113; M. O. Grenby, *The Child Reader, 1700–1840* (New York: Cambridge University Press, 2011), 231. Paul and Grenby admire the cleverness of her color stratagem.
33. Dr. Syntax, *A Picturesque Grammar of the English Language* (London: Wallis [ca. 1820]), Cotsen.
34. Jane Marcet, *Mary's Grammar Interspersed with Stories, and Intended for the Use of Children* (London: Longman, Rees, Orme, Brown, Green, and Longman, 1835), 58–59, 223.
35. Marcet, *Mary's Grammar*, 5–6.
36. Quoted in Bennett, *Hidden Oak*, 43. On Marcet's economic theories, see Bette Polkinghorn, "Jane Marcet and Harriet Marineau," in *Women of Value: Feminist Essays on the History of Women in Economics* (Aldershot, UK: Edward Elgar, 1995), 71–81; Bette Polkinghorn and Dorothy Lampen Thomson, *Adam Smith's Daughters: Eight Prominent Women Economists from the Eighteenth Century to the Present* (Cheltenham: Edward Elgar, 1998); Mary Poovey, *The History of the Modern Fact: Problems of Knowledge in the Sciences of Wealth and Society* (Chicago: University of Chicago Press, 1998).
37. Marcet, *Mary's Grammar*, 79.
38. Endpapers to Marcet's *Willy's Travels* also advertise *Willy's Grammar* (London:

Longman, Rees, Orme, Brown, Green, and Longman, 1845), which is similar to *Mary's Grammar*, featuring everyday scenes for boys, and *The Mother's First Book: Containing Reading Made Easy and the Spelling-Book* (1845). My dates reflect the earliest surviving copies, but it is hard to say whether she published all of these ten years after writing *Mary's Grammar*, or if they were reprinted. The Game of Grammar mentioned in the story consists of 290 cards with counters. Karen Cajka, "Eighteenth-Century Teacher-Grammarians and the Education of 'Proper' Women," in *Grammars, Grammarians and Grammar-Writing in Eighteenth-Century England*, ed. Ingrid Tieken-Boon van Ostade (Berlin and New York: Mouton De Gruyter, 2008), 191–222.

39. Marcet, *Mary's Grammar*, 63–73.
40. The Cotton Mills and Factories Act of 1819 initially limited work hours of children under age sixteen in cotton mills to twelve hours and no night work, which was extended in 1831 and 1833 to factory children under eighteen, and, in 1844, to ten hours for women and children under eighteen. After 1878, children under fourteen worked half-days to accommodate schooling. J. T. Ward, *The Factory Movement, 1830–1855* (London: Macmillan, 1962); Pamela Horn, *Children's Work and Welfare, 1780–1890* (Cambridge: Cambridge University Press, 1994).
41. Richard Altick, *The English Common Reader: A Social History of the Mass Reading Public, 1800–1900* (Chicago: University of Chicago Press, 1957), 83; Murphy, *Working-Class Canon*, 8; Vincent, *Bread, Knowledge and Freedom*, 118–23; Parolin, *Radical Spaces*.
42. Jonathan Rose, *The Intellectual Life of the British Working Classes*, 2nd ed. (New Haven: Yale University Press, 2010), 20–40; Vincent, *Bread, Knowledge and Freedom*, 136; Murphy, *Working-Class Canon*, 17.
43. Murphy, *Working-Class Canon*, 7–25; E. P. Thompson, *The Origins of the English Working Class* (London: Penguin, 1980), 782–92; R. K. Webb, *The British Working Class Reader, 1790–1848: Literacy and Social Tension* (London: George Allen & Unwin, 1955), 34, 83.
44. The 1833 Factory Act legally defined age fourteen as the end of childhood for working-class youth, after which children become "free agents," who contract their labor independent of their parents and collect their own wages. Elizabeth Massa Hoiem, "Radical Cross-Writing for Working Children: Toward a Bottom-Up History of Children's Literature," *Lion and the Unicorn* 41, no. 1 (January 2017): 13–14. After 1878, age fourteen became when children legally end school for fulltime work. On age, labor, and agency, see Holly Brewer, *By Birth or Consent: Children, Law, and the Anglo-American Revolution in Authority* (Chapel Hill: University of North Carolina Press, 2005); Robert J. Steinfeld, *Coercion, Contract, and Free Labor in the Nineteenth Century* (Cambridge: Cambridge University Press, 2001).
45. Marsh, *Word Crimes*, 78–80.
46. William Cobbett, *Grammar of the English Language* (New York: Clavton and Kingsland, 1818), 44, 74, 184.
47. On the radical politics of Cobbett's grammar, see L. C. Mugglestone, "Cobbett's 'Grammar': William, James Paul, and the Politics of Prescriptivism," *Review of English Studies* 48, no. 192 (November 1997): 471–88; James Grande, *William Cobbett, the Press and Rural England: Radicalism and the Fourth Estate, 1792–1835* (Houndmills: Palgrave Macmillan, 2014), 100–3.
48. Cobbett, *Grammar*, 14, 46, 78, 48, 109.
49. Tieken-Boon van Ostade, "Female Grammarians."

50. Anonymous, *A Critical Examination of Cobbett's English Grammar* (London: W. Wright, 1819), 63; Rev. William Lisle Bowles, *Thoughts on the Increase of Crimes, the Education of the Poor, and the National Schools* (Salisbury, Brodie and Dowding, [1815]), 21.
51. Cobbett, *Grammar*, 65.
52. George Jacob Holyoake, *The Logic of Co-operation* (London: Trubner & Co.; Manchester: Co-operative Printing Society, 1873), 7. Despite these differences, *Mary's Grammar* also suggests that girls own what they make: "Well then, we must think of something you possess," suggests Mother, "your work-box, for instance, and you may say I have a work-box." Marcet, *Mary's Grammar*, 254.
53. A prolific author of practical self-education manuals, Cobbett was portrayed in 1820s political cartoons as the "public instructor" holding two-penny trash, with Thomas Paine's coffin on his back. After two years exiled on Long Island, he reportedly brought Paine's bones back to England with him.
54. William Hill, *Fifteen Lessons on the Analogy and Syntax of the English Language, for the Use of Adult Persons Who Have Neglected the Study of Grammar* (Huddersfield: T. G. Lancashire; London: Simpkin and Marshall, 1833), lesson 1, par. 1–3; Cobbett, *Grammar*, 74, 184.
55. Hill, *Fifteen Lessons,* lesson 8, par. 21.
56. Asa Briggs, ed., *Chartist Studies* (London: Macmillan, 1959), 74; quoted in Eileen Yeo, "Christianity and Chartist Struggle, 1838–1842," *Past & Present* no. 91 (May 1981): 139.
57. William Hill, *Educational Monitor, Part I. Spelling and Reading Lessons* (London: Whitaker and Co.; Manchester: J. Galt and Co., 1848), 4, 5.
58. William Hill, *The Grammatical Text Book* (Leeds: Joshua Hobson, 1839), vi–vii.
59. Hill, *Educational Monitor*, 3.
60. Richard Carlile, *An Address to Men of Science* (London: R. Carlile, 1821), 4–5.
61. Carlile, *Men of Science*, 40.
62. James A. Epstein, *Radical Expression: Political Language, Ritual, and Symbol in England, 1790–1850* (New York and Oxford: Oxford University Press, 1994), 124–27.
63. *The New Satirist; or Censor of the Times* (London), issue 2, (November 28, 1941); *Penny Satirist*, vol. 5, issue 212 (Saturday, May 8, 1841). See also *Mirror of Literature, Amusement, and Instruction*, vol. 2, issue 5 (July 30, 1842): 69; "Reviews," *Northern Star*, September 18, 1841, 3. The *Fleet Papers* critique of free trade and the new poor laws was written from jail by "Short Timer" Richard Oastler, called "King of the Children" for organizing factory children's marches for a ten-hour work day, 1832–1833. Although jailed for debt, these charges seemed politically motivated to his allies.
64. Mudie, *Grammar*, viii–ix, xiv.
65. E.g., William Hone's *The Queen's Matrimonial Ladder, a National Toy, with Fourteen Step Scenes*, a pamphlet sold with a prop-up pasteboard ladder toy, satirizing the ladder of learning. Each rung bears a "-tion" word (degradation, coronation, qualification, accusation, etc.), imitating recitation lessons on Latinate words. See Wilson, *Laughter of Triumph*, 320.
66. Using "hinge" for a "conjunction" is supported by the definition for a "universal hinge" in mechanical philosophy, as "'junctures which admit motion of the parts;' or rather, of parts that are connected," Egbert Willis, *Principles of Mechanism* (London: Longman, Green, 1870), 507.
67. Mudie, *Grammar*, x, xiv.

68. W. T., "To the Members and Managers," *The Co-operative*, February 1826, 44; W.T., "To the Members and Managers," *The Co-operative*, January 1826, 25.
69. Robert Owen, *A New View of Society*, 2nd ed. (London: Longman, Hurst, Rees, Orme, and Brown, 1816), 44.
70. Quoted in Brian Simon, *The Radical Tradition in Education* (London: Lawrence and Wishart, 1972), 19.
71. Owen, *New View*, 73.
72. Ophélie Siméon, *Robert Owen's Experiment at New Lanark, from Paternalism to Socialism* (Palgrave: Macmillan, 2017), 1–24.
73. Robert Owen Correspondence Collection, The National Co-operative Archive, Letter no. 25, January 2, 1823. This letter mentions a prospectus used for Mudie's lectures: "I went last night to Lunt's Coffee House, having previously sent a [?] of the Prospectus. There are debates there in the large room every Thursday night. The room is always crowded to excess, the speakers being men of talent." The prospectus survives as the first issue of his new periodical, *The Political Economist and Political Philanthropist* (1823), published the same month that Mudie wrote Owen. The second issue proves that "Labour is the source of wealth" and includes a letter to the editor from someone in Mudie's audience. On Lunt's Coffeehouse, see Markman Ellis, *The Coffee-House: A Cultural History* (London: Phoenix, 2005).
74. Bennett, *Hidden Oak*, 46.
75. Murphy, *Working-Class Canon*, 11–12; Thompson, *Origins*, 782.
76. Emilie Holyoake-Marsh, "Preface," in *A Descriptive Bibliography of the Writings of George Jacob Holyoake* by Charles William F. Goss (London: Crowther & Goodman, 1908), xxv. The preface is by Holyoake's daughter.
77. George Jacob Holyoake, *Public Speaking and Debate*, 1849 (London: Frederick Farrah, 1866), v–vi; George Jacob Holyoake, *A Logic of Facts: or, Every-Day Reasoning* (London: F. Farrah, 1866). Most of Holyoake's textbooks are first issues as cheap serials, followed immediately by books. See Goss, *A Descriptive Bibliography*. Holyoake's publications that I consulted in this chapter are held at The National Co-operative Archive.
78. Holyoake, *Public Speaking*, vi.
79. Variations on the phrase "things as they are" and "things as they might be" appear in social protest literature in the 1790s, including novels about human nature and education, e.g., *Things As They Are; or, The Adventures of Caleb Williams* (1794) by William Godwin; *Hermsprong; or, Man as He Is Not* (1796) by Robert Bage. William Godwin describes a pupil skilled in languages: "Things hold their just order in his mind, ideas first and then words." *The Enquirer* (London: G. G. and J. Robinson, 1797), 45.
80. Wooler, "Modern Charity," *Black Dwarf*, November 20, 1822, 737–40.
81. William Thompson, *An Inquiry into the Principles of the Distribution of Wealth Most Conducive to Human Happiness* (London: Longman, Hurst, Rees, Orme, Brown, and Green, 1824), 337–38. Although beyond my scope, this work comments on intellectual and physical labor, laws, and matter.
82. Simon, *Radical Tradition*, 12–13; Marsh, *Word Crimes*, 60–77.
83. Holyoake, *Logic*, 13.
84. Marsh, *Word Crimes*, 117.
85. [George Jacob Holyoake], *The Cabinet of Reason: A Library of Free Thought, Politics, and Culture* (London, 1850), 2. Thomas Paine, Thomas Spence, Robert Owen,

Thomas Cooper, William Godwin, Francis Wright, Percy Shelly, William Hill, and Holyoake himself.

86. George Jacob Holyoake, *The Child's Ladder of Knowledge* (London: Frederick Farrah, 1864), 2. Holyoake published four infant alphabet and reading books from 1852 to 1854, based on teaching at Sheffield, later recombining contents into *The Child's Ladder of Knowledge* (1864).
87. George Jacob Holyoake, *The Child's First Word-Book: For Teaching Spelling, Meanings, Grammar, and Reading* (London: Holyoake and Co., 1854), preface, 14. The star lesson is also printed in *Child's Ladder* (14) and *The Reasoner*, no. 4 (January 26, 1853): 62.
88. George Jacob Holyoake, *Practical Grammar: Intended for the Use of Those Who Have Little Time for Study*, 5th ed. (London: J. Watson, 1847), 9, 10.
89. Holyoake, *Practical Grammar*, 18, 10.
90. Holyoake, *Practical Grammar*, 15, 8, 72.
91. George Jacob Holyoake, *The Reasoner*, no. 68 (September 15, 1847): 83.
92. George Jacob Holyoake, *The Hand-book of Grammar: For the Use of Teachers and Learners* (London: J. Watson, 1849), back matter.
93. Holyoake, *Hand-book*, 44, 45, 47, 49. William Channing wrote *Self-Culture* and *Elevation of the Labouring Classes*, used in evening courses that encouraged self-education. The philosophical radical Jeremy Bentham supported secular education through his proposed Chrestomathia Institute and funded Robert Owen's New Lanark enterprises. Mrs. Leman Gillies (who used the pseudonyms Mary Rede and Mary Grimstone), was a socialist activist, novelist, and radical journalist who supported women's rights and Wilderspin's infant school movement. Detroisier is a radical founder of mechanics institutes.
94. Gloria Ladson-Billings, "But That's Just Good Teaching! The Case for Culturally Relevant Pedagogy," *Theory Into Practice* 34, no. 3 (1995): 476; Django Paris proposes "culturally sustaining pedagogies," or teaching that cultivates "linguistic, literate, and cultural pluralism as part of the democratic project of schooling." See Paris, "Culturally Sustaining Pedagogy: A Needed Change in Stance, Terminology, and Practice," *Educational Researcher* 41, no. 3 (April 2012): 93.
95. Holyoake, *Practical Grammar*, 37–42; Holyoake, *Hand-book*, 52–53.
96. George Jacob Holyoake, *The Child's Second Letter-Book, For Teaching Reading and Writing at Once* (London: James Watson, 1853).
97. George Jacob Holyoake, *The Logic of Co-operation* (London: Trubner and Co.; Manchester: Co operative Printing Society, 1873), 5–6.
98. *The Reasoner*, no. 65 (August 25, 1847), 470.
99. George Jacob Holyoake, *Mathematics No Mystery, or the Beauties and Uses of Euclid* (London: J. Watson, 1847), 46, 56. Holyoake quotes from George Darley, *The Geometrical Companion* (London: John Talyor, 1828), which locates geometry's practical origins in surveying land, to claim all students use induction to systematize everyday observations.
100. Holyoake-Marsh, "Preface," in Goss, *Descriptive Bibliography*, xx.

CONCLUSION: WILLIAM LOVETT'S CASE OF MOVEABLE TYPES

1. Francis Trollope, *The Life and Adventures of Michael Armstrong, the Factory Boy* (Chalford, EN: Nonsuch Publishing, 1840).
2. Trollope, *Michael Armstrong*, 150, 163, 160.

3. Charles Dickens, *Hard Times: For These Times*, ed. Graham Law (Peterborough, ON: Broadview, 1996, 2003), 48, 242, 140.
4. Dickens, *Hard Times*, 268, 55, 315.
5. "The Monstrous Regiment" is the name of a chapter in Percy H. Muir, *English Children's Books, 1600–1900* (London: B. T. Batsford, 1985). See Norma Clarke, "'The Cursed Barbauld Crew': Women Writers and Writing for Children in the Late Eighteenth Century," in *Opening the Nursery Door: Reading, Writing and Childhood 1600–1900*, ed. Mary Hilton, Morag Styles, and Victor Watson (London: Routledge, 1997).
6. Melanie Keene, *Science in Wonderland: The Scientific Fairy Tales of Victorian Britain* (Oxford: Oxford University Press, 2015), 1–20.
7. Trollope, *Michael Armstrong*, 219.
8. William Lovett, Cabinet-marker and John Collins, Tool-maker, *Chartism; A New Organization of the People: Embracing a Plan for the Education and Improvement of the People, Politically and Socially* (London: J. Watson, H. Hetherington, J. Cleave, 1840), 83.
9. Lovett and Collins, *Chartism*, 55, 18, iii, 83.
10. Lovett and Collins, *Chartism*, 54.
11. Martyn Lyons, *The History of Illiteracy in the Modern World Since 1750* (Cham, CH: Palgrave Macmillan, 2022), 39–57.
12. Jentery Sayers, "Introduction: 'I Don't Know All the Circuitry,'" and Julie Thompson Klein, "The Boundary Work of Making in Digital Humanities," in *Making Things and Drawing Boundaries: Experiments in the Digital Humanities*, ed. Jentery Sayers (Minneapolis: University of Minnesota Press, 2017), https://doi.org/10.5749/9781452963778.
13. Thank you to Emily Knox for bringing the gendering of sewing machines in maker spaces to my attention. Shirin Vossoughi, Paula K. Hooper, and Meg Escudé investigate normative definitions of making that require critical investigation in educational maker settings in "Making Through the Lens of Culture and Power: Toward Transformative Visions for Educational Equity," *Harvard Educational Review* 86, no. 2 (2016): 206–32.
14. Jacqueline Reid-Walsh, "Viewing *What Is This? What Is That?* (1905) and *The Beginning, Progress and End of Man* (circa 1650) under the Microscope: What Do I See?" *Unfolding Metamorphosis: The Learning as Play Blog, Learning as Play* (website), November 29, 2022, https://sites.psu.edu/learningasplaying/2022/11/29/under-the-microscope/. Examples of these flip-up books can be seen on the main site and digital archive, *Learning As Play*, https://sites.psu.edu/play/.

Index

Page numbers in *italics* indicate an illustration.

INDEX

INDEX

INDEX

INDEX

INDEX

INDEX

INDEX

INDEX

INDEX

www.ingramcontent.com/pod-product-compliance
Lightning Source LLC
Chambersburg PA
CBHW020455270326
41926CB00008B/609
* 9 7 8 1 6 2 5 3 4 7 5 5 8 *